Volume 9

DIRECTORY OF WORLD CINEMA
GERMANY

Edited by Michelle Langford

intellect Bristol, UK / Chicago, USA

First Published in the UK in 2012 by Intellect, The Mill, Parnall Road, Fishponds, Bristol, BS16 3JG, UK

First published in the USA in 2012 by Intellect, The University of Chicago Press, 1427 E. 60th Street, Chicago, IL 60637, USA

Copyright © 2012 Intellect Ltd

All rights reserved. No part of this publication may be reproduced, stored in a retrieval system, or transmitted, in any form or by any means, electronic, mechanical, photocopying, recording, or otherwise, without written permission.

A catalogue record for this book is available from the British Library.

Publisher: May Yao
Publishing Manager: Melanie Marshall

Cover photo: Krabat 2008/Brass Hat Films/7 Pictures Film/Kobal

Cover Design: Holly Rose
Copy Editor: Michael Eckhardt
Typesetting: Mac Style, Beverley, E. Yorkshire

Directory of World Cinema ISSN 2040-7971
Directory of World Cinema eISSN 2040-798X

Directory of World Cinema: Germany ISBN 978-1-84150-465-0
Directory of World Cinema: Germany eISBN 978-1-84150-582-4

Printed and bound by Cambrian Printers, Aberystwyth, Wales.

DIRECTORY OF WORLD CINEMA
GERMANY

Acknowledgements	5
Introduction: German Cinema and the Vicissitudes of History	6
Film Pioneers	14
The Films of the Skladanowsky Brothers	
Arnold Fanck (1889–1974)	
Then and Now: *Berlin Symphony*, 1927/2002	
Festival Focus	28
The Berlinale: Berlin International Film Festival	
Scoring Cinema	32
The Music Films of Straub/Huillet	
Fantastic Film	36
Essay	
Reviews	
Adventure Film	68
Essay	
Reviews	
Der Heimatfilm	94
Essay	
Reviews	
Comedy	122
Essay	
Reviews	
Foreigners and Guest-workers	148
Essay	
Reviews	
Queer German Cinema	168
Essay	
Reviews	
Vergangenheitsbewältigung	204
Essay	
Rubble Film	216
Reviews	
War Film	228
Reviews	
Historical Drama	242
Reviews	
Political Drama	260
Reviews	
The Berlin Wall	280
Essay	
Reviews	
Recommended Reading	303
Online Resources	306
Test Your Knowledge	310
Notes on Contributors	313
Filmography	318

ACKNOWLEDGEMENTS

Editing this first volume of the *Directory of World Cinema: Germany* has been no small undertaking. When I agreed to take on this challenge, little did I know that I would find such an amazing scholarly community who share my passion for German cinema and who would meet the task with such enthusiasm and generosity. My heartfelt thanks goes out to all the contributing authors for their committed scholarship, collegiality, punctuality and patience. Without you, this volume would certainly not exist. To Louise Malcolm, who provided expert editorial assistance and kept things ticking along at crucial moments, I extend unending gratitude. I would also like to thank my colleagues and students in the School of English, Media and Performing Arts at the University of New South Wales for generating a supportive and inspirational atmosphere in which to work. I extend a special note of thanks to my friend, mentor and colleague Professor George Kouvaros for his continued encouragement and support. A heartfelt thanks goes to my family and friends for doing without me on those many weekends spent behind the keyboard. And I owe my deepest gratitude to my devoted partner Adrian. Thanks for the morning coffee, the endless cups of tea and always knowing when to make me take a break.

The editorial team at Intellect have, as always been amazing to work with: May Yao, Melanie Marshall and Michael Eckhardt, you have my sincere thanks for your patience, support and expert guidance. A note of thanks must also go to Intellect intern, Emily Chard for the last-minute help with the quiz. I would also like to thank John Berra for his encouragement and advice in the early stages.

Finally, I thank all the German film-makers whose works have entertained, thrilled, mystified and challenged audiences for more than a century.

Michelle Langford

INTRODUCTION
GERMAN CINEMA AND THE VICISSITUDES OF HISTORY

If any national film industry could be said to have weathered the great vicissitudes of twentieth century history, German cinema must spring immediately to mind. After its modest beginnings in the late nineteenth century with the early experiments of the Skladanowsky brothers and a false start interrupted by the Great War, German film-makers, writers, producers and studios have continued to confront tempestuous times: two world wars, the Nazi period and the Holocaust, the Cold War, the terrorist movements of the 1970s, the establishment of the European Union and re-unification are just a few of the events that either sent the German film industry into upheaval or inspired change. Not only has German cinema survived, at times it has even thrived. From the rich aesthetic and commercial success of the Weimar period (1918–33) to the hard-edged politically and socially conscious works of the Young and New German Cinemas of the 1960s to early 1980s, through the 1990s 'cinema of consensus' (Rentschler 2000) and the current era of, on the one hand, the proliferation of small, independent German production companies and, on the other, the spread of international co-productions, German film-makers and producers have shown a great capacity for invention and re-invention.

In the Weimar period following the First World War, the German nation was faced with its own humiliating defeat, political turmoil, high inflation and a massive war debt. The film industry, whose chief pre-war competitors were Denmark and France, now met with strong competition from the United States. In the immediate post-war years, Hollywood dumped both its new product and back catalogue into German cinemas, assisted largely by its block-booking practices and international distribution networks that were well established by the end of the war. With the nation's cinemas awash with relatively cheap Hollywood product, German producers struggled earnestly not only to re-establish themselves, but to compete with the economic and cultural might of Hollywood. In his far-reaching study of the rise and legacy of Weimar cinema, Thomas Elsaesser highlights the important role played by producer Erich Pommer and the UFA (Universum Film Aktien Gesellshaft) studio in the relative success of German cinema of this period. UFA was, for a time at least, able to successfully combine the seemingly opposite imperatives of 'art' and commerce (Elsaesser 2000: 109). Under the helm of Pommer, UFA, which had acquired along with a number of other major studios Decla-Bioskop in 1921, was responsible for the production of some of the most memorable 'art' films of the era, as well as some of the most successful 'genre' films. Amongst its artistic and commercial successes we find one of Germany's first major international post-war hits, *The Cabinet of Dr. Caligari* (Wiene, 1920), as well as numerous films by Fritz Lang (*Destiny* [1921]; *Metropolis* [1927]) and F. W. Murnau (*Nosferatu* [1922]; *Faust* [1926]). Frequently labelled as 'expressionist' cinema, this cycle of films played a number of important roles in the Weimar industry. On the one hand, they appealed to 'high art' and had roots in 'Germanic' cultural traditions such as Romantic art and literature as well as fairy-tales and legends, which lent the films a certain level of cultural specificity and respectability. This was important in raising the cultural legitimacy of film as a medium more generally and making it respectable for consumption by bourgeois audiences. This phenomenon was not unique to Germany as many nations, including the US, struggled to raise the status of cinema out of its lowly beginnings in vaudeville, peep shows and the fairground in order to attract a broader, more literate, respectable and ostensibly more massive audience. In America, this largely involved industry regulation of film content to ensure that films were suited to a family audience, although the tight industry-wide regulations of the Hayes Code were not introduced until 1930. In Germany, there was a drive to align cinema with the arts, and numerous intellectuals and cultural commentators rallied against sceptical, moralising scaremongers in the nation's newspapers and journals during the so-called *Kino-Debatte* (1909–29). Some, including Siegfried Kracauer, Walter Benjamin and George Lukács attempted to come to terms with the ambivalences (between art and commerce) with which the medium of cinema confronted them. If cinema deeply troubled intellectuals and moralists alike (for quite different reasons of course), the industry appeared to manage this ambivalence with greater ease. To some extent the move toward literary and artistic precursors assisted not only to raise the cinema's artistic profile, but could also be used as a way of differentiating German films from international (mostly US and French) imports. This product differentiation would also provide the necessary edge to market German films internationally as somehow uniquely 'German'. It is this marriage of art, commerce and national imaginary that gave rise to some of the films reviewed in the first section of this volume under the heading 'The Fantastic'.

While many accounts of German film history frame works like *Caligari*, *The Golem* (Boese and Wegener, 1920), *Waxworks* (Birinski and Leni, 1924) or *Faust* as 'expressionist' films, I have elected to group them into a rather loose generic category that allows the films in part to transcend their ties to a specific historical moment or artistic movement, and see them in terms of a generic legacy that re-emerges at various moments of German film history. As Elsaesser points out, many of these films carried 'titillatingly sensationalist titles' (2000: 18) which more than hint, I would argue, not only at the rather sensational, fanciful, fantastic, magical and devilish subject-matter, but also at the way they make full use of the tricks and special effects available to the cinematic medium at the time. Indeed, the fact that heavy investment in scientific research and development of special effects techniques helped to bring these fantastic tales to the screen is evidence of the commercial imperatives that drove the production of such 'art' films. This is also borne out in the fact that many of these films serve as precursors to one of the cinema's more denigrated genres: the horror film. In this section, we flash forward to two of the most internationally successful films of more recent German cinema: *The NeverEnding Story* (Petersen, 1984) and *Perfume: The Story of a Murderer* (Tykwer, 2006). Not only do these films take up the rather 'fantastic' subject-matter of the earlier cycle of films in an 'artful' way, they were both underpinned by another powerful and prolific German producer, Bernd Eichinger, who sadly passed away in January 2011 as I was preparing this introduction. It may not be too bold a claim to say that Eichinger was the Pommer of his age: able to move easily between art and commerce, with a unique ability to respond to industrial change. He also proved to have a keen eye toward the internationalization of German film and was a master of the truly transnational co-production, unhinged from any specific national context (see for example the *Resident Evil* franchise 2002–10).

It is my hope that this inaugural volume of the *Directory of World Cinema: Germany* will not only provide a broad survey of the development of specific genres and themes throughout German film history, but that through my decision to include some genres over others, readers will take away one version of the many possible stories that could be told of German cinema and its 116-year history. Indeed, the volumes in the *Directory of World Cinema* series are intended to be representative rather than exhaustive. Each section constitutes a fragment of this story and each film reviewed becomes a yet smaller fragment to then be reconstituted in the minds and imaginations of the reader. It is hoped that my readers may find what Walter Benjamin called 'sensuous' and 'non-sensuous' correspondences and connections between each section and between the films contained therein. To some extent my editorial method has been deeply influenced by the thought of one of the New German Cinema's most important practitioners and theorists, Alexander Kluge. In his films, Kluge developed a montage method that was intended to provoke multiple associations in a spectator's mind. His fragmentary, collage style was based largely on his concept of *Zusammenhang* (literally 'to hang together'). The array of disparate fragments was intended to spark connections in a spectator's mind, and it was there rather than on the screen that the story was finally completed. Kluge was also deeply influenced by the silent cinema of the 1920s, particularly for the way the inter-titles would interrupt the narrative flow of the images. He has written:

> I wouldn't be making films if it weren't for the cinema of the 1920s, the silent era. Since I have been making films it has been in reference to this classical tradition. Telling stories, this is precisely my conception of narrative cinema; and what else is the history of a country but the vastest narrative surface of all? Not one story but many stories. (Kluge 1981/82: 106)

Kluge is not the only German film-maker to speak of the legacy of the cinema of the 1920s. Werner Herzog has also framed himself and his generation as the rightful heirs of the Weimar cinema. This is in part due to the problematic and gaping void in the national imaginary created by the Third Reich (1933–45) and the refusal of any cinematic patrilineage on the part of the post-war generation in West Germany. Herzog's films are rife with oblique allusion and homage to the Weimar period. This is evidenced not only in the most obvious way by his re-make of Murnau's *Nosferatu* (1979), but also by his career-long fascination with adventure and forays into wild and exotic locations. The 'adventure' film takes us back to another strand of the story of Weimar cinema as this, in its many and varied sub-genres, was one of the staples of the commercial end of Weimar cinema. In this iteration of the (hi)story of the German adventure film we begin with the cycle of *Bergfilme* ('mountain films') pioneered by director, producer and avid mountaineer, Arnold Fanck. I see this cycle of films to be related to the fantastic films of the preceding section because of the way the subject-matter helped to push the boundaries and capabilities of the cinematic medium to the extreme; the extreme locations calling for the invention of special lenses, cinematographic techniques and equipment to capture the scope and scale of the location shoots. In her essay on Fanck in this volume, Darlene Inkster provides an excellent overview of the work of this rather neglected German film pioneer whose reputation was marred by his decision to stay on in Germany to continue making films under the Third Reich. It is here too, in the *Bergfilme* that we find other resonances and overlaps between adventure and the fantastic. Sitting right at the intersection of adventure and fantasy, Leni Riefenstahl's directorial debut, *The Blue Light* (1932), cleverly capitalises on its generic hybridity, but also more than hints at a version of an ideal (Aryan) 'Germanness' that has been read as an important precursor to the films she would make under the Third Reich. But rather than heading down this path (I shall outline my reasons below), in this iteration of the story, after looking at some more recent adventure films that take us to exotic and sometimes mountainous terrain – I have already mentioned the importance of Werner Herzog in this trajectory – we move on to consider what is perhaps the most uniquely 'German' of all the 'genres' covered here: *Der Heimatfilm*.

The *Heimatfilm* is one of only a few home-grown genres that grew up in the late Weimar period, and came to dominate German film production in the post-World War II period. The *Heimatfilme* of the 1950s are often seen as a retreat from the horrors of the Nazi period. On an aesthetic level these films represent an escape into bucolic and almost a-temporal rural landscapes: infinitely lush hills and valleys betray little (if any) trace of the country's tumultuous past. These landscapes return, sometimes ironically, throughout German film history, as does the question of *Heimat*, which literally translates as 'homeland', but refers more to a combined sense of place, identity and belonging: it is a concept that lives far beyond the materiality of grassy hills and lederhosen and it has been taken up seriously, ironically, critically and comically in a range of recent films including the highly successful comedy *Grave Decisions* (Rosenmüller, 2006). Indeed Bavaria-based Rosenmüller's commitment to reviving the genre and making it relevant to contemporary times may also be seen as a move to combat the cultural odourlessness of the international and transnational co-production, described by some as the 'Euro-pudding' phenomenon.[1]

Through Rosenmüller we move to a mode that, as Christine Haase points out in her introduction, Germans are not normally known for: comedy. Despite the fact that comedy was another of the most well represented genres of the Weimar period, scant scholarly attention has relegated these films to relative oblivion – and unfortunately there they will remain for this edition of the *Directory* at least. In this section I have gathered together a disparate and rather odd grouping of films that admittedly does not do full justice to the range and scope of German film comedy and its numerous sub-genres and iterations. We do, however, find humour used for ironic and at times critical purposes and as a way of 'coming to terms with the past.' The section opens with Curt Goetz's humorous critique of authority figures, *Napoleon is to Blame for Everything* (1938) with its witty parody of Hitler, a daring move in the Nazi-controlled film industry. It makes a nice pairing with Dany Levy's 2007 film *Mein Führer – The Truly Truest Truth About Adolf Hitler*. I have also elected to situate Alexander Kluge's unclassifiable collage film *The Female Patriot* (1979) here, alongside Michael Verhoeven's dark comedy *The Nasty Girl* (1990) for the way both employ a ludic, Brechtian register to critique history in a general and more particular sense respectively. Importantly, these films prepare us for some of the later sections of the volume that deal more explicitly with German history.

Histories of national cinemas (and indeed national cinemas themselves) are frequently silent on the question of society's more marginalised groups. One of my aims with this volume is to recognise the important role German film-makers have played in giving visibility to a range of ethnic identities. I do so in the section entitled 'Foreigners and Guest-workers.' In part we can see the problems of belonging and 'unhomeliness' experienced by the central characters of films by R. W. Fassbinder (*Ali: Fear Eats the*

Soul [1974]), Helma Sanders-Brahms (*Shirin's Wedding* [1976]) and Werner Schroeter (*Palermo or Wolfsburg* [1980]) to be in part an answer to the exclusively Aryan communities of the *Heimatfilme* of the 1950s. Indeed, in her review of the early *Heimat* film *When the Evening Bells Ring* (Beck-Gaden, 1930), Habiba Hadziavdic highlights the way the film exoticises the local Gypsy community as outsiders. Although not voluminous, the New German Cinema's turn to various *Gastarbeiter* ('guest-worker') themes is somewhat unique in European cinema at the time. In a recent article Wes Felton asks an important and potent question for French film history: 'Where are all the Africans in the French New Wave?' (Felton 2010). In doing so, he points not only to certain lacunae in French film history, but also to the resultant remnants and tensions of French colonialism during the 1960s that may well have kept African faces from French cinema screens. At the very least, the directors of the New German Cinema of the 1970s and 1980s should be commended for bringing the plight of Germany's 'others' to the screen, and in doing so, for producing some of the most important films of that period.

Some of the more recent German films about foreigners should be viewed in light of debates currently raging in Europe around the apparent failure of multiculturalism.[2] It is important to highlight the key role contemporary German-born, German-Turkish film-makers like Fatih Akin and Thomas Arslan play in continuing to portray the struggles of *Gastarbeiter*, migrants and their German-born children on-screen in a German context. Indeed, the bevy of prizes won by Akin's *Head-On* (2004) in Germany alone may indicate a will (at least among the film-going community) to tackle some of these social problems rather than admit defeat. Indications are that this new generation of film-makers, open about their hybrid identities, will continue to make an impact on the German filmscape, especially if the sell-out and enthusiastic reception of debut feature by Yasemin Samdrelli *Almanya – Willkommen in Deutschland* (2011), which premiered out of competition at the 2011 Berlinale is anything to go by. *Hollywood Reporter* reviewer Karsten Kastelan remarked: 'The film does for Turkish-German immigrants and their progeny what *Good-bye Lenin!* did for (or to) East Germans, charmingly poking fun at the respective peculiarities of Turks and Krauts alike without ever being condescending' (2011).

Where many other national cinemas remained silent on the question of its ethnic 'others', even very early German film-makers were concerned with giving face to another of western society's most marginalised groups: the GLBTQ community. As early as 1919 we see the formative traces of a Queer German Cinema that will later, in the 1970s, become the cinematic frontline for gay activism in Germany and around the world. It is a trend that persists today and, as we see in the films selected for coverage in the present volume, contemporary queer cinema in Germany frequently shares the concerns of many of the other 'genres' treated here. For example, both *Lola and Billy the Kid* (Ataman, 1999) and *Unveiled* (Maccarone, 2005) deal with the struggles of Germany's doubly 'othered' identities: queer and foreign. We see in Chris Kraus' *4 Minutes* (2006) an attempt to register a lesbian presence during the Third Reich as its (fictional) central character struggles to come to terms (in the present) with her enforced and self-serving complicity with the Nazis (in the past). Furthermore, in controversial Canadian director Bruce LaBruce's German-produced *The Raspberry Reich* (2004) we find a contemporary queer terrorist film that satirizes the political terrorist movements of the 1970s and pre-empts the more recent 'terrorist chic' aesthetic of a film like *The Baader Meinhof Complex* (Edel, 2008). At the heart of this movement, amidst the turbulent 1970s and 1980s lie the key gay and lesbian film-makers – R. W. Fassbinder, Werner Schroeter, Monika Treut, Ulrike Ottinger and, of course, Rosa von Praunheim – whose approach to queer politics revelled in confronting German audiences with their own homophobia.

It is perhaps fitting that as we make our way through this particular (hi)story of German cinema we travel first through the highly politicised and culturally contested terrain of 'foreignness' and 'queerness,' for these sections register the important political 'turn' made in the 1960s and 1970s with the emergence of the Young and New German Cinemas. Aside from attempting to register a critical view on contemporary German society, one of the most persistent concerns of this generation of film-makers was to critically reckon with the period of National Socialism (1933–45), the Second World War and its aftermath: post-war reconstruction; the West German 'economic miracle'; the East-West divide; the Berlin Wall; and the Cold War era more generally. For this reason I have grouped a number of fairly conventional genre categories under the heading *Vergangenheitsbewältigung* – a term that I will unpack in more detail in my introduction to that section, but which translates as 'coming to terms with the past'. Here readers will find entries on the *Trümmerfilm* ('rubble film'); a short-lived genre ostensibly commencing with Wolfgang Staudte's *The Murderers Are Among Us* (1946), where dramas of post-war life were set against the backdrop of Germany's ruined cityscapes. Other genres covered here include the war film, the historical drama and the political drama. These are followed by another quintessentially German cycle of films: the 'Wall film', that is, films that deal with the physical, political and imagined division of Berlin into East and West, and its eventual re-unification approximately a year after the fall of the Wall in 1989.

Beyond this focus on the Wall as a physical and psychological entity, the changing face of Berlin's cityscape is examined here in Collin Chua's essay 'Berlin: Then and Now' on Walter Ruttmann's *Berlin: Symphony of a Great City* (1927) and Thomas Schadt's re-make (2002). This is complemented by Alina Hoyne's examination of the triumphs and controversies of Germany's largest international film festival: the Berlinale. It is my hope that these two essays will point toward the place Berlin (and Potsdam-Babelsberg) has held for more than a century as a crucial hub for the German film industry (East and West) in all its many and varied manifestations. The emergence of what has recently been referred to as the 'Berlin School' of film-makers, along with the re-establishment of the Babelsberg studios in the 1990s, the presence of two of the country's most important film schools and countless independent production companies (including Tom Tykwer's X-Filme) in Berlin will ensure that the city's key contribution to German film culture continues well into the twenty-first century.

As we find ourselves now well ensconced in the twenty-first century, there continues to be a lively film industry in Germany. Increasingly, however, I find myself using the phrase 'German cinema' with caution when describing this contemporary industry. Since the early 1990s more and more films are being made within and across inter- and transnational configurations of capital, talent and infrastructure so that to mark a film as 'German' becomes ever more problematic. Germany's contribution to international co-productions is solid, based on heavy investment in studio infrastructure and training in the 1990s and the first decade of the twenty-first century. This is further supported by the gradual opening up of some of Germany's regional film subsidy boards and television networks to allow partial (sometimes very substantial) funding of such co-productions. For example, many of Danish director Lars von Trier's pan-European productions have received support from German funding bodies and television stations[3] and indeed, Quentin Tarantino's 2009 hit *Inglourious Basterds* was a US/German co-production. This is also a boon for German-based film-makers and film professionals who may also take advantage of the open market across Europe (obvious complaints about the evaporation of cultural specificity aside). In terms of a nation-based volume such as this, however, the increasing diffuseness of European film-making presents something of a dilemma, as during preparation of this volume there were a few instances where a German-themed co-production had been explicitly flagged in the press as not *necessarily* German and my decision was to exclude it from this volume. A good example is Academy Award winner *The Counterfeiters* (Ruzowitzky, 2007), an Austrian/German co-production entered as Austria's nomination for the awards, but also nominated in a range of categories for the annual German Film Awards. By contrast, I have elected to include other co-productions such as *Unveiled* (2005) (Germany/Austria), *Downfall* (Hirschbiegel, 2004) (Germany/Italy/Austria), *The Harmonists* (Vilsmaier, 1997) (Germany/Austria), *The Edukators* (Weingartner, 2004) (Germany/Austria) and *The Raspberry Reich* (2004) (Germany/Canada) where production, cast and crew are primarily German. This shift away from strictly nation-based film production is in turn prompting a reassessment of our scholarly methods and approaches. Chris Berry (2006), for example, has advocated a move away from the concept of 'national cinemas' to focus more on the varying configurations of cinema *and* nation, and Susan Hayward (2000) has suggested that as national cinemas are 'deterritorialized' and 'reterritorialized' from within and without our understanding of what constitutes national cinema should also shift. The growing body of scholarly work on transnational cinemas is also going some way to account for this phenomenon that, to some extent, lies outside the scope of nation-based volumes such as this. For this volume, I merely wish to suggest that Germany has had many cinemas throughout its long history and will have many more to come, inclusive of those films that are not easily locatable in a strictly 'national' sense, but nonetheless continue to contribute to Germany's rich and vast filmscape.

While I have attempted to include a range of films from (almost) all periods of German film history and across the East-West divide in this volume, with entries ranging from 1913 to 2009, the emphasis lies predominantly on the past: the past conceived in two senses – as film history and as history on film. It is for this reason that we begin with essays paying tribute to important but largely forgotten pioneers of German film: the Skladanowsky brothers – who were Germany's answer to France's frères Lumière – and Arnold Fanck, whose location shooting of epic Alpine vistas remained unrivalled anywhere in the world throughout the 1920s. Fanck's innovative filming techniques were quickly adopted by the Hollywood studios but, unlike many of his compatriot film-makers who left Germany in the 1930s with the rise of the National Socialists, the director remained in his home country, only to have his international reputation tarnished by association, if not necessarily by conviction. I have to admit, however, that this tacit prejudice against the Nazi film industry still prevails in the pages of this volume, this period forming something of a lacuna, with two important exceptions: Curt Goetz's comedy *Napoleon Is to Blame for Everything* (1938), mentioned above, and Carl Froelich's *Heimat*, made in the same year. In any case, I felt that a more rigorous and contextualized attention to this period of German film history would be better left for a future edition of the *Directory of World Cinema: Germany*. Indeed, aside from the widely-acknowledged investment in propaganda, that period may be considered one of the most vibrant for the production of genre films in the strict, industrial sense of the word and so is likely to offer up a rich array of films to survey. For the moment, I hope that readers take away from the present volume an insight into the great diversity of German film culture and industry, and a sense of the alacrity of German film-makers who continue to respond to ever-changing times.

Michelle Langford

Notes

1 This is largely a consequence of the de-regulation of the European television market and pan-European funding/production initiatives such as MEDIA or Eurimages. For a discussion of these in the German context see Randall Halle (2002) 'German Film, Aufgehoben: Ensembles of Transnational Cinema' *New German Critique*, 87, pp. 7-46. One of, or perhaps even the earliest discussion of this phenomenon can be found in William Fisher (1990), 'Let Them Eat Europudding', *Sight and Sound*, 59: 4, pp. 224–27. While Fisher's focus is the impact of pan-European film-making and televi-

sion programming on the French film industry, his argument is equally applicable to the German context.
2. German Chancellor Angela Merkel announced this failure to a meeting of young Christian Democrats on 16 October 2010. This was echoed by British Prime Minister David Cameron in a speech at the Munich Security Conference on 5 February 2011.
3. These include: Filmstiftung Nordrhein-Westfalen, Filmförderungsanstalt (FFA), the national broadasters Westdeutscher Rundfunk (WDR) and Zweites Deutsches Fehrnsehen (ZDF).

References

Berry, Chris (2006), 'From National Cinema to Cinema and the National: Chinese-language Cinema and Hou Hsiao-hsien's "Taiwan Trilogy"', in Valentina Vitali and Paul Willemen (eds.), *Theorising National Cinema*, London: BFI, pp. 148–57.

Elsaesser, Thomas (2000), *Weimar Cinema and After: Germany's Historical Imaginary*, London and New York: Routledge.

Felton, Wes (2010), 'Caught in the Undertow: African Francophone Cinema in the French New Wave', *Senses of Cinema*, 57.

Fisher, William (1990), 'Let Them Eat Europudding', *Sight and Sound*, 59: 4, pp. 224–27.

Halle, Randall (2002), 'German Film, Aufgehoben: Ensembles of Transnational Cinema', *New German Critique*, 87, pp. 7–46.

Hayward, Susan (2000), 'Framing National Cinemas', in Mette Hjort and Scott Mackenzie (eds.), *Cinema and Nation*, London and New York: Routledge, pp. 88–102.

Kastelan, Karsten (2011), '*Almanya – Willkommen in Deutschland*: Berlin Review', *The Hollywood Reporter*, 12 February, http://www.hollywoodreporter.com/review/almanya-willkommen-deutschland-berlin-review-98929. Accessed 18 February 2011.

Kluge, Alexander (1981/82), 'On Film and the Public Sphere', *New German Critique*, 25/26.

Rentschler, Eric (2000), 'From New German Cinema to the post-wall cinema of consensus', in Mette Hjort and Scott Mackenzie (eds.), *Cinema and Nation*, pp. 260–77.

Max Skladanowsky.

FILM PIONEERS THE FILMS OF THE SKLADANOWSKY BROTHERS

Max and Emil Skladanowsky undertook the first projection event of celluloid films for a public, paying audience at the Wintergarten Ballroom in Berlin on 1 November 1895 (shortly before the Lumière brothers' first public projections in Paris), as the concluding part of a variety spectacle showing a programme of their own films with a dual lens film projector, the Bioskop, which they had designed and constructed themselves. Their work, developed in an industrial district of northern Berlin, Prenzlauer Berg, was undertaken within film-historical and urban-historical constraints which eventually led to the forced abandonment of their career in film, less than two years after that first projection event.

The films which the Skladanowsky brothers projected at the Wintergarten Ballroom in November 1895, and on their subsequent film tour until September of the following year, were almost exclusively sequences showing variety performers: together their films assembled a slightly down-market programme of variety acts to those appearing on the main stage of the Wintergarten, so that spectators exposed to those moving images must have felt they were experiencing – through the medium of film and at the evening's end – a concertinaed, phantasmatic variant of the live performances that had just finished. The Skladanowsky brothers' films of the urban life of Berlin, recorded both in the peripheries and at the heart of the city, would be shot only in the following year, and projected only once, for their final projection event in the city of Stettin in March 1897. And the brothers' very first film, shot as an experimental test on the rooftop of a building above the Schönhauser Allee, belongs more to that second set of films than the first. In the film Emil Skladanowsky is seen standing on the building's roof, dressed in a suit and tie and holding his hat; he performs exaggerated corporeal gestures, pitched between gymnastics and clowning, alternately lifting each leg high into the air. The film camera is facing south, towards the centre of Berlin, in the opposite direction to the Skladanowsky brothers' own local district, as though intimating the direction in which their experiments were now taking them. The shadows cast by Emil Skladanowsky's figure indicate that the film was shot around midday, in direct sunlight. Behind his figure, a panorama is visible of factory and brewery chimneys and large tenements, with the distinctive pointed steeple of the nearby Zionskirche prominent in that cityscape. A notable strategy of early film-makers was to focus their cameras on sites in which a maximal concentration of urban traces could be registered by their potential spectator, as with one of Louis Le Prince's first films from 1888 of human and vehicle traversals of Leeds Bridge in England; with the Skladanowsky brothers' film, the gesturing human body is in the foreground of the image, with the Berlin cityscape forming a cohering framework for it. But, as with Le Prince's film of Leeds Bridge, the Skladanowsky brothers' first film was never projected and was not included in the Wintergarten programme. It survived only in fragments, notably in the form of four celluloid frames, two of them exceptionally clear, with considerable detail of the urban panorama behind Emil Skladanowsky's figure, and the other two frames blurred and scratched, holding residues of damage in the form of scorch marks from fire or smoke. The entire film had comprised 48 frames, so if it had been projected at 16 frames per second, it would have had a projection duration of three seconds.

The eight short films projected at the Wintergarten Ballroom were all longer, comprising between 99 and 174 frames, and were each shown repeatedly, in loops. Shot in May 1895, they showed physical spectacles, dances and acrobatics. The first film to be projected each evening simulated an Italian peasants' dance performed by two children; a further film depicted a wrestling contest featuring a celebrated bodybuilder and wrestler of the era, Eugen Sandow, fighting another wrestler named Greiner; the other films showed a boxing kangaroo, an acrobatics display, a human pyramid, a juggler, and a Russian Cossack dance; finally, a film of the Skladanowsky brothers themselves, appearing from either side of the screen, ended the programme. In some cases the films held only a fragment of the complete action, which had either already begun before the camera started to record it or else continued after the film had run out. Other than their shared recording of contemporary variety performers, the programme's film fragments held no linear or interlocking cohesion; together, the films formed a disjointed sequence of moments of eruptive and compelling spectacle similar, in some ways, to the forms of 1960s European and American experimental cinema, such as the films of Kenneth Anger and Kurt Kren. In compiling and filming that programme, even before they had been commissioned to show their work at the Wintergarten, the Skladanowsky brothers evidently devised a content which could be dependably well received at a city centre variety hall, and would allow their spectators, to the maximum possible extent, to recognise, situate and respond to the moving images they were faced with. The brothers' specific choice of performers was clearly influenced, too, by their recent exposure to the Edison company's 'Kinetoscope' individual film-viewing machines designed by William Dickson, which had been installed at another prominent Berlin entertainment venue, Castans Panoptikum, in March 1895, two months before the brothers shot their own films, and which showed similar physical feats and dances.

For the Wintergarten Ballroom projection, the Skladanowsky brothers used filmstrips of 44.5mm-wide unperforated Eastman Kodak film stock, which they meticulously cut and perforated by hand, so that it could run with the minimum disruption in front of the Bioskop's twin lens. The film celluloid was also coated with a special emulsion, devised by Max Skladanowsky and applied with a brush. The films were all shot out-of-doors, either in the garden of the Café Sello in Prenzlauer Berg or those of the venues in which the performers were then appearing, in direct sunlight, to achieve clarity and contrast. But most of the work of preparing both the shooting and projection of the films was undertaken in the Skladanowsky brothers' own workshop, which functioned in that sense as an improvised and formative film studio, prescient in its artisanal dimensions of the studio of the film pioneer Georges Méliès, similarly installed on the urban periphery in the eastern Paris suburb of Montreuil, and in which Méliès began to shoot his hundreds of extravagant film conjurations from March 1897 onwards. The Skladanowsky brothers' workshop-studio also, in some ways, prefigures the spatial form of the far larger Weissensee film studio, constructed in 1913 as a one-storey brick building in a Berlin district adjacent to that of their own workshop, and in which many of the seminal films of early German cinema, such as *The Cabinet of Dr Caligari* (1920), were shot, before that studio abruptly went out of business in the late 1920s in the face of competition from industrial-scale film studios. The derelict Weissensee film studio building was eventually utilised, as it is today, as a subdivided space for numerous artisans' workshops in much the same way as the Skladanowsky brothers' workshop-building operated in 1895. The brothers' first film of Emil Skladanowsky's gestural movements against Berlin's urban panorama was shot only a short distance from that workshop; access to the building's roof could be gained since a friend of the brothers operated his own business there.

The Skladanowsky brothers' final films were shot during the later months of their 1895–96 projection tour across Germany, Holland and Scandinavia, and also immediately after it upon their return to Berlin. By that time the original films shown at the Wintergarten Ballroom had worn out through overuse and had become severely damaged; in addition, the brothers had become aware that they urgently needed new films to seize the attention of their future audiences, and urban film sequences fulfilled that desire. For their new films they used 63mm-wide celluloid film stock. In the centre of Berlin they documented concentrations of horse-drawn vehicles and pedestrians in one of Berlin's main squares, the Alexanderplatz, and along the Unter den Linden avenue; in their own districts of industrial northern Berlin, they filmed at the Schönholz railway station; and also shot a further panorama from the rooftop of the building on which Emil Skladanowsky had performed his gymnastics movements, but this time with the camera facing in the opposite direction – northwards – focused on a busy street corner, the Ecke Schönhauser, and without the foregrounded presence of a human figure. They also shot extremely brief 'fiction' films, depicting choreographed quarrels, such as one filmed in a public garden in Stockholm during the final phase of their projection tour.

In anticipation of future public screenings of their new films, Max Skladanowsky constructed a more sophisticated projector, the single-lens Bioskop-II, during the summer of 1896. But a second film tour proved impossible to arrange. The Skladanowsky brothers demonstrated their new projector and films to the Wintergarten's proprietors, with a view to being commissioned for a second engagement there, in February 1897, but were turned down in favour of rival film exhibitors with more advanced projection devices and films. The only engagement they could secure was in the provincial port-city of Stettin, north-east of Berlin, at the 2,000-capacity Zentralhallen-Theater (later destroyed, like the Wintergarten, by British wartime bombing). The Skladanowsky brothers showed their new city films there for the only time, adding to that programme a new city film shot and then rapidly developed in Stettin during the course of their two-week engagement. It was also the only occasion on which the brothers used their new projector, the Bioskop-II, for public screenings. On 31 March 1897, exactly seventeen months after their first Wintergarten screening, the brothers projected films for the last time. They had been far surpassed, in terms both of their films and projection technology, by a growing number of rival film exhibitors; the Berlin authorities abruptly withdrew their trade license and, after a family dispute, the brothers acrimoniously parted company. As a result, their work fell into oblivion for many years.

A longer version of this article was originally published in the online journal *Senses of Cinema*.

Stephen Barber

Directory of World Cinema

White Hell of Pitz Palü, Sokal-Film GmbH/H.T. Film.

FILM PIONEERS
ARNOLD FANCK
(1889–1974)

18 Germany

Best known for capturing on film exquisite alpine vistas and the extraordinary physical feats of champion athletes, Arnold Fanck has left an indelible mark on popular culture well beyond the borders of Germany. Fanck worked alongside some of the biggest names in German cinema, including G.W. Pabst, Harry Sokal, Max Reinhardt and Carl Mayer, as well as launching the careers of numerous Weimar-era cultural luminaries such as Leni Riefenstahl, Luis Trenker and Hannes Schneider.

As a young student at the Universities of Berlin and Munich, Fanck taught himself photography and honed his mountaineering skills in the Alps. He completed a doctorate in sedimentary geology at the University of Zurich in 1915 then worked for the German army as a photographic technician until discharged at the end of World War I. His first foray into independent film-making began amid the rampant inflation and unemployment that followed. Capitalizing on the international trend of alpinism, Fanck co-founded the Freiburg Mountain and Sports Film Company. Early films, such as *Wonder of the Snow Shoes* (1920) and *Struggle with the Mountain* (1921) concentrated on portraying the art of skiing and starred Hannes Schneider (1890–1955), an expert skier Fanck had met on the slopes some time earlier. This proved to be a turning point for both Fanck's team and for the emerging recreational skiing industry in general. In an attempt to circumvent the stranglehold UFA had on film distribution in Germany at the time, Fanck had taken to screening the films in hired halls and tents at schools, universities and clubs. This stimulated interest in Schneider's fledgling ski school, and by 1923 thousands were flocking to St. Anton for ski lessons, making it necessary for Schneider to employ over twenty instructors to keep up with demand. Around this time Fanck and Schneider co-authored a two-volume book containing hundreds of photographs and reproductions of thousands of frames taken from *The White Art* (1924). Intended as an instruction manual for skiing, these images bear a startling resemblance to Muybridge's analytical research into human motion. The books, which were released in multiple language versions, were highly successful internationally and describe in detail Schneider's now famous 'Arlberg technique' (Fairlie 1957: 161).

Fanck claims that during his early forays into film-making he discovered that he had what he described as an 'innate sense of picture composition' (Weigel 1976: 2), which he believes is something that cannot be taught. To accomplish his particular version of cinematic spectacle Fanck utilized and portrayed some of the most advanced technologies available in the day, often combined with a spirit of experimentation and improvisation. Filters and an assortment of lenses were combined with techniques such as time-lapse photography to enhance the appearance of billowing clouds or lengthening shadows, whilst slow motion was utilized to deconstruct movement. Animation, reconstructed sets, point-of-view shots through imaging devices and on moving objects, backlighting, magnesium flares, wind generators and dynamite were all employed as part of his cinematic toolkit. This had the effect of anthropomorphising nature and embellishing the cinematic spectacle. It also became apparent to Fanck that when it came to editing he was dealing with a completely different set of variables from those used in studio-based productions.

Editing his 'snow and ice' themed movies entailed a good deal of trial and error since he had to learn to match elements such as cross-cutting, movement and tempo. This presented its own unique set of problems. Unlike studio-based productions, which operated primarily on a horizontal plane with constant indoor lighting and conditions, Fanck had to contend with capturing dynamic movement on a variety of inclined planes with constantly changing light and weather conditions. This greatly complicated the shooting and editing process for Fanck and his crew, who had to learn to construct his films to accommodate the vagaries of nature; hence, his early films were based on loose ideas made entirely 'off the cuff' without formal scripts or shooting schedules. Fanck also recognized the need to increase the pace of editing in his films in order to heighten dramatic tension. Even when he had later adopted the practice of preparing formal scripts, Fanck was often forced to abandon segments and improvise in order to accommodate the weather conditions. It was this innovation and moulding of Fanck's cinematic sensibilities to suit the environment which became known as his aesthetic hallmark and made his work so highly influential, setting his work apart from other productions of the era.

The next significant shift in Fanck's films was precipitated by Leni Riefenstahl, a young dancer from Berlin who was keen to act in his mountain films. She had become entranced after seeing *Mountain of Destiny* (1924), a beautifully filmed documentary of the high alpine regions, which featured Luis Trenker. Riefenstahl approached Fanck, and shortly after Fanck wrote *The Holy Mountain* (1926), the first of six mountain films starring Riefenstahl. The incorporation of Riefenstahl into the narrative proved to be groundbreaking for the era and led to the development of more complex plot structures, thus considerably broadening the public appeal of the films. By casting Riefenstahl as young, adventurous, physically competent, attractive, intellectually curious, technically proficient and, for the most part, disinterested in domestic chores, Fanck presented a vision of feminine modernity that is in direct contrast to the oppressive morality tales in genres such as *Strassenfilm* ('street films') that were prevalent in the era. Riefenstahl also claims to have introduced Ernst Udet to Fanck and lobbied for his inclusion in *White Hell of Piz Palü* (Fanck and Pabst, 1929). The depiction of flight, with its dynamic, constantly shifting perspectives and bird's-eye view of the landscape, added highly modernist visual and narrative dimensions to Fanck's *Bergfilm*. The contrast between state of the art technologies and the frozen, primal landscape became integral components in several more of Fanck's films thereafter.

S.O.S. Eisberg (1933), financed by Carl Laemmle Sr. of Universal Pictures in Hollywood, proved to be the most expensive and elaborate production of Fanck's career. Filmed primarily in Greenland, a second version crediting Tay Garnett as director was released due to creative differences. Fanck's next major production was *The Eternal Dream* (1934), filmed in the French Alps. The film lacked the exceptional camerawork and dramatic tension typifying Fanck's earlier productions, primarily because the mountainscape did not feature as prominently in the film.

Daughter of the Samurai (1937)[1] was the last of Fanck's mountain films. Although shot in Japan in an environment vastly different from European alpine environments, the climax of this film, perhaps more than any other, reveals Fanck's preoccupation with innovative cinematic technologies and his professional training as a geologist. The narrative of this film illustrates Fanck's political concessions and may be viewed as a successful attempt to ingratiate himself with the Nazi hierarchy. As a result Fanck was able to make a few 'culture films' in Germany during the remainder of the Nazi era, all of which are bereft of mountain themes, and appear perfunctory and uninspired. Fanck released his last films, both documentary shorts, in 1944.

One of Fanck's most important legacies is that members of his close-knit cast and crew became acknowledged experts in their own right. Luis Trenker and Leni Riefenstahl proved to be Fanck's most famous protégés. Trenker is perhaps best known for *The Prodigal Son* (1934), filmed in the Dolomites and New York City, and *The Emperor of California* (1936), a big budget Western about a German émigré to California during the 1840s gold rush. The film won an award for best foreign film at the 1936 Venice Film Festival. Riefenstahl's directorial debut, *The Blue Light* (1932), won silver at the 1932 Venice Film Biennale and led to the commissioning of films for the National Socialist Democratic Party. *Triumph of the Will* (1935), a record of the 1934 Nuremburg Rally, was much lauded upon its release and subsequently became one of the most studied, criticized and referenced films in the history of the medium. Riefenstahl's record of the 1936 Berlin Olympics, *Olympia Parts 1 & 2* (1938), set the bar for sports reportage and aesthetic rendering of the human body. Both films received numerous international accolades and awards upon their release and, since the end of World War II, have been the subject of rigorous analysis, debate and controversy.

Cameramen who honed their cinematographic skills on Fanck's films and went on to enjoy distinguished careers of their own include Hans Schneeberger, Sepp Allgeier and Walter Riml. All made significant contributions to the German film and television industries and were highly regarded internationally. Walter Riml worked for the US Army immediately after World War II and was engaged as a specialist consultant on films such as *The Great Escape* (Sturges, 1963) and the James Bond classic *On Her Majesty's Secret Service* (Hunt, 1969).

Although Fanck was unable to work in the film industry after the war because of his perceived ties with the National Socialists, his films have influenced generations of film-makers. Despite the positive reception his films received internationally at the time of their release, Fanck's name remains virtually unknown among English speaking audiences. At the German Film Awards in 1964 Fanck was honoured for his outstanding individual contributions to German film.

Darlene Inkster

Note

1. This film was also released as *The New Earth* and *The New Soil*.

References

Fairlie, Gerard (1957), *Flight Without Wings: The Biography of Hannes Schneider*, London: Hodder and Stoughton.
Weigel, Herman (1976), 'Herman Weigel Interview mit Arnold Fanck', *Filmhefte*, Summer.

Berlin: Die Sinfonie Einer Grosstadt.

FILM PIONEERS THEN AND NOW: *BERLIN SYMPHONY, 1927/2002*

Today, in traversing its streets, it is clear that Berlin is a world city.[1] Perusing its urban landscape there is ample evidence of the city's declared ambitions to be the business and cultural capital of Europe in the twenty-first century. Furthermore, in terms of the European and German film industries, Berlin is an important centre, boasting more than one thousand film and television production companies and around 270 movie theatres. The city is also home of the European Film Academy and the German Film Academy, and host to the prestigious annual Berlin International Film Festival (Berlinale), now the largest attended film festival in the world. In addition, the city's urban and historical legacy has made it a popular setting for national as well as international film productions.

It is well known that Berlin's history over the past century has been complex, turbulent and eventful, and the city has been described as 'the capital site of a discontinuous, ruptured history [...] saturated with memories' (Huyssen 2003: 53). Of course, Berlin's past – and even its present – has been mediated to the global spectator through a range of cinematic images and filmic narratives of its urban spaces. A few brief examples can be mentioned.

Run Lola Run (Tykwer, 1998), is an MTV-inspired film with a videogame-like narrative structure, centred on Lola's thrilling race against the clock. The routes that Lola sprints through Berlin are fictional.[2] Instead, Tykwer presents a 'collage of Berlin' (Clarke 2006: 162), constructing a series of false continuities between disparate parts of the metropolis – Berlin is presented like a puzzle, assembled by the director for our bemusement, set to the insistent pulse of a techno soundtrack. *Wings of Desire* (Wenders, 1987) is a cinematic meditation on pre-reunification Berlin as a city wasteland, divided into East and West, caught up in the long struggle of the Cold War, and in the throes of a historicised physical and political schizophrenia, symbolised by the Wall. *The Murderers Are Among Us* (1946), a moody and gripping melodrama that enacts coming to terms with the past, is the first 'rubble film' shot within the ruins of post-World War II Berlin, and the first film to come out of Germany after the fall of Hitler.

Nevertheless, there are two films in particular that are uniquely preoccupied with Berlin. These two films, the two *Berlin Symphony* films (made in 1927 and 2002 respectively), present collages of Berlin, like puzzles we are urged to decipher. These cinematic puzzles are spatial and also temporal. They ask that we are equipped to read the social, historical and ideological traces and narratives inscribed in the urban spaces and human experiences of Berlin, shaped over the years by the implacable forces of modernity and global capitalism, by the legacies of conflict, division and political machination. Viewed in conjunction, these two films allow the past and an always receding present to collide.

In 1927, the director Walter Ruttmann preserved a portrait of Berlin with his documentary, *Berlin, Symphony of a Great City*. An example of the 'city symphony' genre, this remains Ruttmann's best-known film. Ruttmann was heavily influenced by the values of objectivity and factuality associated with New Objectivity painting and photography, a strong current in Weimar cinema after Expressionism. He was interested in the dynamism of movement and shapes, and his work, from the purely abstract *Opus* films (1918–23) to the celebration of urban life in *Berlin* (1927), blurred the boundaries between narrative and non-narrative forms, using the camera as a powerful instrument for representing the visible world.

Made in the silent era in the Weimar period, shot on black-and-white 35mm film over the period of one year, the film premiered in September 1927 at Berlin's Tauentzienpalast, with a specially composed live soundtrack written by Edmund Meisel.[3] Ruttmann's intention was to showcase the German capital's vitality and modernity to allow the viewer to experience the city of Berlin.

The film depicts the life of a city through visual impressions in a semi-documentary style. Without a conventional narrative structure, the sequencing of events implies a kind of loose theme or impression of the city's daily life. The five reel film is divided into five acts, each act announced through a title card at the beginning and end.

We are brought into Berlin by train early in the morning. The city is mostly quiet, but before long there are some signs of activity, and a few early risers can be seen on the streets. We perceive the visceral, accelerating life of the city as it wakes; we travel through the cityscape and are presented with the people, animals and machines that populate it. We see the movement, motion and dynamism of a great European metropolis as it swings into the routine of a typical day, full of bustle and energy. We observe the city's midday rest, busy afternoon life and evening leisure, as calm gradually descends, and the city settles back into slumber.

Despite the apparent chaos and disorder of the flashing images and swift movements, the film is underpinned by a distinct sense of rational order and purpose, conveying the feeling that 'the underlying structure of urban-based capitalism remains intact' (McElligott 1999: 210). Based on the principle of cross section, shots and scenes are dynamically cut together based on relationships of image, motion, point-of-view and thematic content. The film is propelled by rhythm, movement and the city theme. There is very little actual camera movement, and much of the motion in the film, as well as many of the scene transitions, is built around the motion of trains and streetcars.

Ruttmann's *Berlin* is a fascinating, poetic, cinematic capsule of a time and a place irrevocably left behind and now only viewable to us from across an unbridgeable distance. Watching the film is like peering avidly into the past. It is a document of a spectral Berlin that no longer remains, removed not only by the passage of years but also by the ravages and destruction of World War II and the Cold War – when the city was divided, with East Berlin becoming the capital of Soviet-controlled communist East Germany, and West Berlin becoming a political enclave consisting of the American, British and French occupation sectors, and surrounded by the Berlin Wall.

75 years later, the award-winning German documentary film-maker Thomas Schadt would remake the film. Schadt's reinterpretation revealed his impressions of the new face of the metropolis. The urban landscape is given a modern soundtrack by composers Helmut Oehring and Iris ter Schiphorst.

The 1990s had seen the revival of popular star-driven German cinema, firmly focused on values of entertainment and impelled by commercial imperatives. The shift away from art cinema and toward genre films was made possible by new models of film financing and sustained by the changing division of labour between film and television, marking a break with the artistic ambitions and critical intentions of Young German Cinema and New German Cinema in the 1960s and 1970s. Schadt's documentary can be positioned in terms of the re-emergence of a more diverse range of critical filmic narratives and complex images in German cinema in the early 2000s.

While retaining some of the original's basic dramatic principles and characteristics – shooting on black-and-white 35mm film; the lack of a conventional narrative, where the film is organised according to a symphonic structure, with music and images on equal footing; depicting one day in the life of Berlin using several main themes – this is not a slavish remake, and the film strives to establish its own cohesive pictorial language and narrative structure. However, this *Berlin: Symphony of a Great City* (2002) still draws much of its resonance from its precursor.

The power of Ruttmann's images came from the rhythm of his montage technique, which conveyed a sense of movement and speed. Schadt has taken a different tact: long takes, slow contemplative sections, allowing certain details to run for longer. The earlier film's rhythm of progress and development here gives way to a certain melancholy and even a recurring sense of foreboding.

In Schadt's reinterpretation, a contemporary Berlin appears: 75 years older; riven with contradictions; scarred by history; balancing the weight of the past and the demands of the present; simultaneously full of vitality and decay, elegance and ugliness. The 'new' *Berlin*, with the 'old' *Berlin* poised ghost-like in the past, invites us to turn our attention to the multitude of changes the city has gone through over the subsequent decades. The film examines the layers of history and memory preserved and renewed in Berlin, in the spatial organisation of social relations.

Schadt's *Berlin* presents an array of images that bear clear traces of the city's recent history. The daily routine of Berlin is located in different places: in the New Year's Eve celebration at the Brandenburg Gate; in the observation of people going to work, attending sports events, meeting in bars and cafes, lolling around parks, and strolling through department stores; in footage of the fall of the Berlin Wall; the rise of innovative city architecture; in the striking images of the Berlin-Hohenschönhausen Memorial; the redone Reichstag and the new Chancery; the painted remains of the Berlin Wall known as the East Side Gallery; the Olympiastadion; the Love Parade; the Berlinale; and even the zoo.

The Berlin we observe is a city that has undergone a significant transition in the years since the collapse of the Berlin Wall in 1989 and the signing of the Unification Treaty in 1990. In the wake of 1989/90, Berlin was again made the official German capital, and within a decade the face of Berlin has undergone rapid change, giving rise to a new, glittering city.[4] Billions have been spent on spectacular new architecture. There have been heavily debated major development projects, such as the new Potsdamer Platz, the central district constructed in the former no man's land between the East and the West, reconnecting the two halves of the city. Modern housing has been built in run-down areas, and huge, glittering skyscrapers have been erected. However, concerns have also arisen about depleted city finances that could force the closure of some of the city's renowned cultural institutions. There are dirty streets, dilapidated schools and recurring right-wing demonstrations.

The face of the 'new' Berlin has been shaped, on the one hand, by European unification, globalisation and mass migration, and on the other, by increased ethnic and religious resentments and new provincialisms. While the 1990s and the early 2000s have seen a greater tolerance toward ethnic, religious and sexual minorities, and a growing acceptance of pluralism, multiculturalism, and hybridity in social attitudes and cultural practices, there has also been an intensified sense of unprecedented mobility and dislocation resulting in repeated confrontations over issues of immigration, citizenship, and asylum laws, and over the costs and benefits of the neo-liberal world order. Unification resulted in fresh confrontation with the legacies of the past, giving rise to a complex and contradictory culture of remembrance, retrospection and nostalgia.

Ruttmann's original *Berlin* has been recognised as an important artefact of non-narrative experimental cinema, which has exerted an enduring influence on documentary film-making technique. However, it also attracted criticism of the city symphony as a superficial form that displaced politics within its aesthetics. Siegfried Kracauer, for instance, was particularly dismissive of Ruttmann's 'formalism' and 'rhythmic montage' that only managed to set image next to image, failing to critically engage with and understand the significance of its subject matter (1947: 187). The British documentary film-maker John Grierson also specifically mentioned *Berlin* as an example of what documentary should *not* be. For Grierson, despite the visual beauty and power of its images, and the acknowledged dynamism of its editing, Ruttmann's associational montage was found lacking in its capacity to produce documentary insights into daily life (1932: 86).

More recently, Andrew Webber has been equally critical of Schadt's remake because he sees 'the two works closer to each other in their aesthetic-political disposition than might be assumed' (2008: 155). Evelyn Preuss has also argued that Schadt's preoccupation with Weimar images derived from an idealised 1920s Berlin prohibits a proper engagement with Germany's difficult history in the ensuing years (2004: 119–42).

In opposition to these criticisms, the aesthetic strategies of *Berlin* – then and now – can be productively read in socio-spatial terms as presenting specific political analyses. As Henri Lefebvre has instructively remarked, space is a dynamic entity produced by historically contingent social practices (1991). In this way, Berlin can be viewed as 'a disparate city-text that is being rewritten while earlier texts are preserved, traces restored, erasures documented' (Huyssens 2003: 81). Taken together, the two Berlin Symphonies – then and now – help develop a fuller contemporary understanding of an emerging world city that in many ways remains ambivalent about both its built past and its urban future.

Collin Chua

Notes

1. The term was popularised by Saskia Sassen, who recognised that the global economy is no longer dominated by powerful nation-states but instead by world cities acting as the major nodes in a global economic network.
2. The opening scene of Lola's apartment, where the camera zooms in from an aerial view of Berlin, was shot at an existing apartment house on Albrechtstraße, half a block away from the Spree River in the centre of Berlin. But the scenes of Lola running down the street, after she goes through the gate, were shot at various other locations – it would be impossible to actually reach all these places within twenty minutes.
3. Contemporary viewers are generally accustomed to the score composed by Timothy Brock in 1993; the original score by Meisel was for a long time thought to be lost. On 24 September 2007 a restored version of the film was premiered, with the fully reconstructed original score, at Berlin's FriedrichstadtPalast with live orchestral accompaniment by the Rundfunk Sinfonieorchester Berlin. This was subsequently broadcast on the Franco-German TV cultural channel Arte.
4. For a fuller discussion see, for example, Karen E. Till (2005), *The New Berlin: Memory, Politics, Place*, Minneapolis: University of Minnesota Press; Brian Ladd (1997), *The Ghosts of Berlin: Confronting German History in the Urban Landscape*, Chicago: University of Chicago Press.

References

Clarke, David (2006), *German Cinema: Since Unification*, London and New York: Continuum.

Grierson, John (1932), 'First Principles of Documentary', in I. Aitken (ed.) (1998), *The Documentary Film Movement: An Anthology*, Edinburgh University Press, Edinburgh, pp. 145-56.

Huyssen, Andreas (2003), *Present Pasts: Urban Palimpsests and the Politics of Memory*, Stanford, CA: Stanford University Press.

Kracauer, Siegfried (1947 [2004]), *From Caligari to Hitler: A Psychological History of the German Film*, Princeton, NJ: Princeton University Press, p. 187.

Ladd, Brian (1997), *The Ghosts of Berlin: Confronting German History in the Urban Landscape*, Chicago: University of Chicago Press.

Lefebvre, Henri (1991), *The Production of Space*, (trans. Donald Nicholson-Smith), Oxford: Blackwell.

McElligott, Anthony (1999), 'Walter Ruttmann's *Berlin: Symphony of a City*: Traffic-mindedness and the city in interwar Germany', in Malcolm Gee, Tim Kirk and Jill Seward (eds.), *The City in Central Europe: Culture and Society since 1800*, Aldershot: Ashgate Publishing, pp. 209-38.

O'Sickey, Ingeborg Majer (2000), 'Whatever Lola Wants, Lola Gets (Or Does She?): Time and Desire in Tom Tykwer's *Run Lola Run*', *Quarterly Review of Film and Video*, 19: 2, pp. 123–31.

Preuss, Evelyn (2004), 'The collapse of time: German history and identity in Hubertus Siegert's *Berlin Babylon* (2001) and Thomas Schadt's *Berlin: Sinfonie einer Großstadt* (2002)', in Carol Anne Costabile-Heming, Rachel J. Halverson and Kristie A. Foell (eds.), *Berlin: The Symphony Continues. Orchestrating Architectural, Social and Artistic Change in Germany's New Capital*, Berlin: Walter de Gruyter, pp. 119–42.

Sassen, Saskia (1991), *The Global City: New York, London, Tokyo*, Princeton, NJ: Princeton University Press.

Till, Karen E. (2005), *The New Berlin: Memory, Politics, Place*, Minneapolis: University of Minnesota Press.

Webber, Andrew (2008), 'Berlin Symphonies: Movements and Stills', *Berlin in the Twentieth Century: A Cultural Topography*, Cambridge: Cambridge University Press, pp. 152-87.

Cast and crew of *Almanya – Willkommen in Deutschland* with Berlinale director Dieter Kosslick. Photo: Richard Hübner © Berlinale 2011.

FESTIVAL FOCUS
THE BERLINALE: BERLIN INTERNATIONAL FILM FESTIVAL

Every February, in the depths of winter, film-goers and cineastes congregate in warm cinemas to sample the offerings of the Berlin International Film Festival (or Berlinale, as it is affectionately named). Not only is it one of the world's most prestigious and longest running annual film festivals, but it also draws the biggest audiences. According to organisers, in 2010 ticket sales for the almost 1,000 public screenings over the two-week festival exceeded 270,000 and almost half a million theatre visits in total.

As one of the 'Big Three' (Cannes, Berlin and Venice), the Berlinale strikes a balance between red carpet 'glitz 'n' glamour' and its role as talent scout. The festival must attract enough 'talent' to pique media and public interest and make the festival economically viable, while staying fresh and in-step with emerging figures and new developments in film-making. The official section, 'Panorama' and 'Forum' have all played important roles in championing new talent. The French New Wave was recognised early with several awards given between 1959 (*Les Cousins* [dir. Claude Chabrol]) and 1965 (*Alphaville* [dir. Jean-Luc Godard]). In the 1960s it was new Polish film-makers, with Golden Bears to both Polanski and Skolimowski. In the 1980s attention turned to the Fifth Generation Chinese directors with a Golden Bear awarded to Zhang Yimou for *Red Sorghum* in 1988. At the turn of the millennium, Dieter Kosslick (now the head of the Berlinale) championed a new wave of German films.

Although the Berlinale was touted as the 'showcase for the free world' in its early years, American productions dominated, with films such as Sidney Lumet's *Twelve Angry Men* (1957) and Gene Kelly's *Invitation to the Dance* (1956) taking 'unofficial' Golden Bears. In 1951 Disney won two golden Bears with *Cinderella* (dirs. Clyde Geronimi and Wilfred Jackson) and *In Beaver Valley* (dir. James Algar), and in 1958 Walt Disney was presented with an honorary porcelain bear by then mayor of West Berlin, Willy Brandt. By the end of the 1950s the programme took on a more international flavour with over 50 nations' films in competition, helped along no doubt by official recognition given by the International Federation of Film Producers in 1955 and the appointment of an International Jury in 1956.

The first taste of East-West controversy for the Berlinale came in 1956 when the festival's founder and first director, Dr Bauer, protested to senate against the 'unofficial' screening of East German DEFA films in West Berlin under the slogan 'International Understanding'. While Bauer's move caused contention, he won some respect for showing Alain Renais' *Nuit et Brouillard* (1955) in a special screening at the festival: ironically, perhaps, as the film had been dropped from Cannes after the West German government protested that the film, documenting the actions of Germans in Auschwitz, didn't serve 'international understanding'. The following year Orson Welles refused to attend the Berlinale or screen his film *Othello* (1952). Arguments between the 25 members of the working committee over anti-German comments made by Welles two years prior led to the postponement of his invitation, which was sent so late that Welles declined.

But the disagreements of the 1950s were not in the same league as the scandal of 1970, when the competition ended prematurely and no official prizes were awarded. Some members of the jury, led by president George Stevens, resigned after attempting to have Michael Verhoeven's film *O.K.* (1970) excluded from competition. Stevens, who had served during World War II, claimed that the film – in which a Vietnamese girl is raped and shot by four American soldiers – was anti-American. In 1979 Eastern European and other communist delegations and their jury representatives left the festival after a screening of Michael Cimono's *The Deer Hunter* (1978). They claimed the film, which follows a group of Pennsylvanian steel-mill workers at war in Vietnam, was racist and insulted Vietnamese people. Amid the controversy the film's director flew home, while the president of United Artists International, the company that owned the rights, came to Berlin and defended the film. With the support of the American Embassy and the German senate, Donner refused to remove the film from the festival, while Mortitz De

Hadeln (soon to be co-director) stood with the GDR delegation as a sign of understanding and solidarity. The film was well received by audiences.

The Berlinale is not only remarkable due to controversy but also for continuity. Remarkably in its 60-year history the Berlinale has only had four directors. The first was founder Dr Alfred Bauer, author of the definitive catalogue of German sound film *Deutsche Spielfilm-Almanach 1929–1950*, who ran the festival from 1951 to 1976. In 1950, after serving in the Reichfilmskammer (National Film Office) during World War II and assisting the British army's film advisor after 1945, Bauer presented a report to the mayor's office in Berlin, proposing that a film institute – and an attendant film festival – should be founded in Berlin to encourage the re-establishment of the German film industry. Berlin's then mayor, Ernst Reuter, opened the first Berlinale at the Titania-Palast in Steglitz on 6 June 1951, with a screening of Hitchcock's *Rebecca* (1940). For the next 40 years the festival's centre was situated in the heart of West Berlin until, in 2000, the Festival moved to Potsdammer Platz.

In 1976 Bauer turned 65 and was obliged to retire. 38-year-old journalist Wolf Donner, the Chairman of Committee charged with finding Bauer's successor, had to take the position himself after the Committee failed to settle on any one individual. Although overseeing only three festivals, Donner made significant changes, including introducing the children's and 'Panorama' sections, and ensuring that German films were accessible to wider audiences by screening them with English subtitles. In 1978 he made the most influential decision since the festival's inception, to move the Berlinale from June to February, placing it three months before Cannes.

Moritz de Hadeln, in partnership with Ulrich Gregor at the International Forum of Young Cinema (now the 'Forum'), set out to modernise the festival and to make the Berlinale the world's most efficient event. The current director, Dieter Kosslick, whose first festival was in 2002 and who is contracted until 2013, has attracted attention for his new non-competition section on culinary arts and his taste for political controversy. In 2004 Fatih Akin's *Head-On*, which tackles the sensitive issue of integration in Germany, received the Golden Bear awarded to best film. 2008 saw the appointment as jury president of renowned political film-maker, Costa-Gavras, whose jury awarded a Golden Bear to the hyper-violent Brazilian film *Tropa de Elite* (dir. Jose Padilha [2007]). In 2009 controversy surrounded the screening of two documentaries, one on Kashmir in 'Panorama' and another on Iranian President Mahmoud Ahmadinejad shown in 'Forum'.

Beyond such political controversies, the Berlinale has also stood in solidarity with jailed film-makers and political prisoners. This was highlighted at the opening of the 2011 festival when jury president Isabella Rossellini read an impassioned letter from the Iranian film-maker Jafar Panahi. Panahi, who won a Silver Bear for his film *Offside* in 2006, was sentenced to jail for six years in December 2010 along with fellow director Mohammad Rasoulof. Both film-makers were banned from making films for twenty years. An empty white chair bearing Panahi's name was symbolically left empty for the duration of the festival.

Maintaining a balance between the local and the global is key to the survival of the Berlinale. This is reflected not only in the selections made for the main 'Competition' – which is international in scope but of interest to a wide audience – but also the other six sections: 'Panorama' provides a forum for independent and art house productions (including, since 1987, the annual 'Teddy Awards' for queer cinema); while 'Forum' provides a view into other worlds and cultures; German cinema productions are shown in '*Perspektive Deutsches Kino*'; 'Generation' (with its two competitive sections and GK+ and G14+) screens movies with young audiences in mind; 'Berlinale Shorts' shows experimental short films; and 'Retrospective and Homage', curated by the Berlin Film Museum, places contemporary cinema within a historical context, focusing on the life work of a cinema great (a director, producer or star).

The Berlinale doesn't just view itself as a showcase but also as a propagator. This is sometimes expressed symbolically, as in the generational passing of the baton, in which older directors present awards to their younger counterparts, such as Ingmar Bergman to Michelangelo Antonioni. On a practical level it hosts the Berlinale Talent Campus giving around 350 young film-makers from around the world the opportunity to collaborate and meet with experienced film professionals and personalities during a week of workshops and discussions. The Talent Campus is one of the Berlinale's great successes and has been exported to other festivals around the world.

The European Film Market (EFM), the Berlinale's trade centre, is one of the most important events on the international film business calendar, attracting around 130 stands and over 400 exhibitors from all over the world. As well as screenings the EFM hosts lectures and debates, a special sidebar for German cinema, as well as initiatives such as 'Books at Berlinale' and 'Straight from Sundance'. The Berlinale also supports new projects such as the Berlinale Co-Production Market, which to date has helped produce around 80 films, and World Cinema Fund (WCF), a joint initiative between the German Federal Cultural Foundation and the Goethe Institute, which supports films from developing nations.

In recent times, the Berlinale has continued to attract criticism on issues of social justice, some of which is directed at the festival itself. Although the Berlinale budget is around €18 million annually, only twelve people are employed on permanent, year-round contracts. Whilst this figure rises to 1000 workers during the festival, the Berlinale has attracted criticism for relying upon low or unpaid labour. In 2008 activists dressed as superheroes descended upon the red carpet to liberate the workers. A number of nude protests – most notably by students at the 2004 awards ceremony protesting against the introduction of university fees in Berlin – have also drawn media attention.

Despite, or perhaps because of, on-going controversy the future of the Berlinale appears to be secure. It has a healthy number of sponsors, committed grants from the German government and income from the EFM. But, even more significant, it is growing in popularity amongst the general public, with the festival attracting more Berliners every year, new and old alike.

Alina Hoyne

The Chronicle of Anna Magdalena Bach, IDI/RAI/SEITZ.

SCORING CINEMA
THE MUSIC FILMS OF STRAUB/HUILLET

Jean-Marie Straub (b. 1933) and Danièle Huillet (1936–2006) made four films dedicated to music over a period of nearly thirty years. Three were full-length features: *Die Chronik der Anna Magdalena Bach/The Chronicle of Anna Magdalena Bach* (1968), *Moses und Aron* (1974–5) and *Von heute auf morgen/Today to Tomorrow* (1997) – the last two being filmic versions of Schönberg's two operas, one Biblical and one modern. In addition, there is the seventeen-minute *Einleitung zu Arnold Schönbergs Begleitmusik zu einer Lichtspielszene/Introduction to Arnold Schönberg's Accompaniment to a Cinematic Scene* (1972). All share an unusual approach to film sound distinguishing these films from the better known work of New German film-makers such as Fassbinder, Wenders and Syberberg, as also from the aural montage practice of Kluge.

Straub and Huillet moved to Germany from France in 1958 so that Straub could avoid being drafted into the French army during the Algerian War. Early influences on his work include not only Bresson but also Jean Grémillon, whose experiments with soundtrack independence and musical conception of form parallel Straub and Huillet's later work (Roud 1972: 18–19). The deliberate neutrality with which Bresson's actors deliver their lines and his extreme fidelity to his adapted texts are also models for Straub and Huillet's documentary aesthetic. One might say that in their music films they extended Bresson's fidelity to a literary text to musical scores and their historical contexts. The extreme length of Straub and Huillet's long takes, their use of non-professional actors and their documentary use of live sound all go beyond their models, however, and have no real parallel in the work of their German contemporaries. As Barton Byg has shown, 'the relative marginality of Straub/Huillet in treatments of the New German Cinema, with its narrative, "art cinema" label, is based on the supposed "antinarrative" quality of their work as well as their outsider status' (1991: 25). This 'antinarrative' quality is, in turn, usually derived from Brechtian influence, and described in terms such as 'austere' or 'formalist' – which, as we will see, is not entirely accurate.

Die Chronik der Anna Magdalena Bach was their third film, after the short *Machorka-Muff* (1962) and the Böll adaptation *Nicht versöhnt/Not Reconciled* (1964–5). However, they had been pursuing funding for the Bach film since the late 1950s. The film is based on documents about Bach's life, told by his wife in voice-over; Bach is played by the Dutch harpsichordist Gustav Leonhardt, one of the pioneers of the original instruments movement. The looseness of the narrative meant that the shape of the film, the length of its shots, could all be determined by the music. Shot editing is sometimes surprisingly discontinuous, as when in shot 47 we suddenly discover that Bach and Anna Magdalena are much closer to each other in space than the previous two shots suggested. Shots of performance are often at strong diagonals with tracking in or out. Composition of shots and discreet camera movements are systematically, almost musically, varied.

This compositional rigor is taken even further in *Moses und Aron* (1974–5) whose singers were recorded live in the ancient theatre of Alba Fucens in the Italian Abruzzo (the orchestral accompaniment was done in a studio and later synchronized). There are only 77 shots in a 110-minute long film due to Straub and Huillet's desire to avoid breaking apart the continuity of music with cuts. Straub and Huillet read Schönberg's drama of the birth of monotheism in Marxist terms, as a narrative of the liberation of the people of Israel. Any spectacular or mystical elements are thus shown only in distanced form. The paradoxical Divine presence that, as invisible, could not be shown was implied by elements outside the enclosure of the theatre, such as the mountain at the end of the pan in shot 10. As Byg has noted, through the editing and camera movement, 'the spectator is not confined to a point of view but still senses the confinement of the theater space' (1991: 148). Thus, the Israelites' escape from Egypt is shown via 'two long panning shots of the Nile' (ibid: 152).

Einleitung zu Arnold Schönbergs Begleitmusik zu einer Lichtspielszene, to a film score composed in 1930, uses documentary elements – as did *Anna Magdalena Bach* – but now in more heterogeneous fashion: stills of Schönberg, of his painted self-portrait and quotes from his letters, mixed with shots of the murdered Paris Communards of 1871 and sequences of the directors themselves, and Günther Straschek speaking either outdoors or inside. Both black-and-white and colour are used. The spoken commentaries concern Schönberg's career, such as his refusal of an invitation to join the Bauhaus or his exile and his thoughts on anti-Semitism. Since the film states that the composer's film score, which only contains the indications 'threatening danger, fear, catastrophe,' cannot be directly represented, the music's contents are given political and documentary correlatives.

Von heute auf morgen is the most unusual of all Straub and Huillet's filmic opera choices. Schönberg's only comic opera was long neglected both by scholarship and performance, but has made something of a comeback since Straub and Huillet's film. It was not only a comic opera, but also a *Zeitoper*, or 'opera of the age', meaning an opera with specifically documentary quality. Schönberg composed it in 1928–29 in response to other *Zeitopern*, including Krenek's jazz-inspired *Jonny spielt auf/Jonny Strikes Up* (1927) and Brecht and Weill's *Die Dreigroschenoper/The Threepenny Opera* (1928). The opera concerns the midlife crisis of a modern marriage, where both partners – simply titled The Man and The Woman – are tempted to infidelity, yet come together at the end. Straub and Huillet managed the astonishing feat of recording a live performance with full orchestra, again making their cuts match musical articulations of form.

Straub and Huillet's sound practice may be summed up in two aspects: firstly, the function of direct sound, and secondly, the relation of sound and image. Straub and Huillet were fond of quoting Jean Renoir to the effect that if he, or they, had a religion it was that of direct sound. One could argue that in this they are only repeating old-modernist forms of technophobia, or that this position privileges the direct presence of voice or music versus medially modified copy, yet this would be inadequate. Recent work in performance has pointed out that we do not need to see valorisation of the live against the mediated as ontological, but rather as an operative distinction. Live and recorded performances depend on each other, as Straub and Huillet's documentary practice acknowledges.

That documentary sound practice also wears a specific historical signature from the history of recording technology circa 1930. That moment was not only one of the inception of sound film, but also of a shift in radio broadcasting practice. In the US, the Metropolitan Opera would begin its decades-long broadcasts in 1930. Radio broadcasting required a studio acoustic that was drier and harder, more free of resonance, than that of the nineteenth century concert hall. The *Sachlichkeit* or 'objectivity' of radiophonic sound was reflected in the work of Schönberg, whose dry, objective orchestration in the mid-to-late 1920s Adorno compared to photography (1997: 87). This is why Straub and Huillet were so fascinated by the early sound films of Renoir, or the deliberately neutral use of sound by Bresson: their hearkening back to early cinema is not only one to the silents but to early sound film too. Their rejection of all the added reverb and resonance of Dolby and digital recording techniques has a critical or polemical edge. The relative flatness of their monophonic sound is meant as a historical marker, a memory perhaps of Edison's famous 1888 claim that film would 'do for the eye what the Phonograph has done for the ear.'

Straub and Huillet also refuse to eliminate background noise from their recordings. They do so in order to insist not only on the materiality of recorded space, but also on the difference between that space and the listener. As Barry Blesser and Linda-Ruth Salter have argued:

> Sensing the location of a sound source and sensing the experience of an enclosed space are polar opposites. With localized sound, the instrument is external to the

listener, whereas with enveloping reverberation, the listener is inside the sound generation process [...]. (2007: 145)

That is, inside the recording 'apparatus'. It is this illusion of being inside the apparatus that is rejected by direct sound.

Here is also where a Brechtian aspect of Straub and Huillet's sound practice may be found. As Brecht suggested in a piece for the *Berliner Börsen-Courier*, 'you must move with the apparatuses closer to the real events and not simply limit yourself to reproducing' ([1927] 2000: 35). 'Moving closer to real events' does not, however, mean abolishing all distance. In another typescript about radio from 1927, Brecht apodictically states, '[A]rt must intervene where the defect is to be found' (ibid: 38). We might interpret this 'defect' as one in media technology itself, the limitations or aural 'frame' of which are deliberately exposed by the documentary quality of Straub and Huillet's direct sound. This practice marks their difference from Alexander Kluge's audio-visual counterpoint, which is closer to Eisler/Adorno's *Composing for the Film*. Music is neither merely used as a form of authorial commentary, as in Kluge's Godard-inspired practice, nor is it linked with irony or nostalgia for lost cultural values, as in Fassbinder or Syberberg. Rather than being a bearer for cultural semantics, music plays a structural and syntactic role for Straub and Huillet. In this, their sound practice may indeed be described as musical materialism.

Larson Powell

References

Adorno, Theodor (1997), *Philosophie der neuen Musik, Gesammelte Schriften*, Frankfurt: Suhrkamp, vol. 12.
Blesser, Barry and Salter, Linda-Ruth (2007), *Spaces Speak, Are You Listening? Experiencing Aural Architecture*, Cambridge, MA: MIT.
Brecht, Bertolt (1927 [2000]), *Brecht on Film and Radio*, (trans. Marc Silberman [ed.]), London: Methuen.
Byg, Barton (1991), *Landscapes of Resistance: The German Films of Danièle Huillet and Jean-Marie Straub*, Berkeley: University of California Press.
Roud, Richard (1972), *Straub*, New York: Viking.

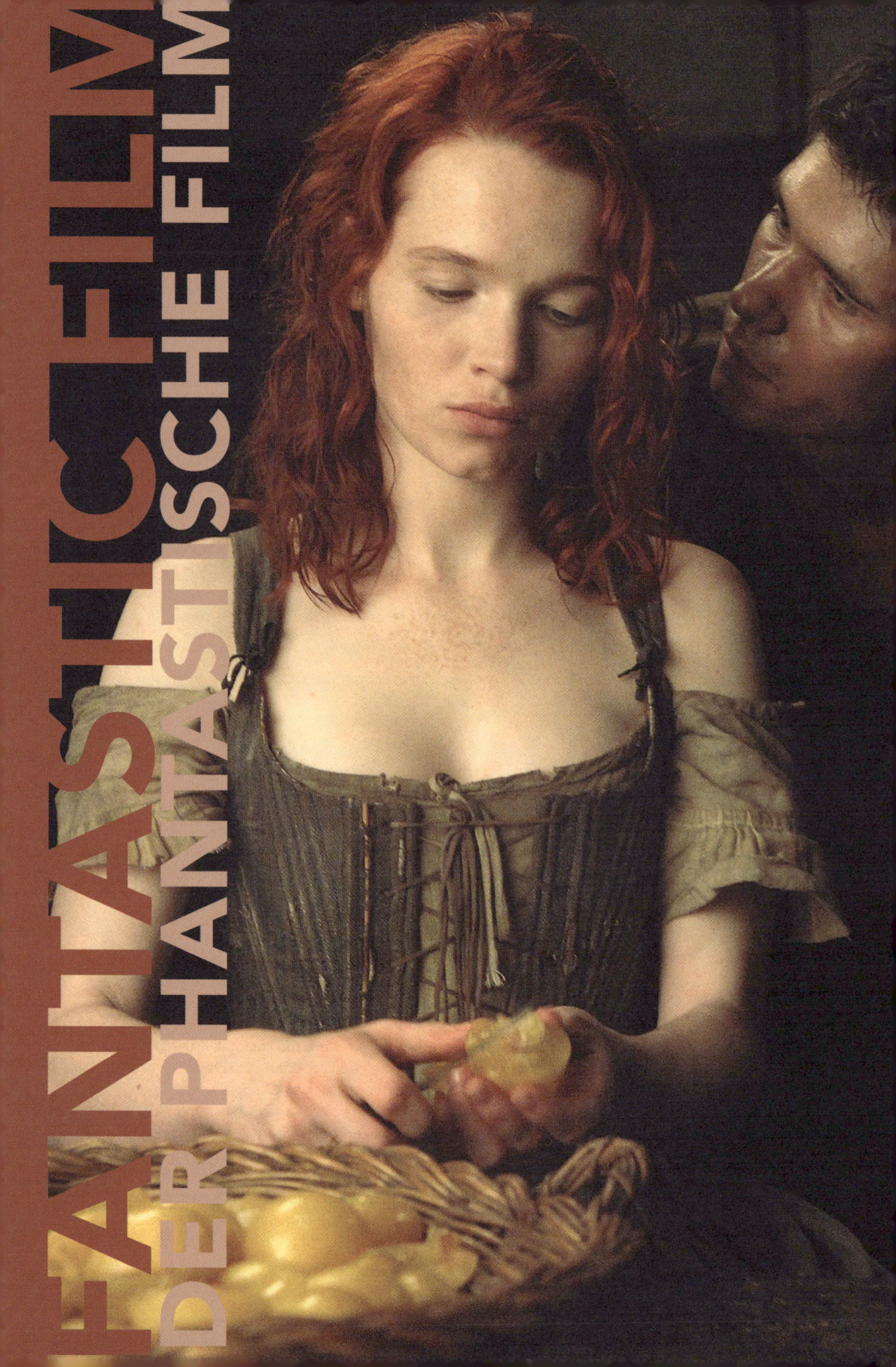

FANTASTIC FILM
DER PHANTASTISCHE FILM

The fantastic film characterizes an affect-laden tradition in German and world cinema, integrating supernatural, fairy-tale and/or science fantasy elements into a fictional diegesis. Introduction of such otherworldly elements by definition requires the innovation of visual effects to achieve a kind of 'sensory surplus' (Lachmann 2002: 26) or non-mimetic mimesis in the viewer; that is to say, the diegesis helps the viewer imagine non-empirical realities, or lets him/her believe for a moment that they actually witnessed an impossible event. The purpose is no less than to induce direct shock and awe in the audience as part of a broader fictional narrative.

One memorable illustration of the German notion of the fantastic film can be found in the title sequence of the popular German Second Channel (ZDF) television programme *Der phantastische Film* (1970–92). A London gas lamp against a shadowy stone backdrop cuts suddenly to Heinz Edelmann's (famous for illustrating the Beatles' *Yellow Submarine* [dir. George Dunning, 1968] film) animation of the profile of a mod-styled white man as he undergoes a series of invasive metamorphoses. A blue alien creature thrusts itself from his mouth, a demon from his nose, his face becoming a mask vaguely resembling a Japanese *oni*. We then see the man from the front, the upper half of his head literally ablaze as he disconcertingly meets our gaze before his whole face shifts upward to become a yelling Cyclops. Switching back to profile as his head slowly moves to the right, horns and oversized ears grow from his head, his hair transforming into a flock of bats and then into the sallow faces of two women. The sequence ends with his head rotating 360-degrees on his neck to reveal a frightening robotic face before it simply blasts off and detonates in the air to become the show's star-emitting title. The warble of an analogue synthesizer combined with an eerie violin melody offers a suitably unsettling accompaniment. In an arresting fashion, all iterations of the fantastic – Gothic horror, science fiction and fantasy – are summarized via the cranium of the presumed white male viewer. The shocks and surprises of the cuts and on-screen metamorphoses immediately filter the show's audience, giving its target demographic horrific payoff while startling others into changing the channel. Long-time fans witness the well-established and familiar catalogue of the monstrous and the uncanny whilst receiving a fresh burst of shock, albeit via a cartoon.

Though frequently based on novels, German fantastic films may be the most firmly entrenched of any genre in the painting medium,[1] particularly in the works of the Romantic and Expressionist movements. Both visual styles emerged as rebellions against Enlightenment expressions of rationality and the individual. Indeed, Romanticism and Expressionism were the societally sanctioned form of resistance against a perceived Weberian 'disenchantment of the world.' The work of Romanticists such as Caspar David Friedrich or Joseph Anton Koch, echoed in F.W. Murnau's *Nosferatu* (1922) or Wolfgang Petersen's *The NeverEnding Story* (1984), resist this disenchantment through empirically plausible dreamscapes that instil awe and mystery, with figures before them unable to master their splendour. On the other hand, Expressionists such as Hermann Warm and Walter Röhrig, who painted the angular sets of *The Cabinet of*

Left: *Perfume: The Story of a Murderer*, Constantin Film Produktion/VIP 4 Medienfonds.

Dr. Caligari (1920), broke with empirical reality altogether, collapsing the gulf between figure and landscape entirely and projecting internal fantasies into impossible worlds of their own. Romantic traditions internal to the film lure a viewer into a fantasy world, while Expressionist traditions render the familiar alien and the discontinuous as the norm.

The German fantastic film recurred throughout film history in discrete, closed cycles. Following early magical shows by Georges Méliès, the Germans abruptly entered into the genre in 1913 with three films: *The Other* (dir. Max Mack), *Das fremde Mädchen* (dir. Max Reinhardt) and *The Student of Prague* (dirs. Stellan Rye and Paul Wegener), all of which revolve around the Gothic intrusion of madness or horror into ordinary peoples' lives. This 'calculated madness' (Lange 1992) reached its apogee following the trauma of World War I with Robert Wiene's *The Cabinet of Dr. Caligari* (1920), in which the ambiguity between figure and landscape, reality and nightmare, 'special effect' and narrative content becomes absolute. Such ambivalence and dark subject matter came into vogue in the 1920s, leading to Germany's innovative dominance of the fantastic film market with *Weird Tales* (Oswald, 1919), Wiene's *Genuine – Tragödie eines seltsamen Hauses* (1920), Paul Wegener's *The Golem* (1920), F.W. Murnau's *Nosferatu* and *Satanas* (1920), and Fritz Lang's *Destiny* (1921), to name but a few German films portraying the unearthly and/or the macabre that seized the global audience's imagination. This Berlin and Potsdam-based explosion of high quality, metaphysical allegories could be attributed to the acute concentration of working artists in the region, cheap labour afforded only due to wild inflation and a desire to distinguish German national cinema products from Hollywood. These films – characterized by their angled sets, high-contrast lighting, stylized acting, discontinuous montage and supernatural or eerie content – left an indelible impression on world cinema, with their descendents best found in the horror and film noir genres.[2] By the mid-1920s, however, the actual movement had both ushered in its masterpieces such as Paul Leni's *Waxworks* (1924), Lang's *Die Nibelungen* (1924), and Murnau's *Faust* (1926) – all fantasy/adventure films with extensive effects sequences – and met its end in the rising costs of production and redoubled competition with Hollywood. Then the beautiful catastrophe of Lang's *Metropolis* (1927) single-handedly trained future fantastic film experts like Robert Baberschke and Eugen Schüfftan, while depriving them of future German work by almost bankrupting the Babelsberg UFA studio that made it. The fantastic genre gave way to several fairy-tale productions (*Märchenfilme*), many of which dovetail with the adventure Genre: Willi Wolff's *Der Flug um den Erdball* (1925), Henrik Galeen's *Alraune* (1928), Lang's *Girl in the Moon* (1929), G.W. Pabst's *Queen of Atlantis* (1932) and Leni Riefenstahl's *The Blue Light* (1932). A *Märchenfilm* ('fairy-tale film') incorporates allegory and adventure into the otherwise forbidding realm of the fantastic film, usually to attract younger audiences and deliver a moral lesson to them in the end. During this time, the fairy-tale ascended to become a staple of the German film industry, as oft recurring as the romantic comedy. Moody investigation-centred features at the time also incorporated expressionist lighting, like Lang's *M* (1931) and Carl Theodor Dreyer's *Vampyr* (1932).

As much of the Expressionist talent wound up in Hollywood, the Nazi period constitutes a relative aporia in the fantastic film: a re-make of *The Student of Prague* (1935) and Joseph von Báky's *The Adventures of Baron Münchhausen* (1943), which Eric Rentschler calls 'an example of fascinating and fantasizing fascism' (1990: 14–23) demonstrate the limits of fantasy under the Third Reich. After 1945 much of the old UFA talent at the Babelsberg Studios would contribute their skills to the East and West German film industries, where the state interests of divided Germany achieved surprisingly direct expression in their respective fantastic films. Paul Verhoeven's colour fairy-tale film *Heart of Stone* (1950) marked the East German DEFA studio's commitment to exacting mimetic detail in its creation of the fantastic, whilst Arthur Maria Rabenalt's *Alraune* (1952) re-make exhibited the West German strategy of using noir lighting and strong acting to make up for a lack of visual effects budget. The DEFA would inherit the studio apparatus to manufacture credible utopian fairy-tales (*The Story of Little Mook* [Staudte, 1953]; *The Singing Ringing Tree* [Stefani, 1957]; *Silent Star* [Maetzig, 1960]), whereas West German operations like the Central Cinema Company (CCC) would inherit the diverse talent stemming from co-production agreements and transnational capital to bring dark horror films into being. UK-German co-produced Edgar Wallace films such as *Face of the Frog* (1960) provide villains with almost supernatural abilities accompanied by visual effects, only to demystify these very antagonists in the end to give the protagonist power over them. The GDR fantastic made movie-goers out of children with films such as *Die goldene Jurte/The Golden Tent* (Dorshpalam and Kolditz, 1961) or *Frau Holle* (Kolditz, 1963), whereas the West German fantastic cycles hooked their citizens as teenagers with B-movies such as *Night of the Vampires* (Ráthonyi, 1964) or the bizarre Spanish-German co-production *Island of the Doomed* (Welles, 1967), though science fiction and the supernatural did occasionally penetrate the New German Cinema with R.W. Fassbinder's *World on a Wire* (1973) or Hans-Jürgen Syberberg's *Parsifal* (1983). The latter movement heavily emphasized theatrical techniques over cinema tricks to achieve the desired fantastic implications

The last three decades of the fantastic in German cinema could not be conceived, however, without the contributions of Bernd Eichinger, a producer who further internationalized German film production by filming *The NeverEnding Story* (1984), *Resident Evil* (Anderson, 2002) and *Perfume: The Story of a Murderer* (2006) in English.[3] Though all the films pay homage to the origins of the German fantastic film in their enchantment and shock effects, their aesthetic and storytelling strategies remain thoroughly grounded in that of international Hollywood: high-concept narratives offering commoditised adventure and violence, foregrounded matte and digital effects, and the postmodern interplay between nostalgia and technophilia. At the beginning of the twenty-first century German co-productions like the fairy-tale/anti-adventure *Krabat* (Kreuzpaintner, 2008) or the sci-fi horror flick *Pandorum* (Alvart, 2009) establish themselves as global, digital cinema productions that are to blend in chameleon-like with other Hollywood fare in order to stand a chance of recouping their investments. Yet even in a thoroughly disenchanted digital age, the promised thrills of the fantastic continue to entice movie-goers, spurring the shock and awe that makes children of us all before our silver and plasma screens.

Evan Torner

Notes

1. This makes German fantastic films distinct from the French and American traditions of magic theatre and carnivals, respectively.
2. See, for example, Peter Nicholls (1984), *Fantastic Cinema*, London: Ebury Press, pp. 14-15; Paul Meehan (2008), *Tech-Noir*. Jefferson, NC: McFarland, p. 23.
3. A notable precedent for this was Bavaria Film Studios' US/French/German co-production *Willy Wonka & the Chocolate Factory* (Stuart, 1971).

The Student of Prague

Der Student von Prag

Production Company:
Deutsche Bioscop GmbH

Directors:
Stellan Rye
Paul Wegener

Screenwriter:
Hans Heinz Ewers

Cinematographer:
Guido Seeber

Composer:
Josef Weiss

Duration:
85 minutes

Genre:
Fantastic
Horror
Romance
Silent

Cast:
Paul Wegener
John Gottowt
Grete Berger
Fritz Weidemann
Lyda Salmonova
Lothar Körner

Year:
1913

Synopsis

The film opens with the protagonist Balduin (played by co-director Wegener) moping in a beer garden while his fellow students party with the alluring Gypsy girl, Lyduschka (Salmonova). Though a brash pupil and talented fencer, Balduin has fallen on hard times, making him easy prey for the evil sorcerer Scapinelli (Gottowt). He offers Balduin great wealth provided that he may take anything he wishes from Balduin's room. Balduin quickly signs the contract, having looked around his sparse room and finding nothing of consequence to lose. The sorcerer then takes his most ephemeral possession: Balduin's reflection, which walks right out of the mirror and leaves the room with Scapinelli. Now in possession of abundant riches, Balduin courts the beautiful Countess Margarita (Berger), who falls in love with him despite being already engaged to Baron Schwarzenberg (Weidemann). His luck in love, however, turns sour as his reflection returns to haunt him at the most inopportune moments, even replacing him in a duel that kills the Baron. Driven mad by his reflection's frequent appearances, he eventually shoots it. But the bullet has no effect, and blood instead streams from Balduin's own chest. Death seems the ultimate price for his devil's bargain.

Critique

Though Robert Wiene's *The Cabinet of Dr Caligari* (1920) has often been cited for kick-starting the German art film after the First World War, the first of its kind will always remain Stellan Rye and Paul Wegener's *The Student of Prague* (1913). In fact, this film beautifully demonstrates the potential marriage of art and technology via the cinema. The story employs common German Romantic and gothic literary tropes – such as the pact with the devil and the *doppelgänger* – institutionalised by Goethe's *Faust* and the writings of Edgar Allan Poe and E. T. A. Hoffman. Screenwriter Hans Heinz Ewers also draws heavily from French writer Alfred de Musset's narrative poem 'The December Night.' Quotations from the poem form both the film's epigraph and its postscript, placing strong emphasis on the *doppelgänger* and devil thematics.

Such a mystical, fantastic story provided the perfect outlet for experimenting with both cinematographic special effects of the time and their combination with strong narrative motivation. It was here that trick photography found a purpose beyond the early 'cinema of attractions' characterised by Georges Méliès or the Skladanowsky brothers. It would be an overstatement, however, to say that *Student* innovated any new special effects techniques, unlike in the 1920s with the films of F.W. Murnau, Arnold Fanck or cinematographer Eugen Schüfftan. Instead, Rye, Wegener and cinematographer Guido Seeber use simple split screens, double exposures and the occasional trick set to show, for example, Balduin's reflection stepping out of a wall mirror. Nevertheless, it was one of the first large-scale applications of such effects in a feature film.

The Student of Prague, Deutsche Bioscop GmbH.

Indeed, the film appears most remarkable when seen as an early example of a German feature length film with a cohesive, motivated narrative structure supported by naturalistic acting. While *Student* relies largely on the one-scene-one-shot formula, with little attempt at camera movement or variation between shot lengths, each scene develops the story using a causal logic that needs little assistance from the title cards. A significant ellipsis in the duel between the Baron and Balduin's reflection would be one striking exception to this structural integrity. Additional narrative incongruities may also have been a result of the reduction of the film's length by approximately 100 metres in 1921.

While most of the interiors were filmed at the Bioscop studio in Neubabelsberg just outside Berlin, the film-makers proudly announce the use of location shooting at various palaces in Prague, including the old Jewish cemetery where, in keeping with the gothic theme, Balduin arranges to meet Margarita in their first clandestine rendezvous, and where Balduin's reflection makes his ominous first appearance to the couple.

Student is perhaps the best known surviving example of the burgeoning German film industry before the First World War, and is often cited as evidence of an unfulfilled promise that Germany could have established a film industry to rival the fast-growing American pre-war industry had production not been interrupted by the outbreak of war in the summer of 1914. It is true that Germany had begun to establish key infrastructure, particularly around Berlin, Potsdam and Babelsberg to support the growth of such an industry, but this is also true of numerous countries in Europe, with important, memorable and narratively sophisticated features (of varying lengths) produced in France, Italy, Denmark and Sweden around this time. Examples include: Louis Feuillade's *Fantômas* (1913); Giovanni Pastrone's epic *Cabiria* (1914), August Blom's *Atlantis* (1913) and Victor Sjöström's *Ingeborg Holm* (1913) to name only a few that certainly overshadow *Student* in scale, ambition and narrative complexity.

Perhaps *The Student of Prague* has been so well remembered for the fact that its cautionary fairy-tale uncannily foreshadows the key fantastic themes of the Weimar Cinema, whose directors added an expressionist aesthetic to the mix that would, after its stunted beginning, see the real rise of the German feature film industry to national and international success in the 1920s.

Michelle Langford

Weird Tales

Unheimliche Geschichten

Production Company:
Richard Oswald Produktion

Director:
Richard Oswald

Producer:
Richard Oswald

Screenwriters:
Robert Liebmann
Richard Oswald

Cinematographer:
Carl Hoffmann

Duration:
112 minutes

Genre:
Fantastic
Horror

Synopsis

At midnight, Death, Devil and Harlot step out of their paintings on the walls of an antiquarian bookshop and start reading horror stories.

'The Apparition': A man and a woman check into a hotel. Overnight, the woman inexplicably disappears and everybody claims that she never existed. Eventually, it turns out that she died suddenly from the plague, a fact that the hotel management tried to cover up.

'The Hand': Two men throw the dice for a woman, but the loser kills his opponent. However, the ghostly hand of his victim drives the murderer to his death.

'The Black Cat': A drunkard kills his wife and hides her body behind a plastered wall in the cellar. Her cat, inadvertently sealed in with her, eventually reveals the deed.

'The Suicide Club': Detective Artur Silas discovers a secret suicide club and is immediately chosen as the next victim. Although frightened, Silas succeeds in outwitting the club's sinister president.

'The Spectre': When a braggart rococo baron attempts to seduce a neglected wife, her husband stages supernatural incidents to expose his rival's cowardice.

At the stroke of one o'clock, Death, Devil and Harlot return to their paintings.

Cast:
Anita Berber
Reinhold Schünzel
Conrad Veidt
Hugo Döblin
Paul Morgan
Georg John
Bernhard Goetzke

Year:
1919

Critique

Weird Tales represents a critical link between the more conventional German mystery and detective films of the mid-1910s and the groundbreaking fantastic cinema of the early 1920s, which became world famous for its eerie atmosphere and unique visual style. In terms of décor, narrative structure and acting, *Weird Tales* is still rooted in the past, but its achievements in terms of mood, lighting and cinematography forcefully herald a new era.

Weird Tales consists of a series of one-reel (approximately twenty minutes long) episodes strung together by a common theme of the strange, eerie and supernatural, as well as a fairly sketchy fantastic frame narrative. By resorting to this structure, which makes *Weird Tales* one of the earliest horror anthology films, director Richard Oswald references the obsolete narrative model of the one-reel short film, and simultaneously complies with the contemporary standard of feature length films. The second unifying element of *Weird Tales* is the three prominent lead actors – Reinhold Schünzel, Conrad Veidt and Anita Berber – who appear in different roles and guises in varying love triangles in each story. Commending each episode's distinctive style and the effective and purposeful creation of a feeling of terror, reviewers at the time perceived *Weird Tales* as quite innovative.

Taken as a whole, however, *Weird Tales* has not aged well. The acting (explicitly lauded by contemporary critics) repeatedly strikes today's viewer as rather laboured. Similarly, reflecting the characteristic predicament of German film-making at the time – namely a fundamental lack of means, including time, money and equipment – the interior sets often look unconvincing and ramshackle. Dramaturgically some episodes seem quite uneven, featuring elaborate expositions and digressive plotlines, but stun spectators with abrupt endings. However, in scenes where performances and visual style transcend the simulation of physical reality and take a psychological and expressive turn, *Weird Tales* reaches new dimensions in terms of cinematic language. Undoubtedly ahead of the times is the necromancy scene in 'The Hand', for which cinematographer Carl Hoffmann (*Dr. Mabuse: The Gambler* [Lang, 1928]; *Die Nibelungen* [Lang, 1924]; *Faust* [Murnau, 1926]) crafted stunning dramatic lighting and special effects. Another highlight of the film is the climactic scene in 'The Suicide Club', where the hero is forced to watch his final minutes count down on a huge clock with glowing numbers, haunted by an extreme close-up of the sinister club president – a device that was highly unusual at the time. In 'The Apparition', Conrad Veidt gives a stirring performance as the bewildered and horrified protagonist confronted with everyone around him emphatically and consistently substantiating evidently false facts. Here, *Weird Tales* effectively anticipates the most chilling and disturbing hallmark motif of numerous Hitchcock films of later decades, including *The 39 Steps* (1935), *Saboteur* (1942) and *North By Northwest* (1959).

Although *Weird Tales* does not rank among of the great masterpieces of German cinema, it is nonetheless an important film.

By exploring a variety of narrative and visual approaches to the strange, eerie and supernatural, *Weird Tales* reveals the emergence of a new filmic idiom founded on fearful suspense and visual expressivity that, in films like *The Cabinet of Dr. Caligari*, *The Golem* and *Nosferatu*, would soon establish the world fame of German silent film.

Katharina Loew

The Golem: How He Came into the World

Der Golem, wie er in die Welt kam

Production Company:
Projektions-AG Union (PAGU)

Distributor:
Universum Film (UFA)

Directors:
Paul Wegener, Carl Boese

Producer:
Paul Davidson

Screenwriters:
Paul Wegener
Henrik Galeen

Art Directors:
Hans Poelzig
Kurt Richter

Cinematographers:
Karl Freund
Guido Seeber

Composer:
Hans Landsberger

Duration:
85 minutes

Genre:
Fantastic
Horror

Synopsis

The Golem: How He Came into the World is set in Prague in the sixteenth century. Emperor Rudolf II (Gebühr) has ordered the Jewish community to be expelled from the city. In order to protect his people, Rabbi Loew (Steinrück) magically animates a clay figure: the golem (Wegener). When the golem, who possesses enormous physical strength, saves the emperor's life, the emperor permits the Jewish community to remain in the city, albeit in a ghetto. Sensing the golem's increasing dangerousness, Rabbi Loew deactivates his creation. Fatally, however, the Rabbi's enamoured assistant reanimates the figure in order to take vengeance on a rival. The golem now turns into a perilous berserker and causes a devastating fire that destroys part of the Jewish ghetto. Having eventually broken through the ghetto walls, the golem meets a little girl who accidentally removes his animating amulet and the clay figure crashes to the ground.

Critique

The Golem: How He Came into the World ranks among the great masterpieces of German silent cinema. Celebrated from the outset as a pinnacle of film art, the film was an instant international success. *The Golem* is first and foremost known for star architect Hans Poelzig's bizarrely ponderous sets, which established an unprecedented unity of thematic and stylistic elements and revolutionized the ties between film and modernist art. Like the magically animated clay figure of the golem, the bio- or even anthropomorphic forms of Poelzig's *Golem*-city epitomize the central motive of the film, namely the magic relationship between the organic and the inorganic.

The driving force behind this production was actor-director Paul Wegener, one of the most distinguished pioneers in German cinema. An expert in East Asian art and a devotee of Eastern religions, Wegener had strong affinities towards exoticism and esotericism. Among the supernatural narratives, fanciful characters and exotic locales which are characteristic for his work, the Jewish golem legend plays a particularly important role as Wegener created three films on the subject: *The Golem: How He Came into the World* was preceded by *The Golem* (Galeen and Wegener, 1915), a tale about a golem's modern day re-animation, and the satire *The*

Cast:
Paul Wegener
Albert Steinrück
Lyda Salmonova
Ernst Deutsch
Otto Gebühr
Lothar Müthel
Loni Nest
Hans Stürm
Dore Paetzold
Greta Schröder
Max Kronert

Year:
1920

Golem and the Dancing Girl (Gliese and Wegener, 1917). Sadly, however, both films are considered lost.

Jewish folklore's golem narratives trace back to both Biblical and non-Biblical sources and underwent various modifications over the centuries. Since the early nineteenth century the golem figure appeared in literary works of both Jewish and non-Jewish authors, primarily in the German-speaking countries. It was not until the 1850s that the creation of the golem became primarily associated with sixteenth century Rabbi Judah Loew ben Bezalel, known as the Maharal of Prague. The first decades of the twentieth century saw a remarkable surge of golem narratives, the most famous of which, Gustav Meyrink's fantastic novel *The Golem* (1915), does, however – contrary to persisting claims – not bear any relation to Wegener's golem films.

Wegener, Poelzig and their collaborators were clearly indifferent towards genuine Jewish history and culture, and their rehashing of anti-Semitic stereotypes appears highly problematic today. The dismissal of historic or cultural accuracy in favour of a specific expressive ambience resulted in what could be described as Jewish-themed fantastic Orientalism. Wegener pointed out:

> It is not Prague that my friend the architect Poelzig built. Rather it is a poem of a city, a dream, an architectural paraphrase on the theme of the golem. The lanes and squares are not meant to recall anything real, they are meant to create the atmosphere the golem breathes. (in Neumann 1996: 66)

The labyrinthine Jewish settlement, consisting of 54 specifically constructed and apparently timeless buildings, almost appears like a living organism. The biomorphic qualities of Poelzig's sets become particularly apparent with respect to the interiors, which are strikingly reminiscent of the human body's internal anatomy. Poelzig developed his organic forms out of the basic shape of the gothic arch, and amalgamated gothic tradition and art nouveau with an expressionist gestus, which recalls the brawny, contorted distortions of gothic shapes characteristic of the style of Catalan architect Antoni Gaudí.

The Golem had an enormous impact on the development of German film art and the fantastic/horror genre more generally. Film historical milestones such as *Metropolis* (1927), *Faust* (1926) and *Frankenstein* (Whale, 1931) unmistakably bear its traces. In addition to its epoch-making historical significance and substantial influence, the stunning imagery and magically sensual atmosphere of *The Golem: How He Came into the World* have retained its powerful appeal to this day.

Katharina Loew

The Cabinet of Dr. Caligari

Das Cabinet des Dr. Caligari

Production Company:
Decla-Bioscop AG

Distributor:
Goldwyn Distributing Company (USA)

Director:
Robert Wiene

Producers:
Erich Pommer
Rudolf Meinert

Screenwriters:
Hans Janowitz
Carl Mayer

Cinematographer:
Willy Hameister

Composer:
Alfredo Antonini

Duration:
71 minutes

Genre:
Horror
Fantastic

Cast:
Conrad Veidt
Werner Krauss
Lil Dagover
Hans Heinrich von Twardowski
Friedrich Feher

Year:
1920

Synopsis

When the quiet German village of Holstenwall is visited by a travelling carnival, events take a sinister turn with a series of mysterious murders. One of the carnival's chief attractions is a fortune-telling somnambulist called Cesare (Veidt), and his master, the mysterious Dr. Caligari (Krauss). When two local friends, Francis (Feher) and Alan (von Twardowski), decide to visit the carnival they become fascinated by Dr. Caligari's claim that Cesare can answer any question he is asked. Alan decides to ask Cesare how long he has to live, to which Cesare replies that Alan will die before dawn the next day. The next morning Alan is found murdered. Francis, along with a mutual friend, Jane (Dagover), and her father decide to investigate further. Under the influence of Dr. Caligari, Cesare attempts to murder Jane but, captivated by her beauty, carries her off instead. Alerted by her cries for help, Jane is eventually rescued by her family, but Cesare, after being pursued by the townsfolk, is later found dead at the bottom of a ravine. Francis, meanwhile, discovers that the mysterious Dr. Caligari is in fact the director of the local asylum, obsessed with an old tale about a monk/mystic who uses a somnambulist to murder people. Caligari is immediately declared insane and imprisoned, but here the story takes a final twist as a result of the film's framing narrative. The final scenes of the film reveal the story to be a figment of Francis' imagination and that he, Jane and Cesare are in fact inmates in the same asylum run by Dr. Caligari. The film concludes that Francis' story is part of *his* madness and delusion.

Critique

The deliberate distortion of reality provided by the film's denouement has been a cause for debate and controversy ever since its release. Siegfried Kracauer has noted that the decision for including the framing narrative was taken by the director, Wiene, as an afterthought and without consultation with the writers (1947 [2004]: 66). It has since been claimed by one of the writers, Janowitz, that the framing scene changed the original concept and symbolism of the film completely, from the tale of a man gone mad through the 'misuse of his mental powers' (Dr. Caligari), to the 'fantasy of a deranged asylum patient' (Robinson 1999: 13). The end result has encouraged views that *Caligari* attempts to give audiences a sinister psychological and visually unorthodox experience that places the film firmly in the canon of the German fantastic film.

The Cabinet of Dr. Caligari has provoked much debate, partly due to the way it exists at the intersection between high and low (popular) culture. As such, *Caligari* has been described as both an art film and as a template for subsequent and more mainstream films that offer dark experiences (noir), fantasy or a similar 'tale of terror' (Prawer 1980). Its aesthetics and artistic design are almost entirely derived from influences prominent in the plastic arts at the time – namely German Expressionism. The painted sets, created by Herman Warm and the painters Walter Reimann and Walter Röhig, provide not just a unique look, but contrive to offer viewers an extra sensory experience that highlights expressionist themes such as anxiety, ambiguity, disorientation, distortion and inner-trauma. With its tacit acknowledgement of a fascination with a modish psychoanalytical theory, both through its design and its narrative, *Caligari* can be construed as a very fashionable film for its time. Equally, the design concept of *Caligari* illustrates how the film deliberately points to its own artifice and, as such, has given weight to those opinions that describe the film as an art film. However, such opinions have given the film a gravitas or seriousness that may not have been intended (Scheunemann 2006). The histrionic acting style in *Caligari*, as well as the *mise-en-scène* and aesthetics of the carnival, highlight a certain amount of kitsch in the film. Similarly, *Caligari* recognized and played to a fascination with the macabre and the uncanny (or *Unheimliche*) prevalent in popular entertainment of the time. The film points to, and arguably attempts to recreate, those experiences of the carnival where fortune telling and mysticism offered an alternative means of expression to a culture of rationalism. Whilst the appeal and popularity of *Caligari* may have been due in part to the novelty of its innovations and its allusions to modernity, its *mise-en-scène*, characters and a certain amount of Romanticism lent the film a familiar feel. As with films such as *The Student of Prague* (1913), *Caligari* hints at influences from more traditional, conventional and popular German fantasy/fiction formats, such as the fairy-tale – a form that was undergoing something of a revival (and revision) at the time (Zipes 1997). The film's *mise-en-scène* of a temporary distortion and suspension of reality not only mirrors filmic processes, but also the effects of the carnival itself. Viewed in its entirety, the film's *mise-en-scène* and plot, as well as its narrative and technical innovations all provide scenarios and examples where accepted conventions, hierarchical structures and barriers are challenged and transcended. The film also offers a fantasy experience that is outside of, and contrary to existing forms and everyday life, providing a 'suspension of official ordering of time and space' (Webb 2005: 121–38). *Caligari*, therefore, employs various techniques, heavily influenced by the arts, which provide a scenario of a distorted reality to tell a fantastic story of what happens when the carnival comes to town.

Kenneth A. Longden

Destiny

Der müde Tod

Production Company:
Decla-Bioscop AG

Distributor:
Weiss Brothers Artclass Pictures (USA)

Director:
Fritz Lang

Producer:
Erich Pommer

Screenwriters:
Thea von Harbou
Fritz Lang

Synopsis

Two young lovers (Dagover and Janssen) encounter an eerie wanderer (Goetzke) at a crossroads. A flashback reveals that this stranger, who is really Death himself, had recently acquired a plot of land next to a nearby cemetery and had enclosed it with a giant, doorless wall. When the young man mysteriously disappears, the maiden soon realizes that Death has taken him. Adhering to the belief that 'love is stronger than death,' she begs Death for the life of her lover. Death, weary of the grief that he inflicts, shows the maiden a vast hall containing all human flames of life. He gives her three chances – represented by three dying candle ends – to defeat him. However, in each of the subsequently unfolding episodes, set in Baghdad, Renaissance Venice and legendary China, the girl fails to save her lover's life. Conceding her one additional final attempt, Death asks the maiden to bring him another life in exchange for her lover's. Yet, as it turns out, even most miserable figures desperately cling to life and the maiden has not the heart to hand over an infant she saves from a burning building. Instead, she decides to sacrifice her own life. In death, she is at last reunited with her lover.

Destiny, Decla-Bioscop AG.

Art Directors:
Walter Röhrig
Hermann Warm
Robert Herlth

Cinematographers:
Fritz Arno Wagner
Erich Nitzschmann
Hermann Saalfrank
Bruno Timm
Bruno Mondi

Composers:
Giuseppe Becce
Karl-Ernst Sasse
Peter Schirmann

Editor:
Fritz Lang

Duration:
79 minutes

Genre:
Fantastic
Thriller

Cast:
Bernhard Goetzke
Lil Dagover
Walter Janssen
Max Adalbert
Wilhelm Diegelmann
Hans Sternberg

Year:
1921

Critique

Destiny is one of Fritz Lang's most poetic works. A powerful *memento mori* constructed from a plethora of visual and narrative references, allegories and symbols and, reverberating the trauma of World War I, the film is simultaneously a wistful ballad conjuring up German Romanticism as the spiritual foundation for a distressed and defeated nation.

The film's original subtitle 'A German folksong in six verses,' describes not only an intended quaint, lyric atmosphere, but also a formal structure. The six verses correspond with six film reels, of which the first two and the last are dedicated to the frame narrative, and the remaining to the three exotic stories within the story. The frame narrative distinctly emulates German Romantic poetry, novellas and fairy-tales, whereas the embedded episodes are modelled after Boccaccio, Shakespeare, *Arabian Nights* and early twentieth century adventure stories. The same eclecticism also prevails visually. The frame narrative recalls imagery of nineteenth century German Romantic and Symbolist paintings by Caspar David Friedrich, Moritz von Schwind and Arnold Böcklin, while nineteenth century Orientalist art, Italian Renaissance painting and the fantastic artificiality of Georges Méliès' early magic films evidently inspired the look of the stories within the story.

Both visually and narratively, *Destiny* constantly evokes death allegories from various, mostly Christian, Ancient Greek and European folk mythologies, referring, for instance, to Death as a gravedigger, Thanatos with the inverted torch or the Rider on the Pale Horse. *Memento mori* symbols like clocks, candles, crosses or skulls are omnipresent. Three architectural elements – walls, stairs and pointed arches – dominate many image compositions and function as partitions, pointers and walkways between worlds. When entering the realm of Death through the film's most spectacular emblem – the boundless wall – the maiden walks up a staircase framed by a giant pointed arch. The resulting image visually combines wall, arch and stairs into a breathtaking icon resembling a stylized candle, in itself a symbol for the finiteness of life.

Like its visual imagery, the film's basic narrative is also highly symbolic. Featuring the same principal cast, roughly the same plotline is reiterated in the frame and all embedded episodes. Lil Dagover in the role of the maiden, the Caliph's sister, a Venetian noblewoman and the imperial magician's daughter repeatedly tries to rescue her lover from the clutches of a tyrant. However, Death, always acting under orders in a subservient position, succeeds in killing him each time. The outcome is always the same, which is why Death is weary. He is not his own master, but an 'agent of Fate', as described by film theorist Siegfried Kracauer. Seeking to expose in German cinema of the 1920s the mindset that eventually would bring about Nazism, Kracauer pointed to the ideological links between totalitarianism and the morbid fatalism depicted in *Destiny*: '[H]owever arbitrary they seem, the actions of tyrants are realizations of Fate' (1947 [2004]: 90).

While Kracauer's assertion is certainly perceptive, it is not surprising that in 1921, only a few years after the horrors and humiliation of World War I, the ensuing German revolution and with the onset of hyperinflation Germans should have perceived fate as inescapable and humans as helpless in view of destiny's infinite power. Although the film's fatalist ideology and overwrought symbolism may justifiably be criticized, *Destiny* must be recognized as one of most profound and poetic reflections of human mortality in all of film history.

Katharina Loew

Waxworks

Das Wachsfigurenkabinett

Production Company:
Neptun-Film AG

Distributors:
Universum Film (UFA) (Germany)
Film Arts Guild (USA)

Directors:
Leo Birinsky
Paul Leni

Producers:
Leo Birinsky
Alexander Kwartiroff

Screenwriter:
Henrik Galeen

Art Director:
Paul Leni

Cinematographer:
Helmar Lerski

Duration:
65 minutes

Genre:
Fantastic
Horror

Cast:
Emil Jannings
Conrad Veidt
Werner Krauss

Synopsis

In the frame narrative of *Waxworks*, a young poet (Dieterle) is hired to write publicity stories for a waxworks display. Smitten by the showman's daughter Eva (Belajeff), the poet writes himself and Eva into each story that he subsequently composes. The first and longest episode is a comedy of errors around Harun al-Rashid (Jannings), mighty Caliph and notorious womanizer, who chases after the beautiful wife of a young pastry baker. Tsar Ivan the Terrible (Veidt), the diabolically cruel protagonist of the second episode, delights himself by clocking the remaining lifetime of his poisoned victims with an hourglass. As guest of honour at a wedding, Ivan extorts the bride to surrender to him sexually by torturing her groom. However, believing he has also been poisoned when faced with an hourglass that supposedly measures *his* remaining lifetime, Ivan eventually goes mad. The final brief episode visualizes the horrors of the poet's psychotic nightmare in which Jack the Ripper (Krauss) chases Eva and him through a cubist urban labyrinth. Back in the frame narrative and the showman's booth, all ends well: after their third imagined adventure as a couple, Eva and the poet finally embrace in real life.

Critique

Waxworks, which represents one of the most significant experiments in stylized film décor in the history of cinema, suffered from an ill-fated production history. Director-designer Paul Leni fought for years for this endeavour, which accumulated his best ideas from other aborted projects. In the planning stage since 1920 and produced during the height of the hyperinflation in 1923, the film was not released until November 1924. Having almost bankrupted its creators, *Waxworks* remained a fragment even in its final, completed form, which causes a perceptible imbalance within the film as a whole. Despite these predicaments, however, the resulting film became Leni's most recognized work, celebrated foremost on account of its breathtaking and unique visual style.

Waxworks consists of a frame narrative and three stories within the story, each of which is distinguished by its distinct design, in

Wilhelm Dieterle
Olga Belajeff

Year:
1924

terms of both cinematography and art direction. The décor is carefully tailored to the respective episode's subject matter and can be traced back to a few basic geometric forms. The comic-grotesque Oriental episode is characterized by large, rounded, pear-shaped and doughy contours, which were inspired by Islamic architecture and also reflect Harun al-Rashid's baroque nature and his rivalry with a baker. Resulting from close framing, the caliph incessantly seems to be bulging out of the frame, which all the more accentuates his flamboyant physicality. The Russian episode, on the other hand, features predominantly low camera angles, which contribute considerably to its oppressive, devious atmosphere of lurking danger. The tall and slim human silhouettes can often only move around if stooped, seemingly crushed by the massive low ceilings and doorways. Onion domes, a typical feature of Russian Orthodox architecture, semi-circular arches and rectilinear polygon shapes dominate this design idiom. As originally conceived, the Russian episode was to be followed by a romance concerned with the unrealizable love between a princess and a chivalrous outlaw, eighteenth century Corsican bandit, Rinaldo Rinaldini. However, the production's financial difficulties led to the elimination of Rinaldini, who yet still appears in the waxworks display of the frame narrative. While each section of *Waxworks* is a masterpiece of production design and cinematography, the most extraordinary is the final five-minute Jack the Ripper episode, which, according to film critic Siegfried Kracauer, 'must be counted among the greatest achievements of film art' (1947 [2004]: 86–87). By layering multiple superimpositions, cinematographer Helmar Lerski virtually eliminated cinematography and set design as separate entities, in favour of cubistic compositions of shreds of painted light. Their distinctive styles notwithstanding, Leni took great care in linking the individual episodes visually. While the Oriental semi-spherical domes and horseshoe arches, and the Russian onion domes and round arches are culturally specific, their graphic shapes are closely related, which creates a strong sense of stylistic unity despite all the diversity in décor.

Leni was reportedly concerned about the extent to which *Waxworks* seems to follow in the footsteps of *The Cabinet of Dr. Caligari* (1920), with which it shares two principal actors (Conrad Veidt and Werner Krauss), the fairground setting, as well as the stylization (though not the style) of its sets. *Waxworks* also uses the same plot formula as Fritz Lang's *Destiny* (1921) and its fantastically organic, bulky décor distinctly recalls that used in *The Golem, How He Came Into the World* (1920). In most cases, such evident affinities would be indicative of an unoriginal, uninteresting imitation. Quite the contrary is true with regard to *Waxworks*, however, which is one of the visually most creative, multifaceted and complex works of German silent film.

Katharina Loew

The Adventures of Prince Achmed

Die Abenteuer des Prinzen Achmed

Production Company:
Comenius-Film GmbH

Distributors:
Universum Film (UFA) (Germany)
University Arts Foundation (USA)

Directors:
Lotte Reiniger
Carl Koch (uncredited)

Screenwriter:
Lotte Reiniger

Art Director:
Lotte Reiniger

Cinematographer:
Carl Koch

Composer:
Wolfgang Zeller

Duration:
65 minutes.

Genre:
Animation
Fantastic
Adventure

Year:
1926

Synopsis

An evil magician offers the Caliph a poisoned gift – a flying horse – in exchange for the hand of his daughter Dinarsade. In order to save his sister, Prince Achmed intervenes. He demands to test the horse but, unable to stop it, is flown away to an enchanted island, ruled by the fairy Pari Banu. Falling in love and defying warnings about the wrath of her demon-servants, he convinces her to follow him home. Their escape is thwarted once again by the magician, who sells Pari Banu to the Emperor of China and banishes the prince to the fiery mountains. With the help of a powerful sorceress and aided by Aladdin and his lamp, Achmed rescues his beloved, fights off the demons and brings everybody safely back. Aladdin can now reunite with his rightful bride Dinarsade, and the two couples appear in front of the Caliph, who gives them his blessing.

Critique

As one of the world's earliest animated features – the first ever to be directed by a woman – *The Adventures of Prince Achmed* has achieved a legendary status in the history of German and international film. Combining stop motion cinematography with the aesthetic potential of silhouette and shadow play, Reiniger and her team (Carl Koch, Walter Ruttmann, Bertold Bartosch et. al.) offer a spectacular demonstration of movement and depth that belies the tremendous effort put into its design: three years of labour, hundreds of thousands of stills, tinted and hand-coloured frames, dozens of backgrounds and elaborate figures painstakingly cut out from paper and lead, shot with an early version of the multiplane camera.

By 1923 Reiniger's list of works already included collaborations with Fritz Lang and Paul Wegener, as well as animation shorts of her own. Yet the challenge of directing a full-length silhouette film is of an entirely different order. To counteract the potential limitations of the genre, Reiniger constructs an action-filled fantasy plot, loosely based on narrative elements from the *Arabian Nights* cycle, and partly inspired by Raoul Walsh's 1924 classic *The Thief of Bagdad*. But rather than 'orientalizing' the subject, *The Adventures of Prince Achmed* pays homage to its roots in non-western forms of dramatic entertainment and traditional storytelling techniques.

At the same time, the film tests the limits and conventions of an artistic practice that, since the eighteenth century at least, had entered the German public imaginary as a fashionable, low-cost means of portraiture, on the borderline between typological representation and individual morphology: the *Scherenschnitt* ('scissor cuts'). In *Prince Achmed* the medium is exploited to the maximum, allowing images to fluidly oscillate between caricature and realistic psychological detail. Especially in close-up profile frames, additional features (eyes, brows) are sometimes introduced to enhance facial expression, although such markers – as the 'monstrous' figure

The Adventures of Prince Achmed, Comenius-Film GmbH.

of the sorceress indicates – may be misleading, posing a challenge to normative readings and binary contrasts of good versus evil.

But, more generally, the film methodically overcomes the aesthetics of stillness predominant in classical *Scherenschnitt* representations. Not accidentally, Reiniger insists on sequences that flaunt the illusion and artifice of movement: full body turns, vanishing acts, magical transformations and mobile landscapes. In this sense, *The Adventures* is also a direct descendant of the early European cinema of attractions exemplified by Méliès.

Despite initial distribution difficulties, the film instantly becomes a sensation, not in the least due to the fact that Reiniger and her collaborators wittingly tapped into both critical and commercial trends. The fairy-tale genre, already popularized by Paul Wegener during the war years, allows here for fantasies of pre-technological innocence, while exploiting a whole gamut of expressionist tensions resulting from the play of shadow and light. But ultimately, it is the creative distillation of forces that meet on the animation board (Ruttmann's abstract method, Bartosch's special effects, Reiniger's realist tone) that lends the composition its unitary shape, placing it at the intersection between mass entertainment and avant-garde experiment.

Ilinca Iurascu

Faust

Faust – Eine Deutsche Volkssage

Production Company:
Universum Film (UFA)

Distributors:
Universum Film (UFA) (Germany)
MGM (USA)

Director:
F.W. Murnau

Producer:
Erich Pommer

Screenwriters:
Gerhart Hauptmann
Hans Kyser, based on the play by Johann Wolfgang Goethe

Art Directors:
Robert Herlth
Walter Röhrig

Cinematographer:
Carl Hoffmann

Composers:
Werner R. Heymann
Erno Rapee

Editor:
Elfi Böttrich

Duration:
106 minutes (German domestic version)

Synopsis

An archangel and the Devil (Mephisto, played by Emil Jannings) wager the entire medieval world over the soul of one man: the aging alchemist Faust (Ekman). Mephisto inflicts a plague upon his city, causing Faust to doubt his faith. The Devil then offers him power for one trial day, which he uses to miraculously cure a victim before the town discovers the satanic origins of his healing powers. Giving the despondent Faust his youth, Mephisto transports him to Parma, where he seduces the beautiful Duchess (Ralph). This permanently seals the pact with Mephisto. Armed with youth and magic, Faust returns to his hometown. There he falls in love with the virtuous Gretchen (Horn). Mephisto arouses her interest in Faust with a golden locket. Faust aggressively courts her and she eventually succumbs to temptation. Mephisto kills her mother and informs her brother Valentine (Dieterle) of the affair, stabbing him in the back as Faust duels him. Gretchen is now ruined, humiliated and pregnant. She bears the child, but it dies during the winter, and she is to be burned at the stake as retribution. Still in love, Faust curses his youth, causing Mephisto to take it away from him before he embraces Gretchen on the pyre. When the Devil and archangel meet again, the latter wins thanks to this love.

Critique

Faust is an opulent, painterly adaptation of Goethe, Marlowe and German folk legends concerning a scholar's deal with the Devil. Its Romantic/neo-Gothic look, spectacular effects and wry performance of the Devil by Emil Jannings left an indelible impression on cinema history, influencing works such as Tod Browning's *Dracula* (1930), Walt Disney's *Fantasia* (1940) and Ingmar Bergman's *The Seventh Seal* (1957). The film's own indeterminate stance on the revered source material, however, prompted a lukewarm reception from the German populace – recouping only half of its 2 million Reichsmark budget – as well as from generations of scholars who note the fine line *Faust* treads between high art and kitsch.

For many cineastes, *Faust* is a phantasmic film. In addition to its obvious dream-like quality, the production was F.W. Murnau's last German film before departing for Hollywood, and a lush demonstration of the UFA at its creative and financial apogee before

Genre:
Fantastic
Drama
Horror

Cast:
Gösta Ekman
Emil Jannings
Camilla Horn
Frida Richard
William Dieterle
Yvette Guilbert
Eric Barclay
Hanna Ralph
Werner Fuetterer

Year:
1926

the advent of the sound film. Shadows of Murnau's foreshortened career, UFA's bankruptcy and the decline of silent cinema haunt images already saturated with apocalyptic portent. In addition, the film's explicitly German national and superstitious character conjures up associations with the nascent Third Reich, refusing us both purely political or film-aesthetic readings despite its otherwise clear good/evil and light/dark dichotomies.

Murnau and Jannings wrested Erich Pommer's international prestige production from the hands of operetta director Ludwig Berger and, despite just finishing an intensive shoot for *Varieté* (Dupont, 1925), managed to exert an exacting level of control over every frame. Few details were overlooked and little spontaneity was allowed. Convincing models constructed by Herlth and Röhrig even compensated for Murnau's departure from his usual on-location shooting. His cinematographer Hoffmann unveiled every camera trick he knew on behalf of the film's experimental vision, building tracks through the miniature town model and adapting light conditions in stationary shots to imitate that of Rembrandt's paintings. Expressive results of this ludic exactitude include Mephisto's black shape engulfing the entire village in his shadow, the exhilarating flight on his cloak, Gretchen's head screaming over an onrushing landscape, and she and Faust kissing whilst being engulfed in flames.

It is thus no wonder that Mephisto himself serves as an agent of the cinema, an impetus to traverse space, time and identity through cinematographic, make-up and other purely spectacular effects. Yet Faust is associated with the book, a fusty medium routinely set alight in various sequences throughout the film. This tension between book and film also reflects Murnau's ambivalence to the complexity of the film's narrative that incensed so many critics at the time: he opts for what Matt Erlin calls 'a peculiar and indecipherable fusion of Goethe and the chapbook' (2009: 164) in the first half, and a superficial *Kammerspielfilm* reading of Goethe and Marlowe in the second half. The prestigious script, written by Kyser and Hauptmann, circulated months in advance yet proved of no utility at the box office. By foregrounding the book adaptation's visuals – after all, the opening intertitle of *Faust* commands us to 'Behold!' – Murnau implies that cinephiles with art history backgrounds were the film's ideal audience, rather than a Weimar bourgeoisie disillusioned with the film's message, let alone with its simplistic emotional appeals.

Nevertheless, *Faust*'s Faustian bargain with the cinematic medium serves as a fantastic archive of the fabled pre-Hugenberg 'UFA-Style'; a mixture of brooding sets, high-contrast lighting, innovative tracking shots and expressionist acting. Christian nationalist images of hometowns and the dark deals that threaten them are animated through the magic of cinema.

Evan Torner

The Story of Little Mook

Die Geschichte vom kleinen Muck

Production Company:
Deutsche Film (DEFA)

Distributor:
VEB Progress Film-Vertrieb (East Germany)

Director:
Wolfgang Staudte

Screenwriters:
Peter Podehl
Wolfgang Staudte, based on the fairy-tale by Wilhelm Hauff

Art Director:
Artur Günther

Cinematographer:
Robert Baberske

Composer:
Ernst Roters

Editor:
Ruth Schreiber

Duration:
100 minutes

Genre:
Family
Fantastic
Fairy-tale

Cast:
Thomas Schmidt
Johannes Maus
Silja Lesny
Friedrich Richter
Trude Hesterberg
Alwin Lippisch

Year:
1953

Synopsis

Street children harass the dwarfish and hunchbacked Old Mook (Maus). He locks them up and obliges them to listen to his story – the story of Little Mook. Orphaned at a young age, Little Mook (Schmidt) searches for the merchant who sells good fortune. With magical slippers and a magical walking stick, he becomes the chief messenger and treasurer at the Sultan's (Lippisch) court. The Sultan's fraudulent and avaricious advisors frame him and have him ousted from the palace. His discovery of magic figs enables him to take revenge on the conniving and corrupt court. Little Mook leaves behind the magic objects and lets them be buried in the desert. After listening to the story of Little Mook, the children all want to help Old Mook, and make a human 'elephant' that carries Old Mook through the little Middle Eastern town.

Critique

Based on Wilhelm Hauff's nineteenth century tale of the same name, *The Story of Little Mook* is a widely celebrated East German children's classic made by the famed director Wolfgang Staudte. Marxist themes of class struggle and critique of capitalism are woven into the film in a subtle manner. Since it is entertaining and politically appropriate yet not propagandistic, the film became a model for future fairy-tale film-making in the DEFA studio.

Staudte changed the original ending, where Mook lives 'very rich but lonely, for he despises other human beings.' Such a misanthropic attitude towards society would not be politically and socially permissible for the GDR. Staudte changed it by having Mook remain true to the lower-class. Little Mook voluntarily leaves behind the keys to rising into the upper-class – the magical objects – when he returns to the life of the working-class. This new ending is more consistent with Mook's disinterest in wealth and power, which is shown throughout the film. With his magic gold-detecting staff, he could have abundant gold at his disposal, and he has theoretically found his 'good fortune.' However, Old Mook tells his audience that he has not found the latter, indicating that wealth and power do not amount to 'good fortune' for him. Mook is ready to find his good fortune with his own hands, without the help of anything magical. This ending prepares the (East German) audience for the daily reality that they face, where no magical slippers or stick are available, and honest and hard work is expected. In the East German context, the pursuit of wealth and power is relegated to being capitalistic in nature, and the values of friendship, love and work ethics are instead promoted.

Embodied in Little Mook, the lower-class is depicted as good-natured, smart and generous. In contrast, the upper-class is described as extremely greedy and insatiably covetous. Princess Amarza (Lesny) is the only uncorrupted member of the palace. Her indifference to riches stands in stark contrast to the courtiers, who resemble Mook's treasure-finding cane that is drawn to gold like a magnet. For the princess, love is the real treasure. The theme that love has no monetary value and wealth comes from true love is prevalent in all East German fairy-tale films.

Old Mook has told a rags-to-riches story where Little Mook initially suffers a great deal of injustice at the hands of other bullying kids, the school master, the relatives, the gypsy woman and the corrupt advisors to the Sultan. Little Mook has made a fool out of the Sultan and his evil staff, and helped the princess marry her true love. Children rejoice in Mook's final victory over the corrupt court, and are deeply moved by his integrity and strength of character in abandoning the magic objects in the desert and starting a working life. He chooses to become one of 'us', a blameless proletarian like his listeners, although he could have lived a luxurious life. For that decision, he is embraced and hailed as a hero by the working-class children. Although there is no change in social structure at the end, the listeners of the story still go away with the sense that the poor have triumphed.

The children fall in love with Little Mook who becomes a figure with whom they can identify. Staudte changed the original frame story by having Old Mook himself narrate. By changing the third-person narrative to a first-person narrative, the authenticity of the tale increases. The children take the story of Little Mook to be Mook's autobiography. His life story has generated immense respect for him. During the narration of the story, Old Mook stops twice at cliffhanging moments and the children are hooked to his story. The narrative strategy Old Mook uses resembles that of Scheherazade, who tells the king half of a story every night, and in the end saves her life. Here, we observe a similarly redemptive and edifying power of narration. Staudte shows his confidence in the life-changing effect of storytelling and in the educational capacity of literature and film.

Qinna Shen

The Dress

Das Kleid

Production Company:
Deutsche Film (DEFA)

Distributor:
VEB Progress Film-Vertrieb (East Germany)

Director:
Konrad Petzold

Synopsis

Two weavers, Hans and Kumpan (Drinda and Lierck), come to a kingdom surrounded by a guarded and seemingly impenetrable wall. By stowing away under a cart, they slip through the city gate. Helped by a kitchen maid named Katrin (Hagen), they are smuggled into the palace, where the emperor orders them to make an amazing outfit that will make everyone fall to their knees. The weavers come up with an ingenious plan to claim that the robe they are making is invisible to those who are stupid or inept. The emperor's immediate servants and ministers are aware that the so-called invisible fabric is a hoax, but they deliberately conceal the fact from the emperor. Unwilling to admit that he cannot see the robe, the emperor heads a procession naked. During the parade, the emperor's kitchen boys present themselves stripped in front of

Screenwriters:
Egon Günther, based on the fairy-tale by Hans Christian Andersen

Cinematographer:
Hans Hauptmann

Composer:
Günter Hauk

Editors:
Ilse Peters (1961)
Thea Richter (1991)

Duration:
88 minutes

Genre:
Comedy
Fairy-tale

Cast:
Wolf Kaiser
Horst Drinda
Werner Lierck
Eva-Maria Hagen

Year:
1961/1991

the crowd and tell the hapless emperor that they are dressed as splendidly in royal attire as the emperor himself. The crowd scatters in laughter and the procession ends abruptly. The emperor asks the foreign minister how many people have laughed and orders 80 per cent of the populace to be banished. The minister recommends that the emperor choose a different people.

Critique

Adapted from Hans Christian Andersen's 'The Emperor's New Clothes,' Konrad Petzold's banned comedy *The Dress* is a political satire, in which the ruler becomes a laughing-stock when the naked truth of his incompetence is revealed. The original tale, in which no-one except a small child discovers the ruse, serves as a poignant portrayal of dictatorship, where no opposition exists to point out the absurd notions of the ruling party. It also satirizes the pretentiousness of the nobility, as well as social hypocrisy, conformity and the blind acceptance of authority. Children are associated with innocence, honesty and boldness. They can break the spell because they can speak their mind without fear of shame or stigmatization.

In the film there is also a child who has no qualms about blurting out the blatantly obvious truth. However, the role of the child is marginal. In the film, the people are not depicted as being as gullible as the emperor. On the contrary, they defy the emperor, secretly or openly. A rumour quickly spreads through the city that the weavers have woven nothing at all. When the weavers tell the two businessmen, Fatty and Skinny, that the clothing is invisible to the stupid, Fatty immediately predicts, gloating, that the emperor is going to head the parade naked. During the parade, some onlookers ignore the ceremony and play cards. The procession climaxes when the two kitchen boys want to make the onlookers laugh and decide to imitate the emperor. The clothes have achieved a result exactly opposite to what the tyrannical ruler had intended. Instead of bringing everyone to their knees, he has made everyone turn against him.

After the Berlin Wall was erected, the film was increasingly suspected to be a parody of the East German state as an isolated dictatorship because the kingdom lies behind a thick and solid wall. The censors demanded that some scenes be cut: in an early episode, the guard who wears a moustache was said to resemble Stalin; in the animated sequences, the cloud puffs up its cheeks to blow wind, allegedly mocking the Soviet Party Secretary Khrushchev. In early 1963, the entire 135 cases of negatives were secretly sent to the State Film Archive. The director could not complete the film until the summer of 1990. When it reached the screen 30 years after its making, however, it had already missed the right audience and political context.

The fact that the film quotes 'The Solution' from Brecht's anti-Stalinist *Buckow Elegies* suggests that its subversion was to some extent intended. The brutal repression of the 1956 workers' uprising by Soviet tanks could partially be the reason for the indirect criticism expressed in this very Brechtian film. Hans and Kumpan wish to honestly earn their bread by making clothes for the emperor. However, it is the emperor's ridiculous expectations that make the task impossible, much like the unrealistic expectations that the East German government had for workers to increase production quotas. The affluent and happy image that the patrol guard presents of the city mocks the reality of poverty, mass exodus and the necessity to build the Berlin Wall in East Germany. The crippled minister of justice suggests a paralysed judicial system. The masked soldiers walking on stilts represent the ostentatiously imposing (East German) military. A viewer would also inevitably associate the secret police with the Stasi. The anti-authoritarian attitudes of the people, provocative at the time, foresaw the eventual implosion of the East German state.

Qinna Shen

Nosferatu the Vampyre

Nosferatu: Phantom Der Nacht

Production companies:
Werner Herzog Filmproduktion
Gaumont
Zweites Deutsches Fernsehen (ZDF)

Distributor:
Werner Herzog Filmproduktion, 20th Century Fox of Germany

Director:
Werner Herzog

Producer:
Werner Herzog

Screenwriter:
Werner Herzog

Cinematographer:
Jörg Schmidt-Reitwein

Composer:
Popol Vuh

Editor:
Beate Mainka-Jellinghaus

Synopsis

Described by Herzog as 'part re-make, part re-version' of F.W. Murnau's silent Weimar masterpiece *Nosferatu* (1922), *Nosferatu the Vampyre* both derives narrative and aesthetic elements from the Murnau original while adding material that takes the film in a strikingly different direction. It follows in part the well-known story originating in Bram Stoker's novel *Dracula*, which was adapted not only by Murnau but also film-makers such as Tod Browning (*Dracula*, 1931), Terence Fischer (*Horror of Dracula*, 1958) and Francis Ford Coppola (*Bram Stoker's Dracula*, 1992). The central thread of *Nosferatu* concerns the triadic relationship that develops around Lucy (Adjani), whose husband, the real estate agent Jonathan Harker (Ganz), is sent to seal a property deal with Count Dracula (played by long-time Herzog collaborator, Klaus Kinski). Dracula lives in a Transylvanian castle but wants to buy a residence in Harker's hometown of Bremen. Upon seeing an image of Lucy in Harker's pendant, Dracula becomes obsessed with her and, after attacking Harker and leaving him locked up in the castle, he sails to Bremen in order to consummate his desires.

Critique

Nosferatu re-works certain narrative patterns and gendered representations that can be traced back to Murnau's film, to German Expressionism more broadly, and to the history of nineteenth century German Romanticism. For example, it is the woman, Lucy, who is represented as the only character who has the pure love and faith necessary to destroy the evil vampire. After Harker's return she reads *The Book of Vampires* and identifies herself as 'a woman of pure heart' mentioned in it. This allows Lucy to sacrifice herself in order to destroy Dracula by luring him to her bed where he drains her life away until the sun rises.

Nosferatu the Vampyre, Werner Herzog Filmproduktion/Gaumont/Zweites Deutsches Fernsehen (ZDF).

Duration:
107 minutes

Genre:
Fantastic
Horror

Cast:
Klaus Kinski, Isabelle Adjani, Bruno Ganz, Roland Topor, Jaques Dufilho, Walter Ladengast

Year:
1979

Nosferatu also enacts gender codes, which can be found in many supernatural horror films that pitch a battle between rational science and superstition. For example, Lucy and the vampire are presented as psychically connected. This is expressed symbolically in the beginning of the film through an experimental assemblage of images that links her with death and the nocturnal. This symbolism culminates in an absurd carnival scene near the end of the film where Lucy confronts the residents of Bremen who, knowing that they are going to die soon from the plague brought by Dracula, are frolicking and feasting in the town square swarming with rats. It is only Lucy who understands what is truly happening, and who is intuitively linked to the vampire, while rationally-minded, educated men, such as Dr. Van Helsing (Landengast), ironically fail to heed the numerous signs of the supernatural.

Judith Mayne observes that the 'single, all-encompassing perspective' of *Nosferatu* is a 'quasi-mystical, visionary celebration of the irrational and the absurd' (1986: 127), a perspective that has a particular, patriarchal quality. It involves presenting Nosferatu as the central character through whom other characters eventually perceive themselves and each other. The patriarchal nature of this identification is particularly reflected in the fact that, even though Lucy destroys the vampire, this act is not powerful enough to end the vampire's curse. It is transmitted to Harker who himself transforms into a vampire. Therefore, Harker's encounter with the vampire does not end in the former's death, but in his transformation into the vampire's heir. *Nosferatu* is thus, for Mayne, a story about fathers and sons.

Herzog has claimed that the very act of re-making *Nosferatu* was a way to re-claim the cultural legitimacy for German cinema that he felt had been lost since Hitler's seizure of power in 1933. It was a way to find continuity with 'true' German masters of Romantic and Expressionist art. Apart from visual homages to Murnau's original there are, for example, allusions to the sublime landscape paintings of Caspar David Friedrich in the scene of Harker's journey to Dracula's castle (in which there is also a fragment from Wagner's prelude to *Das Rheingold*). In other words, the film itself reflects Herzog's own 'patriarchal' story and his quest for lineage. As Thomas Elsaesser suggests, in his films Herzog constructs myths and allegories that reflect an existential search for good and bad father images amidst feelings of isolation and homelessness; a search reflecting the alleged fatherlessness and discontinuity in German national history. The rise of Nazism, followed by the defeat in World War II and the US led Allied occupation resulted in a radical re-working of questions of nationhood in conjunction with 'traditional', patriarchal authority (Elsaesser 1989).

Tyson Namow

The NeverEnding Story

Die unendliche Geschichte

Production companies:
Neue Constantin Film
Bavaria Studios
Westdeutscher Rundfunk (WDR)

Distributors:
Neue Constantin Film (Germany)
Warner Bros. (USA)

Director:
Wolfgang Petersen

Producers:
Bernd Eichinger
Bernd Schaefers
Dieter Geissler

Synopsis

To the dismay of his widowed, workaholic father, Bastian Balthazar Bux (Oliver) is a loner and a dreamer. Chased by bullies on the way to school, Bastian takes shelter in a bookstore, and is drawn to a book bearing an insignia of two interlinking snakes. With uncharacteristic bravery Bastian steals the book, taking it with him to school. He hides in the attic and begins to read. Created by the collective imagination of children, Fantasia is being destroyed by the Nothing, an aggressive black hole fuelled by the aggregate nihilism, apathy, despair and lack of imagination in the real world. The dying Empress (Stronach) enlists the help of Atreyu (Hathaway), a young warrior. To guide him on his quest to find a cure and stop the Nothing he is given the Auryen, an amulet with two intertwined snakes. Atreyu loses his horse in the swamps of sadness and meets a new companion, Falkor, the luck dragon. They travel 10,000 miles to ask the Oracles who can save Fantasia and the mirror shows Bastian's image. Atreyu kills G'mork, the cat-like-creature who controls the Nothing and, with Fantasia almost completely eroded, the Empress pleads with Bastian to save them. Bastian screams his mother's name and in so doing takes on the responsibility of re-imagining Fantasia from a single grain of sand. Returning to the real world Bastian takes revenge on the bullies with the help of Falkor.

Screenwriter:
Wolfgang Petersen
Herman Weigel
Robert Easton, based on the novel by Michael Ende

Art Direction:
Götz Weidner
Johann Kott
Herbert Stradel

Cinematographer:
Jost Vacano

Composers:
Klaus Doldinger (German and English version)
Giorgio Moroder (English version only)

Editor:
Jane Seitz

Duration:
94 minutes (English version)
102 minutes (German version)

Genre:
Fantastic
Adventure
Drama

Cast:
Noah Hathaway
Barret Oliver
Tami Stronach
Moses Gunn
Thomas Hill

Year:
1984

Critique

'Do what you wish' reads the inscription on the back of the Auryen. This mantra serves as the major message of *The NeverEnding Story*. Fans of the book by German author Micheal Ende, on which the screenplay is based, have critiqued the film for deviating from the book and for being overly Americanized. Ende himself attempted, unsuccessfully, to stop filming by suing the makers. The film lacks the depth, sophistication and symbolic intensity of the book, and covers only the first half of Ende's epic novel. However, the film's fast pace indicates that the incorporation of the entire book in a single film may have been an impossible undertaking due not only to the length of the story but also the complex philosophical concepts in the latter parts of the novel.

The film both upholds and contradicts one of its own main themes; namely that the fostering of a unique, personal imagination, independent from the practical concerns of everyday life is an essential and restorative exercise for children and adults alike. More specifically, it suggests that while books assist moral and emotional development in children, formal structures such as work and school, as well as modern technology and mass media can inadvertently deaden the human imagination. As this film, with an estimated budget of around US$27 million, employed what were then cutting-edge modern technologies to visually 'imagine' – or impose, depending on one's interpretation – a singular vision of a world supposedly created from the wealth of human imagination for or upon the viewer, perhaps this film can be read against the message of free and individual imagination that it attempts to deliver. Nevertheless, *The NeverEnding Story* highlights the importance of individual thought, bravery and self-esteem, and reinforces the concept that an individual can face and overcome massive forces, if they only believe in themselves.

Spectacular cinematography and special effects help to realise the sprawling Kingdom of Fantasia, but it is the endearing and colourful characters that populate this fantasy world – attained via a cunning combination of live actors, puppetry and animatronics – that really bring this story to life. A powerful, if not at times overwhelming, electronic soundtrack composed by Klaus Doldinger (along with Giorgio Moroder's memorable theme tune which appears only in the English language version) heightens the fantasy. Those familiar with Peterson's World War II submarine epic *Das Boot* (1981) may be surprised by the fantasy genre and young market for his sophomore film; however, a return to the fantasy genre can be noted in his later works, most strikingly in his Hollywood epic *Troy* (2004).

Alina Hoyne

Perfume: The Story of a Murderer

Das Parfum – Die Geschichte eines Mörders

Production Companies:
Constantin Film Produktion
VIP 4 Medienfonds

Distributors:
Pathé Distribution, Constantin Film

Director:
Tom Tykwer

Producer:
Bernd Eichinger

Screenwriters:
Tom Tykwer
Bernd Eichinger
Andrew Birkin, based on the novel 'Das Parfum' by Patrick Süskind

Art Director:
Laia Colet

Cinematographer:
Frank Griebe

Composers:
Reinhold Heil
Johnny Klimek
Tom Twyker

Editor:
Alexander Berner

Duration:
147 minutes

Genre:
Fantastic
Thriller
Serial Killer

Synopsis

Set in eighteenth century France, Tykwer's film tells the story of Jean-Baptiste Grenouille (Whishaw), an orphan and social outcast with a phenomenal sense of smell. As a boy Grenouille is sold to work in a tannery in extremely hard conditions. Later, he finds work in the shop of a famous perfumer Baldini (Hoffman). Once he learns all he can from Baldini about the craft of perfume-making he leaves Paris for Grasse, a town in southern France famous for its perfume manufacturing. During the journey Grenouille realizes that he has no smell of his own, and hence, to his mind, no identity. As a result, he decides to create a perfect perfume that he could use for himself and become accepted in society. Grenouille starts killing women in Grasse in order to collect their scent. Laura (Hurd-Wood), a beautiful young girl attracts him particularly strongly, and he pursues her relentlessly as she escapes with her father. When Grenouille finally succeeds at killing Laura, he uses her scent to mix his perfect perfume. Captured and taken to Grasse for public execution, he manages to spill a few drops of the perfume over the angry mob gathered in the square. Brought into a state of ecstasy, the citizens of Grasse declare Grenouille an 'angel' rather than murderer and let him walk free, as they indulge in a mass orgy. Although he achieves the social acceptance he always desired, Grenouille realizes that he himself is unable to love. Disappointed, he returns to Paris. He uses his perfume to bring a bunch of homeless drifters into a state of ecstasy in which they devour him.

Critique

The fictional character Grenouille is an interesting crossover between a serial killer, a mad genius and an almost autistic society reject. Tykwer and his co-writer Andrew Birkin made significant changes to the literary original, portraying Grenouille as a more human and sympathetic character, and depicting some of his killings as accidents rather than premeditated crimes. Grenouille is consistently portrayed as the victim of an oppressive society; an underdog whose lack of smell is the source of the dramatic conflict in the story, compelling him to murder his fellow human beings. While Grenouille feels no remorse for his killings, he does not derive pleasure from them, thus appearing more a deranged person than a sadistic killer, with some critics suggesting that his violence comes as a result of his weakened narcissistic ego. It should be noted that, even though Grenouille can hardly be seen as a positive character in the story, the people he meets in his life are portrayed with even less sympathy as brutal, primitive and egoistic.

As critics noted in reference to Süskind's literary original, the eponymous perfume capable of changing people's perception of reality can be seen as a metaphor of the sublime, thus evoking the romantic ideal of arts as the epitome of purity and perfection. Hailed as the ultimate postmodern novel, *Perfume* also contains

Cast:
Ben Whishaw
Dustin Hoffman
Alan Rickman
Rachel Hurd-Wood

Year:
2006

numerous references to Romantic literature, such as Adelbert von Chamisso's *Peter Schlemihls wundersame Geschichte*, E.T.A Hoffmann's *Das Fräulein von Scuderi*, or Heinrich von Kleist's *Michael Kohlhaas*. Tykwer preserves much of the postmodern, pastiche spirit of the literary original, while adding Romantic motifs in the visual style: the sublime, colourful landscapes of southern France bring to mind paintings of Philipp Otto Runge, the 'heroic landscapes' of Joseph Anton Koch, or Caspar David Friedrich's trademark motifs of a *Rückenfigur* ('back-view figure') and a *Wanderer* ('wanderer'). In addition, Frank Griebe's photography makes great use of the chiaroscuro lighting technique pioneered by Weimar directors. Numerous night scenes are portrayed using high contrast lighting and some of the most emblematic shots of the film, such as the opening close-up of Grenouille's nose, or the last scene in which he pours the perfume over himself, are remarkable for their chiaroscuro effect.

One of the main aspects of the film's style is the visualisation of scent. To deliver the visceral, synaesthetic experience of smell Tykwer uses a plethora of stylistic devices, such as expressive close-ups, fast editing, suggestive colours, camera movements following different smells around Grenouille, digital effects, animation and music score. The portrayal of scent on-screen was without doubt the major challenge of the production, but at the same time it offered new possibilities of artistic expression. Before Tykwer several established directors, such as Stanley Kubrick or Martin Scorsese, considered adapting Süskind's novel. The major obstacle was the author's refusal to sell the copyright of the book. After years of negotiations Bernd Eichinger finally acquired the rights. Made on a budget exceeding 50 million, *Perfume* remains one of the most expensive German movies of all time. The critical reception was mixed, but the film became a commercial success in Germany and other European countries.

Klemens Czyzydlo

Krabat

Production Companies:
B.A Filmproduktion
Brass Hat Films
Krabat Filmproduktion

Distributors:
20th Century Fox of Germany
Peccadillo Pictures

Director:
Marco Kreuzpaintner

Synopsis

In the bitter winter of January 1646, the enigmatic Master (Redl) summons the young orphan Krabat (Kross) in his dreams to a remote Black Mill in Lausitz. Krabat is thus spared the ravages of the Thirty Years War, apprenticing in the mill's peculiar operations along with eleven other boys. He befriends the oldest boy Tonda (Brühl), and from him learns both the black sorcery practiced at the mill and of its price: the boys may not have relationships with women or outsiders and cannot physically leave the Master's sphere of influence. Naturally, both young men fall in love with girls in the nearby village. The apprentices use their magic to defend the village against marauders, though Tonda's love interest is revealed during the conflict and the Master has her killed the

Producers:
Jakob Claussen
Nick Hamson
Lars Sylvest
Thomas Wöbke
Bernd Wintersperger
Uli Putz

Screenwriters:
Michael Gutmann
Marco Kreuzpaintner
Otfried Preussler

Art Directors:
Daniel Chour
Christian Schaefer

Cinematographer:
Daniel Gottschalk

Composer:
Annette Focks

Editor:
Hansjörg Weissbrich

Duration:
120 minutes

Genre:
Fantastic
Coming-of-Age
Magic School

Cast:
David Kross
Daniel Brühl
Christian Redl
Paula Kalenberg

Year:
2008

following day. Tonda subsequently becomes the annual sacrifice to fuel the Master's eternal youth. Krabat and his lover Kantorka (Kalenberg) assiduously conspire to escape the Master's power the following year. The Master challenges Kantorka by transforming all twelve apprentices into ravens and having her find Krabat among them. She succeeds and the Master's power is broken, destroying man and mill alike. The surviving apprentices lose their magic powers, perhaps for the better.

Critique

The story of Krabat and the Black Mill, a centuries-old Sorbian legend published as a Czech short story, became one of the most popular German young adult novels of the last four decades, resulting in a 20th Century Fox feature. Such are the terms under which the film *Krabat* evolved, dispelling any notion that this central European magician's apprentice fable is a simple dramaturgical derivative of the *Harry Potter* series.

The feature film is actually the third German-language motion picture of the cult novel, preceded by Celino Bleiweiß' GDR television production *The Black Mill* (1975), and Czech animator Karel Zeman's *Krabat* (1977). Director Marco Kreuzpaintner, one of the book's many fans, considered it both an honour and a fulfilment of a childhood fantasy to be named director of the film – akin to Peter Jackson when 'discovered' by New Line Cinema to shoot *Lord of the Rings* (2001). Like the West German Karl May films of the 1960s, a firmly entrenched children's literary cycle produced both the enthusiastic German creators and audience necessary for the semi-success of a big-budget mainstream production. After all, clever intellectual property mining is not merely a twenty-first century paradigm.

In order to please generations of *Krabat* readers, several key personnel were purposefully engaged in the film from its creation. Dr. Susanne Preussler-Bitsch, daughter of *Krabat* author Otfried Preussler, consulted on the film in terms of her father's 'vision'. Producer Uli Putz and production designer Christian Goldbeck – both veterans of Hans-Christian Schmid's 2006 drama *Requiem* – scouted breathtaking locations in the Carpathian Mountains and then built a full mill complex according to seventeenth century material specifications against the backdrop. Alex Lemke, a Weta Digital VFX artist on *Lord of the Rings* and Uwe Boll's *In the Name of the King* (2007), supervised the fantastical visual effects from the film's earliest stages, incorporating morphing and key frame effects into every aspect of its production. Even the 20th Century Fox logo dissolves into a flock of ravens. In the end, *Krabat* retains the memorable aspects of the novel, the gritty materiality of 'living history' in the seventeenth century, and the visually convincing sorcery that sparks young viewers' imaginations. Hollywood made in Germany becomes attainable through sustained, collaborative work among cutting edge professionals enthusiastic about their source material.

This professionalism, however, also shelters the film from all the risk and excess that might lead to more subversive readings.

Vertiginous landscapes refer more to the *Heimatfilme* or the Winnetou cycle than to the grim surroundings of war-ravaged Lausitz. The homoeroticism of twelve boys condemned to live without women is hastily counterbalanced with Tonda and Krabat's immediate and definitive female love interests. In his subtle portrayal of the Master, Christian Redl eschews the overwrought maniacal laughter characteristic of Zeman's version, but the magical panopticon in which he places his pupils seems thus less sinister and somehow less socially critical as well. The apprentices morphing into ravens convinces the audience of the film's production values, though their subsequent defence of the village with their staves more than gratuitously references the Gandalf-Saruman duel in *The Lord of the Rings: The Fellowship of the Ring* (Jackson, 2001). Genre tropes from contemporary fantasy films, such as faceless goons with swords, fluttering black cloaks and fast-moving tracking shots permeate the work and threaten to age it before its time. For an adaptation of a story that brilliantly allegorizes the old preying on the young and a Foucauldian surveillance society intent on absolute biopower, *Krabat* ends on a remarkably tame note. Nevertheless, the film marks a turning point toward the seamless and necessary incorporation of digital effects into German fairy-tale films.

Evan Torner

References

Elsaesser, Thomas (1989), *New German Cinema: A History*, New Brunswick, NJ: Rutgers University Press.

Erlin, Matt (2009), 'Tradition as Intellectual Montage: F.W. Murnau's *Faust*', in Noah Isenberg (ed.), *Weimar Cinema*, New York: Columbia University Press, pp. 155-72.

Kracauer, Siegfried (1947 [2004]), *From Caligari to Hitler: A Psychological History of the German Film*, Princeton, NJ: Princeton University Press.

Lachmann, Renate (2002), *Erzählte Phantastik. Zu Phantasiegeschichte und Semantik phantastischer Texte*, Frankfurt: Suhrkamp.

Lange, Wolfgang (1992), *Der kalkulierte Wahnsinn: Innenansichten ästhetischer Moderne*, Stuttgart: Fischer Taschenbuch Verlag.

Mayne, Judith (1986), 'Herzog, Murnau and the Vampire', in Timothy Corrigan (ed.), *Between Mirage and History: The Films of Werner Herzog*, New York: Methuen, pp. 110-32.

Meehan, Paul (2008), *Tech-Noir*, Jefferson, NC: McFarland.

Neumann, Dietrich (ed.) (1996), *Film Architecture: Set Designs from Metropolis to Blade Runner*, Munich: Prestel.

Nicholls, Peter (1984), *Fantastic Cinema*, London: Ebury Press.

Prawer, Siegbert Salomon (1980), *Caligari's Children: The Film as Tale of Terror*, Cambridge: De Capo Press.

Rentschler, Eric (1990), 'The Triumph of Male Will: "Münchhausen" (1943)', in *Film Quarterly*, 43: 3, pp. 14–23.

Robinson, D. (1999), *Das Cabinet des Dr. Caligari*, BFI Film Classics Series, London: BFI.

Scheunemann, Dietrich (2006), *Expressionist Film: New Perspectives*, Rochester, NY: Camden House.

Webb, Darren (2005), 'Bakhtin at the Seaside: Utopia, Modernity and the Carnivalesque', *Theory, Culture and Society*, 21: 3, pp. 121–38.

Zipes, Jack (1997), *Fairy Tales and Fables from Weimar Days*, Madison: University of Wisconsin Press.

ADVENTURE FILM
DER ABENTEUERFILM

The German adventure film (*Abenteuerfilm*) is a hybrid genre loosely organized around tales set in faraway places, and focused on the viewer's affective engagement with these places' 'exotic' features and apparent dangers. The word 'hybrid' should compel us not to seek an essential quality in the German iterations of the genre, but rather inductively link sub-genres such as the mountain film (*Bergfilm*), medieval epic (*Ritterfilm*), Oriental melodrama or the anti-adventure according to shared studio and viewer expectations. Like the horror genre, 'adventure' is more a mood than a set of generic prescriptions, an assemblage of 'vicariously exciting experiences undergone by sympathetic but largely fictional characters,' as Douglas Fairbanks, Jr. once put it (in Cameron 1973: 5). It stems from a financial need to inscribe the emotional promise of 'adventure' into other genres such as the fairy-tale or the war film, as well as classify films set in differing settings (jungle, desert, mountain peaks, among others) with radically different plot structures (comedy, melodrama, romance, tragedy, etc.) under an umbrella term that summarizes their overall exoticism to the studios and bourgeois viewers. Regardless of what one thinks of the term *Abenteuerfilm*, however, its stubborn presence in production documents, reviews, academic discourse and informal banter over a century of German national film production prompts us to examine the thread that weaves this patchwork of disparate sub-genres together.

This thread can be seen as a certain geographic imaginary that sutures awe-inspiring indexical reality with imagination-inducing staged reality; the comforts of a capable tourist with the vulnerability of a stranger in a dangerous land; the modern *flâneur* with his horseback-riding, mountain-climbing ancestor. Exoticization, or treating an object or people as unusual for the purposes of condescension or romanticization, also plays a central role in the adventurous encounter. Since Germans have generally identified themselves as 'white' and 'civilized,' the audio-visual preoccupation with non-white people, non-European modes of governance and racialized geographies reflect this sought-after combination of comfort and danger. Racialized people either confirm white supremacy (as 'dying races') or become a second skin to act out white fantasies. Technology employed against nature is also a dominant theme; the forbidding dangers of the uncivilized territory test not only humankind's limits, but also its fancy tools. Reconciliation and/or recognition of nature's power alongside that of the protagonist are often a shared dramaturgical goal.

Such films emerged from the nineteenth century traditions of the pulp novel (*Kolportageroman*) and an Orientalism trend in fashion and design throughout Europe, both corresponding with the apex of European colonialism. The Anglo-American stories of Rudyard Kipling, Rafael Sabatini, James Frederick Cooper and Edgar Rice Burroughs all provided collective myths about what Europe was to its bourgeois readers, recapturing 'lost' notions of honour and courage in the face of industrial modernity. In the German case, Karl May and Fritz Steuben, among others, filtered this bourgeois honour ideal primarily through Native American characters in the American West, frequently appropriating tropes from the German heroic epics (*Heldensagen*) to ennoble and immortalize the protagonists'

Left: *The Blue Light*, Leni Riefenstahl-Produktion.

emotional-ethical world views. Treasures and love were often the goal, but not at the expense of the protagonists' moral integrity.

Conventional typologies for the adventure sub-genres organize them around the various excitement cues and far-flung landscapes offered, but always on the Hollywood altar. Brian Taves divides adventure into the swashbuckler, pirate, sea, empire and fortune hunter sub-genres (1993: 15); Bodo Traber and Hans J. Wulff into the ancient, knight, cloak-and-dagger, pirate and samurai film (2004: 31); Georg Seesslen into ancient, knight, pirate, cloak and dagger and 'last adventurer' (with Fritze and Weil 1983). While such typologies fleetingly acknowledge the importance of Japanese (samurai) or Italian (ancient) contributions to the genre, they neither adequately encompass the German sub-genres, nor the substantial German influence on and engagement with global adventure film productions. After all, it was émigré Robert Siodmak who directed *The Crimson Pirate* (1952), one of the genre's all-time classics, and Joe May's Filmstadt studios in Woltersdorf and Rüdersdorf established a foothold in the genre that only the crises of the Weimar Republic could break. Indeed, the study of the German adventure film reveals the nation's film history in its inconstancy and ambition, its self-sufficiency and co-dependency, its remarkable highs and embarrassing lows. Thus, I submit sub-genres that correspond to the peculiarly German iteration of the adventure film, namely, the Orientalist, empire, mountain, '*Indianerfilm*' and anti-adventure.

The Orientalist adventure melodrama reflects German fantasies about the Near and Far East. Such films feature sets drawn from an incoherent potpourri of Asian traditions, actors in make-up and costumes designed to foreground ethnic/racial Otherness, and the occasional documentary or on-location footage situating the impossibly lavish rooms within geographies abroad. These mostly serialized films reached their popular zenith in the period during and immediately after World War I, with Richard Eichberg's *Der indische Tod* (1915), Harry Piel's *Der Sultan von Johore/The Sultan of Johore* (1917), Ernst Lubitsch's *Sumurun* (1920), Fritz Lang's *The Spiders* (1919/1920), Kurt Gerhardt's *Die Jagd nach dem Tode* (1920/1921), and Joe May's *Die Herrin der Welt/Mistress of the World* (1919/1920) and *The Indian Tomb* (1921, re-made in 1938 and 1959). May's Oriental films came into being largely because of an exhausted 'detective' genre cycle, but the investigation of mysteries and treasure still play a central role. Successful fairy-tale crossovers into the sub-genre included Wilhelm Prager's *Der kleine Muck/Little Mook* (1921, re-made in 1944 and 1953) and Lotte Reiniger's animated classic *The Adventures of Prince Achmed* (1926). This sub-genre notably gained a second life in the 1950s and 1960s thanks to the films' inherent televisuality.

A Weimar and Nazi-era sub-genre without much of a second life, the 'empire' film occupies a maligned position of being an artefact of German colonialism and colonial fantasies: an irrefutable claim. This sub-genre depicts white settlers in colonial Africa and/or South America fighting for peace and justice in spite of the prevailing 'savagery' embodied by the natives, often shot in frond-bedecked sets with working black extras such as Louis Brody. Those films not shot in studios such as *Tropengift* (1919) or *Eine Weisse unter Kannibalen* (1921) were likely shot by entrepreneur Hans Schomburgk, who combined African 'research' with feature film-making that depicted Africans as subhuman and white females as objects of sexual anxiety (Nagl 2009: 227). The sub-genre proved to be surprisingly resilient up until the 1950s, with *Ich hatt' einen Kameraden/The Good Comrade* (Felsing, 1923), *Samba, Der Held des Urwalds* (Bauer-Adamara and Bruckner, 1928), *To New Shores* (Sirk, 1937), *Kautschuk/The Green Hell* (von Borsody, 1938), *The Immortal Heart* (Harlan, 1939), *Carl Peters* (Selpin, 1941), *Uncle Krüger* (Steinhoff, 1941) and *Germanin* (Kimmich, 1943) marking continuity from Weimar through the Nazi period until Eduard von Borsody's pin-up female Tarzan cycle *Liane, Jungle Goddess* (1956). Disparate plot lines and themes over decades still give way to a uniform racialization of the Global South and its inhabitants.

The 'mountain' film, a sub-genre pioneered by Arnold Fanck, Hans Schneeberger and Sepp Allgeier, pushed the encounter of white Europeans with Nature to its visual and emotional extremes. Despite the cycle's limited lifespan, beginning with *Im Kampf mit dem Berge* (Fanck, 1921) and ending ten films later with the US/German co-production *S.O.S. Eisberg* (1933), the sub-genre had a profound impact on world photography and the later work of Leni Riefenstahl (the films' trademark starlet), particularly *The Blue Light* (1932). The films' aesthetics foreground authentic mountain settings with tiny humans overcoming – and being humbled by – awe-inspiring, sunlit Nature. The storylines were usually confined to simple love triangles and rescue dramas so as to highlight Riefenstahl's attractiveness and athleticism. Though the sub-genre's proto-Aryan philosophies clearly stand in the shadow of National Socialism, the photography and daring stunts still fascinate to this day.

The '*Indianerfilm*' is the filmic incarnation of long-held Native American fetishism carried over from the aforementioned pulp literary tradition. The phenomenon was found on both sides of the Wall, with the West German cycle (1962–68), produced by Horst Wendlandt, grounded in the Winnetou stories of Karl May; and the East German cycle (1965–83), led by Günter Karl, grounded in the anti-fascist re-imagining of US history. Both *Indianerfilm* traditions were reliant on co-productions with countries like Italy and Yugoslavia, however, for the necessary rugged backdrops and experienced horse handlers. The American West, shot in Eastern Europe, served as an almost mythic setting to frame Cold War ideology alongside explosions and stunts that have little to do with the Native Americans' actual plight.

Finally, the 'anti-adventure' film arrived in West Germany in the late 1950s with the popularization of existentialism and initial reactions to a postcolonial reality. Anti-adventure films combat notions of a protagonist's psychological transparency, the permeability of the unknown landscape, and the materialist desires of the adventurer. Georg Tressler's production *Ship of the Dead* (1959), for example, cast upcoming star Horst Buchholz as a stateless sailor who searches the world for a place to take him in and finds naught but a sinking ship. The director who properly defined this sub-genre, however, is undoubtedly Werner Herzog, whose prior work in critical documentary fuelled a narrative style ambivalent to audience identification with the protagonists. In films such as *Aguirre: The Wrath of God* (1972), *Fitzcarraldo* (1982), *Cobra Verde* (1987) and *Cerro Torre: Scream of Stone* (1991) Herzog draws on tropes of the empire and mountain sub-genres to advocate an opaque, anxious counter-fantasy to that which those films originally proposed. Nevertheless, the viewer is still given landscapes to exoticize and scenes of human brutality to enjoy.

It is worth noting that the fairy-tale film (*Märchenfilm*), a sub-genre of the fantastic film, often profiles itself as an 'adventure film' as well. It typically draws upon tropes from another adventure sub-genre, such as the empire film for G.W. Pabst's *Queen of Atlantis* (1932) or the Orientalist adventure for Gottfried Kolditz' *The Golden Tent* (1961). The films rely on special effects to attract movie-goers, but offer landscapes and characters inspired by children's adventure stories.

Naturally there are German contributions to the Hollywood adventure sub-genres as well: Lang's *Die Nibelungen* (1924) as a knight film; Bourgeois and Piel's *Zigano – Der Brigant von Monte Diavolo* (1925) as cloak and dagger film; Martin Hellberg's *Die schwarze Galeere* (1962) and Ulrike Ottinger's and Tabea Blumenschein's *Madame X* (1978) as pirate films; or Thomas Frick's *Detective Lovelorn und die Rache des Pharaos* (2002) and Florian Baxmeyer's *Spear of Destiny* (2009) as recent fortune hunter entries reveal a continued desire to engage with Hollywood paradigms and satisfy local German audiences with domestic film products. Nevertheless, in German film history the *Abenteuerfilm* will remain an elusive constellation of thematically related sub-genres at a slight remove from Hollywood. It continues to pose a moving target for film scholars so long as producers, screenwriters and reviewers insist (in writing) that the term somehow describes the film at hand.

Evan Torner

White Hell of Pitz Palü

Die weiße Hölle vom Piz Palü

Production Companies:
Sokal-Film GmbH
H.T. Film

Distributors:
Aafa-Flim AG (Germany)
Universal Pictures (USA)

Directors:
Arnold Fanck
G.W. Pabst

Producer:
Henry Sokal

Screenwriters:
Arnold Fanck
Ladislaus Vajda

Art Director:
Ernö Metzner

Cinematographers:
Sepp Allgeier
Richard Angst
Hans Schneeberger

Composers:
Heinz Roemheld
Giuseppe Becce

Editor:
Arnold Fanck

Duration:
150 minutes

Genre:
Mountain
Adventure

Cast:
Leni Riefenstahl
Gustav Diessl
Ernst Petersen
Mizzi Götzel
Ernst Udet
Otto Spring

Year:
1929

Synopsis

While climbing the dangerous north face of Pitz Palü in the Dolomites, Dr. Johannes Krafft's (Diessl) wife drops into the ravine of a mountain glacier and dies. Three years later a young couple, Maria and Hans (Riefenstahl and Petersen), spend their honeymoon in a cabin at the foot of Pitz Palü. Maria is reading about the tragedy in the logbook when Krafft suddenly appears. Since the accident, he has become restless and plans to tackle Pitz Palü again. As he gets ready for his morning ascent, Hans and Maria join him. On the way to the top, Hans trips and hangs unconscious from a rope that Krafft manages to haul up. Hans has suffered a head injury, however, and they must wait for help to arrive from the village. Meanwhile, a group of inexperienced students climbing the mountain and using a different route are hit by an avalanche and plunge to their deaths. Weather conditions worsen and three days pass before a local mountain guide and old friend of Krafft locates and rescues Maria and Hans. Help comes too late for Krafft, who awaits his death in a small cave on Pitz Palü.

Critique

White Hell of Pitz Palü, a film by director and mountaineer Arnold Fanck, plays out as a contest between humankind and nature. On a narrative level Pitz Palü presents a challenge for Krafft, Hans and Maria, with each character having their own motive for climbing the mountain. Krafft wants to win a race against the younger students; Maria, under Krafft's spell, aims to live up to Krafft's dead wife; finally, Hans tests his manliness against that of Krafft, who has become a rival for Maria's affection. Only the villagers, a religious community whose men come to the rescue of the stranded are wise enough to shun this kind of contest. They appear respectful of the mountain and dare not challenge its mighty presence. For them, as the title of an earlier Fanck film (*The Holy Mountain* [1926]) suggests, it is a holy mountain.

Fanck pioneered the mountain film, a genre whose essence lies in their tantalizing visual properties. *White Hell of Pitz Palü* is a prime example of this aesthetic formula: thinly plotted, the film is notable for its icy Alpine scenery. As in his other films, the sublime glacial backdrops dwarf the people who admire them. These images evoke the work of Romantic landscape painter Caspar David Friedrich, who viewed natural phenomena as overwhelming experiences for the human soul.

White Hell of Pitz Palü pays tribute to Fanck's passion for two inventions that stimulated and expanded human imagination in the first half of the twentieth century: the film camera and the airplane. The extended sequence of a propeller plane filmed against snowy landscapes suggests Fanck is mesmerized by new technologies as tools to render the secrets of nature visible. The many aerial shots offering panoramic views of the mountain and valleys often feature parts of the plane and its pilot (flying ace Ernst Udet manoeuvred

White Hell of Pitz Palü, Sokal-Film GmbH/H.T. Film.

the airplane in this film as well as Fanck's *Storm Over Mont Blanc* [1930] and *S.O.S. Eisberg* [1933]), revealing the location of the cameraman. In this way, the spectator is made aware of the location shooting as both dangerous venture and remarkable achievement. The aesthetic appeal of the locations supports the idea that the mountain film is on one level complementary to the Weimar street film rather than it's opposite (see Rentschler 1996b: 137–61). Both genres share a strong link with modernity, *White Hell of Pitz Palü* drawing on tourism and vacationing as a counterbalance to the hectic city lifestyle.

It is up to the viewer to decide whether the passion for aviation and film-making takes precedence over that for the natural world of the mountains, but scholarship on the mountain film generally asserts that the marriage between natural powers and modern technology aesthetically forebodes Nazi ideology. *White Hell*'s final scenes suggest that humankind should respect the might of the mountain. Even after Maria and Hans's traumatic experiences, Pitz Palü appears as benevolent and inviting as ever, as if to say that the misfortune of the couple was due to their own ignorance.

According to Carsten Strathausen this 'cinematic sublime' in the mountain film creates an 'oscillation between peaceful and dangerous images,' a suture that makes pleasurable the threatening aspect of nature (2001: 181). Utilized in fascist aesthetics, the cinematic sublime has the effect of glorifying the danger of death.

Claudia Sandberg

Storm Over Mont Blanc (or Avalanche)

Stürme über dem Mont Blanc

Production Company:
Aafa-Film AG

Distributors:
Aafa-Film AG

Director:
Arnold Fanck

Producer:
Henry Sokal

Screenwriters:
Arnold Fanck
Carl Mayer (uncredited)

Cinematographers:
Sepp Allgeier
Richard Angst
Hans Schneeberger

Composer:
Paul Desasu

Editor:
Arnold Fanck

Duration:
95 minutes

Genre:
Mountain
Adventure

Synopsis

Set at a meteorological observatory atop Mont Blanc, the narrative follows scientist Hannes (Rist) who falls in love with Hella (Reifenstahl), the daughter of an astronomer who works in the valley below. Hella and her father, Professor Armstrong (Kayssler), visit Hannes in his remote outpost. Shortly thereafter, Professor Armstrong falls to his death in a climbing accident. Hannes suggests the grief-stricken Hella visit his good friend Walter (Wieman), a musician friend who is unwell. A misunderstanding ensues, resulting in Hannes believing that Hella has fallen in love with Walter. The disappointed Hannes remains in the weather observatory over winter rather than face Hella and Walter. Whilst continuing to take readings at an anemometer during a blizzard, Hannes loses his gloves and his hands become frozen, preventing him from making a fire in his hut. He attempts to ski down to the village but is forced to turn back. Hannes discovers the hut is severely damaged by the storm, yet manages to send a message via Morse code, which is intercepted by Hella at the astronomical observatory below. A rescue party is dispatched but Ernst Udet arrives in his plane first and lights a fire to save Hannes from freezing to death.

Critique

Shot in France and Switzerland, *Storm Over Mont Blanc* is perhaps the most fascinating of Fanck's melodramatic *Bergfilme*. Divided into three distinct acts, *Storm Over Mont Blanc* utilizes more depictions of 1930s state of the art technologies than any of Fanck's other cinematic productions.

Act 1 introduces Hannes going about his domestic chores, gathering and transmitting scientific data, whilst admiring the Alpine vista. Depictions of the cabin interior are intercut with shots of the surrounding landscape, utilizing time-lapse and filters that enhance the passage of clouds and changing lighting conditions. This has the pragmatic effect of adding a sense of dynamism to what is, to the naked eye, a static vista; one of the hallmarks of Fanck's visual aesthetic. Hannes' lifestyle and activities conform to traditional Romantic/Victorian notions of masculine endeavour in the pursuit of knowledge by portraying the physical hardship, absence of women and primitive living conditions in an outpost essentially 'untouched' by civilization.

Cast:

Leni Riefenstahl
Sepp Rist
Ernst Udet
Mathias Wieman
Friedrich Kayssler

Year:

1930

The contrast between the hut interior and the frozen landscape serves to reinforce a sense of solitude and elemental forces at work. 'Primal' elements of earth, fire, wind and water are all amply represented and juxtaposed against the human need for shelter, warmth, food and intellectual endeavour. Hannes' life of solitude is punctuated by technologically mediated interactions, which connect him via wireless telegraphy, aircraft and telescope to wider communities. Hella first appears on-screen as the operator of a large industrial telescope in a state of the art astronomical observatory in the valley. This scene is unique among films of the era, since it shows advanced technology being competently and credibly operated by a woman.

Act 2 represents a significant change in pace in which athletic displays of skiing, unusual camera angles and high-energy antics dominate. This act has Hella become involved in a playful 'foxhunt' while on Christmas holidays at the foot of Mont Blanc. Dynamic point-of-view shots, an emphasis on stark contrast, close-ups and long shots, cross-cutting and the juxtaposition of movement typify this sequence. This references Fanck's earlier light-hearted comedies such as *The Big Jump* (1927) and *The White Ecstasy* (1931). Ernst Udet introduces bird's-eye views of the landscape in his monoplane, intervenes in the ski-chase, and later ends up delivering Hella and her father to the summit of Mont Blanc. In the mountain hut Hella displays a keen interest in all things scientific, whilst Hannes and Professor Armstrong good-naturedly assume domestic chores. This constitutes an inversion of traditional gender-based stereotypes.

Act 3 is precipitated by Professor Armstrong falling to his death as Hella and Hannes monitor scientific equipment outdoors. The grieving Hella turns her attention to caring for Hannes' ill friend and begins to doubt her commitment to her scientific career. Thematically, this exposes the contradictions and tensions between modernity and traditional concepts of femininity, and introduces spiritual themes. Hannes assumes Walter and Hella are in love, and so remains gathering scientific data at the outpost over winter. Hannes endures a life-and-death struggle against the elements, echoing Judeo-Christian concepts of martyrdom and redemption through suffering. He eventually manages to transmit a distress signal via Morse code and is rescued.

Storm over Mont Blanc explores the complex interplay between advanced technology and the human condition. It metaphorically critiques the impact of modernity upon social structures, interpersonal relationships and traditional gender-based roles. While advanced technology and the quest to acquire scientific data are shown to profoundly alter social dynamics, the technology is also shown to unite isolated peoples, facilitate survival in extreme environments and help humanity fulfil its intellectual and spiritual potential.

Darlene Inkster

The White Ecstasy – New Ski Miracles

Der weisse Rausch – neue Wunder des Schneeschuhs

Production Company:
Sokal-Film GmbH

Distributor:
Aafa-Film AG

Director:
Arnold Fanck

Producer:
Henry Sokal

Screenwriter:
Arnold Fanck

Art Director:
Leopold Blonder

Cinematographers:
Richard Angst
Kurt Neubert
Hans Karl Gottschalk
Bruno Leubner

Composer:
Paul Dessau

Editor:
Arnold Fanck

Duration:
75 minutes

Genre:
Mountain Film

Cast:
Leni Riefenstahl
Hannes Schneider
Guzzi Lantschner
Walter Riml
Rudi Matt
Lothar Ebersberg

Year:
1931

Synopsis

The young woman Leni (Riefenstahl) from Berlin arrives in the mountainous landscape of Tyrol to learn how to ski. With the help of the skiing instructor Hannes (Schneider), she learns all the important movements and tricks in order to take part in a race in the small town of St. Anton near the mountain, Arlberg. With the help of two clumsy carpenters from Hamburg, she manages to win the competition. One year later she has become a decent skier and takes part in fox hunting together with Hannes. Both have to escape from the hunting skiers trying to pull down their 'silly' ski-hats. They shake off their pursuers in a dangerous ski-chase more than once but a small boy captures Leni and Hannes' hats in the end.

Critique

The White Ecstasy is Arnold Fanck's third and last film about skiing and the mountainous landscape of Tyrol. After the first two, which were shot in 1920 and 1922 as silent films, this last movie is special because of the use of sound and the appearance of the future film-maker Leni Riefenstahl as Leni. All main characters are called by their real first names, underscoring the hybridity between documentary and feature film. With forty professional skiers, including the two Tyrolean ski stars Walter Riml and Guzzi Lantschner playing Hamburg carpenters, Arnold Fanck created authentic images of skiing in the Alps, which thrilled the film-going public in the Weimar period. The competition and the fox hunting, which lasts nearly the whole film, required the invention of new camera techniques. Shooting the snowy landscape without a studio, problems of natural light with all its levels of brightness, the difficult mountainous terrain and weather conditions all lend the film a quasi-documentary element. Fanck often used long shots, slow motion and filmed with a mobile camera to show the art of skiing in a way that had never been seen before.

By focusing on the technical innovation of his camera work, however, he disregarded the plot and the development of the characters. Siegfried Kracauer rightly criticized the trivial story of the film. But slapstick elements prove far more important here. Particularly, the two carpenters from Hamburg, Tietje and Fietje, repeatedly interrupt the spectacular skiing scenes. These humorous interludes place the film in the 'cinema of attractions' constellation as well as that of the detective and adventure genres during the Weimar period. *The White Ecstasy* is certainly not one of Arnold Fanck's best feature films. *The Holy Mountain* (1926) or *White Hell of Pitz Palü* (1929) are far more important in the film-maker's oeuvre. However, the realistic and authentic pictures of the skiing competition with the best skiers at that time made a deep impression on its viewers and the mountain film genre as a whole.

Andy Raeder

The Blue Light

Das blaue Licht

Production Company:
Leni Riefenstahl-Produktion

Distributors:
DuWorld Pictures (USA)

Directors:
Leni Riefenstahl
Béla Balázs (uncredited)

Producers:
Henry Sokal
Leni Riefenstahl

Screenwriters:
Béla Balázs
Leni Riefenstahl
Carl Mayer (uncredited), based on the novel by Gustav Renker (uncredited)

Art Director:
Leopold Blonder

Cinematographers:
Hans Schneeberger
Heinz von Jaworsky

Composer:
Giuseppe Becce

Editor:
Leni Riefenstahl

Duration:
85 minutes

Genre:
Adventure
Fairy-tale
Mountain

Cast:
Leni Riefenstahl
Mathias Wieman
Beni Führer
Max Holzboer
Martha Mair
Franz Maldacea

Year:
1932

Synopsis

Resting at a mountain village inn, a tourist couple finds a girl's portrait pinned to a wall, introducing the legend of Junta (Riefenstahl). The village, located at the foot of the majestic Mount Cristallo, was once plagued by the recurring deaths of its young men. Seduced by a blue light that shone on top of the mountain at full moon, they tried to climb it and paid with their lives. The villagers accused Junta, who lived alone in the mountains, of luring their sons to their deaths, because she was the only one who knew a safe route to the top. Vigo (Wieman), an outsider, helped Junta escape an angry mob and subsequently stayed with her in the mountains. When the moon was full again, he followed the sleepwalking girl and found her sitting in a cave filled with precious stones. Excited about his discovery, Vigo informed the villagers of this treasure and Junta's pathway. They plundered the cave and became wealthy while Junta, distraught upon discovering what happened to her secret hiding place, fell from the cliffs and died.

Critique

The Blue Light established and perpetuates Riefenstahl's controversial persona as a near-mythical genius. Despite the contributions of other talented artists, the film over time came to be credited almost solely to her. Riefenstahl directed *The Blue Light* and plays the lead role of the child-woman Junta, who is both feared and desired. According to the credits, Riefenstahl also produced, scripted and edited the film. She also claimed Junta's story as her own idea, downplaying its actual literary source, Swiss writer Gustav Renker's novel *Bergkristall* ('*Mountain Crystal*'). Neither Arnold Fanck's editorial assistance nor Carl Mayer's scriptwriting found their way into the credits. Furthermore, while the initial release version acknowledged the participation of Jewish-Hungarian writer Béla Balázs, his name disappeared from the credits in subsequent releases (see Rentschler 1996a: 27–53).

Placing the story in the eighteenth century European romantic tradition, *The Blue Light* depicts the intrusion of modernity and nature's tragic demystification. Wanderer and painter Vigo arrives in a community of superstitious and repressed villagers and is disturbed upon meeting Junta, who is innocent and unaware of her sexual allure. With his wide-brimmed hat and flowing overcoat evoking Goethe's *Wilhelm Meister*, Vigo is thirsty for knowledge and scientific explanation. It is his rationalism that ultimately destroys the myth of the Blue Light. Aesthetically, the film harkens back to the early Weimar years, depicting the exterior world as an emotional landscape, evident in the ragged lines of the mountain cave that evoke the expressionism of *The Cabinet of Dr. Caligari* (1920). Carl Mayer wrote *Caligari* and the similar expressionist features of *The Blue Light* may be evidence of his participation in 'Riefenstahl's' film. On the other hand, imbuing natural elements such as water, moon and darkness with yearning and desire recalls

The Blue Light, Leni Riefenstahl-Produktion.

the eeriness of F.W. Murnau's *Nosferatu* (1922). As with Ellen in Murnau's film, Junta's femininity is an irrational force that threatens social order and stability. The romantic notion of the uncanny and inexplicable, and Junta's death as sacrifice for the villagers' prosperity, prefigure the amalgam of modernity and romanticism of the Nazi *Heimat* genre, in which female sexuality is a threat that needs to be removed (see von Moltke 2005: 48–52).

The Blue Light belongs to the *Bergfilm* genre pioneered by Arnold Fanck. Whereas in Fanck's films, mountain climbing is usually structured as a challenge testing male strength, gender dynamics are reversed in *The Blue Light*. Here, nature – Junta – is a female beauty doomed because of the human urge to possess it (Nenno 2003: 61–84). According to this perspective, the film can be seen as a critique of the devastating impact of tourism on the environment.

Claudia Sandberg

S.O.S. Iceberg

S.O.S. Eisberg

Production Company:
Deutsche Universal-Film

Distributors:
Deutsche Universal-Film (Germany)
Universal Pictures (USA)

Director:
Arnold Fanck

Screenwriters:
Arnold Fanck, Friedrich Wolf (uncredited)

Art Directors:
Fritz Maurischat, Arno Richter

Cinematographers:
Richard Angst, Hans Schneeberger

Composer:
Paul Dessau

Editors:
Herman Haller, Andrew Marton

Duration:
86 minutes (Germany)
76 minutes (USA)

Genre:
Mountain
Adventure
Drama

Cast:
Leni Riefenstahl
Sepp Rist
Ernst Udet
Gustav Diessl

Year:
1933

Synopsis

The plot of the original German version of the film revolves around attempts to rescue a stranded polar scientist in Greenland. A search party sets out and discovers Dr. Lorenz, played by Gustav Diessl, near death on a drifting iceberg. With the spring thaw, conditions amongst the disintegrating ice floes have become treacherous. Using Morse code on a wireless radio, the message 'S.O.S Eisberg' is transmitted. A young boy tinkering in a home workshop eventually hears the message. This triggers an international response to the plight of the stranded men. Riefenstahl, playing the aviatrix wife of Dr. Lorenz, manages to locate the stranded crew, but in doing so, crashes her monoplane and also becomes stranded. Facing starvation, freezing conditions and ever-present danger from the calving icebergs, a day-to-day struggle for survival ensues. Eventually, after the death of several crew members, the survivors are located by World War I flying ace Ernst Udet, who plays himself in the film. Udet raises the alarm in a nearby village of Eskimos, who use their kayaks to rescue the expedition survivors.

Critique

The indelible renditions of nature that typify Fanck's *Bergfilme* set his work apart from the predominantly studio-based productions of the era. His work shows evidence of a formal visual structure within the frame, echoing aesthetic constructs typical of nineteenth century Romanticism. Temporal notions of the 'sublime' are constructed in the form of grandiose icebergs, vast icescapes and billowing clouds juxtaposed against the human body and/or advanced technologies. Like the nineteenth century Romantics, Fanck's films were designed to inspire awe in the face of nature. By constructing images which evoke contemplation (often shot from a static point-of-view) and contrasting them with dynamic, fast-paced images (often utilizing a shifting perspective), Fanck's melodramatic *Bergfilme* highlight the nexus between traditional and modern sensibilities. The film references early twentieth century exploration narratives, Victorian notions of heroism, the popularisation of science and applications of revolutionary technologies in the form of wireless radio and flight.

The popularity of Fanck's 'snow and ice' themed movies brought him to the attention of Carl Laemmle Sr. of Universal Studios in Hollywood, who successfully distributed some of Fanck's earlier movies in the US. Taking advantage of popular interest in polar exploration, Laemmle bankrolled the lavish five-month 'Universal-Fanck Greenland Expedition' making it the most ambitious production Fanck ever embraced. Two other feature films were shot alongside *S.O.S. Eisberg*: *The Wedding of Palo* (1934), directed by internationally renowned arctic ethnographer Knud Rasmussen; and *North Pole Ahoy!* (1934), a comedy directed by Andrew Marton. Competition for resources, the loss of valuable equipment and personality clashes between Fanck and Marton created considerable tension on location, which was then communicated back to Universal.

S.O.S. Iceberg, Deutsche Universal-Film.

With the filming in Greenland complete, Universal decided to release a second version of *S.O.S. Eisberg* more closely tailored to the perceived tastes of the American public. Tay Garnett (director) and Tom Reed (writer), who happened to be vacationing in Europe at the time, were hired to put together the English-language version. At Garnett's insistence, further location shooting in Switzerland was conducted. This consisted primarily of footage of a dog-sled team travelling over the icy wastelands, an attempted rape scene and the addition of some superfluous dialogue in and around a sod hut and/or recreated ice cavern. Although credited with directing the American release starring Rod La Rocque and Leni Riefenstahl, Garnett's contribution could at best be described as minimal. A comparative analysis between the two versions of the film reveals that over 80 per cent of the material used in the American film was culled directly from Fanck's German version, including complex montage sequences, central narrative strands and numerous dramatic highlights.

The 58 hours of film directed by Fanck in Greenland became a central component in Universal's stock footage archive and was later used in at least ten B films and serials without acknowledgement. In some instances, entire feature films, such as *Mutiny in the*

Arctic (Rawlins, 1941), or episodes from series such as *The Great Alaskan Mystery* (Collins and Taylor, 1944) were specifically constructed around dramatic highlights lifted directly from *S.O.S. Eisberg*. The recurrent themes and visual motifs derived from *S.O.S. Eisberg* were reworked into different eras and genres, making a significant contribution to the construction of action/adventure films in mainstream Hollywood cinema that is still evident today. The lack of recognition accorded to Fanck's *Bergfilme* in Hollywood appears to be a reflection of Fanck's subsequent membership in the Nazi party, and the prominent roles Riefenstahl and Udet later assumed throughout the Nazi era. *S.O.S. Eisberg* is an intriguing film that was made at a critical historical, technical and economic juncture, deserving a prominent place in any analysis of Weimar film culture or contemporary film studies.

Darlene Inkster

To New Shores

Zu neuen Ufern

Production Company:
Universum Film (UFA)

Distributors:
UFA Film Company
Gloria Filmverleih AG

Director:
Detlef Sierck (Douglas Sirk)

Producer:
Bruno Duday

Screenwriters:
Detlef Sierck
Kurt Heuser, based on the novel by Lovis Lorenz

Cinematographer:
Franz Weihmayr

Composer:
Ralph Benatzky

Editor:
Milo Harbich

Duration:
106 minutes

Synopsis

London, 1846: Gloria Vane (Leander), a famous actress, is sentenced to forced labour in Australia after her wrongful conviction for forging a cheque. This is unbeknownst to the actual perpetrator, her boyfriend and army officer Sir Albert Finsbury (Birgel), who has since also relocated to Australia. While Gloria serves a seven-year sentence in the Parramatta prison, Finsbury enjoys life in the finer circles of colonial Australia. When Gloria asks for his help in escaping, Finsbury refuses. Eventually, Gloria agrees to marry farmer Henry Hoyer (Staal) in order to curtail her jail term. On the way to the farm, she tells Hoyer that she is still in love with Finsbury and flees to Sydney, only to learn that Finsbury is engaged to the Governor's daughter. Tired and heartbroken, she works in a nightclub where she once again meets Finsbury, who tries to persuade her to be with him. Disillusioned, she declares she no longer loves him. Soon after, Finsbury commits suicide while Hoyer finds Gloria and they get married in the Parramatta church.

Critique

To New Shores was part of a Nazi escapist cinema that managed to infuse entertainment with a propagandist twist. While the text made audiences long for exotic worlds, it was also saturated with Nazi *Heimat* values to bring them ideologically back to the Reich. The female protagonist Gloria Vane, portrayed by the major star of Nazi melodramas, Zarah Leander, embodies this tension between desire and reason. While performing on the London stage, she is the object of the male and female gaze alike. Yet her provocative manners are only a part of a stage persona that hides the real Gloria, a sensitive and faithful woman. Male lead Finsbury is presented as a rather dark character, while Hoyer, blond and robust, evokes the sturdy masculinity of Arnold Fanck's mountain

Genre:
Melodrama
Adventure

Cast:
Zarah Leander
Willy Birgel
Victor Staal
Carola Höhn

Year:
1937

film characters. Hoyer's attire resembles the traditional dress code of villagers in Alpine regions and seems ill-suited to the heat of the Australian outback. Hoyer's character and his surroundings embody *Heimat*, a rural community where mankind is kind-hearted, nature-loving and, above all, honest; the very opposite of flamboyant Finsbury. Gloria is Hoyer's perfect match, as she is kind to humans and animals alike. It is in the depiction of these characters as a couple that the 'German' homeland is invoked as the only feasible option. In the end, Gloria recognizes that her emotional wellbeing lies with Hoyer rather than Finsbury. Though Hoyer might not be the love of her life, she exchanges passion for prudency, or in the words of the pastor: 'Let us prefer the soul to the flesh.'

Drawing colonial Australia as an inferior place, *To New Shores* approaches the idea of *Heimat* by mapping it's Other. Aside from the English expatriates who head the potpourri of ethnic groups, the film depicts the Australian population – whether Aboriginal, Asian or Caucasian – as uneducated and dirty. This dichotomy between civilized and uncivilized is highlighted further in the costumes and production design. The simply-cut dresses of the English ladies and the barrack-like living quarters cannot measure up to the conditions in Europe. Compared to London's theatres, the Sydney Casino is small and shabby and its clients prefer gaudy entertainment, unable to appreciate Gloria's artistry. On the other hand, the masterly use of lighting creates an enticing atmosphere and appealing images of seemingly appalling places. In one of his last projects before leaving Germany for the US, where he produced melodrama classics such as *All That Heaven Allows* (1955), Sierck creates a visual subtext that, despite its propagandistic tenor, keeps the escapist yearning alive. Released in Finland, Denmark, France and the US, the temporal and spatial location of the narrative secured *To New Shores* an audience beyond Germany.

Claudia Sandberg

The Tiger of Eschnapur/The Indian Tomb

Der Tiger von Eschnapur/
Das indische Grabmal

Production Companies:
Central Cinema Company (CCC)
Rizzoli Film
Regina Production
Criterion Film (UK)

Synopsis

German architect Harald Berger (Hubschmid) rescues the beautiful Irish Indian dancer Seetha (Paget) from a tiger attack en route to the fictional Indian kingdom of Eschnapur. When they arrive, the lord Maharaja Chandra (Reyer) has Berger design schools and hospitals, while Seetha is to become Chandra's maharani. Berger and Seetha inevitably fall in love, much to the pleasure of Chandra's perfidious half-brother Ramigani (Deltgen) who is planning a putsch. Chandra discovers the love triangle and has Berger fight his way out of a tiger pit. Berger flees with Seetha into the desert, leaving his sister Irene (Bethmann) and her architect husband Dr. Rhode (Holm) confused when they come to visit him. Rhode is immediately commissioned by the Maharaja to build a priceless tomb, in which he will bury Seetha alive. The dancer is recaptured

Distributors:
Gloria (Germany)
American International Pictures (AIP) (USA)

Director:
Fritz Lang

Producer:
Artur Brauner

Screenwriters:
Werner Jörg Lüddecke, based on the novel by Thea von Harbou

Art Directors:
Helmut Nentwig
Willy Schatz

Cinematographer:
Richard Angst

Composer:
Gerhard Becker

Editor:
Walter Wischniewsky

Runtime:
101 minutes/102 minutes (2 Parts)

Genre:
Adventure
Colonial Fantasy
Romance

Cast:
Debra Paget
Paul Hubschmid
Walter Reyer
René Deltgen
Claus Holm
Sabine Bethmann

Year:
1959

by Ramigani's men and returned to the palace. Chandra makes a second attempt to marry her before condemning her to death. Meanwhile, Irene, Rhode and Berger navigate the perils of the maharaja's dungeons. Ramigani initiates the putsch against his half-brother, only to be foiled by maharajah loyalists. Berger rescues Seetha and returns to Germany with her. Embattled and emasculated, Chandra abdicates his crown and becomes an ascetic.

Critique

The trivial Technicolor films *The Tiger of Eschnapur* and *The Indian Tomb* have enjoyed a considerable amount of attention – positive and negative, popular and academic – since their European debut in 1959.

Fritz Lang's two-part Indian epic, or 'Eastern,' was not only the revered director's penultimate production, but also marked the final significant entry in a 50-year-old German adventure genre. Orientalist features such as Paul Wegener's *The Yoghi* (1916) or Franz Osten's *A Throw of Dice* (1929), as well as two other prior versions of *The Indian Tomb* – Joe May's 1921 version and Richard Eichberg's 1938 version – seem to consistently turn up in German film history until Indian independence from British rule in 1948 increasingly rendered iterations of the genre (such as Lang's) to be misleading and kitschy, if not outright racist. Typical tropes included conflicts between European democratic rationality and Indian autocratic irrationality; western technology pitted against Oriental 'magic'; burlesque dancing disguised as Indian dance; snake charming, tiger attacks, elephant rites; and obligatory Germans in brownface. Nevertheless, it was Central Cinema Company (CCC) producer Artur Brauner's fascination with the earlier films that prompted him to ask Lang, who had had ex-wife Thea von Harbou's script contracted away from him by May nearly 40 years earlier, to direct his own version.

Tiger of Eschnapur and *Indian Tomb* were shot in the CCC studios in Berlin-Spandau. For exteriors of the Maharaja's palace and city streets populated by real Indian extras, on-location shooting took place in Udaipur, Rajasthan. The opulent Technicolor strongly reminds one of Max Ophüls' *Lola Montes* (1955), and the wildly fantastical *mise-en-scène* proves just as baroque. The visuals and soundtrack are otherwise encyclopaedic databases of Indian epic conventions. Memorable sequences include Chandra and Berger's homoerotic exchange of a ring; the brutal murder of Seetha's servant girl; Seetha's ill-fated Balinese snake-charming dance; and Irene's descent into the leper cave beneath the palace. This is clearly the cinema of attractions, 1950s style.

The history of both films' reception quite clearly invokes disparate cultural forces at work from the 1950s through the '70s. *The Tiger of Eschnapur* was immediately lambasted in the German press, internally snubbed within the film industry for its meagre box office sales and clearly outmoded aesthetic, and even protested by Indian exchange students in Aachen with respect to Seetha's lack of modesty, which allegedly assaulted their 'national and religious sensibilities.' Yet, with the rise of auteur theory and the *Cahiers du Cinéma*, French intellectuals actually praised the film series for its obvious self-conscious irony toward Orientalist excess. Lang's anti-illusionist 'genius' was perceived between the lines, and any weaknesses characteristically blamed on Harbou's script, as was done with *Metropolis* (1927) and *M* (1931). The French *nouvelle vague* also directly benefited from the films' ticket sales: producer Gérard Beytout famously used the *Tiger of Eschnapur* profits to bankroll Jean-Luc Godard's *Á bout de soufflé/Breathless* (1959). In addition, the advent of television as a mass medium in West Germany permitted the film a long, successful afterlife for domestic audiences during the '60s and '70s. Orientalist fantasies of erotic Indian submission to white German male dominance were to be enjoyed in the privacy of one's own home. Thus, the simultaneous ascendancies of postcolonial politics, film studies and television transformed Lang's re-émigré films into cult objects for a cross-section of French intellectuals and German middle-class adolescents. The widespread impact of the films to this day can be felt every time a German asks an Indian if they have ever been to Eschnapur.

Evan Torner

Aguirre: The Wrath of God

Aguirre, Der Zorn Gottes

Production Companies:
Werner Herzog Filmproduktion
Hessischer Rundfunk (HR)

Distributors:
Filmverlag der Autoren (West Germany)
New Yorker Films (USA)

Director:
Werner Herzog

Producers:
Werner Herzog
Hans Prescher

Screenwriter:
Werner Herzog

Cinematographer:
Thomas Mauch

Synopsis

Aguirre: The Wrath of God is very loosely based on actual historical figures and events from the sixteenth century Spanish campaign against the Incan Empire. It is a story about a mad, tyrannical Conquistador, Lope de Aguirre (Kinski), who, during a large expedition in the Peruvian jungle searching for the mythical land of gold 'El Dorado', orchestrates a mutiny against his superiors. Driven by his lust for wealth as much as manic visions of power, he leads a small group of Conquistadors and slaves on an unknown voyage down the Amazonian tributaries. As the journey continues the group begins to suffer from starvation and fever and eventually, one by one, they start to die from Indian's arrows that shoot at them from out of nowhere. The jungle itself also starts to come alive with their inner visions and distorted dreams. This culminates in the final scene of the film where Aguirre, the last remaining man on the raft, looks toward the sun proclaiming that he will marry his daughter and forge a new dynasty. His body is punctured with arrows and he is inexplicably surrounded by a swarm of small monkeys that have overtaken the raft.

Critique

It has been argued that characters are commonly presented in Herzog's films as existentially alienated from their physical environments, as unable to unify with the world around them. Moreover, this alienation is given visual form through the landscapes and other natural objects in these environments. *Aguirre* is a key

Composer:
Popol Vuh

Editor:
Beate Mainka-Jellinghaus

Duration:
93 minutes

Genre:
Adventure Film

Cast:
Klaus Kinski
Helena Rojo
Del Negro
Peter Berling

Year:
1972

example of this. It is a film that presents the shortcomings of western colonial society, when its technological know-how and cultural assumptions are placed up against the realities of nature and other, non-western cultures. The film depicts the Spaniards' perspective of their environment as an amorphous, unpredictable 'Other' that they fail to master and navigate. This is why, for example, the Indians they encounter in the film tend to be presented as an 'invisible' threatening force, indistinguishable from the jungle, and often shown through their arrows darting across space.

The existence of a gulf between western colonial civilisation and the natural world is evident in Herzog's other fictional Amazonian film *Fitzcarraldo* (1982), where it is also a westernised character's perspective of nature that is shown. This excuses in both films the one-dimensional portrayal given of the indigenous Indians in them, which includes conflating them with nature. This is an important retort to the general claim made against Herzog's films that they naively fantasise about non-western peoples. At least in these two films Herzog is not trying to pretend that such peoples can be experienced by western subjects outside of western discourse.

The presentation of westernised characters cut off from their surroundings also shows how on one level Herzog has unromantic views about nature. In *Aguirre* and *Fitzcarraldo* there is a rejection of the German Romantic ideology, which constructs nature as a repository of culture. In such ideology there is continuity between primordial nature and human community and life: the German forest is a space, which can re-ignite the *Volk*. In films like *Aguirre* nature no longer stores key cultural truths that might lead a community of westernised people back to their ancestral, sociolinguistic roots. This is not to say there are not elements of German Romantic literature, painting and music in other Herzog films, just that there are themes in his work that qualify the moniker 'Romantic, nature poet' that has consistently been attached to him.

While rejecting this aspect of German Romanticism, *Aguirre* is arguably tied to key principles of German Expressionism. As Thomas Elsaesser has argued, the film's characters are inscribed in the material spaces they inhabit and their inner worlds are metonymically signified through external objects (1986: 150). Filmed entirely on location in Peru, characters are always first understood in terms of the physical landscapes they occupy. These landscapes will then ideally be meant to convey the inner state of the characters. This anthropomorphic poetics is conveyed in the film through a combination of realist and anti-realist techniques.

For example, in the opening of *Aguirre* the army of Conquistadors and their slaves are presented as entirely dwarfed by the sublime, cosmic landscape they emerge from. This is achieved in part by the camera framing, and the ethereal, non-diegetic music of Popul Vuh. With Thomas Mauch's rhythmic, handheld moving camera they are then shown in more intimate detail struggling through the jungle terrain. Eventually, through blocking and the use of poetic montage, individual characters like Aguirre are introduced in the context of the torrential, churning rapids and other features of the jungle. As the film progresses, these relations between the inner and outer world become more surreal and hallucinatory to the point that the experiential immediacy of the jungle environment conveyed by Mauch's location shooting converges inexplicably with the stylised, other-worldly construction of the jungle.

Tyson Namow

Tecumseh

Production Company:
Deutsche Film (DEFA)

Distributor:
VEB Progress Film-Vertrieb

Director:
Hans Kratzert

Screenwriters:
Wolfgang Ebeling
Rolf Römer
Hans-Joachim Wallstein

Cinematographer:
Wolfgang Braumann

Composer:
Günther Fischer

Editor:
Monika Schindler

Duration:
109 minutes

Genre:
Indianerfilm
Western
Adventure

Cast:
Gojko Mitic
Annekathrin Bürger
Rolf Römer
Leon Niemcyzk
Wolfgang Greese
Mieczyslaw Kalenik

Year:
1972

Synopsis

Tecumseh is set in the Indiana Territory between 1805 and 1813. The titular hero (Mitic) is a Shawnee raised by the fictional McKew family: Simon McKew (Römer) is like a brother to him and Eileen McKew (Bürger) is all but his wife. Yet injustices perpetrated by white settlers prompt Tecumseh to leave the McKews and form an Indian Confederation. Years pass. The Confederation arms itself for war, which unnerves Governor William H. Harrison (Greese). Simon now works for Harrison and has stockpiled firearms at the McKew farm. Eileen smuggles these weapons to the Confederation, but is then presumed killed in a faked Indian attack, turning Simon against his former friend. Harrison then manipulates the Confederation into a foolish assault against Simon's forces, which Tecumseh cannot prevent. The War of 1812 breaks out. The British General Isaac Brock (Kalenik) turns to Tecumseh for military support against the United States, which the chief is willing to give only in exchange for land lost to Harrison. Eileen turns up alive as the wife of a Canadian fighting the Americans. Tecumseh leads the British forces to victory against Simon's brigade, but loses Brock and the arsenal at the McKew farm. Without Brock, there are no longer land promises for the Confederation or competent battlefield strategies. At the Battle of the Thames, Tecumseh sees their struggle already lost and sends Eileen away with a knife intended for his son before dying.

Critique

In a strange twist of fate, the *Indianerfilm* became overnight the most commercially successful genre at the disposal of the DEFA Studios in East Germany. Exhibited at summer film festivals for mixed-age audiences, the *Indianerfilme* were seen as the socialist popular-genre response to the combined onslaught of American Westerns, West German Karl May adventures, and brutal Italo-Westerns dominating the 1960s film landscape. All the films starred Serbian actor/stuntman Gojko Mitic were shot at least partially in Eastern Europe, and depicted muscular Native Americans being oppressed by and actively resisting American expansionism. They intended to project East German solidarity with postcolonial struggles and the so-called Third World (particularly in Vietnam), and were well received east of the Oder in places like Poland, Bulgaria and Romania.

Out of the fourteen *Indianerfilme* made between 1965 and 1983, *Tecumseh* stands out as perhaps the most historically intricate of them all. This is not to say that the film is historically *accurate*, but it is at least *indicative* of larger geopolitical and historical forces, whilst it stolidly shoulders the redundant burdens of action hero and anti-fascist narratives. Rather than demanding near-pathological sympathy for the suffering and struggles of the Shawnee as in *Tecumseh: The Last Warrior* (Elikann, 1995), the East German version of Tecumseh stands at the centre of a complex web of interpersonal and international relations: he radicalizes politically, only to lose his childhood friend to imperialist ideology; he leads his tribe to military successes, only to be incompetently (and fatally) deployed by the British; he battles racism through tribal nationalism, only to face rejection by more spiritually minded members of his tribe. The Western actually bears the 'too late' temporality of a period melodrama rather than the 'in the nick of time' temporality typical for a simple action film.

Wolfgang Greese's Harrison may symbolically function as little more than a Nazi stand-in – even claiming the war of annihilation against the Confederation to be about '*Lebensraum*' – but Mitic's Tecumseh and the two McKew siblings offer the audience at least some possibility for multi-faceted emotional identification.

Tecumseh was shot in Crimea and the Carpathian Mountains and is particularly successful in terms of Wolfgang Braumann's colourful landscape cinematography. Notable set pieces include a breathtaking beachfront meeting on horseback (in land-locked Indiana, no less), a mounted cavalry confrontation with Black Eagle's tribesmen and several exciting artillery barrages. Shot compositions tend to clearly divide the screen between representatives of American and Shawnee forces, giving the interior scenes an almost Brechtian theatrical quality. There is also a peculiar fetishism of the gun present in the film – seen in the wall of pistols in the McKew cabin and in scenes of Confederation braves meticulously checking rifles – more resembling that of *Winchester '73* (Mann, 1950) than any other *Indianerfilme*, in which the primacy of the hatchet and arrow as socialist weaponry is normally foregrounded.

The film offers a good example of a fundamental tension at the centre of socialist action-adventure films; namely how a believable 'socialist martyr' story might be teased out of what is otherwise a cross between nostalgic stunt show and historic fable. If we read the film's final freeze frame of Tecumseh's martyrdom correctly, both stunt show and fable seem to triumph over the kitsch of overdetermined socialist semantics. This fact made Mitic a star in his day and explains why the DEFA *Indianerfilme* continue to entertain viewers of all ages.

Evan Torner

Fitzcarraldo

Production Companies:
Filmverlag der Autoren
Pro-ject Filmproduktion
Werner Herzog Herzog Filmproduktion
Zweites Deutsches Fernsehen (ZDF)

Distributors:
New World Pictures (USA)
Artificial Eye (UK)

Director:
Werner Herzog

Producers:
Werner Herzog
Lucki Stipetic
Willi Segler

Screenwriter:
Werner Herzog

Cinematographer:
Thomas Mauch

Composer:
Popol Vuh

Editor:
Beate Mainka-Jellinghaus

Duration:
158 minutes

Genre:
Adventure Film

Cast:
Klaus Kinski
Claudia Cardinale
José Lewgoy

Year:
1982

Synopsis

Partly driven by his love of Caruso, ice producer Brian Sweeney Fitzgerald ('Fitzcarraldo') (Kinski) desires to build an opera house in the middle of the Amazonian jungle for Caruso to perform at. He decides that in order to obtain the funds necessary for this venture he will have to enter into the rubber trade. He purchases a large steamship that he calls *Molly Aida*, after his lover, the brothel madam Molly (Cardinale), and sets out on a course to investigate the unexplored Ucayali river system for rubber. In order to reach this system, however, Fitzcarraldo has to devise a plan to bypass torrential rapids. Through studying maps he realises that another river system, the Pachitea, runs parallel to the Ucayali, and that at one geographical point the two systems almost converge. He believes at this location he will somehow be able to move *Molly Aida* from Pachitea into Ucayali. After a difficult journey he eventually reaches this point. He finds that through the use of mechanical technology and the efforts of many local Jivaros Indians he is able to pull the steamship up over the steep mountain that links the two systems. However one night, with the boat at bay on the other side of the mountain, some of the Jivaros' cut the cables *Molly Aida* is attached to. With Fitzcarraldo and a number of other people on board it speeds off down through the Ucayali rapids, at the mercy of the flux of the natural world, and ends up back at the place from which it had embarked.

Critique

The enormous feat of dragging a steamship over a mountainside only to have it return to its original departure point and render the whole enterprise futile conjures up a number of mythological, existential precursors. The ancient Greek plight of Sisyphus, for example, famously contextualised by Albert Camus as one example of an 'absurd man' whose tragic punishment is to endlessly embark upon labour that is, in a metaphysical sense, meaningless. Matthew Gandy has referred to Camus's work to describe the presentation of nature as existentially sublime in Herzog's films; a presentation that shows human characters encountering the radical indifference of nature to their own affairs (1996: 1–21).

Similarly to *Aguirre: The Wrath of God* (1972), it is only colonial, subjective experiences of nature that are shown in *Fitzcarraldo*. The eponymous main character perceives the jungle in an abstract way, as a space that has already been mapped out with charts, and that he believes he can order and transform through the use of technology; such as when he employs the engine of the steamship, in conjunction with a complex network of cables, axles and hoisting-machines, to move the boat up through a pathway cleared along the mountainside. However, like the conquistadors in *Aguirre*, Fitzcarraldo faces resistance from the natural world that he cannot control or amend. A world that includes the Jivaros Indians who

Fitzcarraldo, Filmverlag der Autoren/Pro-ject Filmproduktion/Werner Herzog Herzog Filmproduktion/Zweites Deutsches Fernsehen (ZDF).

are shown as conflated with nature and as having their own agenda that turns Fitzcarraldo's feat into failure.[1]

Yet, this failure is also the sign of a relative triumph. While not able to take possession of what for the western world is unexplored territory, the fact Fitzcarraldo has appreciated it with his own eyes indicates that he has achieved something. This importance of personal vision ties into the critical role aesthetic spectacle plays in the film. For example, spending what money he has left, Fitzcarraldo organises for an opera troupe to perform on *Molly Aida* as she sails along the Iquito River at the end of the film. It is these kinds of extraordinary sights that for Fitzcarraldo make the whole venture worth it.

Such spectacles are meant to evoke something profoundly human. Opera is, for Fitzcarraldo, the means by which human kind's deepest feelings can be expressed. Yet the film also has a non-dramatic structure where opera functions to create autonomous spectacles that have little to do with story or characterisation and more to do with the relationship between artifice, technology and nature; a relationship that involves presenting staged, theatrical tableaus in the natural world of the jungle. It is only at a distance and with an awareness of the constructed nature of the images they are watching and hearing that spectators experience the profound feelings opera is ideally meant to evoke. They are never simply immersed in these feelings.

This function of opera is immediately set up in the beginning of the film with a sequence shot by Werner Schroeter showing a performance of Verdi's *Ernani*. Schroeter creates a theatrical tableau in which the stage and the performers are frontally arranged and framed in static shots that cut up the space into autonomous sections, segmented from everything outside the frame as well as from the greater diegetic flow.[2] These kind of cinematic tableaus are created by Herzog later in the film when, for example, he shows a side-on profile shot of Fitzcarraldo playing Caruso on his gramophone on the *Molly Aida* as she cruises into Jivaro territory.

Tyson Namow

Notes

1. For a discussion of the thematic constructions in *Fitzcarraldo* and *Aguirre* see Lutz P. Koepnick (1993), 'Colonial Forestry: Sylvan Politics in Werner Herzog's *Aguirre* and *Fitzcarraldo*', *New German Critique*, 60, pp. 133–59.
2. For a discussion of cinematic tableaus and Schroeter's cinema see Michelle Langford (2006), *Allegorical Images: Tableau, Time and Gesture in the Cinema of Werner Schroeter*, Bristol: Intellect.

Cerro Torre: Scream of Stone

Cerro Torre: Schrei aus Stein

Production Company:
Sera Filmproduktion

Distributor:
Neue Constantin Film

Synopsis

The film opens with a young climber Martin (Glowacz) winning a sports competition. In a live interview, he is challenged by an older, more experienced mountaineer, Roccia (Mezzogiorno), who claims that Martin, although a great athlete, would not do well in an outdoor competition. Martin takes up the challenge and the two set out to climb Cerro Torre, a mountain in Patagonia considered the most difficult and dangerous in the world. Sport journalist Ivan (Sutherland) follows their contest. In Patagonia they meet a deranged man who calls himself Fingerless (Dourif), is a fan of Mae West, and claims to have climbed Cerro Torre. Too impatient to wait for weather conditions to improve, Martin attempts to climb

Director:
Werner Herzog

Producers:
Henry Lange
Walter Saxer
Richard Sadler

Screenwriters:
Hans-Ulrich Klenner
Walter Saxer
Robert Geoffrion, based on an idea by Reinhold Messner

Cinematographer:
Rainer Klausmann

Editor:
Suzanne Baron

Duration:
105 minutes

Genre:
Adventure

Cast:
Vittorio Mezzogiorno
Stefan Glowacz
Mathilda May
Donald Sutherland
Brad Dourif

Year:
1991

Cerro Torre with Hans. Hans goes missing during the climb, but Martin returns safely to the camp declaring that he reached the top of the mountain. However, he has no evidence to prove it, as he left his camera with Hans, who is presumed dead. Meanwhile, Roccia's girlfriend Katharina (May) leaves him and starts a relationship with Martin. Ivan organizes one more contest between Martin and Roccia. In the second ascent, Martin dies, while Roccia manages to climb to the top of Cerro Torre, only to find out that Fingerless was there before him, leaving there a picture of Mae West.

Critique

Even though Herzog distanced himself from the film, pointing instead to his long-time collaborator Walter Saxer as the script author and creative force behind the production, *Cerro Torre: Scream of Stone* nevertheless exhibits many typical characteristics of Herzog's oeuvre. Much like some of his earlier documentary productions, notably *The Dark Glow of the Mountains* (1984) and *La Soufrière* (1977), the film testifies to the director's fascination with mountains as a site of competition between man and nature. As such, *Cerro Torre* calls to mind the German *Bergfilme* that flourished in the 1920s and the 1930s, inviting comparisons with the work of Arnold Fanck and Leni Riefenstahl. However, while confirming his fascination with mountains, Herzog distanced himself from such comparisons, rejecting the idea of Riefenstahl's *Bergfilme* as a possible influence on *Cerro Torre*.

Instead, the film's protagonists Martin and Roccia bring to mind Herzog's own gallery of 'larger than life' characters, whether fictional, played usually by Klaus Kinski, or real people, such as the world famous mountaineer Reinhold Messner portrayed in *The Dark Glow of the Mountains*. On the other hand, the naïve, deranged but sympathetic misfit Fingerless resembles Bruno S.' characters from Herzog's films *The Enigma of Kaspar Hauser* (1974) and *Stroszek* (1977), thus further strengthening the link with the director's existing work. Fingerless typifies the characteristic Herzogian figure of a simple, authentic person at odds with modern society. He emerges as the quiet hero at the end of the film, while Martin's and Roccia's hubris is punished. Another secondary character who fulfils a similar narrative role, as a counterpoint to the two climbers, is an elderly native woman called Indianerin (Chavela Vargas) who derides Christianity and western civilisation. On a more general level, *Cerro Torre* juxtaposes wild nature with modern civilisation and technology, represented by television crews following the two climbers with their cameras. Herzog portrays nature as a fascinating yet dangerous entity, while the television crews are depicted negatively, as invasive and disrespectful of the environment.

The conflict between man and nature aside, the narrative of the film revolves around the theme of male rivalry. The contest between Martin and Roccia assumes an Oedipal dimension, as a conflict between a young, dynamic and arrogant sportsman and an older and more experienced, but no less arrogant and stubborn, mountaineer. The tension between them intensifies when Roccia's girlfriend Katharina leaves him and starts a relationship with Martin. However, in the end, both men seem little affected by Katharina's presence and her decisions as they entirely focus on the adventure. Therefore, the relationship theme seems a little forced upon the narrative, with the female character introduced as a mere background for male rivalry.

On the level of style, the film impresses with difficult, risky shots made on location in Patagonia. Particularly remarkable is the last scene of the film: shot from a helicopter, it shows Roccia standing on top of the mountain, Martin's dead body swinging on a rope beneath. The camera moves away and circles around Roccia, his diminutive figure becoming less and less recognizable in the wild, snowy landscape – a scene illustrating the idea of nature's greatness and its overwhelming power over man.

Klemens Czyzydlo

References

Cameron, Ian (1973), *Adventure in the Movies*, New York: Crescent.
Elsaesser, Thomas (1986), 'An Anthropologist's Eye: Where the Green Ants Dream', in Timothy Corrigan (ed.), *The Films of Werner Herzog: Between Mirage and History*, New York: Meuthen, pp. 133-58.
Gandy, Matthew (1996), 'Visions of Darkness: The Representation of Nature in the Films of Werner Herzog', *Cultural Geographies*, 3: 1, pp. 1–21.
Koepnick, Lutz P. (1993), 'Colonial Forestry: Sylvan Politics in Werner Herzog's *Aguirre* and *Fitzcarraldo*', *New German Critique*, 60, pp. 133–59.
Langford, Michelle (2006), *Allegorical Images: Tableau, Time and Gesture in the Cinema of Werner Schroeter*, Bristol: Intellect.
von Moltke, Johannes (2005), *No Place Like Home: Locations of Heimat in German Cinema*, Berkeley, CA: University of California Press.
Nagl, Tobias (2009), *Die unheimliche Maschine: Rasse und Repräsentation im Weimarer Kino*, Munich: edition text+kritk.
Nenno, Nancy P. (2003), 'Postcards from the Edge: Education to Tourism in the German Mountain Film', in Randall Halle and Margaret McCarthy (eds.), *Light Motives: German Popular Film in Perspective*, Detroit: Wayne State University Press, pp. 61–84.
Rentschler, Eric (1996a), *The Ministry of Illusion: Nazi Cinema and its Afterlife*, Cambridge, MA: Harvard University Press.
Rentschler, Eric (1996b), 'Mountains and Modernity: Relocating the Bergfilm', in Terri Ginsberg and Kirsten Moana Thompson (eds.), *Perspectives on German Cinema*, London: G.K. Hall; New York: Prentice Hall International, pp. 137–61.
Seesslen, Georg, Fritze, Christoph and Weil, Claudius (1983), *Der Abenteurer*, Hamburg: Rowohlt.

Strathausen, Carsten (2001), 'The Image as Abyss: The Mountain Film and the Cinematic Sublime', in Kenneth S. Calhoun (ed.), *Peripheral Visions: the Hidden Stages of Weimar Cinema*, Detroit: Wayne State University Press, pp. 171–90.

Taves, Brian (1993), *The Romance of Adventure*, Jackson, MS: University Press of Mississippi.

Traber, Bodo and Wulff, Hans J. (2004), *Filmgenres: Abenteuerfilm*, Stuttgart: Reclam.

DER HEIMATFILM

Having a unique place in German film history, the term *Heimat* can be traced back to *Heimat* literature beginning in the late nineteenth century as a counter-culture to the (urban) modernity depicted in Naturalism. Novels by writers such as Hermann Löns, Ludwig Ganghofer and Peter Rosegger perceive the love of and attachment to a homeland as means to escape the supposed loss of individuality and the anonymity of an industrial lifestyle, and to preserve a harmonious, national and cultural identity. While the dominant thematic and stylistic patterns varied in the course of the development of German film, most movies of the *Heimatfilm* genre are set in a postcard idyll, centre around topics such as love, friendship and family, and articulate, in an often simplistic morality, the dialectic of the good 'home/self' versus the bad 'foreign/strange,' which results in an inevitable reconciliation and happy ending. The provincial homeliness of the world is portrayed in the colourful scenery of forests, lakes and mountains, most often in southern Germany, Austria or Switzerland as well as the heath of northern Germany. This concept of preserving a provincial humanity through tradition particularly thrived between 1946 and 1965, when over 300 movies of this genre were produced. Famous UFA actors such as Heinz Rühmann, Otto Gebühr, Willy Fritsch, Paul Klinger, Magda Schneider, Paul Hörbiger, and Zarah Leander, and the post-war rise of a new generation of actors including Heidi Brühl, Sonja Ziemann, Marianne Holt, Romy Schneider, Hanna Schygulla and Angela Winkler added to the success of the genre. Music and easily memorable light-hearted or sentimental songs in movies such as *Heimat* (1938), the operetta-turned-movie *The Black Forest Girl* (Deppe, 1950), *The Heath is Green* (Deppe, 1951), *When the White Lilacs Bloom Again* (Deppe, 1953) and *The Fisher-Girl from Lake Bodensee* (Reinl, 1956) furthermore enhanced the popularity of the *Heimatfilm*.

Early films of the sub-genre of the *Bergfilm* such as Arnold Fanck's *The Holy Mountain* (1926) and *White Hell of Piz Palü* (1929) display the sublime beauty of nature as a trigger for extreme experiences of the human soul, often resulting in tragedies and death. Other movies of that time present the serenity of the countryside as a setting of escapism from modern work life in a Weimar metropolis, e.g. *People on Sunday* (Robert Siodmak; Curt Siodmak; Ulmer; Gliese; Zinnemann, 1930). Similarly, in movies such as *Heimat* (1938), the homecoming of a troubled hero or heroine who strived for an international career marks the beginning of a new and promising life of modesty and family harmony in a provincial setting. In the realm of the 'blood and soil' productions of the National Socialist movement movies such as *When the Evening Bells Ring* (1930) and *To New Shores* (1937) present the concept of *Heimat* as a dichotomy of foreignness/desire and Germanness/reason.

Post-war *Heimatfilme* reflect the experience as well as the hopes and anxieties of West German society at that time. The flight from Pomerania and East Prussia by millions of Germans is presented in *The Heath is Green* (1951) and *Die Mädels vom Immenhof* (Schleif, 1955). These *Heimatfilme* also deal with economic aspirations and focus on privacy during the time of the *Wirtschaftswunder* ('economic miracle'), e.g. the rise and fall of *Mailman Müller* (Reinhardt,

Left: *Beste Gegend*, Bayerischer Rundfunk (BR)/ Monaco Film GmbH.

1953) or the constant financial struggles in the *Immenhof* trilogy (Schleif; von Collande; Leitner, 1955; 1956; 1957). The serenity of an intact rural life, firm values of a patriarchal society, and the often kitschy love dramas in these movies provided complete distraction for the audience from the atrocities and the devastation of World War II.

The critique of 1960's film-makers on post-war German life and allegedly destructive undercurrents in a treacherous *Heimat* led to a series of anti-*Heimatfilme*, in which provincial life is portrayed as a poverty-stricken playground for narrow-minded villagers and ruthless authorities (*Hunting Scenes from Bavaria* [Fleischmann, 1969]). In the tradition of New German Cinema *Heart of Glass* (Herzog, 1979) with almost hypnotic, long shots of the Bavarian countryside bears some iconographic similarities to classic *Heimatfilme*, but centres around internal and social catastrophes. More recently in this counter-culture tradition *The Hypocrites* (Krohnthaler, 2001) is a satirical allusion to hypocrisy, nepotism and *Heimat* sentiments, while in *The White Ribbon* (Haneke, 2009) abused and oppressed children of a village in northern Germany are in the centre of violence and authority on the eve of World War I.

In the late Seventies and early Eighties a widespread concern about the environment, imminent tensions of the Cold War – most visible through the deployment of NATO missiles in Germany – and the return of conservative values during the rule of Chancellor Helmut Kohl shaped a new sense of *Heimat*, nature and customs. Filmic representations spanned from popular TV series in the tradition of the *Heimatfilm* (*Der Landarzt*, 1987–present; *The Blackforest Clinic*, 1985–89), to movies by film-makers such as Joseph Vilsmaier (*Autumn Milk*, 1989) and Jo Baier (*Schwabenkinder*, 2003), which show realistic aspects of rural life and thereby provide modern versions of the *Heimatfilm*. Another example of references to this genre is Edgar Reitz's' trilogy *Heimat* (*Heimat-Eine Deutsche Jugend*, 1984; *The Second Homeland: Chronicle of a Youth*, 1992; *Heimat Three: Chronicle of a Changing Time*, 2004) which, in thirty episodes, presents the life of a family in the Rhineland against the political and social changes between 1919 and 2000. Taking the dimension of a national epic, the films represent a synthesis of classic and critical *Heimatfilm* concerns and present the homeland as visualized historical memory without aiming for idealization.

Other modern approaches to the *Heimatfilm* include the presentation of the tranquil pace of life in rural settings as a counterpoint to erotic suspense and crime (*Winter Sleepers* [Tykwer, 1997]) or as an often concurrently comical and painful search for identity and home in a globalized world (*Schultze Gets The Blues* [Schorr, 2003], or *Good Times* [2007] and *Beste Gegend* [2008], both by Marcus H. Rosenmüller).

Martina Lüke

When the Evening Bells Ring

Wenn die Abendglocken läuten

Production Company:
Georg Ziegler

Distributor:
Leo-Film AG

Director:
Hanns Beck-Gaden

Producer:
Georg Ziegler

Screenwriters:
Hanns Beck-Gaden
Joseph Dalman

Cinematographer:
Karl Attenberger

Duration:
29 minutes

Genre:
Drama
Heimatfilm
Sinti and Roma

Cast:
Hanns Beck-Gaden
Maria Mindzenty
Emmy Kronberg

Year:
1930

Synopsis

This *Heimatfilm* is set in the hills of Bavaria. The central authority figure is the mayor. Good (home, church, family, work, health, etc.) and evil (deceitful Gypsies shown as foreign intruders) are conspicuously at odds, and the triumph of the good is easily foreseeable throughout the kitschy plot. The mayor's son, Hans (Beck-Gaden), is a strong, young, skilled, kind and handsome man with whom pretty and pious Annerl (Mindzenty) is in love. Annerl has long blonde, braided hair and a physically healthy body. She knits at home, loves her parents and goes to church. Meanwhile, in the distance, the camera pans over the hills and a valley, where the Gypsies are shown approaching the village. A young and pretty Gypsy girl catches Hans' attention, while Annerl suffers in silence. The Gypsy girl leaves Hans for a Gypsy lover, infatuated by the mesmerizing tunes of his violin. Ironically, this occurs just after Hans has abandoned his entire family and left the village for her. Broken down, wounded and in despair, Hans returns to the village to his mourning family, who thought they had lost him forever. Again seeing Annerl, he exclaims: 'Ah, Annerl – die *Heimat*!'

Critique

The juxtaposition and featured dissimilarities of the German versus Gypsy essence is manifest in this film. The film is a perfect example of a *Heimatfilm*, with hills and mountaintops providing the backdrop to usual themes of friendship, love and family. In his recent study of the term and film genre *Heimat*, Johannes von Moltke, while recognizing 'multiple rebirths' of the word *Heimat* during the twentieth century, highlights its emphasis on the creation of national identity (*Volk*) and on everything familiar and not foreign. Von Moltke describes *Heimat* as a small world with 'narrowly defined boundaries':

> The localism of *Heimat*, its emphasis on experience, presence, and delimitation suggest that we think of it as place, as a limited terrain that affords its inhabitants respite and protection from incursions originating in the more intangible and abstract spaces beyond its boundaries. (2005: 11)

In this film, the national identity or *Volk* is associated with non-Gypsy Germans (home, community, church, family, work, health, etc.) while the foreignness or non-Germaness is embodied in the Gypsy characters (deceitful and conniving intruders). When the camera pans over the hills and a valley where the Gypsies are shown approaching the village, the viewer is led to anticipate the disruption of the idyllic village scenery. Most every scene set-up functions as a reminder of the deep divide between these two kinds of people; on one hand the German and Gypsies on the other.

The love relationship between Hans and the Gypsy girl is yet another trope illuminating the irreconcilable characters (non-Gypsy versus Gypsy). To attract Hans and make Annerl even more jealous the Gypsy girl dances for Hans. Thus, the image of a dancing Gypsy girl is introduced, alluding to the alleged lascivious and sensuous but vulgar Gypsy nature. The Gypsy girl becomes the embodiment of seduction and sexual fantasy based on her seemingly erotic but treacherous body and mind. The portrayed sexuality of the Gypsy girl further reveals the immense imbalance in power relations, whereby the Gypsy girl in the role of an exotic dancer functions as an entertainer for a non-Gypsy man. Additionally, she is portrayed mostly as a physical creature, her corporeality and instinctual behaviour evocative of the animal-state which purportedly explains her character. The alleged animalistic qualities of the Gypsy girl are best illustrated in the last sequence, in which she leaves Hans for a Gypsy lover, infatuated by the mesmerizing tunes of his violin. Allegedly just as an animal, the Gypsy girl acts instinctually and impulsively, which is symptomatic of her innate visceral nature.

The last scene (Hans' return), signifying more than Hans' joyful reunion with his family and the happy end in which he and Annerl live happily ever after, metaphorically connotes Germany as the fatherland which was lost during his interval with the Gypsy girl and the rest of the Gypsies. The Gypsies are portrayed as people of the road, nomads perpetually on the move, and consistently de-historicized. The folly of de-historicized politics accentuates abstract principles such as nomadism and entertainment, ignoring the history of systematic oppression against the Sinti and Roma people.

Habiba Hadziavdic

People on Sunday: a film without actors

Menschen am Sonntag: Ein Film ohne Schauspieler

Production Company:
Filmstudio Berlin

Distributor:
Filmmuseum Distributie (Netherlands)

Directors:
Robert Siodmak
Curt Siodmak
Edgar G. Ulmer

Synopsis

One Saturday in 1929 near Berlin's Zoo station, Wolfgang, a wine merchant, meets Christl, a film extra, on a street corner. Learning that her date stood her up, Wolfgang invites her, with faux chivalry, for ice cream and they make a date to visit Nikolasee, a nearby lake, the next day. Meanwhile Erwin, a taxi driver, is at home having an argument with his partner Annie, a model. When Wolfgang arrives the men drink beer and share easy conversation. Annie becomes furious, as she wanted to see a film. The following day the two men meet Christl and her best friend Brigitte, who manages a record store, at the Nikolasee. Wolf tries to kiss Christl but she is not responsive so he tries Brigitte. The pair disappear into the reeds, suggesting they have become intimate. Later that afternoon Wolf and Erwin hire a paddleboat and flirt with two other women. Brigitte and Christl look on appalled, but take some satisfaction when the men have to borrow money to pay the boat rental. Brigitte asks to meet Wolf the next Sunday. He reluctantly agrees but Erwin brusquely reminds him that they have other plans. It is clear that the most enduring relationship is that between

People on Sunday: a film without actors, Filmstudio Berlin.

Rochus Gliese
Fred Zinnemann

Producers:
Edgar G. Ulmer
Seymour Nebenzal

Screenwriters:
Billy Wilder
Edgar G. Ulmer
Curt Siodmak, after the story from Robert Siodmak

Art Director:
Moritz Seder

the two men. Erwin returns to his flat finding Annie languishing in bed. The next day everyone is back at work: Erwin driving his cab, Wolf selling wine, Brigitte selling records, and they all wait for next Sunday.

Critique

As well as offering a rare glimpse of life in Berlin in the twilight of the Weimar Republic, this film is groundbreaking for its novel blend of feature film and documentary styles. It was shot on a shoestring by the autonomous 'Filmstudio 29': a team of six young German film-makers – Billy Wilder, Robert Siodmak, Fred Zinnemann, Edgar Ulmer, Curt Siodmak, and Eugen Schüfftan – all of whom went on to careers in Hollywood. The cast of non-professional actors worked with the film-makers over a series of Sundays in 1929.

Cinematographer:
Eugen Schüfftan

Composer:
Otto Stenzeel

Duration:
74 minutes

Genre:
Heimatfilm

Cast:
Erwin Splettstößer
Brigitte Borchert
Wolfgang von Waltershausen
Christl Ehlers
Annie Schreyer

Year:
1930

While *People on Sunday* marked the beginning of many careers, it also, as one of the last silent films produced in Germany, marked the end of an era.

The unaffected performances of the five major characters lend *People on Sunday* a curiously modern atmosphere, one more akin to the understated realism of the *nouvelle vague* than the highly stylized spectacle and melodramatic acting styles of New Objectivity (Pabst, Lubitsch, Lang, Julzi, etc) that dominated German cinema at the time. The shots oscillate between tight close-ups of the main characters and *cinema vérité* style long shots capturing ordinary people going about their daily lives. *People on Sunday* depicts the special place that Sunday holds in the hearts of Berliners, religious and secular alike, as a day for individual recreation and self-improvement. In one noteworthy sequence customers line up for a beach photographer who takes a series of still portraits. These are not glamorous actors, but ordinary people caught in a candid freeze frame (a cinematic technique pioneered in this film).

The majority of scenes are shot outside using natural lighting. In one of the few scenes shot on-set, a sequence of shots with increasing tightness are intercut with a shot of a dripping faucet to heighten the claustrophobic domestic dissatisfaction between Annie and Erwin. They argue over a trip to the cinema, destroying each other's film star pin-up postcards in the process. Even without the audio component, Billy Wilder's witty scripting and his trademark cynicism and unapologetic, unromantic depiction of sexuality, that later made him so popular in Hollywood, can be seen clearly.

'And then on Monday... it is back to work... back to the every day... back to the daily grind... Four... million... wait for... the next Sunday. The end.' This lament, appearing as the closing intertitle of *People on Sunday*, jars with the playful and carefree atmosphere of the film, which is essentially an essay on working class leisure in late 1920s Berlin. When considered against Hitler's sweep to power in the following years, however, this sense of lamentation and loss takes on a more forbidding and sinister tone.

Alina Hoyne

Heimat

Production Companies:
Tonfilmstudio Carl Froelich
Universum Film (UFA)

Distributors:
UFA-Filmverleih GmbH
Ufa Film Company

Director:
Carl Froehlich

Synopsis

In 1885, famous New York Metropolitan Opera singer Maddalena dall' Orto (played by Zarah Leander) is scheduled to perform at a festival in the German residence of Ilmingen. It soon becomes obvious that she is none other than Magda von Schwartze, who left the town eight years ago against her father's wishes to become a singer. After overcoming their painful reluctance to talk to each other, Major von Schwartze (George) and his daughter reconcile. Magda is also able to unite her beloved sister Marie/Mieze (Hellberg) with Lieutenant Max von Wendlowsky (Nielsen) by paying the bond that allows him to marry before achieving the rank of a *Hauptmann*. Leaving his self-imposed isolation behind,

Heimat, Tonfilmstudio Carl Froelich/Universum Film (UFA).

Producer:
Carl Froehlich

Screenwriters:
Harald Braun
Hans Brennert
Otto Ernst Hesse, based on the play by Hermann Sudermann

Cinematographer:
Franz Weihmayr

Composer:
Gustav Lohse

Editor:
Gustav Lohse

Duration:
98 minutes

Major von Schwartze joins his friends from the military again and even organizes a sled ride to the countryside. On this occasion he happens to meet a little girl and, unaware that she is the illegitimate child of Magda, is charmed by her. But the happy family reunion and the hopeful new beginning do not last when Magda is blackmailed by her former lover, the bank director von Keller (Schafheitlin), who threatens to publicly announce their former affair. During Magda's early years in Berlin, von Keller had taken advantage of her loneliness and financial struggles and, after seducing her, returned to Ilmenau. Neither remorseful for the desperation he inflicted on Magda, nor interested in the child that he fathered, von Keller, who faces financial ruin, lusts after Magda's fortune and plans to marry her. Magda's father, who is solely concerned with the honour of the family, pressures Magda to marry the bank director in order to avoid a scandal. She is about to give in when the bank director shoots himself as he faces imprisonment for his dubious financial affairs. In the evening, Major von Schwartze, accompanied by Marie and Max, attends Johann Sebastian Bach's 'Matthäus Passion' at the Ilmingen cathedral. He realizes the

Genre:
Heimatfilm
Drama

Cast:
Heinrich George
Zarah Leander
Hans Nielsen
Georg Alexander
Franz Schafheitlin
Lina Carstens
Ruth Hellberg
Paul Hörbiger
Leo Slezak
Babsi Reckewell

Year:
1938

extraordinary talent of his daughter and accepts Magda's choice of career. In the audience at the cathedral the Major meets the little girl from the countryside again. When she points at the singer and proudly states that this is her mother, von Schwartze is happily reunited with his daughter and granddaughter.

Critique

Five years after the National Socialists' rise to power and just one year before the outbreak of World War II, *Heimat* (1938) questions patriarchal hierarchies, military dominance and Wilhelmine concepts of law and order. The movie is based on the socially critical play by the same name written by Hermann Sudermann, which dramatizes the motif of the prodigal son. In the cinematic adaptation, conflicts of the Schwartze family are more moderate. For example, the Major does not die from a stroke as a result of a final argument with Magda, but rather he is able to build a loving connection to his granddaughter, closing the film on a happy note. In allusion to the figure of Mary Magdalene, Magda's fate changes from being a suffering sinner to a forgiven and even highly respected member of her native soil. Froehlich's movie presents *Heimat* as the site of a happily united family, and as the harmonious balance of freedom and order, private life and public roles, artistic creativity and social-military rules. While art enabled Magda to gain a fortune and internationally acclaimed fame, she lacks inner peace associated with *Heimat*. However, Magda's home town does not resemble the idyllic setting of the later post-war *Heimatfilme*. Except for the progressive, globally oriented Prince Ludwig Wilhelmine, Ilmingen is portrayed as a rigid, old-fashioned place with narrow-minded inhabitants, dominated by the military culture of the princely court. This strict hierarchical order is personified in the patriarch Major von Schwartze who initially considers honour and social status over the happiness of his family. In contrast, Magda represents the New Woman of Weimar Germany, who, like her aunt, the rich but extremely avaricious writer Fränze von Klebs (Carstens), makes a career of her own. Yet, unlike her spinsterish aunt, who remains closely attached to the benevolence of the court, Magda has to leave her *Heimat* and survive hostile environments in the metropolises of Berlin and London. Her sensuality and sexual confidence are most obvious in the chanson 'Eine Frau wird erst schön durch die Liebe' ('A Woman Becomes Only Beautiful By Love'), which scandalizes the society at the court and portrays Magda as the promiscuous outcast. The inner struggles of this modern heroine are represented through classical music; for example, the 'Liebestraum' by Franz Liszt and Christoph Willibald Gluck's 'Orpheus und Eurydike'. The movie closes with the questioning of 'old forms' and of a 'hypocritical world', as Magda's admirer, conductor Franz Heffterdingk (Hörbiger), puts it. The family reunification and the collective attendance of the town at Magda's concert in the cathedral symbolize the acceptance of and the hopes for this new approach.

Martina Lüke

The Heath is Green

Grün ist die Heide

Production Company:
Berolina GmbH (Berlin)

Distributor:
Gloria Filmverleih AG

Director:
Hans Deppe

Producer:
Kurt Ulrich

Screenwriters:
Bobby E. Lüthge, based on the novel by Hermann Lönns

Cinematographer:
Kurt Schulz

Composer:
Alfred Strasser

Editor:
Hermann Ludwig

Duration:
90 minutes

Genre:
Heimatfilm

Cast:
Sonja Ziemann
Rudolf Prack
Willy Fritsch
Marianne Holst
Hans Stüwe
Otto Gebühr
Margarete Haagen
Josef Sieber
Hans Richter
Ludwig Schmitz
Kurt Reimann
Oskar Siemann

Year:
1951

Synopsis

After the end of World War II Lüder Lüdersen (Stüwe), the former owner of a feudal estate in the East, and his daughter Helga (Ziemann) arrive as refugees in the Lüneburg Heath. While living a seemingly happy life on the estate of his cousin, Lüdersen hides a dark secret: he is a poacher. The new forest ranger, Walter Rainer (Prack), is determined to catch him. During his search for the poacher, Walter meets Helga and falls in love. When they both catch Lüdersen red-handed, Helga restrains Rainer from shooting the thief and Lüdersen is able to escape. It becomes obvious that Helga knows about her father's secret. Father and daughter talk things out. Lüdersen admits that the hunting helped him to overcome his longing for his lost *Heimat*. Out of respect for his daughter, however, he promises to now refrain from poaching.

When a policeman is shot, suspicion falls onto Lüdersen, but he can prove that he is innocent. Helga begs him to leave the heath and move to the city, and her father, with a heavy heart, gives in. While a fair is celebrated in the little village, the police scour the heath for the poacher. Lüdersen, taking a last walk through the beloved landscape, encounters the real perpetrator. Both men start a fight and Lüdersen is severely wounded. Walter and the policemen come to rescue him and arrest the poacher, who is also the murderer of the policeman. Helga and Walter are finally happily united.

Critique

The Heath is Green is generally considered to be the first *Heimatfilm* in the uniquely German film cycle to emerge in the 1950s as Germany was attempting to re-build its sense of identity. Portraying the serenity of an intact village life in the Lüneburg Heath and a kitsch love story, the movie provided complete distraction for the audience from German cities in ruins and the hardship of the recent war. In particular, the story of the Lüdersen refugees reflected the experience of many Germans and made *The Heath is Green* one of the most successful movies after World War II. In 1953 the movie was awarded a Bambi for its commercial triumph in the preceding year.

The movie is also a modern adaptation of a 1932 film of the same name, directed by Hans Behrendt. While the original version ends with the death of the wounded Lüdersen, who, in his final moment, is able to unite his daughter and the forester, this *Heimatfilm* portrays a happy ending. The 1951 version also uses Lüdersen's loss of *Heimat* as a result of World War II as his reason for poaching.

Otto Gebühr (playing Lüdersen's cousin Gottfried) and Willly Fritsch (playing a local judge) belonged to the most famous pre-war actors. Otto Gebühr's striking resemblance to Frederick the Great allowed him to portray the Prussian king in sixteen movies of the Weimar Republic and Nazi Germany. Due to his fresh, youthful appearance, his musical talent and his pairing with Lilian Harvey in 1928, Willy Fritsch became a very popular actor in the German film industry. For both actors, *The Heath is Green* offered the chance of a new beginning after the war.

The plot and the popular songs of the movie are based on texts by the 'Poet of the Lüneburg Heath', Hermann Löns. The music, such as the title song, also contributed to the immense popularity of the film at the time of its release. Today the movie can be seen as an outstanding example of the *Heimatfilm* genre and presents an interesting insight into the German post-war mentality.

Martina Lüke

Mailman Müller

Briefträger Müller

Production Company:
Berolina

Distributor:
Universum Film (UFA)

Director:
John Reinhardt

Producer:
Kurt Ulrich

Screenwriters:
Eberhard Keindorff
Johanna Sibelius, based on a story by Ernst Neubach

Cinematographer:
Kurt Schulz

Composer:
Friedrich Schröder

Editor:
Erich Palme

Duration:
95 minutes

Genre:
Comedy
Heimatfilm

Cast:
Heinz Rühmann
Heli Finkenzeller

Synopsis

Postman Titus Müller (Rühmann) returns from his daily rounds with a letter that will change the course of his modest provincial existence. Invited to Italy to visit a rich, eccentric aunt (Hesterberg), he finds himself surrounded by crowds of other 'Müllers' all hoping to claim a share of her money. But Titus is in luck: he inherits the aunt's dog Ambrosia, to whom she has left her entire fortune. Hailed as a hero in his home town, Müller quickly learns to live up to his new status, buying a mansion for his family, flirting with politics and the operetta singer Mirabella (von Almassy). The rags-to-riches affair comes to an end, however, when his wife leaves him, the party-leaders run off with the money and Ambrosia dies. Destitute and alone, he is eventually discovered by a messenger from the Salvation Army. The man leads him to the 'Titus Müller Foundation'; named in his honour for the generous cheque he had casually written out to them, merely in order to impress Mirabella. The happy outcome of that fleeting act of kindness finally allows Titus to reconnect with his family and with his former self.

Critique

Part comedy, part cautionary tale, *Briefträger Müller* is symptomatic of the economic aspirations and moral anxieties of the West German society during the affluent 1950s. The subject – the sudden rise to wealth of a small town *Kleinbürger* (petit bourgeois) – may invite allusions to the *Wirtschaftswunder*-phenomenon, the 'miracle' of Germany's reconstruction in the first years of the economic boom. In this case, however, the prospect of capital accumulation threatens to destroy the very values the provincial everyman is supposed to stand for – modesty, decency, familial harmony – which not accidentally correspond to the ideological model of humanity promoted in *Heimatfilme* of the period. Cast in the role of the postman-turned-millionaire is Heinz Rühmann, whose typically good-hearted, good-humoured characters had ensured his continuous popularity with the public from the 1930s onwards, through the National Socialist era and for decades later.

Gisela Mayen
Susanne von Almassy
Harald Paulsen
Trude Hesterberg

Year:
1953

The key to Rühmann's successful career becomes in the film a pretext for self-referential jokes. So, for example, in an eloquent scene, when commenting on his employment with the Postal Service, Müller declares: 'I outlive all governments, all revolutions.' More importantly, however, the statement also points to a much broader context: the resistance to change and the survival through tradition as the answers of the 'common man' – the average lower middle-class individual – in the face of the fluctuations of time and circumstance. These formulas are tested against the extraordinary trajectory of Titus Müller, whose case can be read both in terms of fantasies of upward mobility and the impetus to conform to the demands of economic progress. Here, the film operates on several levels. The first half in particular sets the stage for light-hearted comedy, with slapstick episodes and musical numbers based on the trials and tribulations of a postal worker's life (the eternal confrontation between mailmen and dogs, the risks that ensue from delivering letters etc.)

With the turn from professional routine to the spectacle of wealth and property, the tone shifts towards social satire, although the narrative does not thereby amount to a radical critique of class hierarchy. On the contrary, if Titus ultimately fails, it is precisely because, while trying to lead the life of the moneyed elite, he discards the simplicity of his original existence and thus forgets about his 'proper' place in the world. The latter half of the film dwells on this crisis and develops it in a melodramatic register, through the return of the protagonist to his abandoned home. It is from here that he will be 'rescued', his position on the social ladder and faith in his own humanity eventually restored. The final act also illustrates the most problematic aspect of the *Heimatfilm*-scenario, since what is validated in the end is the retreat into the de-politicized idyll of privacy offered as a placatory solution against the questions raised in the encounter with modernity and historical change.

Ilinca Iurascu

When the White Lilacs Bloom Again

Wenn der weiße Flieder wieder blüht

Production Company:
Berolina

Distributor:
Herzog-Filmverleih

Synopsis

Financial worries jeopardize the marriage of singer Willy Forster (Fritsch) and seamstress Therese (Magda Schneider). Therese is concerned with having a safe life and works hard to provide a steady income, while Willy cares for his music and hopes for a better future. The couple constantly argue and it seems that both lifestyles and personalities do not fit easily together. Indeed, after an intense fight Willy leaves his wife, not knowing that she is expecting a child. Therese gives birth to a baby-girl, Evchen (Romy Schneider), gets divorced from Willy, and raises her as a single mother. Only her long time friend and admirer Peter Schröder (Klinger) supports her. Fifteen years later, Willy has become the internationally famous singer 'Bill Perry' and returns

Director:
Hans Deppe

Producer:
Kurt Ulrich

Screenwriters:
Eberhard Keindorff
Johanna Sebelius, based on the story by Frotz Rotter

Cinematographer:
Kurt Schulz

Composer:
Franz Doelle

Editor:
Walter Wischniewsky

Duration:
97 minutes

Genre:
Heimatfilm
Drama

Cast:
Romy Schneider
Magda Schneider
Willy Fritsch
Paul Klinger
Götz George
Hertha Feiler
Albert Florath
Trude Wilke-Roßwog
Erika Block
Erna Haffner
Nina von Porembsky

Year:
1953

with his competent manager Ellen (Feiler) to Wiesbaden. He visits Therese, who is now the successful owner of a fashion salon and is engaged to Peter. Evchen, who is a big fan of 'Bill Perry', meets the singer and is later informed by her mother that he is her father. However, both agree not to tell Willy since, for them, his decision to stay or not to stay with Therese should be made solely by feelings of love for Therese, but not out of responsibility for a child. Therese and Willy spend time together and, during a romantic trip to the Rhine valley, seem to get closer again. Meanwhile, Peter and Ellen (who is secretly in love with Willy) experience feelings of jealousy and helplessness. Evchen, who is aware of Peter's intense affection for her mother and considers him as a father figure, is determined to take things into her own hands. While her surprise visit to Willy's hotel fails, Peter and Ellen meet accidentally and are able to compare their situations. Both are convinced that leaving their loved ones might be the only chance to make them aware how much they need them and that Therese and Willy cannot live together. Concurrently, Therese realizes how much she loves Peter. Evchen meets Willy again and he learns by chance that she is his daughter. She convinces him that he should not try to win Therese back. Therese und Peter remain a happily united couple while Willy becomes aware that he is not really interested in Therese, but Ellen. While Willy and Ellen leave for an international tour, Therese, Peter and Evchen remain in Wiesbaden. Evchen is deeply saddened to be left behind by her father but is encouraged by Peter to wait for Willy's visit a year later.

Critique

Unlike most *Heimatfilme* this popular movie explores modern themes such as divorce and independent women. The motif of *Heimat* is portrayed as a symbol for a more conservative, family oriented lifestyle, which is contrasted with Willy's international singing career; more precisely a modern, American way of life, personified by Ellen and Willy, stands out against the culture of the old world, embodied in Therese and Peter. The inter-cultural tone of the movie is set in the opening scene, where the traditional title song is mixed with a Swing version of the piece. Accordingly, it is in the idyllic Rhine valley that Therese and Willy seem to get closer again and reconcile. Soon, the viewer understands that Willy's globally oriented career, presented in the beginning with shots of major cities of the world underplayed with his songs in different languages, does not fit with Therese's attitude towards life and her domestic life in Wiesbaden. Finally the couple realizes that Willy does not fit into the *Heimat* he left years ago, nor does he belong to Therese. Thus, remarkably, in this *Heimatfilm*, the previously married couple is not reunited, but both find success and new love independently. Similarly remarkable for the genre, the leading female protagonists, Therese and Ellen, appear to be stronger and more determined than their male counterparts. The movie, for example, starts with a diligent Therese at the sewing machine in the early morning hours, while Willy, who is later accused of being a selfish child by his female manager, is still in bed and not willing to quit his music for a traditional career. Like the protagonists Therese and Ellen, young Evchen is determined to take matters into her own hands. The extraordinary success and the leading qualities of Therese and Ellen reflect the spirit of the German *Wirtschaftswunder* ('economic miracle') after World War II.

Long shots of over the Rhine valley and its numerous castles furthermore remind the contemporary viewer of Germany's rich natural beauty and long history, and thereby provide feelings of *Heimat*, harmony and peace.

The musical and dance numbers add a similarly bright side to the conflict oriented plot. The title song by composer Franz Doelle was already a very popular song in the Weimar Republic. Furthermore, *When the White Lilacs Bloom Again* is one of the very few *Heimatfilme* that do not play solely in an unspoiled countryside but also in the city, here the city of Wiesbaden. Romy Schneider and, very briefly in a supporting role, Götz George, children of the famous actor couples Magda Schneider/Wolf Albach-Retty and Heinrich George/Berta Drews respectively, made their debut as actors, both being fifteen-years-old. As in the *Immenhof* (1955; 1956; 1957) trilogy, Paul Klinger plays the role of a fatherly friend and noble lover. The movie also marks the beginning of a second career of Magda Schneider and Willy Fritsch, who, before World War II, were among the most popular film stars in Germany.

Martina Lüke

Die Mädels vom Immenhof

Production Company:
Arca Filmproduktion GmbH

Distributors:
Casino Film Exchange
Neue Filmverleih

Director:
Wolfgang Schleif

Producer:
Gero Wecker

Screenwriters:
Erich Ebermeyer, Peer Baedeker, based on a novel by Ursula Bruns

Art Directors:
Hans Auffenberg, Karl Weber

Synopsis

The pony ranch Immenhof, a former estate in northern Germany, is the centre of life for Oma Jantzen (Haagen) and her granddaughters Angela, Dick and Dalli (König, Meissner-Voelkner and Brühl). After World War II, the three siblings, who had lost their parents, arrived as refugees from the East and found shelter with their grandmother. The girls try to support her as much as possible: while Angela deals with the administrative tasks, Dick and Dalli care for the animals. Their happy life in the countryside is overshadowed by financial difficulties. Despite all their efforts, Oma Jantzen does not have enough money to pay for taxes and the estate's forester's lodge already had to be leased to riding instructor Jochen von Roth (Klinger). Currently, the attractive instructor reluctantly gives lessons to mostly spoilt and flirtatious young women, but he plans to establish a stud farm. Von Roth and Angela have also fallen in love and plan a future together. When the summer holidays begin, Dick and Dalli expect the visit of their cousin Ethelbert (Fuchs) from the city, who soon turns out to be an extremely arrogant and spoiled young man. However, the photograph of a beautiful woman in Ethelbert's belongings and his flirtation with one of Jochen von Roth's students raises both interest and jealousy

Cinematographer:
Oskar Schnirch

Composer:
Norbert Schultze

Editor:
Hermann Ludwig

Duration:
87 minutes

Genre:
Heimatfilm
Comedy

Cast:
Angelika Meissner-Voelkner
Matthias Fuchs
Heidi Brühl
Paul Klinger
Margarete Haagen
Josef Sieber
Paul Henckels
Christiane König

Year:
1955

in Dick. As a result of his attitude, Ethelbert soon becomes an outsider among Dick, Dalli and their friends. Finally, Jochen von Roth explains to Ethelbert that he has to change his behaviour if he plans to make any friends at the Immenhof. A heated argument with Dick and a stormy night, in which Ethelbert is able to rescue a foal, provide the opportunity to prove that he has changed and he and Dick become a couple. The money troubles of Immenhof nevertheless remain until, finally, von Roth, who got engaged to Angela, is able to buy the forester's lodge and the Immenhof estate is saved.

Two sequels, *Hochzeit auf dem Immenhof* (von Collande, 1956) and *Ferien auf dem Immenhof* (Leitner, 1957), continue the family saga. *Hochzeit auf dem Immenhof*, set two years after *Die Mädels vom Immenhof*, deals with the dramatic events surrounding a potential bankruptcy of the Immenhof. Ethelbert is able to spark his rich Onkel Pankraz's (Hans Nielsen) interest in a rescue plan for the estate. However, when Margot (Karin Andersen), the daughter of Onkel Pankraz, falls in love with Jochen von Roth, who mourns the death of Angela, her father suspects a fortune hunter and threatens to cancel the rescue attempt, but follows through with the plan to give it as a surprise wedding gift to Jochen and Margot.

Ferien auf dem Immenhof focuses on the struggles of the newly founded pony hotel. Once again, Dick, Dalli, and Ethelbert play the leading roles. When all efforts to attract guests seem to fail, they attempt, with wit and creativity, to advertise the place. In the end, after a series of misconceptions and chaos, the deeply indebted Immenhof is transformed into a prosperous resort.

Critique

Die Mädels vom Immenhof is based on the novel *Dick und Dalli und die Ponies* by Ursula Bruns. The scenic setting at the Rothensande estate and the forest house Dodau in Schleswig-Holstein, the cheerful music by Norbert Schulze, as well as charming presentation of the affectionate Immenhof family and their constant struggle to make it in post-war Germany made the movie an instant success. Oma Jantzen is the amiable, old-fashioned matriarch from Imperial times who is still courted by her aged admirer Dr. Pudlich (Henckels), the local veterinarian. Angela, the reasonable and beautiful older sister, Dick and Dalli represent a light-hearted youth and a new beginning in Germany. During the course of the movies, Dick also transforms from an innocent girl to a loving young woman. Another central figure can be seen with the dashing von Roth. Through his appearance, constantly wearing riding boots, as well as his behaviour, standing for law and order, often speaking in military terms and making crucial decisions for the Jantzen family, he epitomizes the generation of soldiers in World War II. Thus, the *Immenhof* movies embody and reconcile three different generations in German history. As with other *Heimatfilme* the trilogy also contrasts a healthy life in the countryside with a decadent lifestyle in the cities. As depicted in the movie, the wholesome life in the country even has a healing effect, when, for example, superficial city boy Ethelbert turns into a mature young man, who seems then to be rewarded with the love of Dick, or when people stressed by the life in the city find peace at the pony hotel. In all three movies the dramatic circumstances and the sudden rescues from financial ruin resemble the happy endings of fairy-tales and can also be perceived as filmic symbolizations of the contemporary *Wirtschaftswunder*.

The *Immenhof* trilogy remains today among the most popular *Heimatfilm* in German cinema and is shown as a classic each year at Christmas time. The movies provide insight into the hopes and fears in post-war Germany, and reflect social rules and norms of the Adenauer era. In 1973 the first director Wolfgang Schleif decided to reprise the successful series with the movie *Die Zwillinge vom Immenhof*. With the exception of Heidi Brühl, the original cast was absent and the movie had only modest success. A second attempt by Schleif, *Frühling auf dem Immenhof*, in 1974 was even less successful and concluded the series.

Hunting Scenes from Bavaria

Jagdszenen aus Niederbayern

Production Company:
Rob Houwer Productions

Distributors:
Alpha
Radim Films

Director:
Peter Fleischmann

Producer:
Rob Houwer

Screenwriters:
Peter Fleischmann, based on a play by Martin Speer

Cinematographer:
Alain Derobe

Editors:
Barbara Mondry
Jane Seitz

Duration:
88 minutes

Synopsis

By 1968, the Bavarian village of Unholzing is marked by modernity – partially mechanized agriculture, Turkish guest-workers, NATO flyovers – but social attitudes remain conservative. The farm mechanic Abram (Sperr) returns from a short stay in the city, but rumours of his homosexuality lead him first to be mocked, then ostracized. Accused of raping a mentally handicapped boy, he escapes to the forest. In desperation he kills Hannelore (Winkler), a naïve young woman who is pregnant with his child. Jointly hunted down by population and police, his capture restores a superficial calm, symbolized in a closing sequence in which locals dance at the village fair under the shadow of the church tower.

Critique

Peter Fleischmann's *Hunting Scenes from Bavaria* is the best known example of a wave of revisionist critical *Heimatfilme* that turned the genre's *heile Welt* ('whole and healthy world') upside down, revealing the dark side of rural life, its obscurantism and structural violence. The phrase 'hunting scenes from Lower Bavaria' has become a German byword for malevolent undercurrents in village society (the term cropped up, for example, in the reception of Haneke's *The White Ribbon* [2009]), but the film itself is difficult to access, still unreleased on DVD. Fleischmann's critical intent went beyond the local and the rural. In interviews he made clear that his film's mission was to reveal the 'everyday fascism' prevalent in the complacent normality of post-war German life, which he saw as marked by an endemic 'sickness' of neurosis and aggression, ideologically directed towards the weak and the marginal. In this respect the film is a companion piece to his 1967 television documentary *Autumn of the Dropouts*, a rare German example of *cinema verité*, which

Genre:
(Anti-)Heimatfilm

Cast:
Martin Sperr
Angela Winkler
Else Quecke
Hanna Schygulla

Year:
1969

highlighted respectable Munich's loathing for the drop-outs and hippies beginning to congregate in its parks and squares.

Today, *Hunting Scenes from Bavaria*'s documentary aspects and its *mise-en-scène* seem fresher than either its social psychology or its plot, whose schematics is closer to soap opera than to Brechtian *Lehrstück*. Adapted from Martin Sperr's 1965 stage play – Sperr himself plays Abram here – Fleischmann's film moves the action from 1948 to the immediate present. As a portrait of village life on the cusp of its total integration into industrial and spectacular society, *Hunting Scenes from Bavaria* is more subtle and at times more affectionate than it sounds in synopsis. Shot entirely on location in rural Bavaria, the film is a micrology of rural modernization, here captured in visual detail – peasants on the motorway overpass, new washing machine in the background as a farmer's wife cuts a pig's throat – but also on the soundtrack, where farm workers' banter is often drowned by jet engines and agricultural machinery. Moreover, one of the film's strengths lies in turning the residual theatricality of its screenplay – the limited spatial range, the entrances and exits, the dialogue-heavy scenes – into an impressively cinematic rendering of the spatial and social constrictions of village life. Until late in the film, there are no horizons and very few long shots; figures move in a close and cluttered world in which bodies are constantly interfered with and conversations invariably interrupted. The smallest social action is observed and remarked on by passers-by and hangers-around.

The film reaches a dramatic, visual and ethnographic high point in its notorious pig-slaughtering scene. There are startling images of the killing, skinning and gutting of pigs; blood flows, innards are inflated; Hanna Schygulla hacks at a sow's carcass with a hatchet. The scene's choreography of pre-industrial collective work successfully conveys both the arduous physicality of the work and its fluid integration into daily life (children play with the still-warm entrails and head); but it also dramatically stages the inherent violence of the village polis, here focussed on the drunken body of Hannelore, who reels defenceless around the scene, groped and mocked by all. From here, it is only a short step to the final 'hunting scenes,' in which she will die at the hands of another marginalized victim, Abram. *Hunting Scenes from Bavaria* is very much a product of its historical moment, emerging from a flourishing late 1960s culture of dissent and critique. Fleischmann roots his critique of violence in the material world of rural life, its mud and machines, the porous spaces of its micro-geographies. But in creating a compendium of cultural and sexual marginalization, his analysis foreshadows an identity politics to come.

Brían Hanrahan

Heart of Glass

Herz aus Glas

Production Company:
Werner Herzog Filmproduktion

Distributor:
New Yorker Films

Director:
Werner Herzog

Producer:
Werner Herzog

Screenwriters:
Werner Herzog
Herbert Achternbusch

Cinematographer:
Jörg Schmidt-Reitwein

Composer:
Popol Vuh

Editor:
Beate Mainka-Jellinghaus

Duration:
97 minutes

Genre:
Heimatfilm

Cast:
Josef Bierbichler
Stefan Güttler
Clemens Scheitz
Volker Prechtel
Sonja Skiba

Year:
1976

Synopsis

The story of *Heart of Glass*, based on a screenplay by German artist Herbert Achternbusch, concerns the fall of a small, pre-industrial Bavarian village after the death of its glassmaker, Mühlbeck. Mühlbeck was the only person who knew the secret of how to produce ruby glass, a financially and spiritually valuable material for the village. A powerful industrialist, Hüttenbesitzer (Güttler) obsessively seeks to try and unravel the secret of the glass. This includes courting the help of the mountain shepherd Hias (Bierbichler), a prophet who has had visions of both the village's and humankind's destruction. However, as Hüttenbesitzer's search continues he succumbs, along with others in the village, to spells of lunacy, confirming the seer's prophecies. Hüttenbesitzer murders his servant girl and burns down the glassmaking factory.

Critique

While there is this storyline running through *Heart of Glass* it is presented in a way that can disorientate and disengage viewers used to films based on classic, realist techniques. Travelling at a slow, sleepy pace *Heart of Glass* is numb to any dramatic progression and it employs many cinematic tableaus which juxtapose segmented blocks of action. The film also introduces groups of characters who are often not clearly integrated into the story arc. Moreover, these characters are sometimes presented staring off into space, lost in unconscious soliloquies, and therefore unresponsive to each other in their respective encounters. The fact characters do not always address each other may have something to do with the actors' states of mind. Herzog said in interviews before the film's release that he hypnotised all the actors except Bierbichler in order to bring unprecedented performances to the screen. While it is not possible to determine whether the actors are genuinely hypnotised, many do come across as being in various kinds of disembodied states, including at times a strange concoction of sedated delirium; although this impression is also partly created by the non-narrative shot construction and editing.

Eric Rentschler (1986) has pointed out that given hypnotism was a staple trope in Weimar cinema it is surprising that Herzog feels he is exploring unchartered territory. While actors were not literally hypnotised in this cinema, in many films hypnotism played a role in the unfolding of events in the diegesis. Herzog has long championed this tradition of German film-making, claiming to have a spiritual affinity with figures such as F.W. Murnau, whose film *Nosferatu* (1922) inspired his own *Nosferatu* film, which he made in 1979. However, this is less surprising when one remembers that Herzog has equally sought to express 'original' images in his films and to exist outside the canonical traditions of cinema history. In other words, *Heart of Glass* is structured by a duality: Herzog's strong identification with certain film traditions and his desire for 'fresh images' that allow spectators to see with new eyes.

For example, there are elements of the work that evoke the popular, if nonetheless infamous, 1950s *Heimatfilme*. From the perspective of many young West German film-makers, who would go on to form various waves of the New German Cinema, this genre was infamous because it produced conservative, sentimentally kitsch works. Films based on romantic, nostalgic fantasies about provincial, rural German communities and their unified relationships with nature. The popularity of these films was seen as partly symptomatic of the nation's 'collective amnesia' concerning its recent fascist past.

On the one hand, with its Bavarian pastoral imagery, Bavarian dialect and pre-industrial, peasant settings *Heart of Glass* bears some iconographic similarities to the classic *Heimatfilm*. Moreover, its apolitical, pre-modern mythological stance draws some of its sustenance from the broader history of *Heimat* and its anti-modern, anti-urban ideology. On the other hand, however, from its opening, where Hias has an internal vision of the destruction of the world illustrated through sublime images of primeval nature, the tone of Herzog's film steers away from essential elements of the *Heimat* movement: national, cultural renewal and preservation through community and nature. Rather, *Heart of Glass* presents unique, internal visions amongst the ruins of idyllic society. Even when Hias talks about a 'new land' he can see it is a 'land' he imagines which emerges out of the world's end. Moreover, it is a 'land' that may be the re-birth of a mythical world already fallen – in the opening of the film he says this 'land' is like Atlantis coming to the surface. Overall, there is a mood of inevitable catastrophe in *Heart of Glass*, reflected in the non-dramatic structure of the film, where human progress and action is slowed down almost to the point of fading away.

Tyson Namow

Winter Sleepers

Winterschläfer

Production Companies:
X-Film Creative Pool
Palladio Film
Westdeutscher Rundfunk (WDR)
Arte
Mitteldeutscher Rundfunk (MDR)

Distributors:
Bavaria Film International, City Screen

Synopsis

The action of the film is set in a Bavarian ski resort. The relationship of Marco (Ferch), a ski instructor, and Rebecca (Daniel), a translator, is marked by constant conflicts and jealousy. One day René (Matthes), a cinema projectionist, takes Marco's car for a joyride and causes a collision with a truck driven by Theo (Bierbichler), a local farmer. Theo's daughter dies in the accident. René, who suffers from short-term amnesia, returns to normal life unaware of the fact that Theo is now out for revenge, trying to find the person who caused the fatal accident. René meets Laura (Sellem), Rebecca's housemate, who works as a nurse at the town hospital, and the two start a relationship. Meanwhile, Marco's relationship with Rebecca gradually falls apart, and Marco starts an affair with Nina (Tonke), one of his ski students. Theo finds Marco's car buried under the snow not far from the site of the accident. He links Marco as the

Winter Sleepers, X-Film Creative Pool/Palladio Film/Westdeutscher Rundfunk (WDR)/Arte/Mitteldeutscher Rundfunk (MDR).

Director:
Tom Tykwer

Producer:
Stefan Arndt

Screenwriters:
Anne-Francoise Pyszora
Tom Tykwer, based on the novel 'Expense of Spirit' by Anne-Francoise Pyszora

Art Director:
Uli Hanisch

car owner with the accident. Theo confronts Marco as he skis in the mountains, setting his dog on him. Marco panics and in an attempt to escape falls off a cliff. The film ends with René and Laura expecting a baby, while Rebecca and Nina meet accidentally on a train as they both leave town.

Critique

Based on the novel *Expense of Spirit* by Anne-Francois Pyszora, *Winter Sleepers* is a generic hybrid combining elements of the *Heimatfilm*, *Bergfilm* ('mountain films') and erotic thriller. In the distanced, at times humorous, portrayal of two relationships one can also find echoes of a *Beziehungskomödie* ('comedy of relations'),

Der Heimatfilm 113

Cinematographer:
Frank Griebe

Composers:
Reinhold Heil
Johnny Klimek
Tom Twyker

Editor:
Katja Dringenberg

Duration:
122 minutes

Genre:
Heimatfilm
Thriller

Cast:
Heino Ferch
Ulrich Matthes
Floriane Daniel
Marie-Lou Sellem
Josef Bierbichler
Laura Tonke

Year:
1997

which was particularly popular in the post-unification New German comedy wave.

Tykwer's second feature film already displays many characteristic features of his oeuvre. Like his subsequent independent hit *Run Lola Run* (1998) and the 2000 production *The Princess and the Warrior*, *Winter Sleepers* addresses issues of destiny and blind chance, its story starting with a car accident triggering a series of dramatic events and bringing together several unrelated characters. The hypnotic electronic score composed in part by Tykwer himself anticipates the famous techno soundtrack of *Run Lola Run*. The film is made in a very kinetic style, featuring some impressive shots; for example, the flight of the camera over a glacier in the opening sequence, or Marco's endless fall into the abyss at the end, filmed in slow motion, elegant and stylised. As such, the energetic audio-visual style provides a counterpoint to the sleepy atmosphere of the Bavarian *Heimat*-town with its rather tranquil pace of life. Finally, the film introduces an interesting colour code for its characters, the most obvious example being Rebecca who always wears red, which underscores her eroticism.

The film proved a critical success earning a Golden Leopard nomination at the Locarno International Film Festival as well as two German Film Awards, thus firmly establishing Tykwer's position as one of the most promising auteurs of the post-unification cinema.

Critics suggested that the characters in the film, the eponymous 'winter sleepers', can be viewed as representative of Tykwer's

Winter Sleepers, X-Film Creative Pool/Palladio Film/Westdeutscher Rundfunk (WDR)/Arte/Mitteldeutscher Rundfunk (MDR).

generation, christened by Florian Illies as the 'Generation Golf' after the popular car model of Volkswagen. Born between 1965 and 1975, the Golf generation is often regarded as hedonistic and openly consumerist, profiting from the stabilisation of the Kohl era, but at the same time somewhat directionless in life. With ironic distance, but not without sympathy, Tykwer portrays his characters as they live a life of stagnation, unable to take responsibility, instead seeking refuge in a *Heimat* and turning away from social and political issues to the private sphere. As some critics observed, the ostensible escapism of Tykwer's film, with its metaphor of hibernation, testifies to the post-unification trauma of the Golf generation and their defensive attitudes to political change. However, in the last scene of the film Rebecca and Nina leave the sleepy town on a train, a scene that suggests their coming-of-age and a willingness to take responsibility for their lives.

Klemens Czyzydlo

The Hypocrites

Die Scheinheiligen

Director:
Thomas Kronthaler

Producer:
Ismael Feichtl

Screenwriter:
Thomas Kronthaler

Cinematographer:
Micki Stoiber

Editor:
Bernd Schlegel

Duration:
80 minutes

Genre:
Heimatfilm
Satire
Comedy

Cast:
Sepp Schauer
Maria Singer
Johannes Demmel
Werner Rom
Andreas Lechner

Synopsis

Johannes (Demmel) is a young travelling carpenter, specialising in counterfeiting statues of Catholic saints. A major order by the priest Anton Selbertinger (Lechner) brings Johannes to the seemingly idyllic, small Bavarian town of Daxenbrunn, where the mayor, Matthias (Rom), and his corrupt friends in the town administration and local police are pursuing plans to build a fast food rest stop with a highway exit on land owned by the gnarly elderly widow Magdalena Trenner (Singer). Magdalena, who is embittered with the greedy village community as well as with reluctant saints, has no children and lives by herself. Deciding to accommodate Johannes and Theophile (Emina), an asylum seeker from Gambia, on her farm, Magdalena introduces the two men to the town community as the potential inheritors of her land. Matthias and his associates see their plans in danger and threaten Magdalena. The trio of outsiders, however, successfully fights the fast food restaurant project and they become very popular with other marginalized villagers including women, youths and children. After an exuberant party at her house, Magdalena dies happily among her new friends. Johannes presents a fake testament to Matthias and his associates, naming the scouts of Daxenbrunn as the beneficiaries of Magdalena's property. Accompanied by Theophile, Johannes leaves Daxenbrunn and travels to Rome to work on a large-scale order for the Vatican.

Critique

With its numerous references to actual events, Thomas Kronthaler's graduate thesis film is a satirical portrayal of provincial life in modern, rural Bavaria. Inspired by the lively debates surrounding the opening of a McDonald's restaurant near Kronthaler's own Bavarian home town Irschenberg, the author-director depicts

Michael Emina
Wolfgang Fischer
Alfred Jaschke

Year:
2001

a fictitious land struggle in the Catholic town of Daxenbrunn, through which the seemingly righteous community leaders are exposed as hypocritical petty criminals. With its allusions to the corruption scandals under the former Bavarian Prime Minister, Franz Josef Strauss, and the CSU, the long-term ruling party in Bavaria, and to the strong connection between Catholic Church and state, especially in provincial regions, the portrait of conservative and corruption-ridden Daxenbrunn also stands in for Bavaria.

In its parodic use of German *Heimat* genre conventions, *The Hypocrites* satirises ideas of provincial life and identity in rural Bavaria as they have been established in German *Heimatfilme*. Most prominently it subverts binaries such as 'home' and 'foreign,' 'inside' and 'outside,' 'self' and 'Other,' and their connotations with what is morally 'good' and 'bad.' These themes are both central to the 1950s *Heimatfilm* and to its filmic counter-reaction, the anti-*Heimatfilm* of the 1960s and 1970s. There is no clear-cut distinction between heroes and villains in the *Heimat* of Daxenbrunn, where the *Schein* is a central figure. The stock characters of the *Heimatfilm*, such as the mayor, the priest, and the policemen – who represent moral authority in the patriarchal world order of the 1950s *Heimatfilme* – are highly involved in corruption and nepotism in Daxenbrunn. Social outsiders and rebel characters such as the travelling carpenter, the financially and socially independent widow, as well as the 'foreigner'/asylum seeker, who are reminiscent of the villainous heroes of the anti-*Heimatfilm*, profit from their counterfeiting business receiving commissions from high-ranking members of a society from which they themselves are excluded. *The Hypocrites* satirically undermines the dialectical conceptions and illusory concepts intrinsic to both affirmative *Heimat* idylls and anti-*Heimat* utopias. Since categories of 'good' and 'bad' do not exist in the anti-idyllic *Heimat* world of Daxenbrunn, questions of 'morality' underlie entirely the individual's self-interest, which is primarily focussed on personal and economic profit. As the Catholic Magdalena explains to Johannes, even saints are attuned to these ideals: 'There are no false saints, and there are no true saints [...] and only few of them are actually willing to help.'

Special intertextual references to the Western genre on the diegetic level and on the extra-diegetic level, point to an important historical influence of the anti-*Heimatfilm* in the 1960s and 1970s. Diegetic examples are most clearly seen in the comedic presentation of a fight scene between the outsiders Johannes and Theophile and locals at the town pub, and in the comedic shootout between policemen and the district administrator's bodyguards in front of Magdalena's farmhouse. Extra-diegetic examples are to be found in the film score. The parodic and ironic depiction of the impact of American culture on the post-war German search for identity – as illustrated in the ambitious fast food restaurant project of the Daxenbrunn town government – is typical of many recent German *Heimatfilme* written and produced by the 'children' of the 1968-generation (such as Kronthaler himself, who was born in 1967).

Maria Irchenhauser

Schultze Gets the Blues, Filmkombinat/Zweites Deutsches Fernsehen (ZDF).

Schultze Gets the Blues

Production Companies:
Filmkombinat
Zweites Deutsches Fernsehen (ZDF)

Distributor:
United International Pictures (UIP)

Director:
Micheal Schorr

Producers:
Jens Körner
Oliver Niemeier
Thomas Riedel

Screenwriter:
Micheal Schorr

Synopsis

Schultze (Krause) has never left Teutschenthal, the small East German village that he calls home. After being forced, along with his friends Jürgen (Warmbrunn) and Manfred (Müller), into early retirement from his job at a mine, the rotund bachelor finds himself locked into a laconic daily routine, dividing his time between fishing and drinking beer, playing cards and chess, laying on the couch, visiting his mother in the nursing home and polishing his garden gnomes. A passionate accordionist and member of the local traditional polka music club, he is captivated by a tune he hears one night on the radio and becomes obsessed with Southern Zydeco and Cajun culture. He cooks spicy Jambalaya for his friends and scandalizes some of the locals by unveiling his 'Zydeco Polka' style at the 50th anniversary of the music club. When the club members ask him to represent them at a folk music festival in Texas he decides to go, but once there Schultze opts to tour the swamps and lakes of Louisiana by boat instead. Despite speaking next to no English, Schultze immerses himself in the music and culture of the Bayou. Happy in the company of friendly strangers, Schultze dies. Back at 'home' Schultze's colleagues and friends host the funeral where he is honoured with humour and respect.

Art Director:
Natascha E. Tagwerk

Cinematographer:
Axel Schneppat

Composers:
Dirk Niemeier, Thomas Wittenbecher

Editor:
Tina Hillman

Duration:
110 minutes

Genre:
Heimatfilm
Comedy

Cast:
Horst Krause
Karl-Fred Müller
Harald Warmbrunn
Rosemarie Deibel
Wilhelmine Horschig
Anne V. Angelle.

Year:
2003

Critique

Where is home? Is it where we feel the most ourselves? If so, then can we find new homes, far from where we have spent our lives, places that resonate more deeply within us than anything we have experienced before? Michael Schorr's debut feature *Schultze Gets the Blues* ruminates on these questions. The film, like its lead character, is extremely quiet, sweet and slow moving. The gentle interplay of tragedy and comedy slowly generates questions about home and identity that continue to resound like a re-occurring musical phrase throughout the film.

In the first half a series of long shots of dead end images, including disused mining equipment, fences, stop signs and closed railway crossings are intercut with scenes depicting Schultze's daily life. These long shots, which could almost be still photographs, not only set the film's languid pace but also establish that the film is as much a poignant portrait of a small, economically depressed town as it is about Schultze getting the blues. Teutschenthal appears as a town left behind. A place where movement is rare and almost nothing happens. The flat landscape, filled with industrial ruins, could hardly be further removed from the idealised Bavarian 'home' featured in traditional West German *Heimatfilme*.

The overwhelming impression is that a day in Teutschenthal is excruciatingly long. Schultze spends his afternoons alone, shuffling his way around town, perfecting the Polka on his accordion and tending to his *Schreibergarten*, a small private garden for the working-class. The one moment of heightened tension in the film occurs when Schultze plays his Zydeco/Polka for the local residents, to which one man reacts in a racist manner, yelling, 'Stop with that Negro Music.' The use of non-professional actors lends the film a strong sense of documentary authenticity. Only the lead characters are played by actors, while residents of Teutschenthal play themselves, as do the audience and performers at the annual 'sausage festival' in Texas.

Schorr's deadpan comedy and detached but none-the-less observant realism lends a naivety to the characters that populate the town. They too seem to be trapped between eras, a physical manifestation of their environment. Both Schorr's observant realism and his use of documentary techniques work against the production of illusion within and throughout the film and suggest a deconstruction of the illusion or idea of home. The scenes in Louisiana are quietly beautiful and suggest that even without a shared language a stranger can get along on hat-tipping and old world charm. In this 'other' world Schultze finds that he is no more, or less, of a stranger than he is in his home village. The film's ending, though sad, is gentle, honest and uncannily upbeat.

'It's never too late to re-tune your soul' reads the byline for this sweet but never saccharin film. *Schultze Gets the Blues* suggests that even those with dull lives can be interesting characters, and that it is not necessary to change the world to find a sense of place, but rather that home is something that resides within us all.

Alina Hoyne

Good Times

Beste Zeit

Production Company:
Monaco Film GmbH

Distributor:
Constantin Film

Director:
Marcus H. Rosenmüller

Producers:
Nils Dünker, Joke Kromschröder

Screenwriter:
Karin Michalke

Cinematographer:
Helmut Pirnat

Composer:
Gerd Baumann

Editor:
Anne Loewer

Duration:
95 minutes

Genre:
Heimatfilm
Comedy

Cast:
Anna Maria Sturm
Rosalie Thomass
Andreas Giebel
Ferdinand Schmidt-Modrow
Johanna Bittenbinder
Florian Brückner

Year:
2007

Synopsis

Kati and Jo (Sturm and Thomass), two 17-year-old women and best friends since childhood, question whether they would miss their small Bavarian hometown of Tandern if they left. When Kati gets accepted into a year-long exchange programme at an American high school, her days in Tandern seem numbered. Everyday life in the province and at her parents' farm becomes more meaningful to her and she realises that during a year abroad she would miss spending time with her family and friends. She is also anxious not to miss her first romance with the soldier Mike (Brückner). Kati recognises Tandern as 'home', and decides to give up her travel plans. *Good Times* is set in the mid-1990s and it is spoken in the Bavarian dialect.

Critique

Good Times is Marcus H. Rosenmüller's second *Heimatfilm* after his successful debut, *Grave Decisions* (2006), and it is the first part of a trilogy set in the small upper-Bavarian town of Tandern. All three films are based on writer Karin Michalke's youth memories in her native Tandern, and deal with the coming-of-age of two young women, Kati and Jo. The second part of the trilogy, *Beste Gegend*, was released in 2008. *Beste Chance* concludes this *Heimatfilm* trilogy and is scheduled for release in 2011.

What makes the rather unspectacular plot of *Good Times* engaging from a film historical perspective is the representation of 'America' (as an idea rather than as a country). Within the *Heimatfilm* context 'America' often serves as an embodiment of cosmopolitanism. Just like 'the city', 'America' was often depicted as a threatening 'Other' and, as such, challenged representations of 'home' in classic 1950s *Heimatfilme*. In a reaction to the conservative *Heimatfilm* genre of the decade following World War II, 'America' in the anti-*Heimatfilme* of the 1960s and 1970s was imagined as a utopian space promising salvation from the constraints of (the German) *Heimat*. In the 1980s writer-director Edgar Reitz took another prominent anti-American stance in his TV-series *Heimat* (1984), where US society is associated with a lack of culture, rootlessness and consumerism. Rosenmüller, as one of the most important representatives of the new generation of German *Heimat* film-makers, depicts the image of America as a mere fantasy. In the (re)negotiation of the German concept of *Heimat*, at the beginning of the twenty-first century, and within the context of globalisation, America seems to have lost both its utopian and its dystopian potential. Throughout *Good Times*, Kati's plan to go to America remains vague. There is no discussion about why she chose to apply for an exchange programme with an American high school, nor does the film show her preparing for her year abroad. It is no surprise to Kati's friends when she decides to get off the airport bus and to stay in Tandern. Similarly in Rosenmüller's film *Räuber Kneißl* (2008), and in recent *Heimatfilme* by other directors, such as Hans Steinbichler's *Hierankl* (2003), the cosmopolitanism associated with America is no longer seen as desirable.

Although the 'American dream' is ultimately dismissed in many recent *Heimatfilme* such as *Good Times*, it is noteworthy how much attention America and elements of American culture occupy in the renegotiation of home in Rosenmüller's films. Without the pending journey to America Kati would not have been prompted to revisit what home means to her. The American-style country rock soundtrack to *Good Times*, composed by Gerd Baumann – a novelty in recent German *Heimatfilme* – further underlines and embraces the impact of American culture on Kati's life, and by extension, on the German search for identity since World War II. *Good Times* displays nostalgia for the 'otherness' of America against which 'home' can be defined, but which seems lost in a globalised world.

Maria Irchenhauser

Beste Gegend

Production Companies:
Bayerischer Rundfunk (BR)
Monaco Film GmbH

Distributor:
Constantin Film

Director:
Marcus H. Rosenmüller

Producers:
Nils Dünker
Joke Kromschröder

Screenwriter:
Karin Michalke

Cinematographer:
Helmut Pirnat

Composer:
Gerd Baumann

Editor:
Anne Loewer

Duration:
98 minutes

Genre:
Heimatfilm
Comedy

Synopsis

Kati (Sturm) and her best friend, Jo (Thomass), have just finished high school and decide to go on a long-planned trip around the world by car. A car breakdown forces the two 18-year-olds to stay in South Tyrol for a few days. When Kati learns that her grandfather is ill and soon to be hospitalised the two women abandon their travels and return to their families' farms in the Bavarian village of Tandern. Kati is concerned about her dying grandfather and spends time with him and her family. Jo, however, is impatient to resume their journey and starts flirting with Kati's crush, Lugge (Murr), a travelling carpenter, who tells Jo stories from his journey around the world. With the help of her friends, Mike and Rocky (Brückner and Schmidt-Modrow), Kati smuggles her grandfather out of the hospital and takes him into his fields where he dies. Kati is determined to travel after her grandfather's funeral but finds Jo with Lugge. An argument at a football match ensues and Jo books a solo trip to South Africa. After a dramatic reconciliation between the two friends, Kati decides to stay in Tandern while Jo leaves for her trip.

Critique

Beste Gegend (literally 'best region') is the second part of Marcus H. Rosenmüller's *Heimatfilm* trilogy set in the small upper-Bavarian, predominantly Catholic town of Tandern, which follows the coming-of-age of two young women and childhood friends, Kati and Jo. Writer Karin Michalke grew up in Tandern and the screenplays of all three films are based on her experiences.

Like *Good Times*, *Beste Gegend* plays out Kati and Jo's adolescence and deals with questions of home and belonging. The underlying subtext of *Beste Gegend*, the expulsion from paradise, is one of the most common mythological models of *Heimat* narratives in both German film and literature. It defines the main parameters within which the conflict between the two female

Cast:
Anna Maria Sturm
Rosalie Thomass
Andreas Giebel
Ferdinand Schmidt-Modrow
Johanna Bittenbinder
Florian Brückner
Stefan Murr

Year:
2008

protagonists evolves: the childhood home with its connotations of innocence, wholeness, uniqueness and moral superiority is constantly threatened by loss. Home and the values associated with it are set against endeavours to cross boundaries (both geographical and moral). Questions of belonging are translated into a conflict over loyalty to friends and family, and home is a testing ground for Kati's and Jo's friendship.

Numerous allusions to the fall of Mankind also reveal connections between constructions of femininity and home that are deep-rooted in the German concept and history of *Heimat*, as well as in the Catholic tradition. Jo, for example, is modelled after Eve, in contrast to the motherly Kati, who bears traits of Mary, mother of Jesus. Whereas men set out on journeys and come back to the home they are longing for, women stay behind and guarantee the continuity of home for returning men. As a domain historically linked with concepts of the feminine, ideas of *Heimat*, with its associated values, take part in processes of idealisation of the feminine. As a consequence, female self-realisation in the context of *Heimat* has been historically limited (Blickle 2002:83).

Beste Gegend deals with the '*Heimat* dilemma' of the female protagonists, but it does so in a rather ambivalent way, constantly oscillating between affirmation and ironic subversion of the biblical subtext. This ambivalence, which is typical of many recent German *Heimatfilme*, becomes most apparent in the relationship triangle between Kati, Lugge and Jo. Drawing on a standard conflict of the 1950s *Heimatfilm* – which is usually resolved in the marriage of the male character to the female protagonist who is depicted as morally superior ('Mary') to the other ('Eve') – Kati and Jo's quarrel is not based on their shared interest for the same man, but, more broadly, on their colliding views of home and belonging. Lugge, as well as other male characters in *Beste Gegend* such as Mike and Rocky, appear and disappear as mere supernumeraries in the women's quests for their individual self-realisation, and they often bring about comic relief. *Beste Gegend* establishes the *Heimat* as a topic particularly troubling for women, and thus stands as a novelty within the historical context of the conservative *Heimatfilm* genre. The selective use of irony, however, elides Kati and Jo's representations as 'Mary' and 'Eve,' affirming gender constellations that continue to underpin the concept of home.

Maria Irchenhause

References

Blickle, Peter (2002), *Heimat: A Critical Theory of the German Idea of Homeland*, Rochester, NY: Camden.

von Moltke, Johannes (2005), *No Place Like Home: Locations of Heimat in German Cinema*, Berkeley, CA: University of California Press.

Rentschler, Eric (1986), 'The Politics of Vision: Herzog's Heart of Glass', in Timothy Corrigan (ed.), *The Films of Werner Herzog: Between Mirage and History*, New York: Meuthen, pp. 159-82.

COMEDY: DIE KOMÖDIE

The German film comedies discussed in this volume range from the witty, reconciliatory 1938 comedy of manners *Napoleon Is to Blame for Everything* and the melancholic Holocaust tragicomedy *Jacob the Liar* (Beyer, 1975) to the gender-bending, campy *Star Trek/Star Wars* parody *Dreamship Surprise – Period 1* (Herbig, 2004) and Dani Levy's 2007 anarchic and politically provocative satirical farce *Mein Führer: The Truly Truest Truth About Adolf Hitler*, illustrating the vast and diverse array of works that have to fit under the generic auspices of comedy – a rubbery and notoriously imprecise generic term for a field of texts rather loosely connected by a few threads. And while it is a cultural commonplace to assume Germans have no sense of humour, some of the first productions in the country – made in 1896 by the pioneering Skladanowsky brothers in Berlin – were brief comedic sketches; and even if much of German cinematic work from before the 1910s has been lost, evidence points to a fairly prolific early output of humorous productions.[1] Up to this day film comedies regularly top box office charts in Germany, making them reliable earners within the industry. Indeed, fifteen out of the twenty highest grossing German films of all times are comedies, with *Manitou's Shoe* (Herbig, 2001), *Dreamship Surprise – Period 1* (2004), and *Otto – The Film* (Schwarzenberger and Waalkes, 1985) taking the top three spots.

In the broadest sense, film comedy is a format defined by a use of humour in order to elicit laughter from its audiences, with usually, but not always, a happy ending. There are many different types of comic films, differentiated according to form and content (romantic comedy, satire, black comedy, comedy of manners, etc.). In addition, comedic treatment can be applied to any genre, resulting in amalgamated comedy-thrillers, Western-comedies and so on. Working with a broad range of materials, and often in conjunction with diverse genres, comedy can thus be seen as a hybrid form to such an extent as to prompt many scholars to prefer conceptualizing it as a mode of representation rather than a genre proper (King 2002).

German film comedies can be roughly divided into two categories relative to the importance they assign to narrative: comedies that are built around a comedian, such as the *Otto*-films or *Dreamship Surprise – Periode 1* (2004); and comedies that are constructed around the comic situation, such as the comedy of manners *The House in Montevideo* (Goetz and von Martens, 1951) or the 'bromantic' comedy *Men...* (Dörrie, 1985). In comedian comedies, physical gags, ad-hoc jokes and a concentration on sketch-like scenes have the ability to disrupt the narrative or to run altogether contrary to the economic function of narrative; whereas in romantic comedy, comedy of manners etc. narrative plays a much more fundamental part. These two categories resonate with film scholar Geoff King's 'two different conceptions' of comedy, which, he claims, are 'often combined: comedy in the sense of laughter, anarchy and disruption of harmony, and comedy in the sense of a movement *towards* harmony, integration, and the happy ending' (2002: 8). Accordingly, comedy is capable of being both exclusionary and inclusionary, making it a weapon of criticism as well as a means of building *esprit de corps*. However, in German cinema, scholars have

Left: *Short Cut to Hollywood*, Artdeluxe, Bavaria Film, Bavaria Pictures, Capture Film International, Schiwago Film.

argued that it frequently pursued a comedic *Sonderweg* ('special path') over the course of its history (Brandlmeier nd.: endnote 7). According to film scholar Thomas Brandlmeier the national idiosyncrasies of especially early German comedies are particularly discernable in comparison with works from France, Italy and England, but also from countries as diverse as the USA and Russia (ibid). These differences mostly manifest themselves in a 'German shame of physical comedy and the prevalence of affirmative laughter, which is destructive not towards the norm, but towards the other, towards difference' (ibid.). Hence, Brandlmeier regards an 'unshakeable loyalty to the system' as a hallmark of (early) German mainstream comedies, even if conformism also often breeds opposition and counteraction, as is manifest in the works of comedian-directors such as Ernst Lubitsch (examples include his 1913 film *Meyer in the Alps* or *The Merry Jail* [1917]) and Karl Valentin (for example his 1914 *The New Desk*, a grotesque deconstruction of bourgeois order via an object that exemplifies it) (ibid.). Looking at the comedic output of the past decades, it seems fair to say that these seesaw tendencies of conformist and critical comedies continue in Germany to this day.

During the Third Reich comedy was the most popular genre, making up almost 50 per cent of the total cinematic output of more than 1,000 films produced between 1933 and 1945. Arguably offering an escapist departure from everyday conventions and realities, the films oscillate between entertainment, distraction and propaganda, between more subversive gender-bending comedies such as the Lilian Harvey vehicle *Capriccio* (Ritter, 1938) and the more affirmative *Quax the Pilot* (Hoffmann, 1941).

During the 1950s and 1960s a tendency to move comically between (mainly) escapist distractions from the present and (some) critical tackling of the past becomes noticeable. The former is embodied by films such as the ever-popular *Schlagerfilme* ('romantic music comedies') with stars such as Caterina Valente and Peter Alexander (*Love, Dance, and 1000 Songs* [Martin, 1955]) or Peter Kraus and Cornelia Froboess (*When Conny and Peter Do It Together* [Umgelter, 1958]), but also by literally 'escapist' movies playing to many Germans' sense of *Fernweh* ('an ache for distance', 'wanderlust'), such as the trivial *When One Goes Swimming in Tenerife* (Backhaus, 1964). More anarchic and clever if also silly, non-political, and light-hearted are the often brilliant comedies about a petit bourgeois everyman and his struggles with German comic icon Heinz Ehrhard, such as *Always these Bicyclists* (1958) or *The House Tyrant* (1959), both directed by Hans Deppe, and *Our Willi Is the Best* (Jacobs, 1971). However, the strand of critical comedies found some support as well, for example in the brilliant political satire *Aren't We Wonderful?* (Hoffmann, 1958), a film that attempts to analyze what happened in Germany between 1913 and 1955, or the moving and darkly funny 1959 drama *Roses for The Prosecutor* (Staudte, 1959), dealing with Nazism's heritage and aftermath in post-war Germany.

The East German film legacy has its obvious points of contact as well as of departure with the West German filmscape, but the comedy tradition in a country with a state monopolized film industry was clearly more closely supervised and guarded than that in the Federal Republic. The overtly critical productions were often affirmative at the same time, being directed towards the official adversaries of the German Democratic Republic (GDR): the fascist past and class enemies in the West. Yet, subversive works found their way into the cinemas, too: *Carbide and Sorrel* (1963) by Frank Beyer, a gentle picaresque road movie dealing with economic shortages and the survival instincts of an unimportant everyman, poked fun at a social and economic reality that was far from being as perfect as the state described it to be. However, when a comedy proved too subversive, such as Frank Beyer's *The Trace of Stones* (1966), which satirically criticizes the planned economy and incompetent functionaries of the GDR state, retribution was swift and the film was banned three days after it had been released. At the same time, one of the most moving films about the Holocaust, and the only film made in the GDR to receive an Academy Award nomination is Frank Beyer's *Jacob the Liar* (1975), a poetic and mournful production that mixes dream and reality, past and present, to create a tragicomic experience of dignity and humanity, resisting the fascist forces with poise and humour to the bitter end.

Comedy of either persuasion, affirmative or subversive, was not the forte of the Young and New German Cinema in West Germany, which informed much of the country's critical filmscape from the late Sixties to the early Eighties; instead, it was largely left to commercial producers of (mostly shallow) entertainment at the time. There were exceptions of course, for example the works by director Adolf Winkelmann, who delved into the social realities of disenfranchised youths and working-class people in contemporary road comedies such as *On the Move* (1978) and *Lots of Cash* (1981), or Klaus Lemke's comedy romances tackling urban-rural as well as ethnic misunderstandings and prejudices in popular television films such as *Idols* (1976) and *Amore* (1978). The witty intellectualism of a film-maker like Alexander Kluge, whose films such as *Yesterday Girl* (1966) starring his sister Alexandra, or *Artists under the Big Top: Perplexed* (1968) and *The Female Patriot* (1979) with Hannelore Hoger can hardly be classified as comedies; however, they display a level of absurdist humour and social critique that asks us to question where the bounds of the comic mode lie. Certainly, throughout his career, Kluge has harnessed the critical capacity of humour in both his film and television work. Finally, directors such as Peter F. Bringmann pointed towards the way of the future with their solid genre treatments in productions like the working-class comedy *Invitation to Dance* (1977) and the road movie *Theo Against the Rest of the World* (1980), both starring German rock icon Marius Müller-Westernhagen.

Film scholars often diagnose a paradigm shift in German film around the early to mid-Eighties from the rather cerebral works of the New German Cinema to more entertainment oriented and commercial films. Lamented by some for a perceived lack of depth and intelligence, praised by others for greater accessibility, emotional allure and commercial viability, the 1980s saw a resurgence of German genre cinema, for better or worse. Scores of comedian-led films by Otto Waalkes and Dieter Hallervorden, for example, were infantile and silly while also enormously successful with the public, but so too were more intelligent and socially engaged productions such as the relationship comedy *Men...*(1985), or the comic and anarchic reflections on the difficulties and indignities of everyday middle-class life in works by Loriot (aka Victor von Bülow) such as *Ödipussi* (1988) and *Pappa ante Portas* (with Westphal-Lorenz, 1991).

Arguably buoyed by reunification in 1989, the German film industry embraced the comedy genre with even more vigour during the 1990s and into the 2000s, spawning what scholars have labelled the new 'comedy boom'. These contemporary lifestyle films, led by scores of relationship comedies frequently staged in yuppie milieus, and often criticized as solipsistic and banal, such as *Alone among Women* (1991), *Maybe...Maybe Not* (1994), both directed by Sönke Wortmann, or *Jailbirds* (Buck, 1996), arguably reflected the audiences' desire for 'less complicated narratives of Germanness' in the aftermath of profound national sea changes (Hake 2002: 180).

At the same time, countering these more affirmative cinematic tendencies were directors often inspired by an interest in dealing with the East-West German past and the positive and negative impact of the fall of the Wall on German social realities, such as Detlev Buck in the picaresque road movie *No More Mr. Nice Guy* (1993), Wolfgang Becker's darker *Life Is All You Get* (1997) and the funny if melancholy *Goodbye Lenin!* (2003), Leander Haußmann's celebration of youth in *Sonnenallee* (1999), or the rather darkly shaded social comedy-dramas of Andreas Dresen, such as *Summer in Berlin* (2005). However, this is just one tendency in contemporary German film. If anything, comedy in the new millennium has been marked by a diverse eclecticism and the inclusion of many different viewpoints, voices, and agendas. From the success of Turkish-German film-maker Fatih Akin's romantic multicultural comedy *In July* (2000) to the humorous take on the very German genre of the *Heimatfilm* ('homeland film') in *Grave Decisions* (2006), it seems that the contemporary German filmscape offers a place for practitioners of many different styles and persuasions. And once again, comedy in Germany appears to run the gamut from the silly and affirmative, such as the Otto-vehicle *7 Dwarves – Men Alone in the Wood* (2004) or the dumb historical parody *Siegfried* (2005), both directed by Sven Unterwaldt Jr., to the challenging and subversive, such as the black comedy *Shortcut to Hollywood* (Mittermeier and Stahlberg, 2009), which takes on contemporary celebrity cult and the entertainment industry. And for those who like films in-between the rebellious and the conformist there are always some comedies such as the clever and satirical yet harmonious *No Ear Rabbits* (2008) by Til Schweiger, gently poking fun at the very German need to have to categorize culture according to its level of subversion or affirmation.

Christine Haase

Note

1. See, for example, Thomas Brandlmeier (nd.) 'Frühe deutsche Filmkomödie, 1895–1917', *CineGraph FilmMaterialen*, 10, http://www.cinegraph.de/filmmat/fm10/fm10_20.html.

Napoleon Is to Blame for Everything

Napoleon Ist an Allem Schuld

Production Companies:
Curt Goetz-Film
Tobis Filmkunst

Distributors:
Astor-Filmverleih
Bavaria-Filmkunst Verleih

Director:
Curt Goetz

Producer:
Gerhard Staab

Screenwriters:
Curt Goetz
Karl Peter Gillmann

Cinematographer:
Friedl Behn-Grund

Composer:
Franz Grothe

Editor:
René Métain

Duration:
88 minutes

Genre:
Comedy

Cast:
Curt Goetz
Valerie von Martens
Else von Möllendorff
Paul Henckels
Kirsten Heiberg
Max Gülstorff
Willi Schur
Leopold von Ledebur
Maria Krahn

Year:
1938

Synopsis

English Lord Arthur Cavershoot (Goetz) is a passionate Napoleon scholar who badly neglects his wife Josephine (von Martens) for his obsession with the French emperor. When the cranky historian travels to a Napoleon conference in Paris, his smart spouse secretly follows him. Unnoticed by her, the city of love threatens to spark a romance between Arthur and chorus girl Pünktchen (von Möllendorff). Back in his hotel after a night of wild partying, the historian is visited by his research object and idol Napoleon in person. Meanwhile Josephine, who has returned to their castle, hears of her husband's forays into Parisian nightlife, supposedly in the company of an illegitimate daughter hitherto unknown to Josephine. Seeing through her husband, she sends a telegram ordering him and the 'daughter' back to England. After several days of turbulent plotting and scheming, Lord and Lady Cavershoot are happily reunited and decide to adopt Pünktchen whom they have both taken to their hearts.

Critique

Screenwriter, director and actor Curt Goetz (1888–1960) worked for stage and screen in Germany (though he was a Swiss citizen). He was known for his sophisticated witty dialogue and a sometimes frivolously biting, yet ultimately affectionate look at human frailties. It is also on this level that this film, his second work as a film director, is most convincing. What makes the relatively unknown film truly extraordinary compared to other works produced in the same historical context – Nazi Germany – is its capacity to elicit some hearty laughs even from today's audience.

The snappy comedy often emphasises situational humour and offbeat slapstick, and operates with self-reflexive gags and song and dance numbers. Modelled after the American 'screwball comedies' of the time, the movie offers remarkable speed and pointed dialogue, sometimes culminating in lewd jokes.

The world of the film is populated by characters who are strangely obsessed with history. Even Napoleon himself (also played by Curt Goetz) asks Lord Cavershoot in the film's nightmarish key sequence whether the rumour about his wife Josephine's infidelity is 'historical'. The question 'Is this historical?' becomes a kind of running joke through the course of the film. Goetz thus devises absurd situations as ironic comments on a popular stance of the time, an attitude that ascribed special significance to the past, excessively referring to and relying on 'History'.

Similarly, *Napoleon* reflects and ridicules academic preoccupation with the past and its theoretical background of German Historicism. In their attempt to understand great historical figures, the participants of the Napoleon conference take part in a futile quest for objective knowledge based on a male-dominated, affirmative notion of national historiography.

Furthermore, the conspicuous use of certain cinematic techniques points to the typical conventions of historical films. With the marked display of historical paintings and music, opulent sets and costumes, and the story's concern with popular and often anecdotal (half) knowledge about history, *Napoleon* satirically exposes the cinematic strategies common to historical dramas.

There is only one convention of the historical film that is not flaunted in an equally open and exaggerated manner: the tendency of historical films to indirectly reference the period of their production and treat contemporary issues rather than the historical events they purport to be concerned with (Sorlin 1980). The reason why Goetz's film will not self-reflexively expose – and thereby deride – this narrative principle is quite simple: Curt Goetz himself makes full use of this method. The grim dream sequence is revealing. Napoleon's lofty demeanour, his barking diction and rolling R, the feverish look in his eyes and his inferiority complex with women suggest that the film's subject is no longer the historical French emperor, but rather a contemporary German ruler: Hitler. The Napoleonic apparition is essentially a parody of Hitler and thus stands as a unique case in pre-1945 German cinema. It is this kind of explicit reference to the film's historical context and to 'German' themes that constitutes the film's socio-critical potential.

Goetz's mockery of the period's obsession with history, his filmic deconstruction of authority figures and pathos, and his allusions to the regime's circus-like spectacles were carefully calculated blows at National Socialism. In other words, Curt Goetz went quite far. Nevertheless, the movie, produced by the Nazi-controlled Tobis Filmkunst and officially labelled 'artistically valuable,' earned positive reviews by Germany's (forcibly) unanimous press. The critical work was thus integrated into the totalitarian culture industry. But how was this possible? First, Goetz's witty, bold, but ultimately apolitical humorous stings were mostly aimed at the universally human, and lacked the unforgiving urgency shown by other (exiled) critics of the Nazi regime. And second, the German Führer state, having recognized the propagandistic value of entertainment, was in need of gifted film directors, especially in the field of comedy. Curt Goetz, however, couldn't picture his future under the Nazis – only two and half months after the opening of *Napoleon* he and his wife Valerie von Martens left Germany for the US where they tried to establish themselves in Hollywood.

Adrian Gerber (translated by Susie Trenka)

The House in Montevideo

Das Haus in Montevideo

Production Company:
Domnick Filmproduktion (DFP)

Distributor:
Herzog-Filmverleih

Directors:
Curt Goetz
Valerie von Martens

Producer:
Hans Domnick

Screenwriters:
Curt Goetz
Hans Domnick, based on the play by Goetz

Art Director:
Emil Hasler

Cinematographer:
Werner Krien

Composer:
Franz Grothe

Duration:
106 minutes

Genre:
Comedy

Cast:
Curt Goetz
Valerie von Martens
Albert Florath
Lia Eibenschütz
Jack Mylong-Münz
Ruth Niehaus
Eckart Dux
Rudolf Reiff

Year:
1951

Synopsis

Professor Traugott Nägler (Goetz), happily married with twelve children, is the epitome of an honourable man with the strictest sense of morality, principles and discipline, if, lamentably, very little money. He rules his household and his students with a firm hand and a self-righteousness that will soon get its just desserts in this turbulent comedy of morals. Decades ago, Traugott cast his sister out of the family because she became pregnant while unmarried. She fled to South America, made a fortune and, upon her death, leaves everything to Traugott under one condition: a member of his own family must have a child out of wedlock within one year or else all of the money will go to charity. This utterly immoral and reprehensible (yet tempting) offer turns the world of Traugott and his family and his ideas about moral principles topsy-turvy.

Critique

German-Swiss film and theatre writer, actor and director Curt Goetz, born Kurt Walter Götz in Mainz, is considered one of Germany's most talented, prolific and successful comedic screen personalities. He wrote close to a dozen theatre plays, twenty one-act plays, two novels and more than a dozen screenplays. Most of his works were theatre and cinema box office hits. In 1939 he and his second wife, Austrian-born comedienne and actress Valerie von Martens, were in Hollywood when the war broke out and remained in the United States until 1946. He collaborated with directors such as George Cukor, Reinhold Schünzel and Joseph Mankiewicz and several of his comedies were turned into successful American films. The couple returned to Europe in 1946 to re-continue their successful careers at home. *The House in Montevideo* was the second film project they realized after their return and it was at the time Germany's biggest post-war cinematic success.

The film, a satire on bigoted petit bourgeois morals, appears at first in the guise of a harmless family comedy, with von Martens playing Marianne, a traditional, ever-busy, nurturing mother of twelve, and Goetz as Traugott, the strict but loving *pater familias* in charge of education and principles for his sizeable household. Within this narration of conservative and content family life, however, the film openly tackles moral and sexual taboos prevalent in German society in the Fifties. It does so not only by way of the story of the ostracized sister, but in particular through its highly 'immoral' happy ending. The success of *The House in Montevideo* arguably rests on its timely social critique articulated within the generic parameters of comedy, thus making it palatable to audiences on either side of the 'moral divide'.

Traugott, who threw his unmarried sister out after she became pregnant, must now, after her death, attempt to reconcile his principled condemnation of pre-marital sex with the prospect of inheriting a large sum of money, provided a member of his family does exactly what caused him to shun his sister in the first place:

conceive a child out of wedlock. Enter Atlanta (Niehaus), the oldest daughter of the Nägler family, who has an admirer, Herbert (Dux), whom she loves and who wants to marry her. Traugott's moral hypocrisy is quickly exposed as he twists and turns in an attempt to justify his oldest daughter letting herself be impregnated by Herbert first, and then marry him later. The film encourages sympathy for the wayward sister throughout. In doing so, it unmasks bourgeois moral normativity as entirely relative and depending on monetary exchange values, situational ethics and the pivotal question of whether one can afford to uphold it or not. Yet the production takes its critique of socially constructed conventions and taboos even further: at the film's conclusion, the family inheritance is not saved by Atlanta's premature pregnancy, but by the discovery that Traugott and his wife, due to a technicality, were never legally married. Thus, all twelve Nägler children were born out of wedlock, a fact that does not cause Marianne to burst into tears, which could be presumed to be the proper moral reaction to such horrific news, but rather to burst into laughter until tears are running down her cheeks. This anarchic happy ending levels all differences between the supposedly morally superior Traugott and the society he represents and his sister, and celebrates a sexuality and lifestyle based on love, compassion and humaneness rather than societal conventions and institutional approval. The display of such free and liberal thinking anticipates developments of the 1960s and '70s and makes *The House in Montevideo*, especially given its nature as a mainstream and popular movie, a rare cinematic find in 1950s Germany.

Christine Haase

Carbide and Sorrel

Karbid und Sauerampfer

Production Company:
Deutsche Film (DEFA)

Distributor:
VEB Progress Film-Vertrieb

Director:
Frank Beyer

Screenwriters:
Frank Beyer
Hans Oliva

Synopsis

In Frank Beyer's 1963 black-and-white film *Carbide and Sorrel*, the main character, Kalle (Geschonneck) must travel, by whatever means he can find – on foot, with a borrowed bicycle, by hitchhiking – from Dresden to Wittenberg after the Second World War to find carbide essential for welding, which is in turn necessary to re-open a cigarette factory destroyed during the war. In a humorous odyssey, he manages to escape several dangerous situations. He meets an attractive and lonely, young tractor-driving woman named Karla (Böhme) whom he has to leave in order to find the carbide. He makes it to Wittenberg and finds seven barrels of carbide, only to be faced with an even bigger problem: how to transport seven barrels of carbide back to Dresden without a truck. By way of more clever and humorous trickery, including stealing a motorboat from an American soldier, leaving the soldier stranded on a small island in the middle of the Elbe River, Kalle finally manages to get two of the barrels back to Dresden. His friends, who are still trying to re-open the factory, are temporarily content, but

Cinematographer:
Günter Marczinkowsky

Composer:
Joachim Werzlau

Editor:
Hildegard Conrad

Duration:
85 minutes

Genre:
Comedy

Cast:
Erwin Geschonneck
Marita Böhme
Manja Behrens
Margot Busse
Kurt Rackelmann

Year:
1963

Kalle is not: he thinks about Karla, and leaves the factory to return to her.

Critique

One of the major themes in *Carbide and Sorrel* is food and hunger. The film is a humorous portrayal of the post-war German *Hamsterfahrt* ('hamster trip'), in which people would travel into the countryside and barter for food, trading off jewellery and other valuables, sometimes only to have their newly acquired morsels of food stolen or confiscated by the authorities. The fact that Kalle's friends specifically want to re-open the cigarette factory is also telling, as cigarettes were a strong currency on the black market and could be exchanged for food. Kalle, a vegetarian and a non-smoker, forages for food all along the way. He once finds shelter at the home of an overweight and concupiscent widow, who sells her jewellery in order to buy an abundance of sausage for a breakfast with Kalle, who turns down the pork breakfast giving the film part of its title. Literally and metaphorically, Kalle chooses the bitter herb (sorrel) over abundant meat, foraging for himself rather than accepting accumulated wealth. Perhaps the most powerful food-related image in the film is when Kalle forages for mushrooms in a mine-laden forest, risking quite literally life or limb in exchange for a bit of edible fungus, only to have his small pail containing a few mushrooms taken away from him by two passers-by in a truck. This scene provides a lens through which the entire film might be read. Post-war Germany is a minefield, and he needs to find both food and carbide. He repeatedly risks his life on a perilous journey, dodging danger and apprehension around every corner. Even after he safely delivers the two barrels of carbide, he sets himself up for more perilous adventure by returning to Karla.

Also important to the film is the fact that it humorously portrays the painful hunger and poverty surrounding the end of the Second World War. Narrating tragic events humorously in a way that is therapeutic is a trademark of director Frank Beyer, who also directed *Naked Among Wolves* (1963) and *Jacob the Liar* (1975), both of which take place in concentration camps. Beyers's humour is both therapeutic and critical. In *Carbide and Sorrel*, no one is safe from the humour. The film pokes fun at the Americans and the Soviets, as well as the Germans. The American soldier is eager to help but is also loud and easily duped, and the Soviet officers are exaggeratedly obtuse. Furthermore, if the humour amidst destruction, hunger and minefields is not already dark enough, Kalle also has to deliver a eulogy for a deceased man whom he never met – a eulogy that turns out to be quite humorous. Although the plot of *Carbide and Sorrel* is inherently funny, much of the film's humour comes from Erwin Geschonneck's expert acting and exaggerated facial expressions. If nothing is safe from the film's humour, it is also difficult to imagine an audience that would not succumb to continuous laughter upon watching the movie.

Robert Blankenship

Jacob the Liar
Jakob, der Lügner

Production Companies:
Deutsche Film (DEFA)
Deutscher Fernsehfunk (DFF)
Filmové Studio Barrandov
Westdeutscher Rundfunk (WDR)

Distributor:
VEB Progress Film-Vertrieb

Director:
Frank Beyer

Screenwriters:
Jurek Becker
Frank Beyer, based on Becker's novel

Cinematographer:
Günter Marczinkowsky

Composer:
Joachim Werzlau

Editor:
Rita Hiller

Duration:
100 minutes

Genre:
Drama
War
Comedy

Cast:
Vlastimil Brodský
Armin Müller-Stahl
Erwin Geschonneck
Henry Hübchen
Blanche Kommerell
Manuela Simon
Margit Bara

Year:
1975

Synopsis

Jacob Heym (Brodský), a dispossessed restaurant owner, is one of the Jews incarcerated in a Polish ghetto. Thanks to a sardonic Nazi watchman, he must defend himself against a wrongful charge at a police station, where he overhears a German radio announcement about approaching Russian troops. An unwilling hero, he has every intention to retain this information, as it would cost his life should he become known as the source of the news. However, he is compelled to tell a young fellow inmate about the broadcast to prevent him from stealing food and effectively committing suicide, as Nazi guards would shoot him on sight. To assure people of his truthfulness, since no one would believe a Jew could leave a Nazi police station alive, Jacob 'lies' about owning a radio. He and his (imaginary) radio become the source of hope (of liberation) for the ghetto, and he is forced to invent more information about the Russian advancing position. His desperate attempt to gather more news whilst trying to rid himself of this immense burden, without losing face or quashing the hope in the ghetto, along with the interactions between the many inmates, renders this movie comical and poignant.

Critique

Unlike its 1999 remake (directed by Peter Kassovitz) with Robin Williams in the lead role, Beyer's movie offers a sombre, gripping depiction of the ghetto and its tormented inmates. This earlier film is also remarkable for its slow pace both in music and the performances, which underscore not only the difficulties the characters face but also the futility of the work to which they have been relegated; in spite of this, they persist in an effort to survive the dehumanized and dehumanizing conditions.

For the flashbacks the film employs exaggerated and vibrant colours reminiscent of East German fairy-tale films. These serve to explain the relationships between the characters and show us their lives before the Nazis invaded Poland. In contrast, the subdued colours of the present accentuate the life the Jewish inmates lead between forced labour and scarce spare time.

The interactions between the characters are touching and sometimes sad. A young couple, for instance, makes the most of the small living quarters assigned to them. They have to share it with people they do not know and have nothing in common except their Jewish heritage. A restaurateur, a barber, a lawyer, an actor and an electrical repairman are just a few of the people we observe in their quest to survive physically and mentally. To preserve his dignity, the lawyer insists on wearing a tie and jacket to work, even if he is now relegated to hauling supplies in a shipping yard. Jacob's best friend, the barber, manages to keep his barber chair in his small room to maintain this link to the past and a hopeful future. All of them yearn for their simple lives that seem so long ago.

Jacob the Liar, Deutsche Film (DEFA)/Deutscher Fernsehfunk (DFF)/Filmové Studio Barrandov/Westdeutscher Rundfunk (WDR).

Food in the ghetto is strictly rationed. Jacob cuts his bread carefully and savours it immensely when he eats a slice with fresh garlic. In his case, it is even more meagre, since he is hiding and supporting an orphaned sick girl with his paltry allotment. But he is not the only one to risk his life by harbouring her – a Jewish doctor also tends to the girl and supplements her food. The girl's innocence and the way in which everyone tries to shield her from the realities of the ghetto are similarly effective. At her age, however, she does not even know what a radio is, as Jews were prohibited from owning one for most of her lifetime.

Thoughts and dreams of the past and their sense of humour are all that keep the people going until they hear that the liberating Russian forces are nearing. Once this information spreads throughout the ghetto, suicides stop, the people's spirits are buoyed and they once again contemplate the future.

Ultimately, everyone in the ghetto is quietly heroic, enduring psychological and physical hardship. Each resists in his or her own way by trying to lead as normal a life as circumstances permit – banding together when they must protect each other, but also realizing when they must relent in the face of their oppressor and look out for themselves instead of those who are helplessly shipped to what we can only assume are death camps. This movie is a brilliant achievement in the simple and solemn portrayal of its subject matter.

Ruediger Mueller

The Female Patriot

Die Patriotin

Production Companies:
Kairos-Film
Zweites Deutsches Fernsehen (ZDF)

Director:
Alexander Kluge

Producer:
Alexander Kluge

Screenwriter:
Christel Buschmann
Alexander Kluge
Willi Segler

Cinematographer:
Günter Hörmann
Werner Lüring
Thomas Mauch
Jörg Schmidt-Reitwein

Editor:
Beate Mainka-Jellinghaus

Runtime:
121 minutes

Genre:
Collage Film
Absurdist Comedy
Satire

Cast:
Hannelore Hoger
Dieter Mainka
Alfred Edel
Alexander von Eschwege

Year:
1979

Synopsis

Gabi Teichert (Hoger), a history teacher, is unhappy with the way history is portrayed in textbooks and is looking for an alternative, more practical approach to 'uncovering' the past, quite literally digging with a spade and dissecting books with hammers and drills. She also feels very strongly that future generations of students must have a better history to study. Therefore, she seeks to influence the present in order to achieve a better foundation for the future. She infiltrates a congress of the Social Democratic Party and asks questions of delegates in a manner that disrupts the conventional proceedings. Throughout the film her efforts are commented on and complemented by a voice-over narrator – the knee of a soldier who fell in World War II.

Critique

Alexander Kluge was one of the signatories of the Oberhausen Manifesto of 1962, in which young film-makers declared their intention to create a New German Cinema. He has been the most influential and most politically active of this group. *The Female Patriot* is his most radical departure from conventional narrative cinema. He has created a collage of a film that allows no categorisation, identification or definitive interpretation. Each member of the audience should come away with very different meanings, mirroring the way Kluge encourages us to internalise history: unfinished, fragmentary, not as a chronologically ordered collection of facts as found in conventional textbooks. The often absurd, but also strangely affecting juxtapositions in the film work in the manner of Brechtian distanciation, making us laugh and reflect at the same time. An example of this would be the frequent incongruity between soundtrack and image.

The film represents a wealth of material on the topic of Germany, yesterday and today. Seemingly in no particular order there are Gabi Teichert's scenes filmed on 16mm film, archive footage, photographs, paintings, cartoons, drawings, writings – all of them scraps of different representations of German themes and stories.

Gabi Teichert is a spirited protagonist who is obsessed and dissatisfied with the inadequacies of German history to the point of neglecting her students. She spends day and night on her quest, inhabiting her own zone that nobody else can penetrate. The most striking scenes are those of a real party political congress where Gabi listens to and interviews delegates, none of whom has any answers to her probing questions about their efforts to create a better history for future generations. We laugh, not at Gabi and her 'inappropriate' questions, but at the helplessness with which politicians greet them. New German Cinema in general has often been criticised for its lack of light-heartedness and Kluge in particular for his intellectualism, but here, in the clashes between reality and imagination, there is great humour. The visual puns – the digging, the taking apart, the digesting of history – are another source of humour, but they also emphasise the idea that in order to access our buried past we have to literally 'unearth' it.

The soundtrack, too, consists of a collage of a range of different materials. Most notably there is the narrator – voiced by Kluge – who introduces himself as the only remaining body part of lance-corporal Wieland, killed in the battle of Stalingrad (the turning point of World War II). The knee, the connecting, 'in-between,' part of the legs that once moved their owner forward, is a reminder of all those buried and forgotten soldiers, but it is also a metaphor for memory in general, connecting past and present.

One of the stories told by the knee is that of the love between a young man and woman (represented by a photograph), which begins in 1939 and is rudely interrupted by World War II. When the husband returns from a prisoner of war camp in 1953 'they are expected to resume their love story.' Effortlessly Kluge connects history and the private lives of individuals. Later on, by providing witty legal analyses of the Brothers Grimm's fairy-tales accompanied by drawings, he once again goes against the grain of standard interpretations in his search for the German imaginary.

The Female Patriot requires the audience's active attention. The different perspectives, attitudes and opinions are integrated into a tapestry of cinematic signs. With this approach Kluge is trying to foster a new historical consciousness by encouraging an ongoing dialogue between cinematic text and spectator. History is meant to be actively 'grasped', that is to say fully experienced and not passively absorbed. This film is not really about 'coming to terms with' the past, but rather about engaging in a process of constant reflection and regeneration at every level.

Maggie Hoffgen

The Nasty Girl

Das Schreckliche Mädchen

Production Companies:
Sentana Filmproduktion
Zweites Deutsches Fernsehen (ZDF)
Filmverlag der Autoren

Distributors:
Filmverlag der Autoren (Germany)
Mainline Pictures (UK)

Director:
Michael Verhoeven

Synopsis

In this Oscar-nominated film, we follow Sonja Wegmus' (Stolze) trials and tribulations from a naïve girl, daughter and granddaughter to a determined, ostracized young woman and mother. The niece of a local priest, she enjoys many privileges in her hometown of Pfilzing, including receiving exam questions before the day of the test from her teachers. She undergoes many developments but her most profound change occurs after she enters an essay contest with the topic, 'My Hometown during the Third Reich.' None of her elders is happy about her choice but she had heard much about the local resistance movement during the Nazi era and idealistically wishes to study and celebrate it. She is granted access to the local archives but her enthusiastic search soon yields details that fail to add up and she becomes entangled in a net of deceit and conspiracy involving municipal, church and court officials who try to prevent her from exposing what really happened during the Nazi era. The deadline for the essay passes but despite attacks against

The Nasty Girl, Sentana Filmproduktion/Zweites Deutsches Fernsehen (ZDF)/Filmverlag der Autoren.

Producers:
Senta Berger
Michael Verhoeven

Screenwriter:
Michael Verhoeven

Cinematographer:
Alex de Roche

Composers:
Lydie Auvray
Billy Gorlt
Mike Herting
Elmar Schloter

Editors:
Barbara Hennings

Duration:
94 minutes

her character and her family, she remains persistent and discovers that not only was there no resistance, but one of the town's most celebrated and respected citizens was actually a Nazi and, together with a respected priest, denounced a Jewish merchant. Despite expectations the courts support her in her quest and, after her findings are published to international acclaim, public sentiment seems to change in her favour and those that opposed her seem eager to celebrate her in the end.

Critique

This comedy, which may be included alongside earlier films by film-makers of the New German Cinema that attempted to 'come to terms with the Nazi past,' is shot as a retrospective with flashbacks, partially narrated by Sonja, the central protagonist. The opening consists of a disclaimer, denying the movie's foundation on actual events, followed by the opening stanzas of the Middle-High-German epic poem, 'Song of the Nibelungs,' connecting the film to Germanic greatness, which is the same propaganda

Genre:
Comedy

Cast:
Lena Stolze
Hans-Reinhard Müller
Monika Baumgartner
Elisabeth Bertram
Michael Gahr
Robert Giggenbach
Fred Stillkrauth
Barbara Gallauner

Year:
1990

strategy employed by the Nazis in order to build German nationalism. Already the first shots identify one of the major players: the huge, gleaming, white cathedral dominates the scene, while the mature Sonja is but a small speck against it. She is filmed from a low-angle as she stands somewhat elevated on the pedestal of a larger-than-life statue of a male saint. The camera then focuses on graffiti spray-painted on the cathedral, which posits the questions, 'Where were you 39–45? Where are you now?' thus setting up the film's premise.

The many criticisms levelled at the townspeople – representatives of any German town, according to Verhoeven – range from subtle to obvious, including revelations concerning the Catholic church, idolatry, corruption, hypocrisy, anti-American attitudes, discrimination, collusion, control of past knowledge and the news, lingering fascist and nationalist sentiments, gender inequities based on patriarchal Catholicism and, arguably, fascist attitudes toward women's social and domestic roles.

The movie employs alienation techniques to prevent the audience from identifying too closely with the characters. Numerous scenes show Sonja interviewing community leaders in their offices while the town is projected directly behind them, indicating how the individuals are either protecting their own or have to be mindful of what might happen were they not to preserve the code of silence. Other strategies include black-and-white photography, stylized comedic elements, as well as the Wegmus/Rosenbergers' living room travelling through town to signify how they have lost all privacy and are under surveillance due to Sonja's determination to uncover the town's Nazi past.

Resentment against the loss of German lands in Eastern Europe is visible through material taught at school, where Sonja's father teaches such phrases as 'the so-called Oder-Neisse Line' and 'the so-called GDR' indicating the hope of their fleetingness, that these areas be returned to their 'rightful' owners, the *Heimatvertriebene* (literally, 'homeland displaced person') and Germany as it was prior to World War II. Sonja's father himself fled Silesia and, ironically, experiences discrimination as someone who came from the East and therefore does not receive the same rights and privileges as those who have lived in Pfilzing for generations. Thus, he cannot find housing after the war and relies on the generosity of Sonja's uncle. The fact his wife's family has lived there for hundreds of years proves immaterial, as the man's standing outweighs the woman's. Still, he shares the townspeople's nationalist aspirations and condemns Sonja for saying 'OK' or dancing rock-and-roll, as these are manifestations of the invaders and occupiers.

No one remains unscathed. Even the supportive grandmother is prejudiced, praying for God's help when a socialist is mentioned. For example, we learn that she was arrested (and nearly incarcerated) for demonstrating against Nazi removal of crucifixes from classrooms; she throws food to concentration camp inmates and exhibits unwavering support for Sonja. But while these acts may be deemed positive, we must be careful. Certainly, grandma demonstrates when the Nazis try to remove crosses from schools, but not because they starve and maltreat POWs.

This movie, which sparked much debate amongst film critics at the time for its comic approach to such a serious topic, is worth repeated viewings as it contains much wit, humour and so many facets that are difficult to appreciate after seeing it only once. Although he has worked mostly in television, Verhoeven's feature films, including *The White Rose* (1982) and *My Mother's Courage* (1995) also take up the themes of World War II, Nazism, the persecution of Europe's Jewish people and demonstrates his continued interest in coming to terms with Germany's past.

Ruediger Mueller

What to do in case of fire?

Was tun, wenn's brennt?

Production Companies:
Claussen & Wöbke Filmproduktion GmbH
Deutsche Columbia TriStar Filmproduktion

Distributors:
Columbia Pictures
Sony Pictures Entertainment

Director:
Gregor Schnitzler

Producers:
Jakob Claussen
Andrea Willson
Thomas Wöbke

Screenwriters:
Stefan Dähnert
Anne Wild

Art Director:
Jürgen Henze

Cinematographer:
Andreas Berger

Composers:
Stephan Gade
Stephan Zacharias

Synopsis

West Berlin 1987: a group of anarchist squatters record their criminal activities on Super 8 film, including the making of a homemade bomb from a pressure cooker, which they leave in an abandoned villa. When the bomb finally detonates years later in 2000 injuring a real estate agent and a potential buyer, the police concentrate their forces on hunting down the perpetrators. Re-opening old files, they decide to raid the old building where the anarchist gang used to squat and confiscate their cache of old radical films. Tim and Hotte (Schweiger and Feifel), the only two of the original group who have remained committed to revolutionary politics, visit their former comrades to plan the recovery of the incriminating film that shows the making of the bomb. Nele, 'Terror', Maik and Flo (Uhl, Matschke, Blomberg and Schretzmayer), who in the meantime are all leading a bourgeois lifestyle agree to team up for one last mission. They breach security by infiltrating the police barracks disguised as a television news crew, smuggling inside a second bomb in order to destroy the evidence. However, when Hotte, paralyzed since a riot with the police back in the 1970s is trapped in the building without his wheelchair, Tim and the others rush to his aid. The bomb explodes destroying the evidence room, and the group manages to escape taking away only the incriminating film, which they later burn on the underground.

Critique

Part of a wave of films about West German terrorism and its legacy, which includes *The State I Am In* (Petzhold, 2000), *Baader* (Roth, 2002) and the documentary *Black Box BRD* (Veiel, 2001), *What to do in case of fire?* depicts a radical subculture in the 1980s of punk and anarchist squatters, and less directly the issue of political violence and authoritarian state policies in West Germany during the same period.

However, in charting the evolution of the main protagonists from punk and anarchist activists before the fall of the Berlin Wall into

Editor:
Hansjörg Weibbrich

Duration:
101 minutes

Genre:
Comedy, Action

Cast:
Til Schweiger
Doris Schretzmayer
Sebastian Blomberg
Nadja Uhl
Martin Feifel
Matthias Matschke
Aykut Kayacik
Klaus Löwitsch
Devid Striesow
Hubert Mulzer

Year:
2001

managers, lawyers and mothers in the 2000s the film equally deals with contemporary issues, most notably questions about national identity in a reunited Germany, along with the impact of unification on society. *What to do in case of fire?* engages with the process of unification from a specifically West German perspective, showing successful young professionals who found a new life in the modern and cosmopolitan capital, Berlin. The transformation of the anarchist group proceeds in parallel with the historical changes undergone by Germany: abandoning old ideologies and evolving into yuppies they symbolize a new country which has managed to overcome its tragic past and to move forward into a globalised world.

At the same time the film looks back at the 1980s with a deep sense of loss and yearning not only for the period's rebellious youth but also for a lost culture, evoking what is often referred to as '*Westalgie*'. Thus, the portrait of contemporary Germany is attenuated by a feeling of nostalgia for certain aspects of the Bonn Republic, such as its cultural liveliness. While other films about terrorism from the 1970s and 1980s used the issue of political violence and oppressive democracy to show how the Bonn Republic was on the verge of breakdown, *What to do in case of fire?* presents a critical view on the new approaches of the young police officer, privileging instead the old methods of Manowsky, a policeman who experienced the terrorists' hunt and the riots in the streets back in the 1970s and 1980s. On the whole, the film offers a fresh and joyful portrait of Berlin's communes and anarchist culture. With its extensive use of punk music and edited 8mm films, it attempts to build an image of a time when friendship still mattered in opposition to the grey and bland society of the globalised Berlin Republic. In this sense, the character of Maik is emblematic in showing how his new life as the owner of an advertising agency is in fact an empty and boring masquerade. He only rediscovers his enthusiasm and creativity when he rejoins his gang and organizes the incursion into the police headquarters.

What to do in case of fire?'s characters appear nevertheless stereotypical and lacking in psychological depth. An inventory of distinctive figures, with which the audience can easily identify, is instead suggested: the problematic single mother, the successful professional, the timid lawyer and the die-hard revolutionary. Without attempting to reproduce Hollywood products, Schnitzel's film adopts a middlebrow formula and aims primarily for lighthearted entertainment. *What to do in case of fire?* is a quintessentially heart-warming film that proposes a formulaic narrative and simplistic resolution. In its weak critical voice and juvenile nostalgia the film follows in the footsteps of the comedies of the mid-1990s about problematic amorous relationships and identity crises.

Elena Caoduro

Dreamship Surprise – Period 1

(T)raumschiff Surprise – Periode 1

Production Company:
herbX film GmbH

Distributor:
Constantin Film

Director:
Michael Bully Herbig

Producer:
Michael Herbig

Screenwriters:
Michael Herbig
Alfons Biedermann
Rick Kavanian

Art Director:
Christoph Steeger

Cinematographer:
Stephan Schuh

Composer:
Ralf Wengenmayr

Editor:
Alexander Dittner

Duration:
87 minutes

Genre:
Science Fiction Parody
Comedy

Cast:
Michael Herbig
Rick Kavanian
Christian Tramitz
Anja Kling
Til Schweiger
Sky Dumont
Hans-Michael Rehberg

Year:
2004

Synopsis

In 2004 an alien is held captive in Area 51 for a general's first viewing. 'Sir, you've never seen anything so terrible?' The alien is revealed to be Spucky (Herbig) in a hybrid cowboy/*Star Trek*/Vulcan outfit, left behind from the year 2304 after a whirlwind time-travelling rescue mission to save the planet by destroying the UFO that landed in the Nevada desert in 2004. 300 years later Regulator Rogul (Rehberg) has declared war on Earth. In an emergency plenary session, Queen Metapha (Kling) reluctantly agrees to hire the crew of the spaceship Surprise to help defend Earth against the invaders. Captain Kork (Tramitz) and his crew are in the middle of getting in shape and preparing for the Miss Waikiki song and dance competition, a campy concoction of a Hawaian-style Club Med performance, and at first do not want to take on the mission. Instead of beaming the overweighed crewmates up, Schrotti (Kavanian) calls a Space-Taxi driven by Rock (Schweiger, who acts in a straight Bruce Willis/Schwarzenegger mode). They crash land and after a quick debriefing are sent on their way on a time machine sofa. Schrotti stays behind as Queen Metapha takes his place on the couch. Jens Maul (played as Darth Vader with a heavy Saxon accent by Kavanian), the regulator's right-hand man and as it turns out also his son, fashions himself a time machine out of the construction blueprint and moped pieces and gives chase. After two amusing detours through medieval Britain and the old West, the crew indeed arrives in 2004 to have a tiny spaceship bump into them on arrival. Just as the US military is advancing on their position the time machine is set to take off but needs to shed Spucky's exact amount of weight. In a tearful admission of requited love, Kork and Spucky part ways. When the three arrive in 2304, Spucky awaits them in a glorious purple/pink refashioned capital, having survived thanks to his genetic Vulcan/part Galapagos turtle make-up. The story ends at the Miss Waikiki tournament, where the crew performs the theme song one more time.

Critique

Michael Bully Herbig, best known for his record-breaking box office success, the Karl May Western parody *Manitou's Shoe* (2001) and his TV show *Bullyparade* (1997–2002), based *Dreamship Surprise* on the recurring gay fan fiction themed *Star Trek* parodies from his show. Unlike the set-as-a-set design platform of *Manitou's Shoe*, Herbig's aesthetic in *Surprise* is a high-end production design, including convincingly replicated as well as CGI-based iconic interiors and exteriors from the *Star Trek* and *Star Wars* franchises, among many others. In addition, *Surprise* combines German slapstick with superior special effects to create viewing pleasure for multiple generations at the German multiplex; for those in the audience who saw *Raumschiff Enterprise* (*Star Trek*) on German TV in the 1970s, but also younger members coming-of-age with Lucas' *Star Wars* origins trilogy in the 1990s. *Surprise* dials *Manitou's*

Shoe gender-bending up a notch and creates a palimpsestic web of allusions and quotations. The resourcefulness of these allusions and the hermeneutical richness of their socio-political implications make this film a true spectacle. Not only does *Star Wars* wage battle with *Star Trek*, as generations of fans of either franchise have, but placed in the East-West-German context, Jens Maul's time travel on a welded 'tinkered' moped when compared with the West-Germans' 'couch-potato' travelling connects media reflexivity to the memory debate in Germany. Watching either East or West German television or cinema allowed both sides a glimpse not only into an Other(ed) space but also into an Other(ed) time. Herbig is arguing that while both travellers may have arrived at and in the same time and space after unification in 1989, the process by which they got there is as important to analyse as the departure or arrival points. Analysing the process and media-specificity has particular repercussions in the German context, when Regulator Rogul is wearing multiple emperors' clothes: fascist, West German and US, and when East German Jens Maul/Darth Vader is revealed as his adopted son. Critiques of the film that argue against its presentation of stereotypes – gay, Ossie or Wessie – miss the point. What Umberto Eco contends for *Casablanca* (Curtiz, 1942) holds true for *Surprise*: 'the clichés are having a ball.' Besides *Star Wars* and *Star Trek*, Herbig and his co-conspirators rely on a vast fan-archive of US media, both accessed in the original from cinema, DVD and Internet, and in dubbed German versions from satellite/cable TV and local movie theatres: *The Fifth Element* (Besson, 1997), *Back to the Future* (Zemeckis, 1985), *Terminator* (Cameron, 1984), *A Knight's Tale* (Helgeland, 2001), *Men in Black* (Sonnenfeld, 1997), *Independence Day* (Emmerich, 1996), *Taxi Driver* (Scorsese, 1976), and Westerns. In *Surprise*, Herbig's crew erects a multi-layered adaptation system for treating these diverse sources; a system that combines faithful homage (design networks and generic codes), postmodern parody (gay fan fiction), slapstick (literal translations of commands, physical and situational humour), irreverent, accented appropriations (US/Russia axis of *Star Wars* morphs into West/East German axis), and media-specific reflexivity (*Star Wars* becomes an heteronormative fascist empire that is pitted against a queered *Star Trek* team, which saves the day). The musical score by Stefan Raab adds to this already intricate intertextual tapestry by connecting the Hammond-organ playing antics of the Regulator (Star Wars' emperor) to the clavichord-seducing tactics of Lord William the Last (Sky Dumont, who also reprises his role of Santa Maria from *Manitou's Shoe* in a musical interlude in the Wild West).

Sunka Simon

Grave Decisions

Wer früher stirbt, ist länger tot

Production Companies:
Roxy Film
Bayerischer Rundfunk (BR)

Distributor:
Movienet

Director:
Marcus H. Rosenmüller

Producers:
Annie Brunner
Andreas Richter
Ursula Wörner

Screenwriters:
Marcus H. Rosenmüller
Christian Lerch

Cinematographer:
Stefan Biebl

Composer:
Gerd Baumann

Editors:
Susanne Hartmann
Anja Pohl

Duration:
104 minutes

Genre:
Comedy
Heimatfilm

Cast:
Markus Krojer
Fritz Karl
Jule Ronstedt
Jürgen Tonkel
Saskia Vester
Franz Xaver Brückner
Johann Schuler
Sepp Schauer

Year:
2006

Synopsis

Set in a rural Bavarian village, this contemporary comic *Heimatfilm* tells the story of the eleven-year-old Sebastian (Krojer) who believes himself responsible for the death of his mother. Fearing the fires of purgatory, this young Catholic boy spends the film looking for a way to redeem himself of his 'crime'. Or if salvation is impossible, he will find a way of becoming immortal and so similarly avoid the pains of the afterlife. One method he uses to seek redemption is to look for a new wife for his father (Karl) and, ostensibly following his mother's signals from the spirit world, he is led to the primary-school teacher, Veronika (Ronstedt). Unfortunately she is already married to the village DJ, Alfred (Tonkel). Despite this barrier, Veronika and Sebastian's father do eventually fall in love, leaving Alfred out in the cold, contemplating suicide. Ultimately, however, Alfred seems to get over his former wife and we leave him playing air-guitar in his radio station as he broadcasts Sebastian's musical debut. The boy at last appears to be on the way to finding immortality, having learnt the guitar, thereby following in the footsteps of the rock heroes that adorn the walls of Alfred's radio station, all of whom, the DJ assures him, live forever in their music.

Critique

Rosenmüller's film is one of the best known examples of a wave of film-making that reinvented aspects of the German *Heimatfilm* at the start of the new millennium. Translated awkwardly into English as 'homeland', *Heimat* is an extraordinarily emotive and slippery term in German that came into widespread use in the nineteenth century as Germany began to negotiate the challenges of modernity and nationhood. Following from its literary and artistic forebears, the *Heimatfilm* reached its zenith in the 1950s when West German audiences flocked to cinemas to watch escapist, brightly-coloured images of Germany as a rural idyll, where dirndl-clad women and warm-hearted men fell in love and married to a soundtrack of German *Volksmusik*, thus seeming to provide a cinematic embodiment of traditional German family values.

Grave Decisions cleverly and, at times, hilariously plays with this tradition. On the one hand, it highlights a darker, gothic note that was always present in the tradition, even within many 1950s presentations of *Heimat* as a chocolate box fantasy world. On the other, it engages the mores of the anti-*Heimatfilm*, developed by the film-makers of the New German Cinema in the 1960s as a critical riposte to what they saw as a quintessential form of 'Papas Kino' against which they defined themselves. *Grave Decisions* negotiates the tensions between the *Heimatfilm* and anti-*Heimatfilm* in both its form and content. Within the *mise-en-scène* the *Heimat* fantasy of Bavarian rural idyll is juxtaposed with an anti-*Heimat* image of farm life as a muddy and bloody reality. On the level of plot, the cosy narrative one generally expected from a 1950s *Heimatfilm* is challenged. As Alfred and Sebastian disappear into their fantasy world of rock, we are given an inkling of the reasons why Veronika left her husband, preferring the domestic stability of life with Sebastian's family to Alfred's permanent adolescence. Nonetheless, we are not wholly convinced of her insistence towards the end of the film that Alfred is now fine. The neat resolution demanded of the traditional *Heimatfilm* is withheld. That said, the emotional power of the *Heimat* idyll is maintained. Thus, ultimately, the film's suggestion of real world problems, such as marriages that do not necessarily end 'happily ever after', along with its evocation of elements of the *mise-en-scène* from the critical anti-*Heimat* tradition, merely seeks to enhance the authenticity of the fantasy. This is a postmodern *Heimatfilm* that assumes a cine-literate audience who will have an inbuilt ironic distance to this tradition. At the same time it exploits the knowingness of its audience to overcome any cynicism the spectator might have for the *Heimat* genre and to indulge their perhaps unavowed desires for the nostalgic innocence the *Heimat* space always represents.

Paul Cooke

Mein Führer – The Truly Truest Truth About Adolf Hitler

Mein Führer – Die wirklich wahrste Wahrheit über Adolf Hitler

Production Companies:
X Filme
Arte
Bayerischer Rundfunk (BR)
Westdeutscher Rundfunk (WDR)

Distributors:
Beta Film (Germany)
First Run Features (USA)

Director:
Dani Levy

Producer:
Stefan Arndt

Screenwriter:
Dani Levy

Cinematographer:
Carl-Friedrich Koschnick

Synopsis

On Christmas Day 1944 Professor Adolf Grünbaum (Mühe), a famous Jewish actor, is called upon to prepare a New Year's speech for Hitler (Schneider), who is suffering from severe depression. For this purpose, Grünbaum is released from the concentration camp Sachsenhausen, just as later on his wife Elsa (Altaras) and their four children are. Grünbaum has to motivate the Nazi dictator again. Through a secret mirror, Goebbels, Speer, Himmler and Bormann (Groth, Kurt, Noethen and Kroschwald) observe every move Hitler and Grünbaum make. Physical exercise and psychoanalytical analysis are part of the treatment. Again and again, Hitler reiterates in a child-like whining manner the violent humiliations of his father. Grünbaum becomes Hitler's tutor and repeatedly attempts to assassinate him but is kept from doing so by his pity toward him. On New Year's Day the Jewish acting coach has to stand in for Hitler who has lost his voice because he had a severe nervous breakdown after half of his moustache was accidentally removed. Grünbaum thus becomes Hitler's ventriloquist in that he is forced to actually make the speech while hiding under the podium where Hitler is lip-synching and gesticulating to the words. He starts addressing the nation to boost the morale in the final phase of the war. Yet, after a while, Grünbaum starts making fun of the dictator and telling the truth about the Nazi regime, at which point Grünbaum is shot.

Critique

Dani Levy's comedy *Mein Führer – The Truly Truest Truth About Adolf Hitler* (2007) represents a paradigmatic shift in German post-war popular culture. Whereas Adolf Hitler to that point had generally served as an icon and personification of evil, Levy's film

Mein Führer – The Truly Truest Truth About Adolf Hitler, X Filme, Arte, Bayerischer Rundfunk (BR), Westdeutscher Rundfunk (WDR).

Composer:
Niki Reiser

Editor:
Peter R. Adam

Duration:
89 minutes

Cast:
Helge Schneider
Ulrich Mühe
Sylvester Groth
Ulrich Noethen
Stefan Kurt
Adriana Altaras
Udo Kroschwald

Year:
2007

highlighted the way German social attitudes to the Führer had undergone a profound change. In *Mein Führer*, Hitler – played by Helge Schneider – is given the right to be the subject of the narrative, and therefore invites identification, even though his ideology is at the same time denounced. Levy's attempts to portray Hitler as both human and psychopath sparked off a debate in Germany about the limits and dangers of 'humanizing' the Nazi leader and 'trivializing' his role in history. From the Hitler satires and parodies in the 1930s to the films of Charlie Chaplin (*The Great Dictator*, 1940) and Ernst Lubitsch (*To Be or Not to Be*, 1942), Hitler has often been made fun of. Yet, Levy's movie raised the question as to whether Germans themselves could now laugh at him. In the context of the German politics of remembrance of the Holocaust and World War II, the humorous representation of Hitler seems to point to an increasing yearning for 'normalcy' in German self-understanding and historiography.

Levy's film can be regarded as a pastiche of visual memory in German post-war and post-Wall society. The images of Hitler viewers are familiar with in the media – Hitler as hysterical speaker and demagogue, military leader, and anti-Semite, but also as an animal and nature lover, unsuccessful artist, Eva Braun's lover – constitute a visual archive that shapes public memory. Levy satirically re-enacts these well-known images and confronts them. By altering the historical imagery he breaks a taboo in defying the mythology of Hitler as the almighty dictator and the ultimate representation of evil. He is dissociated from the direct context of Holocaust and war, and through the hilarious acting exercises and behaviour therapy led by Adolf Grünbaum – played by Ulrich Mühe – he is presented as a victim of his own needs and drives. With his peculiar Austrian accent, hysterical mannerisms, wearing a yellow tracksuit, losing at one point half of his moustache Hitler is represented in an alienating way as an incorrigible, paranoid and, paradoxically, charming psychopath. This makes him a comical figure whose fantasies of world domination are opened to ridicule. The Nazi leader is reduced to the level of a puerile loser. In one particular scene Hitler is shown in his bath tub while making the Nazi salute and playing with a miniature warship. In another awkward sequence Hitler, being sexually impotent, is unable to make love to Eva Braun. Furthermore, in his acting classes Grünbaum makes Hitler crouch on all fours and bark like a dog, leading his beloved German shepherd Blondi to jump on his back. Levy claims his storyline is based on two important references. On the hand, Paul Devrient, a well-known German opera singer during the Weimar Republic, did indeed help Hitler in the early 1930s to improve his mode of public address. On the other hand, Levy refers to Alice Miller's psychoanalytical interpretation of Hitler's public behaviour in which she suggests obvious traces of severe parental abuse. The topic of childhood trauma due to miseducation and lack of love runs through the film as a central theme, like when Hitler gets into bed with the Grünbaums looking for comfort, love and company. His helpless behaviour and ridiculous posture become symbolic iconography.

It is the controversial representation of Hitler as a pitiful buffoon which involuntarily renders him sympathetic to the audience. Indeed, frequent close-ups on Helge Schneider's face aim at emphasizing and at the same time ridiculing the paranoid fears, hopes and other human emotions shown by the dictator. This technique was equally predominant in Oliver Hirschbiegel's film *Downfall* (2004), which was, in a similar fashion, attacked by a number of intellectuals as being too psychologically benevolent towards Hitler and consequently towards the Nazi regime as a whole. Grünbaum repeatedly pities the Nazi dictator for his miserable youth, incurable depression and uncontrollable hysterical fits of anger. As a result, in *Mein Führer* the maintenance of a balanced perspective in regard to the consciousness of being a perpetrator or a victim proves to be a laborious balancing act. In this respect intellectuals such as the dramatist Rolf Hochhuth, the journalist and author Henryk M. Broder or the vice-president of the Central Council of Jews in Germany, Dieter Graumann, have emphasized that as a comedy *Mein Führer – The Truly Truest Truth About Adolf*

Hitler seems to question the Holocaust as a fundamental civilizational caesura. Against the indictment of belittling the Holocaust and performing a reactionary re-interpretation of sacred symbols of genocide and repression, Levy – himself of Swiss-Jewish descent and winner of the Ernst Lubitsch Prize and the German Film Prize for *Go for Zucker!* (2004), an ironic comedy on contemporary German-Jewish life – has again and again stressed the politically subversive potential of humour, much more so than tragedy, in the context of films about the Third Reich.

Arvi Sepp

Short Cut to Hollywood

Production Companies:
Artdeluxe
Bavaria Film
Bavaria Pictures
Capture Film International
Schiwago Film

Distributor:
Senator Film

Directors:
Marcus Mittermeier
Jan Henrik Stahlberg

Producers:
Matthias Esche
Marcos Kantis
Philipp Kreuzer
Martin Lehwald
Marcus Mittermeier
Jan Henrik Stahlberg

Screenwriter:
Jan Henrik Stahlberg

Art Director:
Peter Dang

Cinematographer:
David Hofmann

Composer:
Rainer Oleak

Synopsis

Johannes Selinger (Stahlberg), an insurance salesmen, and his two life-long friends, Christian (Kottenkamp), an alcoholic veterinarian, and Mattias (Mittermeier), a bankrupt used-car salesman, who spend their evenings playing kitschy pop to empty bars have nothing going for them. Now in their mid-thirties, Johannes decides that they will rebrand themselves 'John F. Salinger and the Berlin Brothers' and seek fame in the United States. The 'unique selling point' of their act is to be John's eventual death, live on television, making the man the ultimate 'reality TV' star and using his gradually growing celebrity to market their music. Constructed as a mock documentary, the film charts the development of the 'John F. Salinger Show,' as it becomes known to the world, from his initial 'teaser' act of self destruction – Christian amputates John's little finger, the film of which is used to drum up media interest – through the band's staged terrorist attack on a small-town cafe to increase the hype around the story, to a series of increasingly dramatic amputations and his final death. With fame, however, John finds love, leading him and his friends to question what they are doing, as 'real life' intervenes and undermines the original aim of their 'reality' project.

Critique

The reception of the film in Germany was overshadowed by a hoax staged by Stahlberg. On 10 September 2009, two weeks before the film was due to open and the day before the eighth anniversary of the attacks on the World Trade Centre and Pentagon, Stahlberg contacted the German Press Agency (DPA) posing as a journalist for the fictional network *KVPK-TV*, reporting an attempted suicide attack on a café in the town of Bluewater, California by a German rap band dressed as Arab terrorists. Backed by reports appearing on Twitter, entries on Wikipedia, as well as videos on Youtube and Myspace, the journalist pointed the DPA to his network's website which contained eyewitness accounts of the attack along with US contact numbers. Every aspect of this was a fiction: the television network did not exist, neither did the band. No attack took place and the numbers linked back, via Skype, to Stahlberg and his team

Editors:
Stine Sonne Munch
Sarah Clara Weber

Duration:
95 minutes

Genre:
Comedy

Cast:
Jan Henrik Stahlberg
Marcus Mittermeier
Christoph Kottenkamp
Marta McGonagle
Asli Bayram
Allison Findlater-Galinsky

Year:
2009

in Germany. The hoax was quickly 'uncovered' as a publicity stunt for the 'band,' but not before hundreds of worried Germans had tried to contact emergency services, causing outrage both for the trouble the stunt produced and its timing, which was seen to be in extraordinarily bad taste. The outrage increased as it was subsequently revealed that the band publicity hoax was itself a hoax, and the stunt was aimed at promoting the film *Short Cut to Hollywood*.

The construction and impact of the 'Bluewater Attack' goes to the heart of the film, as well as Mittermeier and Stahlberg's approach to film-making more generally. Short Cut to Hollywood is their second joint feature, following from a similarly quirky quasi-documentary about a vigilante undertaking an obsessive quest to correct the minor misdemeanours of his fellow citizens, *Quiet as a Mouse* (2004), a film which also adopted 'guerilla' tactics – epitomized by the 'Bluewater Attack' – in both its production and marketing. In their second feature, however, such tactics become the very point of the film itself. For the Directors:

> Form has beaten content. No one asks 'why?' anymore. And if another unknown television personality lies down in a terrarium full of spiders no one laughs at him for being an idiot. Instead he just sells twice as many records.

Thus, the film explores the very status of 'reality' in 'reality TV', repeatedly pushing the boundaries of what the audience finds acceptable. This begins with the representation of the first amputation of John's little finger, an operation presented in horrific detail. As the narrative unfolds, we become more accepting of the film's premise and so John's further self-mutilation becomes less shocking. Consequently, the film resorts to other tactics to challenge its own narrative logic, including John's gratuitous performance of Hitler in response to a Jewish television executive's request that he refrain from smoking, the man's father having died of lung cancer. There is no reason for a specifically anti-Semitic plot twist here, other than to shock, breaking the audience out of its now comfortable suspension of disbelief and reminding us of the 'real' world outside the theatre.

Paul Cooke

References

Brandlmeier, Thomas (nd.), 'Frühe deutsche Filmkomödie, 1895–1917', *CineGraph FilmMaterialen*, 10, http://www.cinegraph.de/filmmat/fm10/fm10_20.html. Accessed 2 February 2011.

Hake, Sabine (2002), *German National Cinema*, First Edition, Austin: University of Texas Press.

King, Geoff (2002), *Film Comedy*, London: Wallflower Press.

Sorlin, Pierre (1980), *The Film in History: Restaging the Past*, Blackwell, Oxford.

FOREIGNERS AND GUEST-WORKERS
FREMDE UND GASTARBEITER

Beginning in the late 1960s the directors of the New German Cinema brought the plight of *Gastarbeiter* ('guest-workers') to the screen as part of their engagement with a range of social and political issues facing post-war German society. In 1955, as its economy was booming, Germany had signed the first of a number of international treaties aimed at satisfying the demands of its expanding labour market. Guest-workers who were recruited mainly from Greece, Italy, Portugal, Spain, Yugoslavia, Morocco, Tunisia and Turkey were never conceived of as immigrants: theoretically such workers were employed on rotation and were to return to their countries of origin after spending a year or two in Germany; guest-workers were housed away from the German population in barracks, and typically travelled to Germany alone, leaving their families behind. The policy of labour rotation was never properly implemented, however, and by 1973, when an official moratorium on recruitment was declared in response to an economic slump, many guest-workers had come to consider Germany their home and had brought their families to join them. The guest-worker protagonists of the New German Cinema – Moroccan Ali from Rainer Werner Fassbinder's *Ali: Fear Eats the Soul* (1974), Turkish Shirin from Helma Sanders-Brahms' *Shirin's Wedding* (1976) and Italian Nicola from Werner Schroeter's *Palermo or Wolfsburg* (1980) – are lonely, exploited creatures who are not fully individualised and fulfil the function of representing their fellow countrymen and women on-screen. Their linguistic handicap shapes their relationship with the strange new world in which they find themselves. In these early films dealing with guest-workers and foreigners, the trauma of the country's Nazi past is shown to impinge upon its post-war relationship with ethnic and national minorities, with the racial hierarchies of the Nazi era echoed in new social hierarchies with undeniable racial undertones. The films' critiques of rational capitalism, which invites in 'guests' like Ali, Shirin and Nicola but denies them their humanity by treating them as mere labourers, is also implicit. Violence and misfortune feature to a significant degree: Fassbinder's Ali collapses with a stomach ulcer, Sander-Brahms' Shirin is murdered by her pimp and Schroeter's Nicola commits murder himself. The small, opaque hospital window in the final scene of *Ali: Fear Eats the Soul* is a fitting symbol of the hopelessness and despair conveyed by these three films.

By the 1980s guest-workers in Germany had begun to find their artistic voices in the fields of literature, cinema and the fine arts, and were no longer reliant on a sympathetic German gaze to represent them. In 1986 a Turkish-German film-maker, Tevfik Başer, emerged to add his *Forty Square Metres of Germany* to the engagement begun by the New German Cinema. Başer's film tells the story of a Turkish immigrant, Dursun, who keeps his wife, Turna, confined to their tiny apartment in an attempt to keep her away from the temptations of German society. It would not be until the late 1990s, however, with the first film in Thomas Arslan's trilogy about the Turkish community in Germany – *Brothers and Sisters* (1997) – that directors with hybrid identities became a force to be reckoned with in the German film industry. By this time Germany had grudgingly and belatedly accepted its status as an *Einwanderungsland* ('immigrant country'). Citizenship laws began to change, simplifying the

Left: *The Edge of Heaven*, Anka Film/Dorje Film/Norddeutscher Rundfunk (NDR).

process of obtaining permanent residence and applying for German citizenship. Prior to these changes citizenship had still predominantly been defined on the basis of *jus sanguinis*, or ethnic belonging. German-born children of non-European Union immigrants are today considered German and may retain their second citizenship into young adulthood, at which point, however, they are obliged to relinquish one of their two nationalities. This situation is a serious bone of contention in the Turkish community.

While German society and government remains ill at ease with cultural hybridity, the new generation of film-makers live and embrace it. Fatih Akin, the son of Turkish immigrants, became a national celebrity in 2004 with his Berlinale-winning *Head On*, and followed this with a further drama, *The Edge of Heaven* (2007). *The Edge of Heaven*'s Nejat, a Turkish-German professor of German literature, epitomises the small but growing Turkish-German middle-class. Nejat is only a generation removed from his guest-worker father, Ali, but a world away from the Ali on Fassbinder's screen. Akin's characters are variously German, Turkish, or Turkish-German: their cultural identities, if not always freely chosen, are certainly complex, and this is reflected in their linguistic abilities and preferences. English enters Akin's films as a global linguistic space that breaks down the Turkish-German binary. The violence that afflicted the guest-workers of the New German Cinema has not gone away, but both *Head On* and *The Edge of Heaven* have open endings that hint at reconciliation and redemption, rejecting the pessimism of the past and mirroring the new, more hopeful reality of German society.

Another young director from a non-German background, Alejandro Cardenas-Amelio, whose parents were Latin American exiles, returns to the enclosed spaces of *Ali: Fear Eats the Soul* and *Forty Square Metres of Germany* in his film *Berlin – Buenos Aires* (2008), which is set in a West German *Wohngemeinschaft* ('communal apartment') in the 1970s. In contrast to Akin's global cities and frequent border crossings, Cardenas-Amelio's *mise-en-scène* creates a narrow world, making the point that social exclusion can be a self-imposed state for the exile who longs for home.

The gendered experience of foreignness is a theme that extends from the New German Cinema to the present day. In many ways, Akin's Sibel (*Head On*), who lives in twenty-first century Hamburg, enjoys fewer freedoms than Sander-Brahms' Shirin, left to police her own morality in 1970s' Cologne. Shirin and Sibel, Turna and Yeter (*The Edge of Heaven*), and Fariba in the asylum drama *Unveiled* (2005), reviewed elsewhere in this volume, are all subject to discrimination, exploitation and violence.

Since the 1990s, when the legal situation of immigrants in Germany began to improve, genre films have seized on the stereotype of the foreigner and put it to work in romantic comedies and police dramas, directed largely but not exclusively, by ethnically German directors. These films include Dorris Dörrie's *Happy Birthday, Türke!* (1992), Martin Eigler's *Friends* (2000), Anno Saul's *Kebab Connection* (2004) Stefan Holtz's television film *My Crazy Turkish Wedding* (2006) and the 2011 Berlinale hit *Almanya — Willkommen in Deutschland* (Yasemin Samdereli). Fatih Akin, who co-wrote the screenplay for *Kebab Connection*, recently made his own contribution to the comedy genre with *Soul Kitchen* (2009), the tale of a Greek-German battling to save his restaurant from closure.

There is one important respect in which recent German cinema depicting 'foreigners' mirrors German public debate: the diverse national and ethnic backgrounds of the foreigners depicted in the New German Cinema have given way to a cinematic world whose 'Others' are predominantly Turkish and Muslim. It is to be hoped that future cinematic portraits of Muslims in Germany will help dislodge the discursive turn revealed in recent, controversial comments made by Thilo Sarrazin, former Social Democrat politician and ex-member of the board of the German Federal Bank, who in 2009 dismissed the Turkish and Arabic-speaking populations of Berlin as having no productive function other than 'selling fruit and vegetables' and producing 'head-scarf wearers' (Sarrazin 2009: 198–99).

Chantal Wright

Ali: Fear Eats the Soul

Angst essen Seele auf

Production Companies:
Filmverlag der Autoren
Tango Film

Distributors:
Filmverlag der Autoren
New Yorker Films (USA)

Director:
Rainer Werner Fassbinder

Screenwriter:
Rainer Werner Fassbinder

Cinematographer:
Jürgen Jürges

Editor:
Thea Eymèsz

Duration:
93 minutess

Synopsis

Emmi (Mira), a widowed cleaning lady in her sixties, enters a bar in Munich frequented by foreigners where she meets Ali (ben Salem), a considerably younger Moroccan guest-worker. Ali accompanies her home and the two sleep together. A relationship begins which results in marriage. When Emmi breaks the news of the marriage to her children, they react with disgust. Emmi and Ali find themselves increasingly isolated and decide to go away on holiday to escape their problems. When they return, Emmi finds that she has returned to some sort of social acceptance; her neighbours, the local shopkeeper and her children all want something from her and are therefore prepared to accept her relationship with Ali. Ali's loneliness worsens as Emmi's situation improves and she becomes less understanding of his problems. Ali turns to drink, gambling and the sexual and culinary comforts offered by the owner of the bar where he first met Emmi. When Emmi and Ali attempt reconciliation, Ali collapses from the pain of a stomach ulcer and is hospitalised. The doctor warns Emmi that many guest-workers suffer from stomach ulcers caused by stress and that few of them make a proper recovery.

Critique

Ali: Fear Eats the Soul (1974) was Fassbinder's international breakthrough, winning him a FIPRESCI prize at Cannes in 1974.

Ali: Fear Eats the Soul, Filmverlag der Autoren/Tango Film.

Genre:
Drama
Romance

Cast:
Brigitte Mira
El Hedi ben Salem
Barbara Valentin
Irm Hermann
Rainer Werner Fassbinder
Walter Sedlmayer
Karl Scheydt

Year:
1974

The film is, in part, an homage to the 1955 Hollywood melodrama *All That Heaven Allows* directed by Douglas Sirk (who was born in Germany to Danish parents). *Fear* transposes Sirk's post-war New England setting to 1970s Munich; Rock Hudson's broad-shouldered working-class gardener metamorphoses into El Hedi ben Salem's Moroccan guest-worker. Although the parameters of what are socially unacceptable shift in Fassbinder's translation the basic theme of exclusion by society remains the same.

Fassbinder walks a middle line between the sentimental language of Hollywood film with its appeal to the emotions, and the alienating techniques of Brechtian theatre with its appeal to the intellect. The slogan which fills the screen as the opening credits roll, 'Happiness is not always fun,' indicates what lies ahead. From the opening shot of Emmi entering the bar, closed framing, static groups of silent onlookers and flashes of garish colour are used to emphasise the isolation of individuals and couples within society. In the scene that occurs just before Emmi and Ali go on holiday, the couple are depicted sitting at a table in an empty beer garden. The camera cuts between them – filming the couple first from a distance and then from behind Ali's back as Emmi speaks to him – and an unsympathetic collage of observers. Emmi sobs and shouts angrily at the impassive onlookers. The brilliant yellow of the seats is the only colour in this social landscape devoid of human warmth. Despite the reserve of *Fear*'s camera, which frequently observes its subjects through door frames, windows and staircase railings, the viewer cannot help but empathise with both Emmi and Ali. They are sympathetic if flawed characters whose relationship is built not on communication – for Ali speaks only *Gastarbeiterdeutsch*, the pidgin German used by guest-workers which is referenced in the film's ungrammatical German title – but on mutual need and loneliness. The feeling of hopelessness conveyed by the closed framing and the film's pessimistic ending encourage the viewer to think about what would need to change in order to make Emmi and Ali's 'happiness' more fun.

Ali is not a well-rounded portrayal of a guest-worker in Germany and cannot compete with the complexity of the Turkish-German characters in Fatih Akin's films, made in a very different Germany some thirty years after Fassbinder's *Fear*. Fassbinder argued that this naïve depiction was necessary to uphold the child-like nature of Emmi and Ali's relationship. In fact, to do anything but objectify Ali would be to remove the *raison d'être* of the film, which is to show that any society defines itself in terms of what it is not, and that its excluded 'Others' are destined to be misunderstood. Ali's objectification and exclusion occurs in a society that is still coming to terms with its Nazi past: and which city could better symbolise this ambivalent relationship than Munich? When the newly married couple go out for their wedding lunch, Emmi excitedly leads Ali to Hitler's favourite restaurant where they dine alone, filmed coldly through a door frame as they sit side-by-side, their struggles with the menu observed by a condescending waiter. Emmi is a more complex character than Ali, a bundle of political contradictions, the widow of a Polish forced labourer but also a former member of the Nazi party. This complexity does not express itself in language, however, as both Emmi and Ali are veritable fonts of platitude, perhaps another reason why Fassbinder begins his film by telling us that happiness is not always fun.

Todd Haynes' *Far From Heaven* (2002) was inspired by Sirk's *All That Heaven Allows* and Fassbinder's *Fear*.

Chantal Wright

Shirin's Wedding

Shirins Hochzeit

Production Company:
Westdeutscher Rundfunk (WDR)

Distributor:
Arbeitsgemeinschaft Kino

Director:
Helma Sanders-Brahms

Producer:
Volker Canaris

Screenwriter:
Helma Sanders-Brahms

Art Director:
Manfred Lütz

Cinematographer:
Thomas Mauch

Composer:
Ömer S. Livanelli

Editor:
Margot Löhlein

Duration:
120 minutes

Genre:
Drama
Feminism

Cast:
Ayten Erten
Jürgen Prochnow
Aras Ören
Aliki Georgouli

Year:
1976

Synopsis

In order to be reunited with Mahmood (Ören), a man she was promised to as a young girl, 20-year-old Shirin (Erten) leaves the life she had in a small village in Turkey in search of him. Not knowing Mahmood's whereabouts, Shirin makes her way to Germany, only knowing that he is somewhere in Köln. After a difficult journey, she quickly becomes acquainted with the new life she finds in Köln. Shirin learns the language, makes friends with co-workers, and has a place to stay in the living quarters designated for foreign workers. Yet when she gets fired from her job at the factory, her situation becomes hopeless and prostitution becomes the only way for her to survive. Shirin runs into Mahmood one night in the living quarters of the male foreign workers after being dropped off there by her pimps to make money. There she realizes that the life she could have had with Mahmood is no longer possible and faces a hopeless situation and a tragic end.

Critique

Director Sanders-Brahms provides a unique twist to the depiction of the migrant guest-worker experience in Germany during the 1970s: she tells the story from a female perspective. Consequently, the central theme of the film is women's experience in a male world that is complicated further by migration. In such a world, women, no matter where they are or come from will need to depend on one another for safety. Shirin's story is emblematic of such a network of women that help other women whenever they can, especially because Shirin's journey would not have been possible without her female helpers. These helpers appear in numerous stages of the journey: in order to catch the bus from her village to Istanbul, Shirin needs money, which a random woman on the bus gives to her; while in Istanbul, she meets a woman who takes her in while she settles her documents that would enable her to enter Germany as a guest-worker; and finally in Germany, her numerous female co-workers consult her about the lifestyle women lead in Germany, information which helps ease her transition from a life in the village to a life in a large city. The large amount of narrative attention that is paid to women in the film is characteristic of what can be referred to as Sanders-Brahms' feminine film aesthetic. This aesthetic agenda tends to privilege women with its demands

Shirin's Wedding, Westdeutscher Rundfunk (WDR).

to highlight the urgency to tell stories about women, stories that cannot encompass the problems women face without focalising them through women's experiences.

Sanders-Brahms depicts men in the film differently from the women, especially since the men try to disturb this complex network with their sexual desire. The male figures are shown as greedy capitalists, rapists or emotionless beings, while the women are emotional, caring and selfless beings. The stark contrast between men and women is only exacerbated with each step Shirin comes closer to Mahmood in the film. Her situation finally becomes nearly hopeless when she loses her job in the factory. As a guest-worker she was able to be a legal resident of Germany, but without a job she loses her legal standing. In order to avoid being deported Shirin needs to find a job, but instead realizes that she is not qualified to fill some positions, and racism prevents her from getting others. Shirin suffers especially because she is a woman, and Sanders-Brahms makes sure that the spectator is aware of this throughout the film. Men are privileged over women in the workforce, regardless if they are German nationals or foreigners, and the film addresses this by showing how only women are fired from their jobs and the men still remain employed. The privilege is further thematized with the unsettling of Shirin's safe realm by a rape. From here onward she is unable to recuperate and her situation progressively worsens.

Prior to the rape, Shirin follows a very traditional, conservative lifestyle in which she shields herself off from any male desire, represented by the use of her headscarf. She refuses to remove the scarf even in the presence of women. The scarf symbolizes the tradition she left back in the village that she strongly holds on to in the city; however, the conservative values she is upholding all crush underneath her after the rape. From this point forward, she shows her hair, and, convinced that Mahmood no longer wants her after having lost her virginity, is driven into prostitution. During the final moments before her death, Shirin has no control over her life: she gets thrown into a room full of men to make money for her pimps. She is locked in the world of men, quite literally, in which her purpose is to serve them sexually. With no-one left to help her, and after seeing Mahmood among these men, Shirin wants to take her own life. But her pimp, who shoots her down, takes even this last privilege away from her. Shirin's transformations throughout the film are illustrative of a woman faced with a constant need to defend herself from the impositions and dangers she encounters in men.

Ervin Malakaj

Palermo or Wolfsburg

Palermo oder Wolfsburg

Production Companies:
Thomas Mauch Filmproduktion
Zweites Deutsches Fernsehen (ZDF)
Artco-Film

Distributor:
Prokino Filmverleih

Director:
Werner Schroeter

Producers:
Thomas Mauch
Eric Franck

Screenwriters:
Werner Schroeter
Giusseppe Fava
Orazio Torrisi

Synopsis

Nicola (Zarbo), a young Sicilian man from Palermo is a victim of Sicily's high unemployment rate. During the first part of the film we follow him around Palermo, visiting the people and places that are meaningful to him before he sets off on the long journey to Wolfsburg, Germany to join the ranks of the foreign *Gastarbeiter*. Once in Germany Nicola manages to find a job in the Volkswagen factory and accommodation in a *Gastarbeiter* dormitory. He also meets and falls in 'love' with a young German woman, Brigitte (Tig), on the rebound from an abusive relationship, but soon we realise that she is just using Nicola to get back at her boyfriend. That evening Brigitte's boyfriend and another young man taunt Nicola, making him feel even more angry, rejected and alienated. Nicola lashes out, killing them both. He is put on trial, at which point the film begins to radically depart from a realist aesthetic, to highlight the absurdities and ironies of a German justice system unable to understand or account for cultural difference.

Critique

With this film, Schroeter becomes one of a handful of directors of the New German Cinema attempting to bring stories of cultural difference and the *Gastarbeiter* experience to the screen. Schroeter structures the film into three acts, each with its own distinctive aesthetic. The episodic structure is reminiscent of a Christian Passion play, and indeed Schroeter literalizes this link by intermittently

Palermo or Wolfsburg, Thomas Mauch Filmproduktion/Zweites Deutsches Fernsehen (ZDF)/Artco-Film.

Cinematographer:
Thomas Mauch

Editors:
Werner Schroeter
Ursula West

Duration:
173 minutes

Genre:
Drama, Guest-worker

Cast:
Nicola Zarbo
Otto Sander
Ida Di Benedetto
Magdalena Montezuma

cutting to images of a Passion play being performed in amateurish fashion. These have no direct link to the diegetic world, but encourage us to see Nicola as an allegorical figure; a melancholy martyr representative not only of a single individual, but of a whole generation of men who went to seek their fortunes in Germany.

The first episode takes place in Palermo and is shot in a style reminiscent of the neorealists. As Nicola visits various friends and relatives to tell them of his decision to seek work in Germany, each provides him with words of advice. In turn Nicola gathers together memories and impressions, intangible fragments of his identity that he will take with him to Germany. This presentation of Nicola as a kind of surface or screen upon which these impressions are recorded is emphasised through the many shots of Nicola looking onto a situation from the edges, rather than interacting fully in a situation. During this episode we are also presented with some stories of the men who went before him, and the impact on the wives

Antonio Orlando
Brigitte Tig

Year:
1980

and children they left behind in Italy. It is these impressions that return to him and are effectively re-screened as surreal spectres of his homeland during the courtroom sequence.

During the central episode attention turns to Nicola's interactions with a few Germans and a range of other guest-workers who are mostly Italian and Sardinian, and all speak a range of dialects. Each appears in their own way to long for home and family. Here the film's aesthetic texture shifts slightly, with the *mise-en-scène*, colour palette and framing becoming more reminiscent of that used by R. W. Fassbinder in his own *Gastarbeiterfilm*, *Ali: Fear Eats the Soul* (1974). Like Moroccan Ali in that film, Nicola is subject to discrimination, not least by the German wife of a distant uncle, who refuses to help him on the evening he arrives in Wolfsburg. Nicola does find an ally in Giovanna (Di Benedetto), the strong, matronly Italian woman who owns the local *Kneipe* ('bar') where much of the action takes place. She takes Nicola under her wing, as, it is suggested she has done for many who have come before him, but ultimately is unable to protect him from his tragic response to the young men's racist taunts.

Nicola's trial comprises the film's entire final episode, which takes on a highly theatrical and rather disorienting style that in many ways mirrors Nicola's own disorientation and disconnection from this very foreign place – Germany. Nicola looks on silently as a series of bizarre events take place in the courtroom: while witnesses are being questioned the judges pull faces and slump on the bench; the victims' mothers perform strange, repetitive gestures in the gallery – first they fight, and then they kiss. All the while, an interpreter simultaneously translates the proceedings between German, Italian and the Sicilian dialect resulting eventually in an incomprehensible cacophony of languages. It becomes almost impossible for the spectator, and Nicola to follow what is going on. Faster montage sequences bring a disarray of memory-images to bear on the proceedings in which Nicola's defence lawyer (played superbly by long-time Schroeter collaborator Magdalena Montezuma) argues that Germany and Sicily represent vastly different worlds that cannot be judged with the same criteria. The film ends leaving the case unresolved, but leaving the viewer with an image of an opening window through which Schroeter directs us to contemplate the many cultural divides that separate the world at large.

Michelle Langford

Happy Birthday, Türke!

Production Companies:
Cobra Film GmbH, Zweites Deutsches Fernsehen (ZDF)

Distributor:
Senator Film

Director:
Doris Dörrie

Producers:
Gerd Huber, Renate Seefeldt

Screenwriters:
Doris Dörrie, based on the novel by Jakob Arjouni

Cinematographer:
Helge Weindler

Composers:
Markus Lonardoni, Peer Raben

Editors:
Raimund Barthelmes, Hana Müllner

Duration:
109 minutes

Genre:
Mystery, Noir

Cast:
Hansa Czypionka
Özay Fecht
Doris Kunstmann
Lambert Hamel
Ömer Şimşek
Ulrich Wesselmann
Christian Schneller
Meret Becker
Emine Sevgi Özdamar
Nina Petri
Stefan Wigger

Year:
1992

Synopsis

Kemal Kayankaya (Czypionka), private investigator, is celebrating his birthday alone in his office when a new client enters: a Turkish woman named Ilter (Fecht), who is sporting a purple headscarf, quickly removed when she realizes that Kayankaya is Turkish in name only. Kayankaya, the son of Turkish guest-workers in Germany was orphaned as a small child, raised by German foster parents and therefore has no ties to the Turkish community. Ilter hires Kayankaya to investigate the disappearance of her husband, Ahmed (Özdamar), and to re-examine the circumstances surrounding the death of her father, Wasif, who died in a car accident around the time of Ahmed's disappearance. Kayankaya learns that Wasif and Ahmed, whom he locates but who is stabbed to death before Kayankaya has a chance to question him, were involved in the drug trade, as were senior members of the Frankfurt police. In a showdown at the apartment of Paul Futt (Hamel), a high-ranking police officer, Kayankaya proves that Futt arranged Wasif's death; Wasif and Ahmed had been trying to back out of their business arrangement with the corrupt police. Ahmed's stabbing, however, was not the action of the Frankfurt police force but of Ilter's brother Yilmaz (Simsek). When confronted by Kayankaya, Yilmaz admits the killing; he blamed Ahmed for the family's disintegration. Yilmaz indicates that Ilter is aware of his guilt but is willing to cover it up for the sake of the family. Kayankaya, too, keeps Yilmaz's deed a secret.

Critique

German author Jakob Arjouni created the character of the not so Turkish detective Kemal Kayankaya in 1986. Arjouni's surname and choice of protagonist led many critics to believe that the author was Turkish, whereas Arjouni is, in fact, a pseudonym. In Doris Dörrie's adaptation of Happy Birthday, Türke!, which is the first in a series of four Kayankaya novels, Kayankaya was played by non-Turkish actor Hansa Czypionka, appropriately enough for a character who is Turkish only in name and looks. Caught between the German and the Turkish communities, Kayankaya experiences prejudice from both sides. He is subject to the full range of German racist behaviour, but has also learned to turn German preconceptions of Turks to his own advantage. Depending on the demands of the situation, he switches between a number of different linguistic registers ranging from broken Turkish-German to fluent German delivered with a Turkish accent, to his own Frankfurt-accented version of his native tongue. His utter lack of familiarity with the language and cultural practices of the Turkish community bemuses his client Ilter, who buys him a Turkish-German dictionary and then storms out of his apartment after they argue, uttering the words 'You're Turkish. I thought you would understand me.' Neither national group is able to see beyond Kayankaya's name and appearance. The detective's relationship with his sexually attractive client takes on shades of a mother-son relationship as the narrative progresses, even though their age difference is not significant. Ilter brings Kayankaya Turkish food, she attempts to clean his apartment, sings – at his request – a Turkish song which he remembers his deceased mother singing; and, in the scene that follows their sexual encounter, he presses his head to her bosom in a gesture that suggests the orphan is seeking maternal comfort.

A noir, the film is a departure from Doris Dörrie's usual preference for the gender/relationship comedy, though there is a flash of sexual humour in the peccadilloes of Futt's bosomy wife. The film's production values do not appear to have been the highest, although the bleached view of an ugly Frankfurt marked by train lines, high rises and motorways is very much in the noir tradition, as is the high-angle camera focusing on floors and feet. Germany does not come off well in the film, depicted as a fundamentally racist society where even the prostitutes refuse Turkish clients. Retired policeman Löff's (Wigger) anecdote about his humane treatment of an egg thief during the Third Reich hides his complicity in the regime behind an act of incidental charity and suggests that, at least among a certain generation, the country has not progressed far in its coming to terms with the past.

Notably, *Happy Birthday, Türke!* features music by Rainer Werner Fassbinder's long-time musical collaborator Peer Raben, and a cameo performance by Turkish-German novelist Emine Sevgi Özdamar, who plays Wasif's widow.

Chantal Wright

Brothers and Sisters

Geschwister – Kardesler

Production Companies:
Trans Film
Zweites Deutsches Fernsehen (ZDF)

Distributor:
Trans Film

Director:
Thomas Arslan

Producers:
Kaete Caspar
Alberto Kitzler

Screenwriter:
Thomas Arslan

Synopsis

Brothers and Sisters covers approximately ten days in the lives of the offspring of a Turkish-German family in present-day Berlin. The film follows the three siblings, Erol (21) (Yigit), Ahmet (18) (Savas Yurdreri), and Leyla (16) (Turhan) through their daily lives, starting with a letter to Erol informing him that he has been called up for military service in Turkey and ending with the family accompanying him to the airport. In the intervening days we follow the different paths that the three siblings have chosen for themselves and the reaction of their parents to them.

Critique

Thomas Arslan's *Brothers and Sisters* is the first part of a trilogy in which he explores issues of identity formation within the Turkish community in Germany. The so-called 'guest-workers' who where called in from 1954 onwards to help rebuild the country were for a long time expected to return to their countries. While the German authorities and the general population found it very difficult to acknowledge and debate for decades the fact that Germany is a country of immigration, the immigrants themselves have had to

Cinematographer:
Michael Wiesweg

Editors:
Thomas Arslan
Bettina Blickwede
Heidi Reuscher

Duration:
82 minutes

Genre:
Drama

Cast:
Fazli Yurderi
Tamer Yigit
Savas Yurderi
Serpil Turhan

Year:
1997

deal with difficult social and economic issues. Language barriers, educational underachievement, discrimination and ghettoisation are major problems, mainly for the Turkish minority because of their greater cultural and religious differences. Conflicts exist between the German and Turkish populations, but also within Turkish families, when their sons and daughters follow different paths to those of their parents. These conflicts have been taken up in film culture, initially with an emphasis on awareness-raising. R.W. Fassbinder was the first film-maker to do so in his *Katzelmacher* (1969) and in *Ali: Fear Eats the Soul* (1974). Since the mid-1980s film-makers from immigrant backgrounds (mostly Turkish-German) have begun to represent themselves, in the main still focusing on problems. Thomas Arslan, however, is determined to represent a process of normalisation and to explore the opportunities that cultural hybridity affords.

Thus, the ethnically mixed family background (Turkish father, German mother) of the brothers and sisters of the film's title is shown to provide both conflict and opportunities, with an emphasis on the latter. The young people have choices. Ahmet has chosen to integrate into German society completely; he has a German passport, is following a path to higher education and has a German girlfriend. He is in many ways opposed to his brother's lack of direction and sees Erol's choice of Turkish citizenship as a sign of failure – which it may well be, since Erol, being unemployed, is steeped in street culture and its trappings of petty crime. Generally speaking, though, the two brothers' arguments revolve around issues that any 'normal' siblings would have. This is clearly Arslan's intention: to show for the most part 'normal' family relationships. Leyla is in an apprenticeship and is aiming for an independent life. For her there is no conflict between cultures. She uses her culturally hybrid status to full advantage and has negotiated a very sophisticated identity. For example, she switches effortlessly between Turkish and German as the situation requires and she has both Turkish and German friends. At present there is a potential boyfriend from a Turkish background, but viewers could similarly imagine a German partner for her in the future. In the third part of Arslan's trilogy, *A Fine Day* (2001), the main character, also played by Serpil Turhan, does indeed have a German boyfriend.

The theme of cultural hybridity is in evidence from the start: over the title sequence we see Ahmet waiting for an urban train at a station called 'Kottbusser Tor'; the soundtrack comprises hip hop with English lyrics (rapped by Savas Yurderi); and we hear diegetic voices in Turkish. The setting is thus clearly marked as Berlin's East Kreuzberg district, the area with the highest concentration of immigrant populations in Germany. In observational, almost documentary style, the camera follows the protagonists around, and picks up, almost accidentally, signifiers of cultural hybridity. One example is a quite wonderful visual pun. On his way to school Ahmet stops at a kiosk which, as a small island within this German city, is marked as part of Turkish culture: it sells Turkish newspapers and Turkish is spoken. Ahmet asks for 'a Snickers and a Coke.' This scene points to the layer of global culture, which is seen to form part of the characters' lives, indeed is an important influence on their identity. Later on we encounter Leyla in a music shop, listening to hip hop on headphones and immediately afterwards shifting into Turkish with her girlfriend in order to be able to gossip about a young German man standing nearby.

In his use of non-professional actors, simple narrative, black-and-white cinematography and the often restlessly moving, observational camerawork Arslan is clearly influenced by the French *nouvelle vague*, particularly by Truffaut and Rohmer. The fact that he also wrote the screenplay and edited this film adds to its sense of immediacy and realism.

Maggie Hoffgen

Friends

Freunde

Production Companies:
Cine Licht Camera Rental GmbH
Deutsche Film- und Fernsehakademie Berlin (DFFB)
Moneypenny Filmproduktion GmbH
Zweites Deutsches Fernsehen (ZDF)

Distributor:
zoomfilm.de

Director:
Martin Eigler

Producers:
Sigrid Hoerner
Anne Leppin
Martin Walz

Screenwriters:
Martin Eigler
Sönke Lars Neuwöhner

Cinematographers:
Michael Mieke
Ulrike Meier
Philip Vischer
Bettina Warnecke
Robert Wedemeyer

Synopsis

Policeman Nils (Fürmann), bitter because of the ostracism he experienced in his neighbourhood when he joined the police force, volunteers for a drugs raid on a bar run by his childhood friend Tayfun (Yildiz). During the raid Nils has a crisis of conscience and removes a packet of drugs to protect his friend. The police discover the theft. To avoid going to prison, Nils agrees to report on the activities of the mainly Turkish gang that operates out of Tayfun's bar. He runs across his ex-girlfriend and childhood friend Caro (Paul), who is now Tayfun's girlfriend, and the two rekindle their relationship. Nils' girlfriend Rebekka (Kuggler), a chronic insomniac, overdoses on sleeping pills but survives. Nils realises that Tayfun is behind the hit on an undercover policeman who had infiltrated the gang. When the gang carry out a robbery using a van that is being tracked by the police, and Tayfun's younger brother is shot dead in the subsequent police raid, Nils' status as a spy is confirmed. Tayfun is arrested when he confronts Nils in his apartment. As Tayfun is led away by the police, Nils draws an unloaded gun. The police shoot him dead.

Critique

Friends (2000) is a conventional thriller that pitches cops against robbers and ends in a shoot-out (of sorts). Tayfun's gang is made up largely, but not exclusively, of Turks or Turkish-Germans. The police force is comprised largely, but not exclusively, of white Germans. Aside from the cliché of the ethnic minority gangster, the film presents a surprisingly harmonious view of race relations in Germany. In contrast to Doris Dörrie's 1992 noir *Happy Birthday, Türke!*, in which the police force and society at large are portrayed as fundamentally racist, in *Friends* Turkish-Germans and Germans live side by side in what appears to be an integrated society. Nils, Tayfun and Caro are shown playing together as children in the film's extended opening sequence. Romantic relationships between Turkish-German men and German women seem common. Nils

Composers:
Moe Jaksch
Johannes Kobilke
Tom Reiss

Editors:
Dirk Grau
Daniel Gawrilow
Gilda Rosskamp

Duration:
100 minutes

Genre:
Thriller

Cast:
Benno Fürmann
Christiane Paul
Erdal Yildiz
Michael Gwisdek
Irene Kugler
Erhan Emre
Matthias Schweighöfer
Susanne Bormann
Aykut Kayacik
Murat Yılmaz

Year:
2000

greets Tayfun Turkish-style, with a kiss on both cheeks, and in one scene where Tayfun and Nils are watching a basketball game Nils speaks a few words of Turkish, a rarity for a German character in a contemporary film. The plot centres on the archetypal divide between police and criminal rather than on ethnic tensions, and personalises this conflict through its adoption of the love-triangle as a central plot device. Despite the film's attempts to portray an ethnically integrated society, however, the camera nonetheless works to promote the viewer's identification with the ethnic German, as Fisher convincingly argues. In the scene where Tayfun is arrested 'the prostrate ethnic Turk' is shown 'in a deliberate full shot at a high-angle that emphasizes his prone nature before the policing, disciplinary gaze' (Fisher 2003: 411). When Nils is arrested he is pushed up against a wall rather than to the floor.

Friends sports a glossy aesthetic. There are two shots of Nils' face submerged in or emerging from water: once in his bath tub while the doorbell is ringing and the police are waiting to arrest him for pocketing drugs during the raid, and once in a sink in Tayfun's bar, from which he emerges to find Tayfun observing him from behind. We also see Nils listening to music on headphones, unaware that Caro is ringing the doorbell to his flat. The meeting between Caro and Rebekka, which takes place on this occasion, causes Rebekka to become unsettled and eventually leads to her overdose. In all of these scenes Nils appears to be fleeing from reality or at the very least unaware of the outside forces that are about to exert their influence on him. Water – whether it is in Nils' bath tub, in a sink, in the lake where Nils goes rowing with Caro and kisses her (she remarks that it would have been safer to have gone swimming) or in the pool where Rebekka swims early in the morning when she has not been able to sleep – is always a place of refuge and safety. Aside from the film's contemporary aesthetic and the licence plates, which indicate that the action is taking place in Berlin, there is no indication of when or where the story is situated. The lack of a specific milieu and of any historicity contribute to the film's apolitical feel.

Chantal Wright

Head On
Gegen die Wand

Production Companies:
Arte
Bavaria Film International
Corazón International
Norddeutscher Rundfunk (NDR)
Panfilm
Wüste Filmproduktion

Synopsis

Cahit (Ünel), a forty-year-old Turkish-German alcoholic, and Sibel (Kekilli), a young woman from a conservative, working-class Turkish-German family, meet in hospital in Hamburg following their respective suicide attempts. Cahit, depressed after the death of his wife, had driven his car into a wall at top speed. Sibel, who was attempting to escape her oppressive family, had slit her wrists. Sibel persuades Cahit to enter into a fake marriage so that she can leave the parental home and enjoy her sexual freedom with a variety of men. Their agreement works until Cahit and Sibel fall in love and Cahit

Distributors:
Timebandits Films (Germany),
Soda Pictures (UK)

Director:
Fatih Akin

Producers:
Stefan Schubert
Ralph Schwingel

Screenwriter:
Fatih Akin, based on his book

Art Directors:
Sirma Bradley
Nergis Çaliska

Cinematographer:
Rainer Klausmann

Composers:
Alexander Hacke
Maceo Parker

Editor:
Andrew Bird

Duration:
121 minutes

Genre:
Drama
Romance

Cast:
Birol Ünel
Sibel Kekilli
Catrin Striebeck
Güven Kiraç
Meltem Cumbul

Year:
2004

kills one of Sibel's sexual partners in a fit of jealousy. When Cahit goes to prison Sibel promises that she will wait for him. She moves to Istanbul to live with her cousin Selma (Cumbul). Sibel's self-destructive behaviour results first in her rape and then in a savage beating. When Cahit is released, he goes to Istanbul to find Sibel, who now has a partner and a little girl. The two lovers spend the night together in Cahit's hotel, and Sibel promises to accompany Cahit on his journey to Mersin, the town of his birth. Sibel does not turn up at the bus station and Cahit boards the bus alone.

Critique

Turkish-German director Fatih Akin's Berlinale-winning feature *Head On* shows the full complexities of Turkish-German identity among the second generation of immigrants. Cahit Tomruk's Turkish is 'totally fucked', as his future brother-in-law remarks, and the alcoholic, who earns his living by clearing away beer bottles in a club, certainly seems to identify more with the anti-bourgeois Germans of the punk generation than with the '*Kanaken*' – a pejorative German term for Turks that occasionally falls from Cahit's lips – who populate Sibel's world. Whereas Turkish-born Cahit seems rootless, Sibel, born in Hamburg, is functionally bilingual and anchored in the Turkish community. Cahit's best friend Seref (Kiraç) is a Turkish bachelor; Sibel, initially at least, admires her cousin Selma, whose emancipated lifestyle as a single woman in Istanbul is far removed from Sibel's oppressive experience of the Turkish community in Germany. The permutations of Turkish-German identity and culture are endless, the film seems to be saying, and Turkey is not the backward country the European Union would have us believe. Istanbul is a city of freedom for both Sibel and Cahit – in Sibel's case, this includes the freedom to self-destruct. The protagonists' respective voyages to Turkey should not be seen as a return to their roots for neither of them are truly Turkish, but more properly cultural hybrids; nor is it an implicit condemnation of Germany, but a relocation to a strange country where both can embrace a new life.

Head On is also, and perhaps above all, a tragic love story. This is signalled by the musical *entr'actes* which frame the film: Selim Sesler and orchestra, along with the singer Idil Üner 'watch' and accompany Cahit and Sibel's story from the banks of the Bosphorus with music and song. The Brechtian framing asks us to consider this very modern tale as a conventional love story and adds an intellectual dimension to what is otherwise a conventional, if powerfully, filmed drama that appeals primarily to the emotions. Akin's love story manages to juxtapose scenes of disturbing violence – Cahit's joyous dance with bleeding hands held aloft and Sibel's near death from a beating on the streets of Istanbul – with lighter, often extremely humorous scenes: Cahit and Seref's concern over the alcohol content of the chocolates that are to be presented to Sibel's parents; Cahit answering the door to his flat stark naked, having struggled up from the sofa where he has been sleeping off his hangover.

The film's ending is a quiet tragedy after the major tragedies that have accompanied Sibel and Cahit through their love story. Sibel chooses the life she has rather than a life with Cahit, perhaps out of consideration for the relationship between her daughter and her new partner. Cahit boards his bus to Mersin alone, strong enough now to face a future without Sibel. A happy ending would arguably not have suited this couple and the tender scenes of them making love in Cahit's Istanbul hotel room prior to their separation somehow mitigate the melancholy.

Akin's Germany is de facto culturally hybrid and multilingual. The soundtrack to *Head On* marries East and West, traditional and modern, and is an essential part of the film's *mise-en-scène*. Turkish, German and English – the globalised language that Cahit adopts when neither Turkish nor German fulfil his communicative needs – mix on-screen and in the characters' lives, belying Germany's official status as a monolingual country.

Chantal Wright

The Edge of Heaven

Auf der anderen Seite

Production Companies:
Anka Film
Dorje Film
Norddeutscher Rundfunk (NDR)

Distributor:
Pandora Filmproduktion (Germany)
Artificial Eye (UK)

Director:
Fatih Akin

Producers:
Fatih Akin
Klaus Maeck, Andreas Thiel
Jeanette Würl

Screenwriter:
Fatih Akin

Art Director:
Seth Turner

Cinematographer:
Rainer Klausmann

Synopsis

Nejat (Davrak) is a Turkish professor of German literature, his father, Ali (Kurtiz), a Turkish widower, both living in Germany. Ali offers Yeter (Köse), who works as a prostitute to finance her daughter's studies, a new life with him. When he is violent against and accidentally kills Yeter, Nejat goes in search of her daughter, Ayten (Yesilçay), who is a political activist in Turkey. He cannot find her but stays in Istanbul, running a German bookshop. Meanwhile, the girl, on the run from the Turkish authorities, escapes to Germany to find her mother. She meets Lotte (Ziolkowska) and her mother Susanne (Schygulla). Lotte and Ayten fall in love. When Ayten is deported back to Turkey and imprisoned, Lotte follows her in order to help. However, tragically, Lotte is killed. Susanne comes to Turkey to grieve and to make contact with Ayten. Instead, she meets Nejat in his bookshop. The complex narrative ends with Nejat making peace with his father, whom he disowned after Yeter's death.

Critique

Fatih Akin is Germany's best-known Turkish-German film-maker and he consistently manages to unite critics and audiences in Germany, Turkey and beyond – a rare achievement. This is reflected in the awards that his films have garnered, including the Golden Bear at Berlin for *Head On* (2004), *The Edge of Heaven*'s predecessor and first part of a loose trilogy described by the film-maker as 'Love, Death, and the Devil.'

One meaning of the original title *Auf der anderen Seite* (des Lebens) ('On The Other Side [of Life]') is captured in the English-language title, *The Edge of Heaven*. However, the English title misses important connotations implicit in the German title. One of

Composer:
Shantel

Editor:
Andrew Bird

Duration:
116 minutes

Genre:
Drama
Guest-workers

Cast:
Baki Davrak
Tuncel Kurtiz
Nursel Köse
Nurgül Yesilcay
Hanna Schygulla
Patrycia Ziolkowska
Nurgül Yesilçay

Year:
2007

these relates it to Akin's previous film, *Head On*, literally 'Against the Wall' ('*Gegen die Wand*'). In this sense *The Edge of Heaven* can be understood to be the 'other side' of the first part of the trilogy – beyond the wall against which the character of *Head On* crashes. In addition, the central characters of Nejat and Cahit can be seen as two sides of the same person: where Cahit is passionate, impulsive, even self-destructive, Nejat is calm, caring, with a spiritual quality about him.

Whereas the two protagonists of *Head On* are driven by obsessive passion for each other, *The Edge of Heaven* is a much more restrained film. The ensemble film structure, in which the fates of six characters are explored, is a departure from the highly concentrated, passion-fuelled tour de force of *Head On*. Extreme turmoil of the main characters leads to healing, forgiveness and transcendence. Death is the central theme, both in a real sense and in the metaphorical sense of dying and re-birth.

The Edge of Heaven is an intricately woven tapestry of fate and humanity, which not only take in big themes such as love, death and redemption, but also cross-cultural experiences of its variously German, Turkish or Turkish-German protagonists. We are privy to a variety of cross-border exchanges between Germany and Turkey, some of which are the result of individual decisions of some characters (paralleling Akin's own explorations of his cultural heritage); others are demonstrations of state power, as in Ayten's and Najet's father's deportation from Germany to Turkey. The two most striking crossings are those of Yeter and Lotte's coffins as they are transported back to their respective countries of citizenship. This is shown in silent images in which the coffins are loaded onto planes.

A dense narrative texture has been achieved by concentrating mainly on the actual journeys of the characters after important decisions have been taken or after events have led to a crisis. The original idea was to present the narrative strands strictly chronologically; in other words, by cross-cutting between the characters whenever events took place simultaneously. Only in post-production did the film-makers realise that this would not work because it would not allow the audience to understand and identify with the characters and their fates. Therefore, it was decided not to interrupt the individual stories, rather to link them by visual motifs such as planes taking off and landing, and by inserting chapters such as 'Yeter's death' and 'Lotte's death.' Nejat's central role is underlined by the opening and closing scenes, which are identical: a slow pan takes the eye from a small hut to a petrol station, where a young man is buying fuel and some snacks from the shop in which melancholy Turkish music can be heard. In the opening shots it is not revealed who the young man is, but the scene is set: we are in rural Turkey. At the end of the film we know that he has come to make peace with his father.

Maggie Hoffgen

Berlin – Buenos Aires

Die Tränen meiner Mutter

Production Companies:
Filmworker
Creado Film

Distributors:
Farbfilm-Verleih (Germany)
Valuefilms Licensing (Worldwide)

Director:
Alejandro Cardenas-Amelio

Producers:
Nicolas Grupe
Dirk Hamm

Screenwriters:
Cuini Amelio-Ortiz
Alejandro Cardenas-Amelio
Christoph Silber

Cinematographer:
Florian Schilling

Editor:
Renata Salazar-Ivancan

Duration:
91 minutes

Genre:
Melodrama

Cast:
Adrian Gössel
Fabian Busch
Rafael Ferro
Erica Rivas
Alice Dwyer
Joachim Paul Assböck
Kristian Kiehling
Toñi Gomis Chaparro
Volkmar Kleinert
Roman Russo

Year:
2008

Synopsis

2008: Alex (Busch) visits his dying father Carlos (Ferro) in Buenos Aires. Towards the end of the 1970s, the Argentine military had abducted Alex's uncle, the brother of his mother Lizzie (Rivas); Lizzie, Carlos and Alex fled to West Berlin. Their new home was an open plan loft in an old factory building, which they shared with several individuals: photographer Jürgen (Assböck) and his girlfriend Anita (Chaparro), one-eyed cinematographer and womanizer Micha (Kiehling), introverted Sik (Dwyer), paraplegic con artist Günter (Kleinert) and Andrea (Russo), an aspiring film-maker and Günter's carer. Lizzie was a journalist with a busy schedule, while Carlos, a graphic artist, made a living from occasional blue-collar jobs or as a street painter. The parents' relationship suffered as Carlos was homesick for Argentina, but Lizzie decided never to return there. Carlos's affair with Anita initiated the break-up of Alex's extended family: Sik disappeared, Jürgen died in a car accident, Anita and Carlos moved to Argentina, and Günter and Andrea relocated to Italy. Fast forward to 2008 Buenos Aires: Alex sits at Carlos's deathbed and subsequently forgives him for leaving his wife and son.

Critique

Inspired by his own biographical background, *Berlin – Buenos Aires* is Alejandro Cardenas-Amelio's first feature film. The Argentine director was born in Peru in 1977 and immigrated to Germany for political reasons in the 1980s. Spatially and temporally framed by images of contemporary Buenos Aires that Alex views from a taxi window, the film delves into his childhood memories. Arriving in West Berlin – depicted as an enclave of punks, squatters and other outsiders – Alex finds an extended family among a similarly odd social mixture. The outside world enters the lives of the factory loft inhabitants only occasionally through newspapers, radio and television; an aesthetic device that dates the narrative (Helmut Kohl winning the elections in 1982, AIDS becoming a concern in West Germany, the 1986 soccer World Cup championship in Mexico). In a self-reflexive manner, *Berlin – Buenos Aires* conceives of film-making as a dream that one follows, a passion with visual images, or simply as a source of income. At times the space resembles a film studio or transforms into a makeshift cinema: an old projector screens Weimar film classics watched by an audience sitting on kitchen chairs in front of a screen made from bed linen. Florian Schilling's fluid camerawork supports the imaginative quality of this place.

The conflict between Carlos and Lizzie is explored in spatial terms. As the breadwinner of the family Lizzie is immersed in her work as a journalist and is therefore often absent. She has cut her ties with Argentina because of the atrocities that befell her family. Carlos, on the other hand, lives like a hermit; the house becomes his protective shell from the outside world. His predicament as an unemployed immigrant and his wife's success emasculate him, triggering his affair with Anita. In its spatial symbolism, the film can be read as a counter-example to Tevfik Ba er's *Forty Square Metres of Germany* (1986), where a Turkish woman is locked up by her husband in a small apartment. In Cardenas-Amelio's film the doors are open, living space is plentiful and Carlos is expected to use it. Instead of exploring the reasons for Carlos' homesickness and his refusal to engage with his environment, the film views the condition of the exile as a self-pitying state of mind. When a grown-up Alex returns to Buenos Aires, his estranged and disconnected feelings towards Argentina reflect the film's indifference to Carlos's cultural identity. Germany has become 'normal' and 'us', while Argentina is strange and 'Other'. By spatially dividing 'Germans' and 'Argentines', the film reinforces cultural stereotypes as valid reasons for feeling displaced.

Claudia Sandberg

References

Fisher, Jaimey (2003), '*Globalisierungsbewältigung*'/'Coming to Terms With Globalization: Global Flows and Local Loyalties in Contemporary German Cinema', *Genre*, 36: 3/4.

Sarrazin, Thilo (2009), 'Klasse statt Masse', *Lettre International*, 86, pp. 198–99.

QUEER GERMAN CINEMA

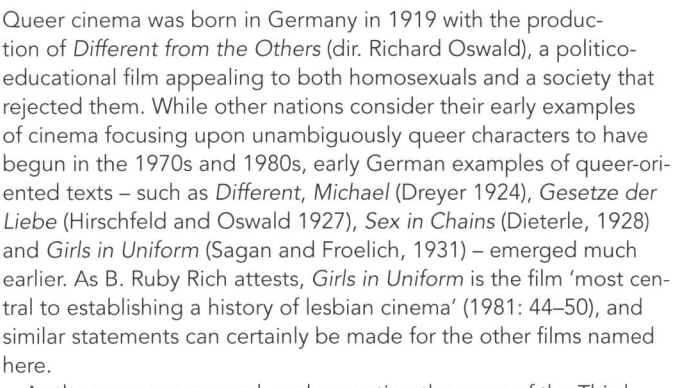

Queer cinema was born in Germany in 1919 with the production of *Different from the Others* (dir. Richard Oswald), a politico-educational film appealing to both homosexuals and a society that rejected them. While other nations consider their early examples of cinema focusing upon unambiguously queer characters to have begun in the 1970s and 1980s, early German examples of queer-oriented texts – such as *Different*, *Michael* (Dreyer 1924), *Gesetze der Liebe* (Hirschfeld and Oswald 1927), *Sex in Chains* (Dieterle, 1928) and *Girls in Uniform* (Sagan and Froelich, 1931) – emerged much earlier. As B. Ruby Rich attests, *Girls in Uniform* is the film 'most central to establishing a history of lesbian cinema' (1981: 44–50), and similar statements can certainly be made for the other films named here.

As the years progressed, and excepting the years of the Third Reich, Germany continued to lead the world in the production of films featuring queer characters and relationships. As the 1970s dawned, queer auteurs such as Rainer Werner Fassbinder and Rosa von Praunheim broke new ground. Each of these directors were unapologetic in their engagement with queer characters and politics, as can clearly be seen in the provocative title of von Praunheim's *It is Not the Homosexual Who Is Perverse, but the Society in Which He Lives* (1971), a film advocating visibility politics. Several of Fassbinder's films, such as *The Bitter Tears of Petra von Kant* (1972), *Fox and His Friends* (1975) and *Querelle* (1982), feature complicated and dark queer relationships, and can perhaps be seen as the precursor to the new queer cinema movement that emerged in the United States in the 1990s.

Madame X: An Absolute Ruler (1978) also gained significant critical attention, likewise thematizing power relations within the context of a queer, postmodern pirate film. Another important queer German film from the 1970s is *The Consequence* (Petersen, 1977). This work depicted the dire consequences of homophobia, adapted from an autobiographical novel by schoolteacher Alexander Ziegler.

The 1980s saw expansion upon such representations, with films such as *Taxi zum Klo* (Ripploh, 1981) providing an examination of the queer life of the period. *Berlin Blues* (1983) saw von Praunheim continue his innovations with an avant-garde queer musical. Also directed by von Praunheim, *A Virus Has No Morals* (1986) engaged with the pressing issue of HIV/AIDS. Avoiding the melodrama of later films engaging with the subject, von Praunheim's work is experimental, political and strangely prophetic.

Celebrated German film-maker Werner Schroeter's film *The Rose King* (1986), like the work of Schroeter's compatriots, depicts a queer love riddled with sadism and symbolism. During the same period the work of auteur Monika Treut first came to public attention with *Seduction: the Cruel Woman* (with Elfi Mikesch, 1985), *Virgin Machine* (1988) and *My Father is Coming* (1991). In these films Treut explores the terrain of sexual/gendered fluidity and sadomasochism, encouraged no doubt by the contemporaneous sex wars, and 'variously discover[s] new ways of expressing how multi-centred realities can be,' challenging 'static views of identity alignment' (Kuzniar 2000: 159). Treut's transnational settings and address assisted in

Left: *Lola and Billy the Kid*, Boje Buck Produktion/Westdeutscher Rundfunk (WDR)/Zero Film GmbH.

bringing diverse international audiences to her work, highlighting the popularity of co-production and diverse settings that increased in later work by German film-makers focusing on queer issues.

A key theme emerging in queer German cinema has been that of re-envisioning the past lives of Germany's homosexuals. Films such as *November Moon* (von Grote, 1985) and *Aimee & Jaguar* (Färberböck, 1999) are both set during the tumultuous period of the Second World War. Farberbock's interpretation of Lily Wurst's autobiographical story is framed as an aesthetically beautiful romance despite its negative outcome, and the film gained significant international popularity. Both *Aimee* and *November Moon* feature Jewish lesbian characters, acknowledging the fear and suffering of multiple German minority communities during this period, and recognizing the differential positions of lesbians and gay men during Nazi rule.

Colonel Redl (Szabó, 1985), a German/Hungarian/Austrian co-production, also took up such themes, with its narrative based on the true story of a homosexual officer blackmailed on the basis of his sexuality. *Legend of Rita* (Schlöndorff, 2000) engages in representing lesbian relationships, likewise within a particular historical context – in this case featuring a character from within the Movement 2 June, a terrorist movement of the 1970s allied with the Red Army Faction. Other films, such as *Gallant Girls* (Teufel, 2002), depict a past of feminist communes and the situational feminist lesbianism that arose in such environments; while von Praunheim's *The Einstein of Sex* (1999) re-envisioned the life of Magnus Hirschfeld and his associates, bringing to the screen a slice of queer history frequently overlooked.

A dark world for queer characters is depicted in such films as *Coming Out* (Carow, 1989), made in the former East Germany, which explores a gay schoolteacher's journey toward self-identification; while the period film *Love in Thoughts* (von Borries, 2004) also featured an angst fuelled narrative based on real-life murders. *Oi! Warning* (Ben Reding and Dominik Reding 1999), in contrast, was set in contemporary times, depicting a world of skinheads, punks, and violence.

As of the late 1990s various examples of queer German cinema began to emerge, with a sophisticated understanding of queer identity as intersectional with issues of race and nationality. The work of Angelina Maccarone, whose film career began with the made-for-television *Kommt Mausi Raus?!* (with Scherer, 1995), featured such characterisations in her later works *Everything Will Be Fine* (1998) and *Unveiled* (2005). The latter's engagement with the difficulties faced by an immigrant living illegally in Germany is likewise explored in *Kleine Frieheit* (Yavuz, 2003).

Lola and Billy the Kid (1999) brought into focus representations of Turkish-German queer identities, an engagement continued in Fatih Akin's *The Edge of Heaven* (2007). The sexual and racial identities of the protagonist of *Return to Go* (Sanoussi-Bliss, 2000) are further complicated by his HIV-positive status. The characters in these films engage not only with a world hostile to their queer identities, but one in which the characters' very status as Germans is rejected by racist elements of a predominantly white society.

In *Ghosted* (2009), Treut takes queer border crossing to a new level in her film set in both Taipei and Hamburg, with a tale that unhinges the boundaries between life and death. Each of these films represent a new age of queer cinema, where sexuality is not the primary 'issue' of the film, and border crossing is further developed as a theme. This is the case too with such films as *4 Minutes* (2006), where sexuality takes a secondary role to incarceration, both literal and metaphoric, and performance is used as a motif of queerness, as is argued here by Mueller.

Along with such independent work, and in keeping with contemporary movements in queer-focused cinema from around the world, German film also moved towards genre film in such films as Rolf Silber's *Regular Guys* (1996), which engaged with the discovery of attraction and romance from within a hybridized form of the crime genre. *Killer*

Condom (Walz, 1996) likewise blurred distinctions between the comedy and horror genres within the context of a parodic B movie.

Films such as *Guys and Balls* (Horman, 2004) stepped away from such hybridity, taking the prototypical sport genre of an underdog team versus a stronger one and turning it into a queer soccer team challenging a homophobic group of soccer players to a match. In doing so it interrogated notions of queer masculinities, as well as being one of the few films worldwide that represent queer polyamourous relationships. An example of a queer travel film can be seen in *Longing* (Brüning, 2003), which was primarily set in Brazil, while the frequently queered genre of the prison film became even more explicit in *Locked Up* (Andreas, 2004).

Coming-of-age films such as *Summer Storm* (Kreuzpaintner, 2004) and *Sonja* (Liimatainen, 2006) reached out to younger audiences, with the former including not only a coming out story, but examples of young and proud gay Germans. While such films rendered queer youth sexuality explicit, less direct homoeroticism remained in German film, as can be seen, for example, in the depiction of the brutal teens in *Out of Hand* (Urthaler, 2005).

There has not, however, been an unambiguous shift into the more normative genre film, with directors such as Bruce LaBruce blending politics with pornography in their work, including *The Raspberry Reich* (2004). This work not only blended genres but also hearkened back to the more avant-garde history of German queer cinema. Likewise, *Agnes and his Brothers* (Roehler, 2004) also lacked a definitive position in terms of genre, representing a transsexual character in a fairly mainstream comedy/drama situated within a familial context.

A little over 90 years since the first example of queer German cinema was released, German cinema has continued to produce work focusing on queer characters, themes and relationships. Not just a key pioneer of queer representation within film, as the years have progressed German cinema has also continued to push boundaries, both aesthetic and thematic, and both the number and diversity of queer filmic texts from Germany have increased. As we move into the future, no doubt we will continue to see innovative work produced by German film-makers that will explore the shifting intricacies of queer life.

Rebecca Beirne

Different from the Others

Anders als die Andern

Production Company:
Richard-Oswald-Produktion

Distributors:
Filmmuseum München

Director:
Richard Oswald

Producer:
Richard Oswald

Screenwriters:
Richard Oswald
Magnus Hirschfeld

Cinematographer:
Max Fassbender

Composer:
Joachim Bärenz

Duration:
50 minutes

Genre:
Drama
Aufklärungsfilme ('educational film')
Queer Cinema

Cast:
Conrad Veidt
Reinhold Schünzel
Fritz Schulz
Anita Berber
Magnus Hirschfeld

Year:
1919

Synopsis

The film centres on the relationship between Paul Körner (Veidt), a virtuoso violinist, and his student Kurt Sivers (Schulz) – a relationship disrupted by Franz Bollek (Schünzel), who extorts Paul under Paragraph 175 of the German penal code prohibiting sex between men. Flashback scenes depict Paul's difficult encounters with school authorities, the medical establishment, and blackmailers in the homosexual subculture. Furthermore, the film is interrupted by an extended illustrated lecture by Magnus Hirschfeld on sexual intermediacy. Paul is ultimately sentenced to one week in prison under the Paragraph, and his concert agency cancels his tour and terminates his contract on account of the ensuing scandal. After Paul poisons himself, Kurt joins him at his bedside, along with both Hirschfeld and members of Paul's and Kurt's families. Hirschfeld urges Kurt to become an activist rather than another suicide case.

Critique

Surveys of queer German cinema often begin with Austrian-Jewish director Richard Oswald's *Different from the Others*, a film many scholars characterize as the first to explicitly thematize homosexuality (Steakley 1999: 181). Furthermore, texts on the turbulent reception history of the film lend it not only a precocious, but also a precursory quality; the backlash against the film and its eventual censorship are seen to anticipate the reactionary and exclusionary politics of the Nazi regime. Rather than positioning the film as a precocious or precursor text, however, I would place it in the context of the concerns of Europe's 'long nineteenth century,' including scientific discourses of race and sexuality, ideologies of the nation-state and body politic, and debates over the role of photography and cinema in the Enlightenment project. Additionally, instead of prioritizing the film's homosexual thematic, I would instead emphasize the inextricable linkage of homosexuality and Jewishness in both the film and the debates it provoked.

The turbulent reception history of *Different from the Others* may seem surprising given the film's discernible strategies to grant respectability to abject figures and lend legitimacy to its own project. One notes, for example, that the film evokes the Hellenic tradition and aesthetic, which served as the basis for the German masculine ideal and a leading model for national self-representation beginning in the nineteenth century (Mosse 1985: 16). Additionally, Oswald's film disavows its own hypnotic suggestiveness and insists on the didactic power of the visual, particularly through inclusion of an illustrated lecture by sexologist Magnus Hirschfeld and frequent use of iris shots. Finally, *Different from the Others* appeals to Enlightenment ideals via Hirschfeld's lecture and notable references to the Oscar Wilde trials and the Dreyfus Affair, which serve as exemplary instances of *Justizverbrechen* ('judiciary injustices') such as the one that the film's protagonist confronts.

Despite these strategic efforts, Oswald's *Aufklärungsfilm* ('Enlightenment' or 'educational film') crystallized widespread anxieties around cinema, Jewishness and homosexuality, all of which were perceived as contaminous and unwieldy elements of the German body politic. Thus, in an alarmist report of a tumultuous screening of the film in Berlin, the *Deutsche Zeitung* observed that a scene featuring cross-dressed characters prompted cries such as 'Should we Germans let ourselves be contaminated by the Jews?' A contemporaneous response to this article in *Film-Kurier*, tellingly entitled 'Homosexuality and Judaism: The Newest Method of Agitation Against the *Aufklärungsfilme*,' noted 'the almost unbelievable fact that the blame for homosexuality is now also placed on the Jews' (Friedmann 1919).

In my analysis, while the retraction of Germany's censorship laws after World War I enabled the release of *Different from the Others*, the film was later banned from public exhibition on account of discourses prevalent at the time of Germany's defeat. Indeed, the film was released directly after the Great War, which called Enlightenment ideals into question and promoted both anxieties around masculinity and theories that Jews and other groups had sabotaged the war effort from within the country's borders. Despite the film's gestures towards national ideals of manliness and bourgeois norms of respectability, detractors zeroed in on its apparent espousal of a mode of homosexuality coded as effeminate and Jewish. I would thus argue that in the wake of both the 'long nineteenth century' and the Great War with its deleterious effects on the body politic, Germans were disinclined to tolerate a film associated with two groups whose abjection fostered a sense of national coherence.

Nicholas Baer

Girls in Uniform

Mädchen in Uniform

Production Company:
Deutsche Film-Gemeinschaft

Distributors:
Bild und Ton GmbH (Germany)
Filmchoice (USA)

Directors:
Leontine Sagan
Carl Froelich

Producers:
Carl Fröhlich
Friedrich Pflughaupt

Synopsis

Girls in Uniform, based in Christa Winsloe's play *Yesterday and Today*, portrays the experiences of Manuela von Meinhardis (Thiele) in Fräulein von Nordeck zur Nidden's (Unda) boarding school. The biggest difference between the text and the movie being that Manuela survives in the movie whereas she commits suicide on stage. The institution runs on strict Prussian values, preparing the girls for their final destination – to be mothers of soldiers. Manuela, having lost her mother, latches on to the school's most popular teacher, Fräulein von Bernburg (Wieck). In contrast to the principal who rules with fear and intimidation, Bernburg uses her students' adoration to motivate them to achieve and perform within the value system of the status quo. Manuela's attraction to Fräulein von Bernburg grows until she can no longer control herself and reveals her feelings for her teacher at a party to celebrate the students' performance of Schiller's *Don Carlos*. Dressed as Don Carlos, in

Screenwriters:
Christa Winsloe
Friedrich Dammann, based on Winsloe's play

Art Directors:
Fritz Maurischat
Friedrich Winkler-Tannenberg

Cinematographers:
Reimar Kuntze
Franz Weihmayr

Composer:
Hanson Milde-Meissner

pants, Manuela steps outside the restrictive gender roles of the boarding school and publicly professes her love for Fräulein von Bernburg to an audience which also includes the principal. Since Manuela's coming out threatens the status quo of the boarding school, the principal isolates the girl until her guardian can pick her up, because she needs to permanently remove the threat that Manuela poses. Unable to bear the prospect of losing her beloved teacher Manuela tries to commit suicide by throwing herself down the main stairwell in the school, but is saved by the other girls. Fräulein von Bernburg, too, joins them, after having defended Manuela's attraction to the headmistress by arguing for the existence of a thousand different forms of love. The survival of Manuela breaks the spell of the headmistress, so that in the final scene of the movie the girls no longer curtsey, but openly defy her authority.

Girls in Uniform, Deutsche Film-Gemeinschaft.

Editor:
Oswald Hafenrichter

Duration:
98 minutes

Genre:
Drama

Cast:
Hertha Thiele
Emilia Unda
Dorothea Wieck
Hedwig Schlichter
Ellen Schwanneke

Year:
1931

Critique

Girls in Uniform is part of the radical and innovative cinema of the Weimar Republic and a classic of queer cinema even today. Celebrated as an all female movie, with an all-female cast, a female director and a female screenwriter, albeit under the guidance of a male producer, the film ties into the German feminist movement of the Twenties and Thirties. In the early Seventies the movie was rediscovered by the feminist movement and made its way into women's film festivals, which led to renewed academic interest and wider distribution of the movie. With its critique of the Prussian militarism and the *Untertanenmentalität* ('subservient mentality') that goes along with it, the film gains prophetic status when read against the ascending Third Reich with its cult of leadership and obedience. Although the women in the movie live in an all female world, patriarchy provides the normative framework for the events portrayed in the movie. The opening scene invokes core institutions of patriarchy such as the church and the military. Omnipresent symbols such as the Prussian eagle and the bugle portray patriarchy as an inescapable backdrop. In this repressive and restricted context Manuela's coming out poses a major threat because it introduces uncontrollable elements such as emotions and eroticism. The movie thus exemplifies the theoretical discussion of sexologists at the time, in which lesbianism is described as sexual intermediacy; 'a concept […] which posits the existence of a third sex (comprising and conflating androgynes, hermaphrodites, homosexuals, transsexuals and transvestites)' (Kiss 2002: 48). Visually, the transgressive nature of the attraction between Fräulein von Bernburg and Manuela is represented in blurred images, most noticeable when the two women gaze at each other. These vague images obscure boundaries and pose a serious threat to a hierarchical system that depends on containing people by clearly labelling them. That Manuela's coming out happens when she wears pants adds to the sense of transgression that she embodies. Her pants place her in the area of sexual intermediacy; as a woman in men's clothing she engages in a playful deconstruction of gender and sexuality, where female characters and audience members can be attracted to other female characters.

Isolde Mueller

It Is Not the Homosexual Who Is Perverse, But the Society in Which He Lives

Nicht der Homosexuelle ist pervers, sondern die Situation, in der er lebt

Production Companies:
Bavaria Atelier
Westdeutscher Rundfunk (WDR)

Director:
Rosa von Praunheim

Producer:
Werner Kließ

Screenwriters:
Rosa von Praunheim
Martin Dannecker
Sigurd Wurl

Cinematographers:
Robert van Ackeren
Rosa von Praunheim (uncredited)

Editor:
Jean-Claude Peroué

Duration:
67 minutes

Genre:
Queer Cinema
Drama

Cast:
Berryt Bohlen
Bernd Feuerhelm
Ernst Kuchling
Norbert Losch

Year:
1971

Synopsis

Naïve country boy Daniel (Feuerhelm) moves to Berlin and encounters a thriving gay community. First, he meets Clemens (Bohlens), a more experienced lover, who takes Daniel under his wing. The two, in love, try to simulate a heterosexual marriage-like relationship, which falls apart after four months. Seduced instead by a rich, older man, Daniel moves into his villa, and is there introduced to a high society group of closeted men. The tables turned, Daniel is then betrayed by his lover. Dismayed, he leaves and finds a job in a local gay bar, becoming the most eligible bachelor in town. Here he learns to invest time in his outer appearance and in fashion. Thereafter, Daniel visits the gay scene on the beach looking for a pick-up, followed by gay bars, leather bars, public toilets and drag shows. At the end of the film, Daniel meets Paul at a transvestite bar, and follows him to a meeting of gay men. They try to convince Daniel that he must become an 'independent gay,' who is out, develops himself intellectually and emotionally, as well as someone who is active in the gay rights movement.

Critique

In essence, this film is at once a polemic and pedagogical caveat and political manifesto. By showcasing slices of gay life in Berlin, director Rosa von Praunheim aims to demonstrate the fact that, as the title suggests, the homosexual is not perverse, but instead just another human being. Perhaps surprisingly von Praunheim makes the argument, through his depictions of the locales in which gay men submerge themselves (the closeted men's club, the bar, public toilet and the S&M scene), that these locations, as the only safe meeting places for gays, do not necessarily promote healthy or happy human beings. Instead, gay men run to the men's club to try and control their sexuality through music and the arts. On the beach and in bars gay men are reduced, through external and even internalized homophobia, to mere objects of voyeurism and bodily pleasure for others. All other values of self worth become secondary to outer appearance and fashion. As explained by the voice-over narrators, who do most of the talking in the film, homosexuals have been forced to hide their sexuality from society, and have been subsequently pushed underground. Separated into groups according to the way in which each person deals with his fugitive state, gay men willingly spend time in desperate, dirty or even dangerous locations in order to meet other men. In a nutshell, von Praunheim argues that society oppresses the homosexual man to such a degree that he can only realistically meet his own kind in perverse places, where they are ultimately deprived of their humanity. The film ends with a call to arms: 'Out of the toilets, into the streets! Freedom for homosexuals!'

Like many of von Praunheim films, this too caused a scandal. Aired for the first time on German public television in 1973, Bavaria's conservative local channel refused to broadcast it. Despite its poor cinematography, the film has received some scholarly attention, focused largely on von Praunheim's message encapsulated in the title of the film, which has notably become an oft-used catch phrase of the gay liberation movement.

What makes von Praunheim's work so provocative as a queer director is his fearlessness, what others call audacity, to not only point the finger at society, but also at the gay community itself as guilty of homophobia. Von Praunheim has played this role as leader and moral compass in other films, including *A Virus Has No Morals* (1986), where he scolds the gay community for their apathy towards HIV/AIDS. Von Praunheim's incorporation of a would-be manifesto for gay liberation, outlined by the men's group in the film, is particularly compelling. Historically speaking, this film captures a German call to action for gay rights; first, following the student protests of 1968 and, perhaps more importantly, the Stonewall riots in 1969. In von Praunheim's manifesto his tenets call for the organization of better bars, better doctors and legal protections in the work place. Even more significantly, they call for a united front with the women's rights movement and even the Black liberation movement and the Black Panthers. The fact that von Praunheim included the Black Panthers calls upon a historically unlikely connection to be made in Germany at that time, and therefore signifies a remarkably far-reaching move on von Praunheim's part.

Samantha Michele Riley

The Bitter Tears of Petra von Kant

Die Bitteren Tränen der Petra von Kant

Production Companies:
Filmverlag der Autoren
Tango Film

Distributors:
Filmverlag der Autoren (West Germany)
New Yorker Films (USA)

Director:
Rainer Werner Fassbinder

Synopsis

This film, based on Fassbinder's stageplay, is highly theatrical: a five-act structure (with fade-outs/fade-ins between acts) and a single set like the original. Only the ending differs. We open on Petra (Carstensen), a successful, recently divorced 36-year-old fashion designer, and Marlene (Hermann), her long-suffering, non-speaking servant and co-designer. Soon, Sidonie (Schaake), Petra's friend, arrives and they discuss their rival views of relationships, freedom and love. Later, Sidonie's 23-year-old, working-class friend Karin (Schygulla) joins them and Petra immediately desires her. Petra and Karin subsequently seduce each other, and agree to a working/sexual relationship, all to the rhythms of Marlene's typewriter in the background. Six months later Karin admits to having an affair with a black man, 'just for fun.' Petra is shattered. Karin leaves Petra to return to her husband, who has come back from Australia. As Petra drinks through her birthday she receives visits from her daughter (Mattes), her mother (Fackeldey), and Sidonie – who present her with a doll that resembles Karin. Petra berates them for being prostitutes and lechers and tramples her own tea set. Everyone leaves. In the final act, Petra turns to Marlene almost tenderly and says, 'Tell me about yourself.' Marlene packs her suit-

Producers:
Rainer Werner Fassbinder
Michael Fengler

Screenwriter:
Rainer Werner Fassbinder

Cinematographer:
Michael Ballhaus

Editor:
Thea Eymèsz

Duration:
124 minutes

case, including a handgun and the Karin doll, and leaves without a word.

Critique

A more appropriate title for this film might be *The Silent Gestures of Marlene*, as it is dedicated 'to him who here becomes Marlene,' and we learn most about the characters, their situations, and *becoming* through her articulate silences and gestures. Marlene's first gesture begins the human action of the film when she enters Petra's bedroom/studio and opens the blinds. As the sun falls across Petra's face she says, 'Marlene [...] be more considerate [...] please!' This is the only time we hear Petra say 'please' to

The Bitter Tears of Petra von Kant, Filmverlag der Autoren/Tango Film.

Genre:
Operatic Melodrama

Cast:
Margit Carstensen
Hanna Schygulla
Irm Hermann
Katrin Schaake
Eva Mattes
Gisela Fackeldey

Year:
1972

Marlene. Marlene turns to listen to Petra as she begins to tell about her dream. However, Petra stops and demands Marlene bring the phone. This sadomasochistic rapport is the norm of the film. Petra abuses, chides and belittles Marlene until the final act. Marlene bends to Petra's will until her final exit, the concluding gesture of the film that undermines all previous assumptions about that rapport.

The Bitter Tears of Petra von Kant (1972) draws out the tensions within relationships across sexualities and the power dynamics among love, desire and social contracts. It depicts a female homosocial space within patriarchy through a diegesis in which men only appear through paintings, newspapers and stories. It is concerned with class differences and the cruelty of capitalism and marks the ways these systems of oppression enact violence on the body. It is also a film that focuses our attention on the force of lying, the violence that attends this force and the gestures that may resist it, even when they are not visible to the liar.

Petra orders her world from her bed in the centre of this white room, a whiteness interrupted by bold colour arrangements. On one side, a wall-sized mural of Poussin's 1629 'Midas and Bacchus' and its nude phallus frames her. On the other side is Marlene's work area and the collection of nude, white female mannequins

The Bitter Tears of Petra von Kant, Filmverlag der Autoren/Tango Film.

that mirror/mock the faces and bodies of the women. At the centre of it all, Petra and her lies seem to control the world around her. In the first act, she lies in the letter she dictates to Marlene. (Fassbinder's acknowledgement of his debt to Joseph Mankiewicz's *All About Eve* [1950]). In Act 3, after Karin resists telling Petra she loves her, Petra tells her, 'Lie to me,' and Karin says, 'I love you.' Petra even lies to herself; she is the great pretender. ('The Great Pretender' by The Platters is the song Petra plays as Marlene packs her bag and leaves.)

Here, lies are about control, discipline and attention. These are the lessons Petra promises and gives to Karin. Lies order chaos, anarchy and neglect. However, lies are also fragile structures that give way under the pressure of gestures that resist and reveal them. Such resistance is the effect of Marlene's gestures – first on us and then on Petra at the end of the film.

Marlene's gestures do not so much reflect or refract Petra; rather, words are rejected and repaid with gestures. Marlene's gestures speak back to Petra's rhetoric even when Petra does not see them: Marlene's hand pressing a windowpane; her tears rolling down her cheeks; her compulsive typing and then sudden halting; her mistaken turn at the midpoint of the film; her look when Petra spits in Karin's face; and her twitching hand that even she may not notice betray the disordering of Petra's world. In the final scene Petra claims she will give Marlene 'what you're entitled to: freedom and fun.' Marlene stoops and kisses Petra's hand. In her final attempt at control, Petra asserts, 'Not like that. Tell me about yourself.' In response, Marlene rises, packs and walks out, leaving Petra alone on her bed, where she had lain at the beginning of the film.

Brian K. Bergen-Aurand

Fox and His Friends

Faustrecht der Freiheit

Production Companies:
City Film
Tango Film

Distributor:
New Yorker Film (USA)

Director:
Rainer Werner Fassbinder

Producer:
Rainer Werner Fassbinder

Synopsis

Franz 'Fox' Biberkopf (Fassbinder) is a fairground performer put out of work by a police raid. Convinced it is his lucky day Fox buys a lottery ticket, which wins him 500,000 DM. With his new money comes a new set of friends, a new lover, Eugen (Chatel), apartment, car and partnership in a business. But only his old friends seem to recognize that Fox is being taken advantage of by this new circle, especially Eugen. Almost immediately, Eugen begins to critique the way Fox dresses, behaves, eats and carries himself. He persuades Fox to invest 100,000 DM in the family business, telling him he will become a partner. He convinces him to buy new clothes and new furniture and to pay for a three-week vacation in Morocco. All the while, Fox tells Eugen he loves him. Eugen never responds. Fox becomes ill and begins taking Valium. A short time later, he breaks up with Eugen, who steals everything, locks Fox from their apartment, and invites his old lover to return. Left with only a car he cannot sell for a fair price, Fox overdoses on the Valium and

Screenwriters:
Rainer Werner Fassbinder
Christian Hohoff

Cinematographer:
Michael Ballhaus

Composer:
Peer Raben

Editor:
Thea Eymèsz

Duration:
123 minutes

Genre:
Melodrama
Queer Cinema

Cast:
Rainer Werner Fassbinder
Peter Chatel
Karlheinz Böhm
Kurt Raab
El Hedi ben Salem
Rudolf Lenz
Karl Scheydt
Harry Baer
Christiane Maybach

Year:
1975

dies in a subway station. In the final scene, as his friends abandon his body to avoid involvement, two boys rifle through his pockets and steal his jacket.

Critique

'Für Armin und alles anderen.' ('For Armin and all the others')

This dedication marks the opening of Fassbinder's highly regarded essay on friendship, money and love – three themes his films never seem to abandon. One of the film-maker's most sympathetic character studies, surprisingly this later film (Fassbinder's twenty-fifth) is his first direct depiction of a homosexual love story between men. For all its sympathies (and comedic first half) though, the film turns to the dark sides of these relationships and the humiliation and final destruction of its main character, played by Fassbinder, in what has often been seen as an ambivalent acknowledgement of his relationship with Armin Meier, who would commit suicide in 1978. While Fassbinder had often focused on male friendship or homosexual relationships as an alternative to the failures of marriage, here the gay characters offer no antidote.

Fox and His Friends is most often understood as a display of the negative. From the opening fairground scene, where paying a fee will gain you admission to the freak show, to the final moments, where Fox's dead body is robbed of all its belongings in an empty, silent subway station, the film dwells on a society ready to exchange any person for any price. It is no mistake the music at the end echoes the music at the start. Everything and everyone is a commodity here. Everything and everyone has its price. Some are higher and some lower, but nothing is outside this economy. Eugen is the obvious example because he values Fox only as long as Fox has money, and Eugen uses this money to take control of everything around him, including his family's printing factory. Furthermore, Max is happy to profit from the couple's ostentatious furniture purchases. Eugen's friend is happy to sell them an overpriced apartment. Philip (Baer), Eugen's other lover, is happy to sell Fox expensive clothing at his boutique. Eugen's family and their lawyer do not hesitate to swindle Fox with a 'standard contract.' At the end of the film, Max and Klaus (Scheydt) (Fox's former lover) are plotting to smuggle drugs when they come across Fox's body. Even Hedwig (Maybach), Fox's alcoholic sister, demands money from him after he loses everything. And finally, Fox too is as guilty as the rest, as we see him and Eugen 'buying' a lover in Morocco (played by Fassbinder's former lover, the Algerian actor El Hedi ben Salem) and bullying a hotel employee because he is a paying guest. Relationships here are like the twisting and spiralling architecture, baroque furniture or gaudy apparel throughout the film. Nothing is direct. Everything lies behind a turn or corner or within a shallow decoration that reveals the overwhelming despair of humans turned to things bought and sold.

Although many critics compare Fox with Petra von Kant, seeing them as two images of homosexual obsession and self-destruction, the stronger comparison might be made between Fox and Maria Braun. While he repeatedly claimed that it was beside the point that *Fox* was about gays, he also noted that '[H]omosexuality is probably a factor in all my films [...] not all have a gay subject, but they all have the point of view of one gay man.' Neither Fox nor Maria is defeated by their sexuality, per se, but by the economics of interpersonal relations. Perhaps by seeing Fox and Maria as two characters who love but are cheated at love by *contracts*, we can see Fassbinder was more closely aligning homosexual men and heterosexual women than has previously been acknowledged.

Brian K. Bergen-Aurand

Madame X: An Absolute Ruler

Madame X – Eine absolute Herrscherin

Production Companies:
Autorenfilm-Produktionsgemeinschaft
Zweites Deutsches Fernsehen (ZDF)

Director:
Ulrike Ottinger
Tabea Blumenschein

Screenwriter:
Ulrike Ottinger

Cinematographer:
Ulrike Ottinger

Art Director:
Tabea Blumenschein

Editor:
Dörte Völz

Duration:
147 minutes

Genre:
Adventure
Melodrama
Queer Cinema

Synopsis

A woman's voice beckons to a diverse array of women: '*Chinese Orlando* – stop – to all women – stop – offer world – stop – full of gold – stop – love – stop – adventure at sea – stop – call *Chinese Orlando* – stop.' The message goes out to a German forest ranger Flora Tannenbaum (Skoda), an artist Josephine de Collage (Rainer), an American housewife Betty Brille (Lutze), a clinical psychologist Karla Freud-Goldmund (von Cube), an Italian model Blowup (von Lichtenstein), an Australian pilot Omega Centauri (Mona), and a native of Tai-Pi, Noa-Noa (Janz). All join the crew of the Chinese junk *Orlando* ruled by Madame X (Blumenschein). Along the way they pick up Belcampo (Taylor), a cast-away of ambiguous sex. The crew learn of Madame X's lover Orlando, how she was drowned by a giant octopus and how Madame X lost one of her arms trying to save her. The crew is challenged to 'win over' the cold-hearted dictator. The pirate ship lures, captures and destroys a 'ship of leisure' only to be destroyed in turn by jealousy and betrayal. In the end all the passengers but Belcampo and Noa-Noa die, but in this context death is merely a metaphor for change and rebirth.

Critique

Ottinger's first feature parodies the traditionally male genre of the pirate film and uses it to critique patriarchal power structures. The film is also a critique of feminism and the women's movement at the time. On board the ship a strict hierarchy is in place with Madame X as the absolute ruler (as indicated by the title). Ottinger has argued that the women's movement also centred around such figures, recreating the very structures of power it was attempting to dismantle. Ottinger was criticized for what was seen as an attack on feminist ideals but contended that self-critique was necessary for the political strength of the movement. The film also critiques the exclusionary practice of 'women only' spaces and participation in political action, as well as throwing depictions of 'lesbian' sexuality into question through the figure of Belcampco, whose sex will determine whether or not he/she is able to stay on board

Cast:
Tabea Blumenschein
Monika von Cube
Roswitha Janz
Irena von Lichtenstein
Lutze
Mona
Yvonne Rainer
Claudia Skoda
Mackay Taylor

Year:
1978

the *Orlando* (if a woman she can stay, if a man he'll be thrown overboard). Belcampo is 'tested' by the clinical psychologist Karla Freud-Goldmund to determine her/his sex and subsequent fate. Along with the rest of the crew Belcampo lampoons the test to the point of absurdity, and gender binaries, as constructed by patriarchal psychology, are shown to be severely limiting and constraining. As a result of the test, however, it is decided that Belcampo is enough of a 'woman' to stay on the ship. The women are enticed to the ship with promises of, amongst other things, love. Since it is a homosocial ship of women this is an offer of lesbian love, which the women engage in wholeheartedly, but love also becomes a source of jealousy and discord.

Deliberately working against classical narrative style, the narrative is disjointed and fragmentary. The film does not try to create a seamless 'reality' but instead constructs a highly theatrical space where these broad representations of 'women' play out a melodrama of love, jealously, power struggles and betrayal. The sound is post-dubbed and is often mismatched with the visuals. The film is awash with quotations, aural and visual, literary and cinematic, including bits of soundtrack from several Hollywood movies. The choice to post-dub the sound was initially prompted by the film's miniscule budget, but later became a deliberate stylistic choice for Ottinger in her bigger budget films. The costumes and make-up are theatrical with Madame X's outfit resembling leather fetish wear or something from a science fiction film. The performance styles are also highly theatrical, recalling both pantomime and silent film acting with the holding of broad gestures and expressions. It is also apparent that the ship is never on the 'high seas' but rather Lake Constance (the location where most of film was shot). The film's theatrical costumes and performances, post-dubbed sound that doesn't match the visuals, obscure aural and visual quotations, jump cuts, surreal and absurd imagery and lack of coherent narrative all encourage a detached rather than immersed mode of viewing. In this sense the film seems to take up some of Laura Mulvey's arguments about how male centred Hollywood conventions should be subverted in terms of style as well as content (1989).

Ottinger's work has come to be considered by some, if in a marginal sense, to be part of New German Cinema. The film was made on an incredibly small budget with funding provided to the project substantially less than those of her (mostly) male art cinema counterparts at the time. The position of *Madame X*'s and indeed much of Ottinger's representations of queer sexuality sits in some ways apart from representations of lesbian sexuality. In *Madame X* this is partly to do with gender-queer or transgender representations, as well as dominance and submission and sadomasochistic role-playing, both of which throw conventional representations of lesbian sexuality into question.

Louise Malcolm

Querelle

Production Companies:
Planet-Film
Albatros Filmproduktion
Gaumont

Distributors:
Scotia (West Germany)
Triumph Releasing Corporation (USA)

Director:
Rainer Werner Fassbinder

Producer:
Dieter Schidor

Screenwriters:
Burkhard Driest
Rainer Werner Fassbinder
Kurt Raab (uncredited), based on the novel by Jean Genet

Art Director:
Walter E. Richarz

Cinematographers:
Xavier Schwarzenberger
Joseph Vavra

Composers:
Peer Raben

Editors:
Juliane Lorenz
Rainer Werner Fassbinder (as Franz Walsch)

Duration:
108 minutes

Genre:
Thriller
Detective Story

Cast:
Brad Davis
Franco Nero
Jeanne Moreau
Laurent Malet
Hanno Pöschl
Günther Kaufmann

Synopsis

Querelle (Davis) is a sailor and smuggler aboard the *Vengeur*, who arrives in Brest and meets his brother, Robert (Malet). Robert is passing time as the lover of Lysiane (Moreau), co-owner with her husband Nono (Kaufmann) of the Feria, an infamous local brothel. At the Feria, you can have your fortune read by Lysiane and throw dice with Nono for your pick of the prostitutes. But if you lose, Nono gets you. Querelle and his accomplice, Vic (Schidor), smuggle opium ashore to sell to Nono. In a double cross, Querelle kills Vic and keeps the money. Then, Querelle purposely loses to Nono. Meanwhile, Gil (Pöschl), a dockworker, kills another worker who has insulted his honour. Querelle is fascinated by their connection and vows to help Gil escape. Instead, Querelle betrays him to the police to be executed. Then, Querelle takes revenge on his brother by sleeping with Lysiane. But Querelle leaves her to return to the ship and surrenders himself to the Captain, who has always desired him. Or, is it all a dream? At the end, Lysiane turns over a new card and declares to Robert, 'You haven't got a brother.' We see Querelle reflected in the mirror behind her, and the film fades to the deck of the ship where the sailors move in reverse as they leave port.

Critique

> 'Each man kills the thing he loves' (from Oscar Wilde's 'The Ballad of Reading Gaol')

Unlike most critics, I was pulled into *Querelle* (1982) on my first viewing. The colours are garish and the sets fake: oppressively heavy yet paper-thin. The bodies are doubled, redoubled and replicated until they start to resemble one another and you have trouble telling characters apart: Hanno Pöschl plays Robert and Gil. The voices and voice-over become repetitive, dull, and heavy. The costumes are flamboyant and excessive, flowing yet revealing an overabundance of muscle and hair. The lighting is diffuse and unrealistic: candles do not flicker, a cut-out yellow sun never moves on the horizon. The intertitles fade to white, and one strangely timed freeze frame of Lysiane's face never let us forget we are watching a film. One oft-repeated line of a song, 'Each man kills the thing he loves,' echoes through every scene and imbeds itself in your memory. The dialogue is stiffly recalled or reported rather than delivered. Erect phalluses and testicles are strewn about the visual field: rising in stone from the city walls, etched in the glass of the Feria, or hastily graffitied on the sides of bridges and buildings. The final action is a repeat of the first scene in reverse. The Coda is a page from Jean Genet, from whose novel, *Querelle de Brest*, the film is adapted.

For some, there is little here to engage the seasoned viewer of Fassbinder's work and much to caution the novice. And yet, it is arguably his strongest depiction of the fluidity and repetition

Burkhard Driest
Dieter Schidor

Year:
1982

through which male bodies and masculinities move. *Querelle* is not like other identity-based gay and lesbian film-making emerging in the early 1980s, where the goal is to produce a positive image to foster a sympathetic audience. In fact, it is the film's obsession with the struggle of male bodies to differentiate and yet connect themselves that is so enthralling. In some ways *Querelle* is a return to Fassbinder's anti-theatre roots. In others it is his queerest, most deviant, perverse film because it refuses sympathetic or positive portrayals, instead passing through an indeterminate, polymorphous and unproductive queer time and space.

Querelle depicts a port town where the stone walls abut the sea. It is filled with hard bodies and hard surfaces. Yet, it is also filled with saliva, sweat and blood. Perversion and longing, love and betrayal, death and sex compete here. Bodies blend together, walkways lead nowhere or only double back on themselves. Querelle and the others double cross one another in every other scene. This is a queer film about a queer town and a queer bunch of characters, indeed. The film focuses on two brothers, linked through kinship and also through incest at an early age when, according to the voice-over, they would meet 'late in the evening in the shared bed in their room.' They repeat these encounters and their relation with their mother (also possibly incestuous) through their exchange of Lysiane and their self-hatred and rejection of being 'just fairies.' Repetition and return, like the waves breaking against the walls of the city. In the end the film rewinds itself to start again, to repeat what has just happened. And it is here, in this final shot of the men aboard the *Vengeur* that we get the image of the phallo-fraternity of friendship between men.

Each man kills the thing he loves not just by murdering it but also by repeating and replacing it so that he is just like all the others and it lives forever. *Querelle* is a rebuke of narcissism and homosexual self-loathing. However, it is also an argument about the fluidity beyond homosociality and homosexuality that resists such a future based on preservation or reproduction. Indeed, it is possible to suggest that the film is just as concerned with self-sacrifice as it is with the sacrifice of those around us. It is, after all, only when Querelle and the Avenger leave that laughter returns to the Feria.

Brian K. Bergen-Aurand

City of Lost Souls

Die Stadt der verlorenen Seelen

Synopsis

American expatriate and erotic trapeze artists Judith Flex and Tron von Hollywood arrive in the bohemia of West Berlin during the Cold War. Looking for work, they stumble upon a seedy restaurant, the 'Burger Queen,' owned by Angie Stardust, a black, pre-operative transsexual drag queen from Harlem. Here, the wait staff dance on the counter tops covered in rotting food, vomit and trash. The campy entourage, who also live in Angie's equally

Production Companies:
Hessischer Rundfunk (HR),
Sender Freies Berlin (SFB)

Director:
Rosa von Praunheim

Producer:
Rosa von Praunheim

Screenwriter:
Rosa von Praunheim

Art Director:
Inge Stiborski

Cinematographer:
Stephen Köster

Composer:
Holger Münzer

Editor:
Rosa von Praunheim

Duration:
91 minutes

Genre:
Queer Cinema
Musical
Comedy

Cast:
Wayne County
Angie Stardust
Manfred Finger
Judith Flex
Helga Goetze
Tron von Hollywood
Gary Miller
Tara O'Hara
Joaquin La Habana

Year:
1983

derelict hotel, includes Gary Miller, a black, erotic, interpretative dancer; Tara O'Hara, a feminine transvestite; Joaquin La Habana, a gender-bending, black, Latino actor, and the transsexuals Lila and Lola. Back at the Pension Stardust, where the Americans shack up, the housemates are plagued by various mishaps: the restaurant is robbed, and Gary burns the hotel to the ground, taking his own life and Tron's. The film culminates, however, with a more felicitous set of events, including Loretta getting a job as an actress in the 'Theatre of the West'; and Lila being offered her own TV show in East Germany as a communist rock star. In the final scene the friends unite (even from beyond the grave) to celebrate Lila's premiere, broadcasted live on television from East Berlin.

Critique

Like *The Rocky Horror Picture Show* (Sharman, 1975) and *Hedwig and the Angry Inch* (Mitchell, 2001), *City of Lost Souls* is a campy, cabaret-style, queer musical, directed by one of the most important figures in Queer German Cinema, Rosa von Praunheim. Known for his over-the-top, queer and politically charged films, von Praunheim's *City of Lost Souls* proves no exception. The plot is thin, made mostly of satirical dialogues and musical performances. Yet, through the mechanism of camp, the film engages with more serious political issues, including post-war politics and anxiety, fascism, anti-Semitism and questions of sexual, gender, racial, political, religious and geographically situated identities.

Through the mechanism of camp as a form of cultural critique, the film also incorporates citations of American cultural icons, such as those of Burger King, television footage of Ronald Reagan and the American flag. Cold War relations are explored through the lives of American expatriates living in Berlin. Judith and Tron seek work as *Gastarbeiter* ('guest-workers'), only to encounter red tape from a West German bureaucracy. Judith, who also narrates parts of the film with an unapologetic American accent and a documentary-like authority experiences her own sense of *Vergangenheitsbewältigung* ('coming to terms with the past') as a Jewish American dating a neo-Nazi. East/West German politics are also probed; in particular towards the end of the film when Lola willingly moves to the East to start her own pro-communist television show. A critique of religion is enacted through Tron's mental breakdown, after which he becomes a born-again Christian healer and then appears to commit suicide in the hotel fire; his sacrifice taking on a religious, albeit problematic connotation.

The film also showcases the queer lifestyles of the characters, which while far exceeding the bounds of normalcy, all the while reaffirm the perversity of the hetero-norm. For instance, Gary, who leads an erotic, or rather sexual healing group, is arrested by the police for his immoral sexual and gender-bending behaviour, and ultimately charged to leave Germany forever. Static notions of gender and sexuality are also challenged through the exploration of the character's own identities, including those of transvestites, transgendered folk, transsexuals, bisexuals and homosexuals, as well as the idea of a 'third sex.' Other taboos explored include kinship relationships between a male-to-female transgendered person and a lesbian, transvestites, the young and old, as well as transnational and trans-racial relationships across conflicting religious and political positions. *City of Lost Souls* is sexually explicit, bordering on what may be considered pornography. Made clearly before the advent of HIV/AIDS, sex is shown as something to be enjoyed without restraint, if not as a means to obtaining a kind of revolutionary, yet peaceful catharsis.

City of Lost Souls has been largely ignored and/or forgotten by academic film scholars with the exception of Queer German Cinema scholars such as Alice Kuzniar, who, while praising von Praunheim's work in general, dismisses this film for its 'silliness.' Also, Johannes von Moltke writes briefly about von Praunheim's use of camp, and specifically his predilection to using American icons in his films. At the most, *City of Lost Souls* has taken on a kind of cult status as a queer musical. At the very least, the film has been read as a perverse example of avant-garde *trash*, if not as a kind of von Praunheim family home movie.

Samantha Michele Riley

A Virus Has No Morals

Ein Virus kennt keine Moral

Production Company:
Rosa von Praunheim Filmproduktion

Distributors:
Filmwelt (West Germany)
First Run Features (USA)

Director:
Rosa von Praunheim

Producer:
Rosa von Praunheim

Screenwriter:
Rosa von Praunheim

Cinematographer:
Elfi Mikesch

Composer:
Marran Gosov

Synopsis

A Virus Has No Morals is made up of perverse vignettes tied together thematically around HIV/AIDS. Each locates the virus stereotypically: in the bathhouse, park, bedroom, doctor's office, laboratory and hospital, at a drag party, in the jungles of Africa and even in an AIDS concentration camp. Highly satirical, each sketch draws out the public's prejudice and ignorance of HIV. For instance, gay bathhouse owner Rüdiger Kackinski (von Praunheim) hides safe sex posters and condom machines, afraid he might lose business. Professor Dr. Blut (meaning 'blood') (Hasenäcker) enjoys making AIDS jokes and traumatizing seropositive patients, claiming the virus is psychosomatic and shame is the best defence. Nurses bemoan their days of uninhibited sex with patients, rolling dice instead to guess which AIDS patient may die next. At the other end of this muddled spectrum a psychologist (Blum) tries to help patients come to terms with the virus, encouraging them to act out their own death and funeral. On a more serious note, a band of revolutionaries called the Army of the Sick and Impotent fight for real facts and funding for research. The film ends with a call for political activism.

Critique

In line with director Rosa von Praunheim's radical public 'outings,' *A Virus Has No Morals* is also a kind of 'outing' of AIDS and its bitter reality. When the film premiered in the mid-1980s scientists and the public were just learning about the nature of the virus.

Editor:
Michael Schäfer

Duration:
84 minutes

Genre:
Queer Cinema
Black Comedy
Drama

Cast:
Dieter Dicken
Maria Hasennäcker
Christian Kesten
Eva-Maria Kurz
Rosa von Praunheim
Ina Blum
Thilo von Trotha

Year:
1986

Yet, von Praunheim already recognized the dangers of both the virus and the conservative politics developing around the topic, and in particular their impact on the gay community. In true form von Praunheim pushes the limits of satire into the grotesque to make his point. This dark comedy highlights the ignorance of public perception and the hysteria developing around the idea of gay men being progenitors of the virus. The film also draws parallels between the control of gay men's bodies and sexuality vis-à-vis HIV and AIDS in the 1980s, and the way in which bodies of all kinds (e.g., Jews, homosexuals, the disabled) were regulated and destroyed in Nazi concentration camps. In *A Virus has No Morals*, gay men are reduced to objects or rather guinea pigs – quarantined, experimented on and eventually exiled. Also acting as a pseudo-documentary, with the inclusion of snippets of real newspaper articles, supplemented with a (fictional) radio cast about the future of AIDS, von Praunheim predicts the virus's pandemic potential. He also anticipates the formation of direct action advocacy groups such as ACT UP. The moral of the film is encapsulated in the refrain of a song sung by a choir of drag queens dressed up as nurses: 'You have your fate in your own hands.'

In retrospect, queer film scholars generally understand von Praunheim's intentions as carnivalesque, sadomasochistic, but sincere. The film's montage of sketches and song and dance routines qualify it as the progeny of a kind of avant-garde musical. Contemporary critics, while registering von Praunheim's intentions to entertain and inform, appeared however more shocked than motivated by his message. In 1987, the *New York Times* pinned the film as more disturbing than funny, accusing von Praunheim of dealing 'in doom.' One can easily understand how critics were angered by the seeming insensitivity of the script. For example, the bathhouse owner, reflecting on his life after AIDS, tells the camera 'this disease makes me horny'; an admission foregrounding the already political and morally problematic position gay men occupy when they choose to have unprotected, so-called 'barebacking' sex. Case in point – von Praunheim follows this admission with one even more telling: 'Sex is life and I believe in life,' which brings home the fact that the politics of HIV/AIDS is also one of queer sexuality and selfhood, entrenched in an ethics of life and death.

Samantha Michele Riley

Virgin Machine

Die Jungfrauenmaschine

Production Companies:
Hyena Films
Norddeutscher Rundfunk (NDR)

Distributor:
First Run Features (USA)

Director:
Monika Treut

Producers:
Monika Treut
Elfi Mikesch

Screenwriter:
Monika Treut

Cinematographer:
Elfi Mikesch

Editor:
Renate Merck

Duration:
85 minutes

Genre:
Comedy
Queer Cinema
Feminism

Cast:
Ina Blum
Marcelo Uriona
Gad Klein
Peter Kern
Dominique Gaspar
Susie 'Sexpert' Bright
Shelly Mars

Year:
1988

Synopsis

Hamburg journalist Dorothee Müller (Blum) is afflicted with a belief in romantic love, and is researching the genetic and hormonal origins of this 'fantastic illusion.' Her relationship with her repulsive boyfriend, Heinz (Klein), is a failure and she has fallen in love with her half-brother. Ostensibly on a search for her mother who had left for America years before, Dorothee lands in San Francisco's Tenderloin district where, like her namesake in *The Wizard of Oz* (Fleming, 1939), she encounters three characters who help her to navigate the journey through a new, queer terrain. First to welcome her is Dominique (Gaspar), a world traveller currently working for Marvin Moss, the 'king of porn.' Next she meets Susie Sexpert (Bright), a strip club barker, who, in one of the film's most memorable scenes enthusiastically presents her dildo collection. Finally, Dorothee responds to a television commercial that promises a cure for romantic love and goes on an epic date with Ramona (Mars), a sex therapist and drag king. Upon receiving the bill for the evening, she can only respond with hearty laughter. In the last scenes of the film, Dorothee performs at a women's strip club and throws photographs presumably from her Hamburg life into the San Francisco Bay.

Critique

Released in 1988, Monika Treut's *Virgin Machine* can be read as part of the larger feminist and queer responses to the general conservatism that characterized the Reagan-Thatcher years. The film's assertion of a politics of pleasure, and specifically a politics of female pleasure that is articulated in the context of the San Francisco sex industry, locates it within the at times polarizing 'sex wars' of the late 1970s and 1980s. From the televised reports of Pope John Paul II's visit to California to the cameo appearance of Susie 'Sexpert' Bright, an early contributing editor to the lesbian sex magazine *On Our Backs*, the film's historical context permeates *Virgin Machine*'s fictional world serving as a persistent visual and auditory reminder of the political stakes of the film's present. In the German context, the making of the film coincides with the height of the pornography debates in West Germany when Alice Schwarzer launched the 'PorNo' campaign in the pages of the feminist magazine *Emma*. Again through the intrusion of the television, the Hamburg sequence of the film features footage of an American feminist discussing pornography, urging women to 'forget this anti-porn stuff.' Scholars have pointed out that the film's anti-identitarian impulses and thematization of drag also generally anticipates queer theory and Judith Butler's foundational work *Gender Trouble* (1990), in particular. Here, Butler argues that far from being a pre-existing natural fact, the category of woman is continually being constituted through a series of performative acts, repetitions that ultimately serve to naturalize sex and gender while at the same time disguising their production as social artefacts. Ramona's strip club performance parodying male masturbation has been read in the context of Butler's much-heralded example of drag functioning to unmask gender as an imitation without origin. In interviews, Treut has voiced her scepticism of identity politics and feminism, and has repeatedly expressed her disbelief in an 'identity concept.'

Treut's theoretical rejection of categories is reflected in the construction of the film itself. The work is a postmodern pastiche of cinematic styles, traditions and citations, and it abounds in playful collisions between low and high culture. Beginning with the title itself, *Virgin Machine* on the one hand evokes the realm of the pornographic at the same time that it references Heiner Müller's play *Hamlet Machine*; it was reportedly inspired by the 1970s art exhibit '*Junggesellenmaschinen/Les machines célibataires*' ('Bachelor Machines') (in Flinn 1996: 52). The film is at times visually reminiscent of the photographic style of the *Neue Sachlichkeit* ('New Objectivity'), which characterized the art cinema in the latter half of the Weimar Republic. *Virgin Machine*'s non-diegetic inserts of biological processes and mechanized human figures link it to experimental traditions, yet it freely cites from the popular realm as well. Dorothee's ex-boyfriend Heinz delivers a disturbing monologue on the 'hixploitation' classic *The Texas Chainsaw Massacre* (Hooper, 1974); the film's conclusion is a feminist reworking of Madeleine's near-drowning in *Vertigo* (Hitchcock, 1958); and the television, which is often heard blaring in the background, enables Dorothee's initial contact with Ramona. As visually, thematically and politically complex as *Virgin Machine* is, Treut reminds the spectator throughout that movies are also tremendously fun to watch. From the exceedingly likable eccentrics who populate San Francisco's sex industry to the humorous performance of male masturbation simulated using a bottle of beer (complete with foamy climax), fun is what links the film to a larger queer project that aims to decouple sexual pleasure and identity. Ultimately, the film resists the lesbian and gay coming out narrative, which assumes the existence of an authentic self that can only be revealed through an inwardly focused process of self-discovery. Instead, sexuality is turned outward as the pleasurable experience of spectatorship and performance, of production and consumption, and of simulation and play.

Alison Guenther-Pal

My Father is Coming

Ein Bayer in New York

Production Company:
Hyena Films

Synopsis

Vicky (Kästner), a young, aspiring actress who is down and out in the East Village, is visited by her father from Germany (Edel). While her dad effortlessly scores a job in a commercial and a date with an ex-porn queen, Vicky loses her waitressing job and searches for her sexual bearings. Although she is attracted to both a lesbian and a male-to-female transsexual, she foolishly undertakes to trick her father into believing that she is leading a happily married life with

Distributor:
Tara Releasing

Director:
Monika Treut

Producer:
Monika Treut

Screenwriter:
Monika Treut
Bruce Benderson

Cinematographer:
Elfi Mikesch

Composer:
David Van Tieghem

Editor:
Steven C. Brown

Duration:
82 minutes

Genre:
Comedy
Romance
Queer Cinema

Cast:
Alfred Edel
Shelley Kästner
Annie Sprinkle
Michael Massee
David Bronstein
Mary Lou Grailau
Fakir Musafar

Year:
1991

a man. Ben (Bronstein), though, is flamboyantly gay and her father can't be deceived. In this comedy of errors each character explores his or her shifting sexualities and desires. By the end, father and daughter come to mutual understanding and respect for each other's lifestyles.

Critique

Following upon her earlier feature length films, *Seduction: The Cruel Woman* (1985) and *Virgin Machine* (1988), *My Father is Coming* consolidated Monika Treut's status as one of the major directors of the New Queer Cinema. This movement was characterized by low budget, independent productions by auteurist directors who unabashedly explored edgy sexualities and gender experimentation. *My Father is Coming* is a fine example of how this innovative cinema pushed the boundaries of fixed sexual and gendered identities. The main character, Vicky, never self-identifies as lesbian or straight but instead recognizes her fluid attractions to both another woman and a male-to-female transsexual. Joe (Massee) talks about the reasons for his gender switching and why he wants the body to conform to his desires. Meanwhile, Vicky's roommate, Ben, rhapsodizes about gay Latino men. Annie Sprinkle, playing herself, talks to Vicky's father about the erotic appeal of transsexuals. And Hans, as the older and heavy-set father, is also openly portrayed as expressing sexual desire and curiosity. Towards the end of the film he encounters Fakir Musafar, a performance artist who achieves ecstasy through body piercings. True to the comedic genre, as the characters intermingle in the course of the film, each person cheerfully learns to live and let live.

In addition to openly exploring transgressive sexualities, *My Father is Coming* also thematizes the crossing and confusion of national borders. Hans has come to New York bearing gifts of German Oktoberfest wieners and 'German technology' – a dust-buster for Vicky's apartment! Others deftly mock his sense of cultural superiority and imperialism, but he quickly learns and begins to immerse himself in his new surroundings, alive to slices of the alternative life New York has to offer him. Unlike Vicky, who has difficulty playing any role convincingly, Hans ends up being a successful actor. He demonstrates that nationality, just like gender and sexuality, is a matter of performance or drag. His German accent and beer-belly land him a spot in a commercial. Stereotypes of whatever sort – gender, sexuality, age, and nationality – exist to be played or camped up. Only then can they be deconstructed. The oppositions – male/female, gay/straight, parent/child, and native/foreign – thereby become undone.

As an independent film-maker and after *My Father is Coming*, Treut found it increasingly difficult to obtain funding for feature length narrative films. She turned to making documentaries and produced several that recorded the lives of strong, independent women, including *Didn't Do it for Love* (1997) on a New York based dominatrix, and *Warrior of Light* (2001) on a human rights activist working with HIV-positive children in Rio. Treut also pursued the theme of transgender first introduced in *My Father is Coming* in the documentary *Gendernauts: A Journey through Shifting Identities* (1999). In 2009 Treut finally released her next feature length fictional film, *Ghosted*, which, like *Virgin Machine* and *My Father is Coming*, deals with the topic of lesbian attraction across national boundaries.

Alice A. Kuzniar

Lola and Billy the Kid

Lola und Bilidikid

Production Companies:
Boje Buck Produktion
Westdeutscher Rundfunk (WDR)
Zero Film GmbH

Distributors:
Delphi Filmverleih Produktion,
Good Machine International
K Films

Director:
Kutluğ Ataman

Producer:
Martin Hagemann

Screenwriter:
Kutluğ Ataman

Art Director:
Mona Kino

Cinematographer:
Chris Squires

Composer:
Arpad Bondy

Editor:
Ewa J. Lind

Duration:
95 minutes

Genre:
Drama
Queer Cinema

Synopsis

This film is partly about the love story between two of the main gay male characters Lola (Mukli) and Bili, also known as Bilidikid (Yildiz). Alongside Şehrazat (Perk) and Kalipso (Ozdemir) Lola is a drag performer in a group called *Die Gastarbeiterinnen* ('the female guestworkers'). Bili and his brother, İskender (Yilmaz), are hustlers. Lola has two brothers, whom the viewer encounters: an older brother, Osman (Mete) and a younger brother, Murat (Davrak), whom one first sees in a gay cruising spot. Lola has never met Murat, because she was forced to leave her home when she was younger because she was gay. There are also three xenophobic, young, white German males, Rudy (Herren), Hendryk (Irrek) and Walter (Andres) who harass and intimidate Lola and attack Lola and Murat. İskender brings into the plot a thread of his budding relationship with an older, aristocratic, white German man, Friedrich (Gerber), whom İskender met after a sexual encounter in a park. Friedrich's mother, Ute (Keller) is very involved with his affairs. The relationship between Lola and Bili finds tension in Bili's continuing hustling, as well as his desire for Lola to undergo a sex change operation. In Bili's eyes the latter would allow them to live normally 'as man and wife.' After Murat's brother, Osman, tries to force him to have sex with a female prostitute, Murat runs away from home. Murat then meets Bili, who introduces him to the world of hustling in public men's rooms. After Lola is found dead, floating in the Spree River, Murat finds out from Şehrazat and Kalipso that Osman raped Lola upon discovering that he was gay. In their belief that the three xenophobic young men are responsible for Lola's death, Bili and Murat lure them into an abandoned factory. After Bili castrates Rudy, he kills Hendryk but not before he is fatally wounded. Murat discovers from Walter, who has escaped alive, that none of them was responsible for Lola's death. Murat knows that it was Osman who had killed Lola. Murat confronts Osman, thereby informing his mother of the circumstances surrounding Lola's death.

Critique

Lola und Bilidikid was Turkish-born Kutlu Ataman's second film and his only one set and produced in Germany. Ataman's work as an artist and documentary film-maker in Turkey, Great Britain and

Cast:
Baki Davrak
Erdal Yildiz
Gandi Mukli
Michael Gerber
Murat Yilmaz
Inge Keller
Celal Perk
Mesut Ozdemir
Hasan Ali Mete
Willi Herren
Mario Irrek
Jan Andres

Year:
1999

the United States is visible in *Lola* as the artful creation of various scenes combines with his aim of bringing to light the lives of marginalized populations. The film was originally to be produced and filmed in Turkey, but financing was more readily available in Germany, making the German focus an alteration of the original project. Nonetheless, the film served a distinct and necessary purpose of highlighting the gay Turkish(-German) subculture in Germany, and Berlin in particular. The film, however, is overloaded with dramatic material that limits the overall success of the film's narrative. The acting, cinematography and plot create a filmic world that is at times reminiscent of Westerns and melodramas. The film often features dark sets, scenes shot at night, haunting music and overcast weather, all of which contribute to its sombre and sometimes eerie atmosphere. The focus on Turkish(-German) gay subculture fascinated critics and reviewers, most of whom received the film positively. Some hailed the arrival of a new generation of (Turkish/Turkish-German) film-makers creating new and noteworthy films around this time. These film-makers (e.g. Fatih Akın, Thomas Arslan, and Yüksel Yavuz) aim to take films beyond the common trope of racial minorities as victims.

This film appeared amid the public debates of the late 1990s surrounding German and double citizenship, making it all the more intriguing, as the public discussions likely coloured audiences' and critics' reception. In 2000 German citizenship laws changed to allow for individuals born on German soil to non-German parents, who have resided in Germany legally for at least eight years, to apply for German citizenship (Adelson 2005: 7). Ataman's film is thus a part of a contemporary trend, which contributed to increased visibility of Germany's largest racial/ethnic minority. This film, however, remains unusual among its counterparts because of its treatment of race and (transgender) sexuality against a German background.

Kyle Frackman

The Einstein of Sex: Life and Work of Dr. M. Hirschfeld

Der Einstein des Sex: Leben und Werk des Dr. Hirschfeld

Production Companies:
Argus Film Produktie
Arte

Synopsis

This docudrama re-enacts events in the life of the early twentieth century German-Jewish sexologist Dr. Magnus Hirschfeld (1868–1935) (von Wangenheim). In childhood, Hirschfeld demonstrates an interest in sexuality, drawing pictures of copulating animals. What his father deems a scientific study turns into a physical one with his foster brother, Richard (Peter Ehrlich). After his father's death, and through his uncle's support, Hirschfeld begins studying medicine. The students are taught to classify homosexuals as mentally ill. Fearing the same, Robert leaves Hirschfeld, who uses his loss as the impulse to study sexuality. He opens a clinic as a doctor of psychology. After losing a closeted patient to suicide and another to blackmail, Hirschfeld starts building a scientific case against

Hessischer Rundfunk (HR)
Rosa von Praunheim
Filmproduktion
Studio Babelsberg
Vrijzinning Protestantse Radio
Omroep (VPRO)

Distributor:
Ventura Film

Director:
Rosa von Praunheim

Producers:
Rosa von Praunheim
Dietmar Schings

Screenwriters:
Chris Kraus
Valentin Passoni
Rosa von Praunheim
(uncredited)
Friedel von Wangenheim
(uncredited)

Art Director:
Peter Kothe

Cinematographer:
Elfi Mikesch

Composer:
Karl-Ernst Sasse

Editor:
Mike Shephard

Duration:
100 minutes

Genre:
Queer Cinema
Biography
Drama

Cast:
Friedel von Wangenheim
Gerd Lukas Storzer
Tima die Göttliche
Olaf Drauschke
Ben Becker

Year:
1999

Paragraph 175, which criminalized homosexual acts in Germany. Furthermore, Hirschfeld writes books on sexuality, founds the Scientific Humanitarian Committee and, finally, opens his Institute for Sexual Research in 1919. Intimately, Hirschfeld maintains few relationships, fearing for his reputation. However, Baron Hermann von Teschenberg (Storzer) and Karl Giese (Drauschke) are his two great loves, and the transvestite, Dorchen (Göttliche), remains his faithful caretaker. His later life is devoted to lecturing abroad, during which time the Nazis burn down his institute on the grounds of his religion and homosexuality.

Critique

Among Rosa von Praunheim's oeuvre, *The Einstein of Sex* is one of his most expensive productions, as well as one of his more serious works in a series of docudramas, showcasing what von Praunheim arguably considers leaders, heroes and martyrs in queer history. Following *I Am My Own Woman* (1992) – an autobiographical documentary of a famous transvestite in Berlin who survived World War II and lived to tell the tale – von Praunheim reaches further back in time to the end of the nineteenth century to extend this queer historiography. In terms of cinematography and acting this (categorically speaking) low-budget film is clearly below par. Shot with a digital camera, the film has the feel of a telefilm; and like many, if not most, of von Praunheim's films, images of nude men abound, interacting in erotic situations similar to those performed in soft porn.

Still, while most popular film critics have dismissed the work entirely, queer scholars recognize von Praunheim's courage to tackle, as he has done many times over, difficult tales of gender and sexual oppression – those stories that history books relegate more typically to footnotes. While many queer persons today may not know his name, Magnus Hirschfeld did play a pivotal role in gay rights activism in Germany at the turn of the century. He was famous throughout Berlin for his unorthodox research interests and methods, and of course, for his Institute for Sexual Research.

Yet, as is von Praunheim's style, he remains critical in his storytelling. For instance, Hirschfeld is portrayed as a man who paradoxically, if not hypocritically, encouraged others to accept their homosexuality as natural. He encouraged prestigious people to support gay rights openly at the (potential) cost of their careers; however, Hirschfeld himself never publicly came out as gay. Instead, von Praunheim paints Hirschfeld as a sometimes-selfish monomaniac, oftentimes prioritizing his work over his family, colleagues and lovers. Also, the source of funding for his institute is clearly problematized in the film. Hirschfeld receives money from a rich Middle Eastern family to perform a sex change operation on a hermaphrodite. Initially, he appears to morally object to the surgery, arguably because his platform is for acceptance, and not the destruction or re-heteronormalizing of queer persons and their bodies. Still, he agrees to take the much needed money and performs the operation.

The Einstein of Sex: Life and Work of Dr. M. Hirschfeld, Argus Film Produktie/Arte/Hessischer Rundfunk (HR)/Rosa von Praunheim Filmproduktion/Studio Babelsberg/Vrijzinning Protestantse Radio Omroep (VPRO).

In sum, von Praunheim paints a multi-layered portrait of the oppression and prejudice homosexuals and queer persons had to endure during the early twentieth century in Germany, placing the blame most solidly on Paragraph 175. At the same time, along with his critique of bygone eras, von Praunheim surely wants to provoke his viewers to reflect on the present politics surrounding gay rights as well.

Samantha Michele Riley

Return to Go

Zurück auf los!

Director:
Pierre Sanoussi-Bliss

Producers:
Frank Löprich
Katrin Schlösser

Screenwriter:
Pierre Sanoussi-Bliss

Cinematographer:
Thomas Plenert

Editor:
Gudrun Steinbrück

Duration:
95 minutes

Genre:
Comedy
Drama
Queer

Cast:
Pierre Sanoussi-Bliss
Matthias Freihof
Dieter Bach
Paul Gilling
Bart Klein

Year:
2000

Synopsis

Sam (Sanoussi-Bliss) is a newly diagnosed HIV-positive, poor, black, East German man living in a run-down apartment in Berlin. Sam's relationships with his friends and lovers comprise the support system that helps him through this difficult time. The viewer learns of Sam's relationship with his ex-boyfriend Manne (Klein), who dies of AIDS-related complications. A constant companion and eventual roommate is Sam's best friend, Bastl (Freihof). Despite and because of serious events in the story, Sam forms new connections with a former and future boyfriend and friend, Rainer (Bach), who is later blinded in an automobile accident. Bastl brings in his own love interest in the form of Mike (Gilling), a British artist who also moves into the decrepit apartment. Two nearly constant occupations of Sam's are his effort to record an album of trite East German *Schlager* ('hit') songs, and his writing of a version of his and his friends' narrative, which the viewer sees unfolding in the film. Towards the end of the film, the trio of Sam, Bastl and Rainer drive to gay-friendly Denmark for a beach vacation. After contemplating life and its difficulties, the three friends drive back toward Germany, victorious and reinvigorated.

Critique

Return to Go presents a number of complicated social issues, which both the characters and the viewer must encounter over the course of the film: Otherness; race and racism; sexuality and homophobia; HIV/AIDS and the fear of the disease. Within and around these themes, binaries and the importance of time and space become crucial elements in the unfolding of the narrative. The two most prominent themes of the film are race and sexuality, and these are treated rather differently. The more prominent of the two is race, as it is the source of both implicit and explicit criticism. For example, racism is treated explicitly in a scene in which Sam directly confronts and challenges a gawking white grocery store employee. Implicitly, other scenes are visually constructed to point to the film's goal of thematizing race; for example, only black faces appear on a TV that Sam is watching, or the stark contrast between Sam's skin colour and that of a facial treatment mask. Sexuality, on the other hand, is treated with a greater sense of certainty in the world of the film. Whereas Sam faces ostracism due to his race, he finds security and comfort in the predominantly gay social scene depicted in the film.

The film also plays with time and space in a number of interesting ways. We see clocks running backward and characters barely missing each other. Through the introduction of non-urban Danish landscape, the film draws on a trope that is common in gay and HIV/AIDS-themed films; namely, a journey to the country as 'balm' for an ill person (Hart 2000: 67–80). Indeed, the film recalls other traits of HIV/AIDS films. For example, the trio's time in Denmark is interspersed with shots of what appear to be home movies of the vacation. We are reminded of scenes from *Philadelphia* (Demme, 1993), for example, in which friends and acquaintances watch old home movies of the recently deceased protagonist. But despite these similarities, the film's ending diverges from the typical AIDS-movie ending. *Return to Go* ends more or less happily and optimistically as the friends travel back to Germany, 'back to go,' as the title suggests. Critics praised the film, although a few expressed some unease at the lightheartedness with which the film's themes are treated (Jahn 2001: 22). One of the few German films to thematize the experiences of black Germans, *Return to Go* uniquely shows the link between different kinds of marginalization like race and sexuality, while also repeating the social criticism (and AIDS satire) of film-makers like Rosa von Praunheim.

Kyle Frackman

The Raspberry Reich/The Revolution is My Boyfriend (hardcore version)

The Raspberry Reich

Production Company:
Jürgen Brüning Filmproduktion

Distributors:
GMfilms (Germany)
Strand Releasing (USA)

Director:
Bruce LaBruce

Producer:
Jürgen Brüning

Screenwriter:
Bruce LaBruce

Cinematographers:
James Carman
Kristian Petersen

Editor:
Jörn Hartmann

Synopsis

Set in present-day Germany, *The Raspberry Reich* narrates the contradictions and dreams of a Berlin wannabe terrorist group, who plan to liberate the masses from the bourgeois repression, including heterosexual monogamy, through a queer intifada. Gudrun (Sachße), the group's leader and chief ideologue, forces her boyfriend, Andreas (Monroe), to have sex with another man, and ignites her followers with slogans taken from the writings of sexologist Wilhelm Reich and philosopher Herbert Marcuse. The radicals engage in urban guerrilla activities and kidnap Patrick (Rupprecht), the son of a wealthy German industrialist. When they discover that their victim has been disowned by his father for his homosexuality, the terrorists start panicking. The tensions created by Gudrun's despotic character causes the dissolution of the group: Patrick escapes with one of his guards and becomes a bank robber; Che (Fettig) enlists in a terrorist training camp in the Middle East; Gudrun and Andreas start a family and have a baby girl, who they name after Ulrike Meinhof, one of the first generation members of the Red Army Faction (RAF) terrorist group.

Critique

The Raspberry Reich combines various genres, including political parody, satirical comedy and porn, with a high camp sensibility and an exuberantly transgressive video clip aesthetic, illustrated in the practice of pastiche flashing images, on-screen titles and driven montage. Its irreverent humour represents a cultural attempt to re-engage with the memory of the RAF from a contemporary perspective, but ultimately relies on established stereotypes. With this film, Canadian director Bruce LaBruce reveals how the 1970s West German terrorism is back in vogue in the new millennium, and how the traumatic memory of those events has been transformed into artefacts of popular culture, free from political meaning or historical

Duration:
90 minutes

Genre:
Queer
Satire
Adult
Comedy

Cast:
Susanne Sachße
Daniel Bätscher
Andreas Rupprecht
Dean Monroe
Anton Z. Risan
Daniel Fettig

Year:
2004

contextualization. In this sense, very few commentators would have expected that less than a decade after the dissolution of the left-wing terrorist organization such impertinent reconsideration could have been possible.

Although graphic in its depictions of sexual acts, *The Raspberry Reich* is far from ordinary gay porn, as its sex scenes are overlaid with intertextual references and revolutionary slogans, which comment on the recent 'terrorist chic' phenomenon, including the appropriation of revolutionary imagery by popular culture, as in the proliferation of Che Guevara merchandise. During sex, Gudrun declares, 'Out of the bedrooms into the streets!' or 'Heterosexuality is the opiate of the masses,' which undercut the expectations of the porn format. Gudrun's pronouncements parody theories about politics and sexuality developed in *Eros and Civilization* (1955) by Herbert Marcuse, which had a great influence in the 1960s. Instead of arousing audiences, the film's pornographic images comment on the capitalist process of exploiting revolutionary discourse for commercial ends and assimilating romanticized forms of terrorism. In addition, the particular attention paid to the T-shirts with RAF logo and to the wallpapers featuring Andreas Baader, Ulrike Meinhof and Gudrun Ensslin connects the film to the so-called 'Prada-Meinhof' clothing phenomenon in the 1990s, when the fashion industry began to rediscover terrorist iconography on the catwalk and in photo shoots.

In its radical conflation of politics and erotica, and its focus on a (homo-)sexual *amour fou*, *The Raspberry Reich* has echoes of *Last Tango in Paris* (Bertolucci, 1972), where the exploration of sexual practices is actuated only to politicize the attack on bourgeois ideology. In this case, the taboo act of breaking the heterosexual monogamy pact between Gudrun and Andreas is at the same time the annihilation of the scope of the 'sacred family,' and the revelation of the claustrophobic power relations within the bourgeois institution.

LaBruce's film pays homage also to the Eastern European tradition of politicized art movies, such as *WR: Mysteries of the Organism* (Makavejev, 1971), through a radical juxtaposed editing of archival footage and interviews with Reich and his wife and visual satirical quotes. The opening scene of *The Raspberry Reich* in particular, which features masturbation with a gun, is a direct quote of the first episode of Makavejev's film.

Elena Caoduro

Unveiled

Fremde Haut

Production Companies:
MMM Film Zimmermann & Co.
Fischer Film

Distributors:
Ventura Film (Germany)
Wolfe Releasing (USA)

Director:
Angelina Maccarone

Producer:
Ulrike Zimmermann

Screenwriter:
Judith Kaufmann
Angelina Maccarone

Cinematographer:
Judith Kaufmann

Composers:
Hartmut Ewert
Jacob Hansonis

Editor:
Bettina Böhler

Duration:
97 minutes

Genre:
Queer Cinema
Drama

Cast:
Jasmin Tabatabai
Navid Akhavan
Anneke Kim Sarnau
Hinnerk Schönemann

Year:
2005

Synopsis

Persecuted for her affair with a married woman, Iranian translator Fariba Tabrizi (Tabatabai) flees Tehran to Germany seeking asylum. Ashamed to reveal the sexual nature of her claim, she states political reasons instead. Without documented proof, her request is swiftly denied. Awaiting deportation at the Frankfurt airport, she meets Siamak (Akhavan), another Iranian refugee. Out of guilt for the arrest of his brother and in fear of deportation, Siamak commits suicide. After discovering the body, Fariba decides to assume his identity. She is granted refugee status in his place and placed in refugee housing, where it becomes clear that asylum means having to live in cramped quarters for an indefinite period of time. Looking for a way out, Fariba finds illegal work in a cabbage factory. Masquerading as a shy Muslim man, Fariba endures xenophobic banter from her German colleagues. The female co-workers, however, and in particular Anne (Sarnau), are intrigued. Anne falls in love with Fariba as a man, and eventually as a woman. Her male co-workers are not as open-minded. Upon discovery, a brawl ensues and the police arrive. Fariba's illegal status exposed, she is deported back to Iran. Yet, still resolved to start anew, Fariba rips up her passport on the plane ride home and reassumes a male identity.

Critique

Several scholars have explored *Unveiled* predominately under the auspices of migration.[1] More specifically, some have demonstrated how the narrative sheds light on the way geographical border crossings give rise to corporal ones in terms of race, class, nation, religion, gender and sexuality. First, the film highlights the difficulties faced by the LGBTQ community in terms of (European) immigration. Self-identified as a lesbian, Fariba must flee Iran to avoid arrest and even possibly the death penalty. The film's original title, *Fremde Haut*, also calls attention to the transitory nature of identity or, in this case, the possibility of transitory embodiments of identity. In German, *fremde haut* can mean 'foreign skin,' 'strange skin,' or even 'unknown skin' or 'alien skin.' In this respect, Fariba must assume an alternate national identity in order to survive, or literally save her own skin. She willingly seeks asylum in Germany. Yet, suffering from internalized homophobia, Fariba cannot proclaim her lesbian identity to German immigration, who may have granted her asylum on the grounds of sexual orientation persecution. Even at the end of the film, when Fariba is deported back to Iran, where she could possibly start a new life (as a woman), she chooses instead to transition (again) to become a man. One may interpret her decision in two ways: either Fariba finds her desire for women psychologically rectified (and legally sanctified in Iran), if and only if she is a man; or Fariba discovers, through her impersonation of a man, that she now prefers to identify as a man or as transgendered, more so than as a woman. In any case, when Fariba is disrobed, or rather as Anne unbinds Fariba's breasts, Fariba is clearly uncomfortable, shuddering under Anne's gaze of her exposed female/feminine body. Even when Fariba finds herself in locations where she may safely express the gender identity of a woman, she does so reluctantly.

In terms of race and religion, Fariba continues to perform the role of a devout Muslim, in face of prejudice and social ostracization as exemplified by the working-class, white and presumably Christian-identifying Germans in the small factory where Fariba works. Problematically, the translation of the film's title into English as *Unveiled* overshadows the film with the arguably clichéd religious connotation of the oppressed, veiled Muslim woman, and this at the expense of the obvious and more prominent issues of sexual and gender oppression at play.

That which is truly 'unveiled' in this film is the interlocking systems of oppression, which coerce people to reveal or cover up certain identities as they navigate the altering geographical and corporal terrains of various times and spaces. This sense of restrictions and permissions, as stops and go's, is further emphasized symbolically by the film's overarching colour scheme of greens and reds (the colours of the Iranian flag), notably take on alternating connotations, complicating this dichotomy: the green of the German police; lighting in the refugee holding compound; the field where Fariba buries Siamak and the fields where the women have their first date; the cabbages and the green factory, and Fariba's own outfits/disguises. Alternately, red is the colour of the sweater of her roommate who secures her work; Anne's outfits, scooter and bed; the red light district (where Fariba is recognized as a woman); and the colour of the Avis car rental, where Fariba steals a car to buy a fake passport. The film ends with Fariba tearing up her deportation papers, placing Siamak's red Iranian passport in her back pocket, and removing her head covering to reveal her male persona, including the grey-green jacket. Here, we may read the conflicting colours again symbolically, whereby the red of the passport might signal the dangers that await her in her homeland; and contrastingly, the grey-green costume gestures towards another beginning.

Samantha Michele Riley

Note

1. See Deniz Göktürk, David Gramling and Anton Kaes (eds.) (2007), *Germany in Transit: Nation and Migration 1955–2005*, Berkeley, CA: University of California Press.

4 Minutes

Vier Minuten

Production Companies:
Kordes & Kordes Film GmbH
Südwestrundfunk (SWR)
Bayerischer Rundfunk (BR)
ARTE
Beauftragter der
Bundesregierung für
Angelegenheiten derKultur und
der Medien (BKM)

Distributor:
Piffl Medien (Germany),
Peccadillo Pictures (UK)

Director:
Chris Kraus

Producers:
Meike Kordes
Alexandra Kordes

Screenwriter:
Chris Kraus

Cinematographer:
Judith Kaufmann

Composer:
Annette Focks

Editor:
Uta Schmidt

Duration:
112 minutes

Genre:
Drama

Cast:
Monica Bleibtreu
Hannah Herzsprung
Sven Pippig
Richy Müller
Vadim Glowna
Jasmin Tabatabai
Stefan Kurt
Nadja Uhl

Year:
2006

Synopsis

4 Minutes traces the relationship between the 80-year-old piano teacher Traude Krüger (Bleibtreu) and her young protégé, Jenny (Herzsprung). The two women meet in a correctional facility where Jenny serves time for having murdered her (male) partner and where Traude has spent most of her adult life, first as a nurse during the Third Reich, and now as a volunteer piano teacher for the inmates, including Jenny. Traude and Jenny are cast as opposites, which creates conflict between them, but is also a basis for attraction between the two unequal women: where Jenny is aggressive, violent, destructive and drawn to contemporary music, Traude is controlled, distanced, repressed and decidedly in favour of the classics. The person who bridges but also complicates the oppositional positions between Traude and Jenny is Hannah (Kathrin Kestler), Traude's dead lover, who was executed as a communist during the Third Reich. Her courage and humanity in the face of adversity make her a role model for both women. Although she is represented in flashbacks only, her absence shapes Traude's life and, in turn, Jenny's too.

As outsiders – Traude among the administration of the correctional facility and Jenny among the inmates of the prison – and because of their love of music, both these women are natural allies, joined in their fight against the restrictive environment of the prison. The friendship between the two women is signified in several scenes where they become interchangeable. At one point, for example, Jenny and Ms Krüger trade their clothes to make Jenny presentable for a concert, so that each one of them literally walks in the other's shoes.

Jenny's success in various piano competitions creates a backlash in the prison. When Jenny defends herself in a fight with other prisoners, she loses her performance privileges, so that Ms Krüger has to break her out of prison in order to take part in a competition for young musicians. Just in time, the two make it to the final, decisive competition. With the police waiting in the background to take her back to prison, Jenny plays her interpretation of Schumann, which finally earns her Ms Krüger's respect and acceptance.

Critique

4 Minutes makes intelligent use of multifaceted characters to prevent thinking in black and white. Jenny and Traude Krüger challenge binary opposites that would allow them to be either good or bad, feminine or masculine, guilty or innocent. Her stepfather's abuse makes Jenny as much a victim as a killer. Ms Krüger appears prim and proper at first glance, but she too feels guilty because she denied being anything more than a piano teacher for Hannah, her lover during the Third Reich. Both Jenny and Traude have to unlearn this reductive thinking. Ms Krüger has to accept Jenny's murderous side and Jenny has to give Ms Krüger credit for her acts of resistance. This concept of identity as a process is captured best in acts of performance, a theme in several other queer movies, such as *Girls in Uniform* (1931). In *4 Minutes* both women are at first reluctant performers because father figures initially defined this role for them. Jenny was pushed into her career by her stepfather and Ms Krüger struggled under the supervision of her mentor Furtwängler. To resist objectification, they refuse to perform. Their friendship allows them to reclaim their artistry and their identity. In the beginning of the movie Ms Krüger performs hidden on a balcony in the chapel of the prison with her back to the audience; her connection to Jenny is established through a mirror in which she can watch her audience indirectly. During the Third Reich, this was also a space she shared with her lover Hannah, intricately linking sexuality and performance. Performance by performance, Traude and Jenny are freer to look at each other, until the end of the movie, when the two women are sustained by looking at each other in public. Now they also direct the way they are being looked at. Under Ms Krüger's openly admiring gaze Jenny publicly performs classical music the way she likes, thus maintaining her independence while playing what Traude chose for her. The applause of the audience affirms that they are being seen for whom they are. Difference no longer means antagonism, since Jenny's 'performance is about shared intimacy and its collective negotiation and exchange' (Villarejo 2001: 329). In the final scene Ms Krüger can accept Jenny's affection because she understands that Jenny's performance can be both an act of defiance as well as a demonstration of trust and love.

Isolde Mueller

References

Adelson, Leslie (2005), *The Turkish Turn in German Literature: Toward a New Critical Grammar of Migration*, New York: Palgrave Macmillan.

Flinn, Caryl (1996), 'The Body in the (*Virgin*) *Machine*', *Arachnē*, 3: 2, pp. 48-66.

Friedmann, Walther (1919), '*Homosexualität und Judentum*', *Film-Kurier*, 33, 1 July.

Göktürk, Deniz, Gramling, David and Kaes, Anton (eds.) (2007), *Germany in Transit: Nation and Migration 1955–2005*, Berkeley, CA: University of California Press.

Hart, Kylo-Patrick R. (2000), *The AIDS Movie: Representing a Pandemic in Film and Television*, New York: Haworth Press.

Jahn, Pamela (2001), '*Sex zwischen Tanke und Altbauwohnung; So klein, so schön kitschig: In den Filmen* Zurück auf los *und* Chill Out *ist Berlin schwules Idyll und heterosexuelle Seelengemeinschaft zugleich*', *taz, die tageszeitung*, 27 March, p. 22.

Kiss, Robert J. (2002), 'Queer Traditions in German Cinema', in Tim Bergfelder, Erica Carter and Deniz Göktürk (eds.), *The German Cinema Book*, London: British Film Institute, pp. 48-56.

Kuzniar, Alice A. (2000), 'Lesbians Abroad: The Queer Nationhood of Monika Treut et. al.', *The Queer German Cinema*, Stanford, CA: Stanford University Press, pp. 157-73.

Mosse, George (1985), *Nationalism and Sexuality: Respectability and Abnormal Sexuality in Modern Europe*, New York: Howard Fertig.

Mulvey, Laura (1989), 'Visual Pleasure and Narrative Cinema', in Laura Mulvey (ed.), *Visual and Other Pleasures*, Basingstoke: Macmillan, pp. 14-30.

Ruby Rich, B. (1981), '*Mädchen in Uniform*: From Repressive Tolerance to Erotic Liberation', *Jump Cut*, 24: 25, pp. 44–50. http://www.ejumpcut.org/archive/onlinessays/JC24-25folder/MaedchenUniform.html. Accessed 12 February 2011.

Steakley, James (1999), 'Cinema and Censorship in the Weimar Republic: The Case of *Anders als die Andern*', *Film History*, 11, pp. 181-203.

Villarejo, Amy (2001), 'Queer Film and Performance', *GLQ: A Journal of Lesbian and Gay Studies*, 7, pp. 313-33.

VERGANGENHEITSBEWÄLTIGUNG

From Rubble to Terror: German Cinema's Coming to Terms with the Past

In 2004, Oliver Hirschbiegel's *Downfall* burst onto the world's cinema screens to critical and commercial acclaim. This film, which aimed to take viewers into Hitler's private world, depicting his failing physical and psychological state in the final days of his life set in parallel to the dying days of the Nazi regime and World War II, also garnered a fair degree of criticism. Critics accused Hirschbiegel for personalising and individualising the figure of the dictator through his uncritical commitment to a realist mode of representation.[1] According to some critics, to humanise Hitler risked promoting identification with him and in turn, according to Christine Haase might 'start to explain "away" the ultimate evil inherent in [Nazi] ideology and actions' (2006: 191). In addition to noting the implied moral responsibility of the film medium in its rendering of 'history' in her analysis of the divided critical reactions to the film, Haase argues that what was at stake for both sides of the debate was *Downfall*'s claims to authenticity and verisimilitude: lauded by some, highly problematic for others. Many critics maintained that an anti-realist mode would have been inherently more appropriate for the representation of the '"unfathomably" evil criminals associated with the Nazi regime' (ibid.: 196). Haase suggests, however, that it is not the realist mode in itself that is problematic, nor the fact of representing Hitler's very human, quotidian moments, but rather the film's 'failure to acknowledge the existence of any representational dilemma' (ibid.: 197). In other words, according to her assessment, the film could have addressed such a dilemma not so much through the adoption of an anti-realist style, but through a meta-cinematic discourse that could interrogate and prompt viewers' critical engagement with the film's 'realist' representational mode. In effect, what *Downfall* confronts us with is the film's own failure to acknowledge its own cinematic heritage. As a commercial venture the film invests heavily in a form of 'reactionary' historical revisionism, rather than the more radical, leftist historical-materialist approach taken by its cinematic forebears. In doing so, it seems to 'forget' the *Trauerarbeit* ('mourning work') and efforts to 'come to terms with the past' undertaken by numerous proponents of the Young and New German Cinemas from the 1960s to the 1980s. Through this essay, I therefore wish to re-situate *Downfall* within the legacy of this film-historical context.

Before looking in more detail at this context, let us pause to consider the concept of *Vergangenheitsbewältigung*, which frames the diverse set of films included in the following four sections of this volume: rubble film, war film, historical drama and political drama. Translated into English variously as 'mastering the past' or 'coming to terms with the past,' the term has primarily come to refer to the process of working through the acts, effects, consequences, memories and indeed the guilt associated with the Nazi era, including and especially the Second World War and the Holocaust. In post-war Germany under Allied occupation, however, the tendency was to repress this important process in favour of two complementary processes: 'denazification,' which brought with it an active form of repression or denial; and reconstruction, which, in addition to the

Left: *Downfall*, Der Untergang.

physical process of re-building also involved, in the Western Zone, a political re-alignment with the values of liberal democracy, and, in the Eastern Zone, a critique of fascism as a way of promoting communist ideals. These processes had little to do with managing, processing and 'coming to terms with' the manifest damage and disintegration that was inflicted on others by Nazism and the war, and which the German population must have felt acutely at war's end amidst the rubble of their cities and in the face of a shattered sense of identity and belonging that had been carefully constructed and codified by the Nazi propaganda machine.

In 1967 psychoanalysts Alexander and Margarete Mitschlerich published a groundbreaking study entitled *The Inability to Mourn: Principles of Collective Behaviour* in which they drew on Freudian psychoanalytic theories to investigate the reasons behind what they perceived to be a general lack on the part of Germans to individually or collectively confront and engage emotionally with the actions and consequences of the Nazi period. They argued that the German people's response to the loss of Hitler, who 'had become the embodiment of their ego-ideal' and thus a 'loved object' in a psychoanalytic sense, should have manifested as a form of 'melancholia,' which would, under normal circumstances give way to mourning as a way of working through and coming to terms with the loss (A & M. Mitscherlich 1975: 26). However, they observe, '[T]hat so few signs of melancholia or even mourning are to be seen among the great masses can be attributed only to a denial of the past' (ibid.: 28).

Numerous scholars of German cinema have noted a parallel lack of engagement with the past in the cinema of the post-war period that lasts at least until the early 1960s when we see the stirrings of this repressed past beginning to return.[2] Instead, throughout the 1950s we see a general turn toward the spatio-temporal safety of the *Heimatfilm* and other genres such as historical pageants that took audiences back to seemingly less troublesome periods of German and Austro-Hungarian history. A good example would be the *Sissi* trilogy produced in Austria between 1955 and 1957, directed by Ernst Marischka and starring Rommy Schneider in the title role as a Bavarian princess. On top of these 'local' productions, Hollywood distributors took advantage of the Allied occupation to flood West Germany with an entire back catalogue of American products that German audiences had been denied during the war. These imports provided a powerful and pervasive means of retreating from the immediate German past.

The Rubble Film

While the *Heimatfilme* and historical pageants of the 1950s appeared to retreat from the recent past, a small wave of films made in Germany's ruined cities attempted to record some of the experiences of upheaval and dislocation felt by the urban population and by soldiers returning from the front. The short-lived cycle of films (1946–49) known as *Trümmerfilme* ('rubble films') represent German cinema's first, albeit somewhat limited, attempts to survey the immediate aftermath and consequences of the war. To some extent the limitations were imposed by the occupying forces, which initially decommissioned the entire German film industry, conscious of the key role film had played in spreading propaganda and fostering Nazi ideology. After a year-long embargo on German film production the cameras began to roll again, but this time each of the occupying forces that divided Germany into four zones (British, French, US and Russian) kept a tight control of film-making, including access to equipment and film stock, and took pains to ensure films conformed to the ideological dictates of the respective zone in which they were made.

The first of these, *The Murderers Are Among Us* (1946), was made in the Soviet zone after its director Wolfgang Staudte, who had worked in the Nazi film industry, had been denied permission to film it by the Americans. Unlike many rubble films, *Murderers* was something of a box office success. Set amongst the rubble of post-war Berlin, the film functions as a *Heimkehrer* narrative (a narrative of 'return'); in this case a returning soldier, whose memories of traumatic events he experienced during the war return to haunt him, and which the spectator experiences via flashbacks. But this 'home' to which he returns is certainly no *Heimat*. As Eric Rentschler asks, 'How can a landscape of rubble become a site of *Heimat* (home) for this depleted *Heimkehrer*?' (2010: 12). Interestingly, however, the film largely unfolds within a domestic space; a bombed-out apartment occupied by the soldier (and former doctor) Hans Mertens and a young woman, Susanne, a concentration camp survivor. While the walls and windows barely offer any protection from the devastated world outside, it is inside, in the interactions between the two characters, that the film shows a process of psychological reconstruction taking place in parallel to Susanne's efforts to transform the space into a habitable home. Outside the walls Hans is constructed as a 'good' German through his efforts to bring his former commander and war criminal to justice. As with so many of the male characters in the rubble films Hans is figured as a victim of the Nazi regime, effectively establishing a Manichean divide between good and evil, and lending the film a degree of melodramatic intensity that abstracts the narrative from coming to terms with the causes and consequences of Nazism.

Indeed, as Rentschler observes, '[A]lthough Hitler is referred to on occasion, his name is never expressly mentioned in any of the *Trümmerfilme*' (ibid.). This suggests that although these films serve in Gertrude Koch's formulation 'to foster reconstruction by reinstalling a work ethic and reaffirming diligence, honesty, punctuality, moderation,' they did not ultimately engage in or model the kind of mourning work necessary for the nation to begin the process of *Vergangenheitsbewältigung* more directly (ibid.: 10-11).[3] At best, according to Elsaesser, they 'offered an audience prepared to be contrite the comfort of fatalism and self-pity' (1989: 250).

Aesthetically, the rubble films recall but diverge significantly from the films of the Italian neorealists, with which they are often compared largely because they were produced contemporaneously and in similarly war-ravaged cities. Despite the use of some location shooting to establish the setting in one or other of Germany's ruined cities – Berlin, Frankfurt, Cologne, Dresden or Hamburg – in contrast to the neorealist films, which were almost exclusively filmed on location, the rubble films were mostly shot in studio sets built to look like the bombed-out interiors of offices and apartment buildings. They were similarly shot on grainy, hard to get film stock; however, they never quite achieve the subtlety or 'poetic realism' of the neorealist films. Instead, many examples of this German film cycle borrow heavily from the dominant aesthetics of the Weimar period, producing at times a blend of expressionism – with stylistic devices such as chiaroscuro lighting or oblique camera angles – and the dramatised social realism of the *Straßenfilm* ('street film') with its roots in the artistic movement known as *Neue Sachlichkeit* ('New Objectivity'). Additionally, as Elsaesser notes, the rubble films 'showed echoes of the film noir genre as practiced in Hollywood during the 1940s by German émigrés, particularly where a thriller format was employed or a flashback structure' (ibid.). Rentschler argues that the return to the cinematic styles of the earlier era constitute a significant 'departure from the polish of Universum Film AG (UFA) productions under Nazi rule.' As such, he finds correspondences between the rubble film and the 'aesthetic resistance' practiced by directors like Helmut Käutner under the Nazi's between 1943 and 1945, with films like *Romance in a Minor Key* (1943). Käutner's own *In Those Days* (1947) makes an important contribution to the post-war rubble cycle. It is therefore primarily this common impulse to assert a stylistic difference from the Nazi past that the rubble film shares with neorealism, which may itself be set in stark contrast to the glossy melodramas, or 'white telephone films' produced under Mussolini. Rentschler writes, 'Both *Trümmerfilme* and neorealist productions reflect the belief that a changed world demands new ways of seeing and different means of representation' (2010: 11).

In light of the Mitschlerich's thesis that Germans and Germany repressed rather than mourned the past, it is perhaps not surprising that the rubble film and its tentative attempts to work through the past were short-lived, replaced instead by a cinematic aesthetic that to some extent mirrored that of the Nazi era, ironically producing a series of re-makes of films made during that period. It would not be until the early 1960s that a new generation of film-makers would seek new ways of seeing and, in doing so, by the late 1960s set in motion a wave of films that more actively attempted to come to terms with the past, frequently from the perspective of the present. In doing so, they would also virulently critique the 'forgetfulness' of their parents' generation, their failure to mourn, their embrace of rearmament and flagrant retreat into the hyper-consumerism enabled by the *Wirtschaftswunder* ('economic miracle') that saw the rapid recovery of the German economy after 1949 under Chancellor Konrad Adenauer.

As early as 1962, a group of 26 German film-makers, writers, artists and intellectuals formally articulated their desire to overhaul the German film industry, proclaiming, 'The old film is dead. We believe in the new one' (in Rentschler 1988: 2).[4] They did this in February 1962 at the annual Oberhausen short film festival, where they presented and signed the 'Oberhausen Manifesto.' The festival, which began in 1955 and promoted stylistic and formal experimentation, had already served as a platform for young film-makers to explore the new ways of seeing offered by the film medium outside of mainstream commercial feature film production. The festival therefore provided the perfect platform for the manifesto, which called for the establishment of an entirely new conception of cinema to be established, based on new intellectual, formal and economic criteria. On one level the manifesto served as a launching pad from which to commence lobbying for economic reform and state support for diverse film-making practices including a shift from a commercial to what Thomas Elsaesser has called a 'cultural mode of production.'[5] On another level, this involved developing a new kind of audience. By the early 1960s, the cinema-going public in Germany, as elsewhere, experienced a major shift in its demographic, and movies also faced tough competition from television. While the work of the Young and New German film-makers was not necessarily directed toward mainstream youth audiences, through film journals and newspapers as well as alternate screening venues, they tapped into a growing community of politically-aware youth, activists and labour groups whose energy would eventually ignite the rallies and protests that spread throughout Europe and many parts of the world in the late 1960s. On yet a third level, their new conception of what cinema could be encompassed a radical re-think of both the creative and storytelling possibilities of the medium. The Young and New German film-makers that emerged around this time embarked on a much more radical and deliberate wave of aesthetic resistance than the directors of the post-war rubble film could imagine let alone sustain. This renewal of what German film could be also provided greater opportunity and motivation for film-makers to engage in the process of coming to terms with the past.

Among other things, this entailed challenging conceptions of cinematic 'realism' and questioning the possibility of representing a singular or incontestable historical 'truth' on film. Importantly, many were intensely critical of their parents' generation apparent inability to address questions of guilt or responsibility for what had occurred two decades earlier. Borrowing from a French review of Alain Resnais' *Last Year at Marienbad* (1961), German critic Hans Dieter Roos, writing for the film journal *Filmkritik* announced, '*Papas Kino is Tot*' ('Daddy's cinema is dead') (1962: 7–11), thus instigating the kind of cinematic patricide that was implicitly advocated by the signatories of the Oberhausen Manifesto and taken up by many of the directors of the Young and New German Cinemas in the decades to follow.

The proponents of the New German Cinema largely eschewed conventional genre films. Instead, their works tended toward either a hard-edged politicised 'realism,' or else experimented with various approaches to fragmenting and disrupting conventions of narrative cinema. In this latter camp, we find film-makers like Alexander Kluge, Werner

Schroeter and Hans Jürgen Syberberg. In the former, figures like Edgar Reitz, R. W. Fassbinder, Margarethe von Trotta, Jutta Brückner and Helma Sanders-Brahms.

This section of the *Directory* attempts to trace some important themes and concerns that were introduced into the German cinema scene by these developments. I have elected to focus on the 1970s and early 1980s when the movement was at its height, and then to survey how these issues have subsequently been dealt with by successive generations of German film-makers into the first decade of the twenty-first century. There is a single question that hangs over all the entries in this section: how has the question of coming to terms with the past been dealt with by these generations of film-makers? I have elected to organise the remaining sub-sections around fairly broad and recognisable genres, although most films reviewed here certainly exceed or even defy such categorisation. Following coverage of the post-war rubble film, we move on to look at films that deal directly with themes of the Second World War to historical dramas that encompass a broader period encompassing pre-war, wartime and the post-war period to the present. The section concludes with films that I have grouped under the banner of 'political drama' with the majority of films focusing on the terrorist movements of the 1970s.

The War Film

In his book *From Hitler to Heimat: The Return of History as Film*, Anton Kaes notes that between 1948 and 1959, a total of 224 war films were shown in West Germany (1989: 17). According to Marc Silberman more than half of these were from the United States and Britain, with German and Austrian productions making up approximately 40 per cent (1995: 129). The majority of the German productions were made after the mid-1950s. Coinciding with Chancellor Adenauer's plans to re-arm Germany, these productions were heavily subsidised by the government and largely served as 'state propaganda for remilitarization' (ibid). Needless to say, very few, if any, of these could be considered to engage in the process of coming to terms with the past; instead, according to Silverman, they served to confirm 'for spectators an imaginary relation to the past that exonerated feelings of guilt and responsibility' by constructing simplistic dichotomies between good and bad Germans and altogether avoiding the question of responsibility (ibid.: 131). Among these, one of the earliest German-language war films to be distributed in Germany was the Austrian production *The Last Ten Days* (Pabst, 1955), a film that, like *Downfall*, is set in Hitler's bunker in the dying days of the war and is based on testimony from the Nuremburg trials as well as the memoirs of Hitler's secretary, Traudl Junge. Like the rubble film, *The Last Ten Days* aesthetically resists the retreat into the atemporal rural landscapes of the *Heimatfilm* and, in doing so, uses Pabst's signature noir aesthetic to great effect in order to construct an image of Hitler's highest officers, injured soldiers and nurses as they descend into a veritable orgy of drink and debauchery. In stark contrast to *Downfall*, the off-key anti-realist, often melodramatic mode obtained through exaggerated performance, oblique camera angles and expressionist chiaroscuro lighting serve the film's purpose of constructing the Nazi officers as evil and sexually depraved, showing Hitler's deteriorating physical and mental state, and depicting the bunker as a veritable hell in which these characters rightfully belong. In the same year, Pabst directed *Jackboot Mutiny* (1955), a film about an event made familiar to contemporary audiences in the Tom Cruise star vehicle *Valkyrie* (Singer, 2008): the attempt by German army officers to assassinate Hitler on 20 July 1944.[6] There is no question that this film was deliberately trying to recuperate the idea of the 'good German' to counterbalance the overwhelmingly pervasive image of the evil Nazi. This recuperative measure is explicitly stated in the opening voice-over, which is spoken with the authority of a newsreel over images of war. It tells us that the events we are about to see were an attempt to 'save Germany's honour and good name in the world.' The film stars prominent Austrian-born actor and director Bernhard Wicki in the role of von Stauffenberg, the would-be assassin.

We begin this brief survey of German cinema's coming to terms with the war with Bernhard Wicki's own highly successful anti-war film *The Bridge* (1959), which attempts to show the senselessness of war as a group of teenage conscripts schooled in the Hitler Youth ideology are sent to fatefully defend a bridge in April 1945, as Germany is on the verge of defeat. As Jaimey Fisher asserts in his review, although the film is politically light in its refusal to take a recuperative approach, it does serve as an important transition to the more critical and politically engaged films of the 1960s and 1970s. In a follow-up piece to the Oberhausen Manifesto, Alexander Kluge noted that the Young German film-makers were 'seeking close contacts with' a range of 'outstanding film-makers' who were among only a handful to make significant and socially committed films in the immediate post-war era (1962: 11). Among those named are Bernhard Wicki, Wolfgang Staudte and Helmut Käutner, whose films are included here and elsewhere in the pages of this volume.

Although the consequences of the war were ever-present in the mostly contemporary settings of the films of the Young and New German Cinemas, they did not immediately seek to represent the war or the Holocaust. This is perhaps a result of the over determination of the war film genre as state propaganda during the 1950s and the Nazi era, along with the general eschewal of genre films in favour of more experimental and radical approaches to film form and style. As we will see in the next section, the war is most frequently depicted by this generation as one event amidst a much broader historical context; a strategy that allows for a greater historical consciousness to be gained. Among the sparse offerings of films that focus primarily on World War II, we find Volker Schlöndorff's remarkable, Oscar-winning 1979 adaptation of Günter Grass' novel *The Tin Drum*. The film's disruptive, unsettling, ludic mode effectively serves to assault the viewer's senses and disrupt old viewing habits, while still holding on to a narrative logic (albeit a rather complex one) that made it palatable for relatively mainstream audiences. The central protagonist Oskar – who was fabulously born with the mental capacity of an adult and wilfully stunts his growth at the tender age of three – serves as an allegorical spectator-in-the-text through whose oblique, and at times perverse, way of seeing the world allows viewers to gain a new, fractured perspective on Nazism and the many horrors this ideology and those who followed it inflicted on the world.

By the early 1980s, Wolfgang Petersen introduces a more commercial genre-based approach to war with his internationally successful anti-war film *Das Boot* (1981). Trained at the Munich Film School, and beginning his career in television, Petersen's approach marks a stark departure from the highly politicised and formally innovative New German Cinema approach. In terms of the task of coming to terms with the past, what *Das Boot* most contributes to German film history is its assertion of Germany's right to represent its own, dark history to the world. In this sense, it must be seen as a response to Hollywood's more than three-decade monopoly on the topic. But neither the 1980s nor the 1990s would see German film-makers make a sustained contribution to the war genre. The few notable exceptions include Michael Verhoeven's *The White Rose* (1982) about the German anti-Nazi resistance movement; Polish-born Agnieszka Holland's German, French, Polish co-production *Europa, Europa* (1990) about a Jewish boy who survives the war and the holocaust by masquerading as a Hitler Youth; Joseph Vilsmaier's *Stalingrad* (1993); Volker Schlöndorff's *The Ogre* (1996); and Max Färberböck's *Aimee & Jaguar* (1999). By the turn of the millennium, however, we do see a veritable increase in a diverse range of films set during the war including Margarethe von Trotta's *Rosenstrasse* (2003), *Downfall* (2004) and Schlöndorff's *The Ninth Day* (2004), all discussed in this section. This millennial increase may, in part, be attributed to heavy investment in the German film industry in order to open it up to the increasing opportunities for internationalisation and, indeed, numerous Hollywood and 'Europudding' war films – including Polanski's *The Pianist* (2002) and *Enemy at the Gates* (Annaud, 2001) – have been co-produced and filmed on location in Germany or at the Babelsberg or Bavaria studios. What is clear from this brief survey is that neither the war film nor the anti-war film proved to be a terribly adequate or sustainable site for German cinema's coming to terms with the past, although Volker Schöndorff's important and ongoing contribution is certainly noteworthy.

Historical Drama

If the highly conventionalised war film genre proved rather limiting to German cinema's attempts at engaging in *Vergangenheitsbewältigung*, films that sought to dramatise German history through a wider historical frame that also encompassed the present proved more successful. For the generation of film-makers born at the end of the war and who came of age in the 1960s, film and its critical potential, unlocked by the Oberhauseners, also became an important site for examining their parents' generation's 'inability to mourn.' While the New German Cinema's interest in history stretches at times far beyond the turn of the twentieth century, I have elected to focus the selection of films in this section on those that look back only as far as the early twentieth century, and do so precisely in order to analyse the social, political and historical forces that led to the rise of the Third Reich, took Germany to war, committed the atrocities of the Holocaust and then on toward the 'economic miracle' (*Wirtschaftswunder*) in the 1950s and beyond. Formative attempts may be found in the early 1960s with the short satirical film on post-war remilitarization in the Adenauer era, *Machorka-Muff* (Huillet and Straub, 1963) and *Not Reconciled* (Straub, 1965), both adaptations of works by Heinrich Böll. *Not Reconciled*'s elliptical and fragmentary narrative enigmatically treats the themes of guilt, militarism, war and generational conflict by juxtaposing the perspectives of three generations, and shifts time frames in non-linear fashion between the present (the late 1950s) and the past from the pre-World War I period onwards. These films by French émigré directors served as important models for the New German film-makers. Although a film not directly about the past, Alexander Kluge's first feature, *Yesterday Girl* (1966), begins a near obsession with his project of understanding history 'from below.' The film's German title, *Abschied von Gestern*, literally means 'taking leave of yesterday,' but this is not a gesture of forgetfulness. Rather, Kluge encourages us to acknowledge the extent to which the past resides *in* the present.

It is fitting, therefore, that we begin this section with Edgar Reitz's *Zero Hour* (1977). Its focus, on a small village over the course of a few days after the end of the war in 1945, actively resists the monumentalizing of history that often takes place in the historical drama. Additionally, Reitz's view of this moment from the perspective of the late 1970s, when Germany was in the grip of severe disillusionment and social unrest, seems to suggest that while Germany's 'zero hour' offered great promise for renewal this would only be achieved (economically) at the expense of submitting to a new occupying force and forgetting the past. In the same year, Theodor Kotulla made *Death is My Trade* (1977), one of the first German films to directly examine the Holocaust from the perspective of one of its perpetrators: an Auschwitz commandant. Importantly, this film preceded by more than a year the broadcast of the American television mini-series *Holocaust*, which first aired in Germany in January 1979. This television series about a Jewish family caught up in the Holocaust would have an immense impact on the German cultural scene, and ignited heated debates about who had the right to represent this dark chapter in German history, and the means by which that history should be represented. In many ways, more than the German films being produced in Germany at this time, *Holocaust* reminded Germans what the Mitschlerichs had revealed more than a decade earlier: they had failed to mourn.

In February 1979, R. W. Fassbinder's first instalment of his BRD trilogy, *The Marriage of Maria Braun* was premiered at the Berlinale. Through a highly melodramatic mode deeply indebted to the Hollywood melodramas of Douglas Sirk, Fassbinder provides an analysis of this lack of mourning as his protagonist, Maria Braun (a kind of German Everywoman), makes a meteoric rise from post-war rubble woman to veritable *Wirtschafts* wonder woman in the space of just ten years (1945–54). Using the melodramatic mode ironically and Maria as a clear allegory for Germany's economic miracle, Fassbinder shows how Maria's success came at the expense of the suppression of her emotions ('I don't have time for tears,' she says at one point), so much so that her story could only end explosively and tragically. While the film's historical setting takes us only up until 1954, Fassbinder is clearly asking his viewers to view this history from the perspective of the present – the late 1970s – amidst the rise of social movements and terrorist factions critical of what this generation saw as the increasing authoritarianism of German society. This period is also dealt with in Jutta Brückner's 1980 film *Hunger Years in a Land of Plenty*, which similarly uses a woman and her journey through puberty into womanhood to take a critical look at the effect of growing up in a highly repressed and repressive society where children grow up internalising and embodying their parent's buried past. The title alludes to the yearning of a generation for emotional richness and openness to match the country's economic prosperity.

In the East, too, although severely restricted in their representations of the past by East German censorship and the mandate that film should promote communist ideals, a few key film-makers attempted to open up public debate about the past. One of East Germany's most important directors (alongside Frank Beyer and Konrad Wolf), Rainer Simon, attempted this in 1980 with his film *Jadup and Boel*, which was banned until 1988. Like many of the West German directors, evidenced here by films such as *Peppermint Peace* (Rosenbaum, 1983), or *The Nasty Girl* (Verhoeven, 1990) (discussed in the comedy section), Simon confronts the history of the post-war period 'from below' as *Alltagsgeschichte* ('history of the everyday') in order to pose moral questions that were intended to prompt an assessment of the nation's conscience on both sides of the Wall.

By the 1990s this urgent assessment and questioning of the past seems to diminish from German cinema entirely. Eric Rentschler calls this period the 'cinema of consensus' for its retreat into conventional, crowd-pleasing genre films. As we saw with the war film (and will see shortly with the political drama) in the 2000s, this history becomes less a topic to be grappled with conceptually, politically or aesthetically, than a backdrop for gripping drama (Rentschler 2000: 260–77). Of course, producer Bernd Eichinger looms large in this era; his production of Caroline Link's international success *Nowhere in Africa* (2001) brings the largely untold story of Jewish refugees who fled to Africa during the Nazi period to mainstream audiences. While it lacks all of the political edge of the earlier historical dramas in this section, it does share a concern with the history of the everyday, and, perhaps more importantly, reminds us that Jewish stories had largely remained absent from the works of the New German film-makers. I include it here as just such a reminder.

Political Drama

As mentioned above, the 1970s in Germany (as elsewhere) was an era of protest, unrest and terrorism. It was fuelled by the coming of age and to maturity of a politically conscious generation rejecting the conservative Cold War politics and repressiveness of their parents and grandparent's generation. The emergence of various home-grown left-wing terrorist groups in West Germany in the 1970s sparked, on the one hand, a series of kidnappings of wealthy German industrialists (some of whom were ex-Nazis) and violent attacks against large corporations, and, on the other, a severe crackdown on civil liberties by authorities and the propagation of a culture of fear and conspiracy by the press. For German artists and intellectuals the increasingly repressive nature of the public sphere that emerged as a heavy-handed response to the terrorist movement signalled a return of what had been repressed rather than dealt with in the aftermath of the war. The 'denazification' and reinstalment of many high-ranking bureaucrats into positions of power in business and government was problematic for artists and terrorists alike. While the majority of the West German film-makers, intellectuals, writers and artists did not condone the violent path taken by the terrorists – like the left-wing student groups, feminists, the civil rights movement and gay rights activists who all emerged with a significant voice in this period – they did see a clear connection between the Nazi period, post-war amnesia, the economic miracle and Germany's now deeply ingrained social problems. Much more than the war films or historical dramas, it was the films about terrorism and the culture of fear and paranoia that emerged with it that really try to come to terms with the consequences of the past in the present. For Volker Schlöndorff, German post-war writers Heinrich Böll and Günter Grass paved the way for his own, politically charged cinematic confrontation of the past and the present. He adapted two of Böll's works for the screen (as did Straub and Huillet). Prior to his adaptation of Günter Grass' novel *The Tin Drum*, Schlöndorff made the Böll adaptation *The Lost Honour of Katharina Blum* (1975), co-directed with his wife Margarethe von Trotta. In it they capture the climate of intense paranoia in Germany when a woman is accused of being a terrorist sympathizer. The film comes down hard on the treatment of her by the police and press alike. Three years later Schlöndorff filmed a script by Böll for his contribution to the radical docu-fiction-essay film *Germany in Autumn* (Kluge; Schlöndorff; Fassbinder; Brustellin; Sinkel; Rupé; Cloos; Reitz; Mainka; Schubert; Mainka-Jellinghaus, 1978), collectively produced by some of the most prominent figures of the New German Cinema. More than any other film of its era, *Germany in Autumn* makes a multifaceted statement not so much about terrorism itself, but about the pervasive remnants of the country's authoritarian past in the present.

Several other New German Cinema directors also made contributions to this cycle of terrorist films including R. W. Fassbinder (*The Third Generation*, 1979), and Werner Schroeter, with his oblique gesture toward this topic in *Day of the Idiots* (1981), starring Carole Bouquet as a woman who goes mad after denouncing her neighbours as terrorist sympathizers. The spectres of the past haunt her as she feels increasingly alienated and repressed by what she perceives to be a society obsessed with order and control. Margarethe von Trotta's *The German Sisters* (1981) looks at what is left behind – a sister and a son – after RAF member Gudrun Ensslin's suicide in Stammheim prison in the 'German autumn' of 1977. The German title of von Trotta's film – *Die bleierne Zeit* – casts the 1970s as a 'leaden time' full of insidious oppression that drives Ensslin's sister in the film to seek the 'truth' of Gudrun's apparent suicide so that she may gift this truth to Gudrun's young son, and by implication the next generation, who will no doubt grow up with little memory of these events, particularly if the mainstream German press has any say in this.

In this vein, the section then proceeds to survey films that look at the legacy of the terrorist campaign with a spate of films produced around the turn of the millennium like Schlöndorff's *Legend of Rita* (2000) and Christian Petzold's *The State I Am In* (2000), which asks the question: what happens to ex-terrorists once the radical times have abated and they are now raising families? A similar question is asked by the young 'anti-capitalist' would-be radicals of Hans Weingartner's *The Edukators* (2004) when they confront an ex-activist who has entered the mainstream and left behind his radical past in favour of a fully capitalised lifestyle. In tension with these films of the early 2000s that still attempt to look critically at the terrorist movements of the 1970s and their aftermath, we find the widely successful *The Baader Meinhof Complex* (2008) that, like *Downfall*, partakes of a certain 'commercialisation' of history as entertainment by adopting a Hollywood style narrative form and glossy aesthetic that does not ask its viewer to think critically about its content. Instead, some have argued that the significance of the radical politics that it purports to represent is lost under a commercial production value that has been variously described as 'Prada-Meinhof' or 'Terrorist Chic,' somewhat ironically, standing at odds with the anti-capitalist stance of the RAF movement. Such films even fail to draw comparisons or connections with our current era of global terrorism and the ensuing War on Terror.

Sitting amongst these political dramas about terrorism we also find Marc Rothemund's *Sophie Scholl: The Final Days* (2005) about the arrest and 'trial' of prominent member of the White Rose anti-Nazi resistance movement. Although the film does not draw this comparison directly, from the perspective of the Nazis Scholl was indeed a 'terrorist' and their treatment of her parallels closely the treatment of the RAF terrorists in the 1970s. Interestingly, it was one of the few internationally successful films produced entirely in Germany in the late 2000s, bucking the trend toward high-budget, high-concept international co-productions exemplified by *The Baader Meinhof Complex*, *Downfall* (2004) or *Perfume* (2006). *Sophie Scholl* may here be paired with Dennis Gansel's *The Wave* (2008), as they deal respectively with the question of right-wing extremism in the past and the present. However, where *Sophie Scholl* affirms the necessity to stand up heroically to oppressive, dictatorial regimes which are, for contemporary audiences of the film, safely sequestered in the past, Gansel's film asks whether Germany could ever be taken over by an autocratic regime again. Although based on an American novel and social experiment, its adaptation to the German context seems logical and topical given the rise of neo-Nazi movements in the last decade or so. With its youth focus and high school setting the film attempts to address and provoke a new generation for whom the war and Nazism is but a distant event that (these days) they only ever see dramatised in the movies.

Michelle Langford

Notes

1. For an excellent summary of the range of critical responses to the film, both positive and negative see: Christine Haase (2006), 'Ready for his close-up? Representing Hitler in *Der Untergang* (*Downfall*, 2004)', *Studies in European Cinema* 3: 3, pp. 194-195.
2. The first wave of such approaches to German cinema include: Timothy Corrigan (1983), *New German Film: The Displaced Image*, Austin: University of Texas Press; Thomas Elsaesser (1989), *New German Cinema: A History*, New Brunswick, NJ: Rutgers University Press; Anton Kaes (1989), *From Hitler to Heimat: The Return of History as Film*, Cambridge, MA and London: Harvard University Press; Eric L. Santner (1990), *Stranded Objects: Mourning, Memory, and Film in Postwar Germany*, Ithaca and London: Cornell University Press.
3. Rentschler cites Gertrud Koch, (1978) "Nachkriegsfilme als Werke der Restauration: Einige Thesen zur Ideologiedes 'Trümmerfilms' in Deutschland," *Kirche und Film* 31, no. 2, pp. 6–9.
4. The full English version of the text is available in Eric Rentschler (ed.) (1988), *West German Filmmakers on Film: Visions and Voices*, New York and London: Holmes & Meier, p. 2.
5. For a more sustained consideration of this point see Thomas Elsaesser (1989), *The New German Cinema: A History*, pp. 36–46.
6. This topic was also treated in a range of other productions including the German TV film *Stauffenberg* (*Operation Valkyrie*) (Baier, 2004), which preceded *Valkyrie* by several years.

References

Corrigan, Timothy (1983), *New German Film: The Displaced Image*, First Edition, Austin: University of Texas Press.

Elsaesser, Thomas (1989), *New German Cinema: A History*, New Brunswick, NJ: Rutgers University Press.

Haase, Christine (2006), 'Ready for his close-up? Representing Hitler in *Der Untergang* (*Downfall*, 2004)', *Studies in European Cinema*, 3: 3, pp. 189-200.

Kaes, Anton (1989), *From Hitler to Heimat: The Return of History as Film*, Cambridge, MA and London: Harvard University Press.

Kluge, Alexander (1962), 'What do the "Oberhauseners: Want?', in Eric Rentschler (ed.) (1988), *West German Filmmakers on Film: Visions and Voices*, New York and London: Holmes & Meier, p. 11.

Koch, Gertrude (1978), 'Nachkriegsfilme als Werke der Restauration: Einige Thesen zur Ideologiedes "Trümmerfilms" in Deutschland', *Kirche und Film*, 31: 2, pp. 6–9.

Mitscherlich, Alexander and Mitscherlich, Margarete (1975), *The Inability to Mourn: Principles of Collective Behaviour* (trans. Beverley R. Placzek), New York: Grove Press.

Rentschler, Eric (ed.) (1988), *West German Filmmakers on Film: Visions and Voices*, New York and London: Holmes & Meier.

Rentschler, Eric (2000), 'From New German Cinema to the Post-Wall Cinema of Consensus', in Mette Hjort and Scott MacKenzie (eds.), *Cinema and Nation*, New York: Routledge, pp. 260–77.

Rentschler, Eric (2010), 'The Place of Rubble in the *Trümmerfilm*', *New German Critique*, 37: 2, pp. 9-30.

Roos, Hans Dieter (1962), '*Papas Kino is Tot*', *Filmkritik*, 1, pp. 7–11.

Santner, Eric L. (1990), *Stranded Objects: Mourning, Memory and Film in Postwar Germany*, Ithaca, NY: Cornell University Press.

Silberman, Marc (1995), *German Cinema: Texts in Context*, Detroit: Wayne State University Press, pp. 129–31.

RUBBLE FILM
DER TRÜMMERFILM

Left: *The Murderers Are Among Us*, Deutsche Film (DEFA).

The Murderers Are Among Us

Die Mörder sind unter uns

Production Company:
Deutsche Film (DEFA)

Distributors:
Sovexport-Film GmbH (Soviet zone)
Internationale Filmallianz (IFA) (French zone)
Herzog Filmverleigh (British and American zone)
Artkino Pictures (USA)

Director:
Wolfgang Staudte

Screenwriters:
Wolfgang Staudte
Eberhard Keindorff (uncredited)
Johanna Sibelius (uncredited)
Fritz Staudte (uncredited)

Cinematographers:
Friedl Behn-Grund
Eugen Klagemann

Composer:
Ernst Roters

Editor:
Hans Heinrich

Duration:
85 minutes

Genre:
Coming to Terms with the Past
Der Trümmerfilm

Cast:
Ernst Wilhelm Borchert
Hildegard Knef
Arno Paulsen
Elly Burgmer

Year:
1946

Synopsis

The Murderers Are Among Us follows a medical doctor, Hans Mertens (Borchert), through the surreal cityscape of early post-war Berlin. Mertens' experiences as a soldier have so traumatized him that he can do little save drink and sulk when his medical skills are sorely needed. The opening sequences establish Germany's and Mertens' devastated state with memorable location shots of the ubiquitous rubble that dominated Germany's cities after the war. Mertens lives in a bombed-out apartment to which the rightful inhabitant, a young female concentration camp survivor named Susanne (Knef), soon returns. *Murderers* then traces Mertens' struggle for personal reconstruction. Prominent among the demons Mertens must confront is his old army commander Brückner (Paulsen), who ordered the massacre of Polish villagers on Christmas Day, which viewers witness in a flashback. Mertens struggles between confronting Brückner about his sins and killing him for his crime: at the precise moment he plans to shoot Brückner in the rubble a mother begs him for help with her sick daughter, whom Mertens saves – his first tentative steps back to practicing medicine. Later, when Mertens concocts another plan to kill Brückner, Susanne restrains him. In the end Brückner is imprisoned while Mertens and Susanne happily move beyond the past together.

Critique

As one of the few 'rubble-films' that became well known, *Murderers* was the first German feature film made after World War II. Although it was made in the Soviet Occupational Zone (SBZ), and with the approval of the Soviet military authorities, it was started so early that DEFA, the East German film studio, had not yet been created. The writer/director, Wolfgang Staudte, who had worked in the Nazi-controlled UFA studio, first approached US officials but, given the belief that cinema had been central to the Nazis' propaganda programme, Staudte was told that no German would make a feature film for many years. Soviet officials had a different model for Nazi culpability, one that emphasized 'two Germanys,' in which economic and political elites had duped the working-classes, which meant bourgeois artists like Staudte could return to work more quickly. The result was *Murderers*, one of the most popular and aesthetically successful German films of the period 1946–51.

Part of this success derived from the film's memorable depiction of post-war Berlin. With its use of some location shooting amongst the rubble, the film parallels in many ways the Italian neorealist films that had considerable impact in Germany and around the world at the end of the war: both this German film and the Italian films emphasized changed cityscapes and the alternative social relations pervading them in the wake of the war.

At the level of plot, the most pointed conflict is between Mertens as the regular soldier (who happens to be a doctor), and his former commander, Brückner, who ordered the massacre of the Polish villagers. The two represent two post-war modes of dealing with the past: Mertens is completely traumatized and dysfunctional, while Brückner is rich, happy and successful from post-war profiteering, recycling military equipment into much-needed household objects. The figure of Brückner – the entrepreneur as war criminal – seems transparently ideological given the Soviet line on Nazism as a result of two Germanys (the workers' and the bourgeoisie's), and the GDR's subsequent association of fascism with capitalism. The film's happy ending seems suspiciously convenient and even contrived; not surprisingly, as it was changed from the original script, in which Mertens shoots Brückner and the film closes with Mertens' trial, whose ultimate verdict remains ambiguous. The Soviet censors, however, required that Staudte change the ending to discourage vigilantism; a concession to the chaotic social moment and proof of the difficult legal context.

This theme of coming to terms with the past entails, at a more subtle level, the revitalization of Mertens via the negotiation of gender and gender relations that were transformed by the war and its traumatic aftermath. Brückner's screen time is actually quite limited; the plot largely narrates how post-war males would require the unshakeable desire and love of post-war women, who were, of course, likely to be just as traumatized. But the film emphasizes how such traumatized men might reject their post-war social duties while women should, by the logic of such films, immediately take up theirs to help support men returning from the war. Carefully depicted and policed gender difference thus rests at the very heart of this transformation of men's post-war 'reconstruction.' Early sequences enact not only male lack and male alterity, but also the inversion of the dominant specular relations between the sexes. From the first scene in which Mertens looks at Susanne, his gaze is undesirous; it is unhealthy and inadequate. Her presence humiliates and tortures him: he buries his head on his arm, stifling any desiring gaze, at the moment she looks lovingly at him. The film deploys in Susanne the normative but unrealistic ideal of the self-abnegating 'rubble-woman.' She is a woman who cleans up the ruins and provides for the household without ever leaving the apartment. Instead, the movie proscribes for Susanne a tough-lipped desire for male lack. From the moment she sees 'what type of man' Mertens is, her desire for him is unshakable, and she ultimately nurses him back to psychological wholeness. Such a representation of the post-war rubble-woman seems all the more reductive given that the film never details the nature of Susanne's concentration camp internment. In many ways, this tension between post-war men and women stands in for, or eclipses, German crimes against humanity that the Allies' re-educational programme was foregrounding at the same time.

Jaimey Fisher

Somewhere in Berlin

Irgendwo in Berlin

Production Company:
Deutsche Film (DEFA)

Distributors:
Sovexport-Film GmbH
Progress Film-Verleigh GmbH
Central Cinema Corportation

Director:
Gerhard Lamprecht

Screenwriter:
Gerhard Lamprecht

Cinematographer:
Werner Krien

Composer:
Erich Einegg

Editor:
Lena Neumann

Duration:
80 minutes

Genre:
Social Drama
Der Trümmerfilm

Cast:
Charles Brauer
Harry Hindemith
Hedda Sarnow
Hans Trinkaus
Paul Bildt
Fritz Rasp

Year:
1946

Synopsis

This film traces the struggles of two so-called 'rubble-children,' Gustav (Brauer) and Willi (Trinkaus) in post-war Berlin. Gustav's father (Hindemith) is still missing from the war, while Willi, his friend, has neither father nor mother, and is exploited by the corrupt Birke (Bildt) to steal food. The film then further underscores the fragmented family life of rubble-children by having the boys meet a whole army of other children who have convened among the rubble, without any adult supervision, to play war.

Into this chaotic social situation wanders Gustav's father in a conspicuously tattered uniform, at first not recognized by his own son. When Willi observes how his friend's father struggles with conspicuous depression and despair, he steals food from Birke to nurse him back to health. Birke is furious and throws Willi out of his house. Parentless and now alone, Willi decides, when teased by the other boys, to prove his courage by scaling a towering ruin, from which he promptly plummets. Gustav's father visits Willi on his deathbed and promises him that they will build it all up again. The film closes with an image of father and son pounding away on the rubble to rebuild the former's garage.

Critique

In a way similar to the first post-war feature film, *The Murderers Are Among Us* (1946), this second feature after World War II (made by DEFA in the Soviet Occupational Zone) also foregrounds the reconstruction of traumatized returning soldiers amidst the social chaos of post-war Berlin. Perhaps even more than *Murderers*, the film emphasizes how the conflicts taken up in the film reflect widespread social problems that are typically not just 'somewhere,' but anywhere 'in Berlin.' Also similar to *The Murderers Are Among Us* is the selective use of memorable location shooting to thematize the ubiquitous rubble of Germany's post-war cities, which serve as stark symbols for the challenges, both psychological and social, that Germans would face after World War II. Finally, also as in *Murderers*, these shots of the rubble become conveniently abstract, even abstruse, symbols for the past and its crimes. Rather than any direct representation of the victims of the war or Holocaust, the past is represented primarily through the trauma that the returning German soldier manifests, but that neither he, nor this plot, ever very specifically articulates.

The focus of *Somewhere in Berlin*, however, is not so much, as in *Murderers*, on how the rubble-women would have to put aside their own concerns to help reconstruct Germany's traumatized men, but instead on the social problem of rubble-children, who often had not seen their fathers for years, and who had also frequently lost their mothers in the bombings and battles in Germany's cities. Both of these fates are central to the plotting of *Somewhere*: at the start of the film, Gustav brings home an adoptive, if corrupt, man to replace his missing father; while his best friend Willi is an orphan exploited by one of these era's recurring types – the small-time criminal taking advantage of the relative lawlessness of the early post-war period.

Somewhere in Berlin does share with *Murderers* an aesthetic, almost film-historical strategy as well. Like *Murderers*, the film deliberately returns to the less politically problematic cinematic traditions of the Weimar era. Like Wolfgang Staudte, the writer/director Gerhard Lamprecht also wanted to circumvent the sort of films produced by the very successful Nazi film industry by taking up a topic and style of the pre-World War II era. But, while *Murderers* deploys a somewhat expressionist style with shadow, murder and intrigue, *Somewhere in Berlin* explicitly invoked a hugely successful children's story and film of a later Weimar moment more akin to New Objectivity, namely, Erich Kästner's 1929 *Emil and the Detectives*, which Lamprecht himself made into a film in 1931 from a script by Kästner, a young Billy Wilder and some uncredited work by Emeric Pressburger. It was not only the children at the centre of the plot which underscored this return to the 1931 film; the conceit of a wallet stolen by a character played by perennial spook Fritz Rasp also made these links – a circumventing of the Nazi era in favour of Weimar citations – very clear. The film's strategy of coming to terms with the past by only vaguely depicting it and then returning to the Weimar era is clear at the surface of the plot and its casting.

Jaimey Fisher

In Those Days (or Seven Journeys)

In jenen Tagen

Production Company:
Camera-Filmproduktion

Distributors:
Britischer Atlas-Filmverleih (British zone)
Herzog-Filmverleih (American zone)
Prisma-Filmverleih (French zone)
Sovexport-Film GmbH (Soviet zone)

Director:
Helmut Käutner

Producer:
Helmut Käutner

Synopsis

Germany lies in ruins at the end of World War II, and two young men ponder the nature and fate of humanity as they pick through the remains of a wrecked automobile. As they lament the loss of so many people during the war the car begins to narrate its story in seven vignettes. A number scratched into the windscreen provides the starting point as the car is delivered to its first owner in January 1933, the month in which Hitler came to power. A range of small objects found in the wreck link the car to its various owners and their fates. The seven episodes mirror events in the Third Reich, including the flight into exile of the first Jews in 1933, the banning of 'degenerate' artists, the 1938 November pogrom, the rounding up of resistance members and, finally, Germany's military collapse in 1945 and the mass exodus from the country's East. Despite the descent into tragedy and desolation, the film manages to reach something of a happy end as the car's last journey brings a widowed young mother and her infant to the relative safety of the Western occupation zone and the fabled rebirth of a new Germany.

Critique

In Those Days was the first post-war film made in what was to become the Federal Republic or West Germany. It was shot in

Screenwriters:
Helmut Käutner
Ernst Schnabel

Art Director:
Helmut Beck

Cinematographer:
Igor Oberberg

Composer:
Bernhard Eichhorn

Editor:
Wolfgang Wehrum

Duration:
111 minutes

Genre:
Coming to Terms With the Past
Der Trümmerfilm

Cast:
Erich Schellow
Gerd E. Schäfer
Karl John
Winnie Markus
Erich Weiher

Year:
1947

and around the ruins of Hamburg and, like its contemporary, *The Murderers Are Among Us*, makes telling use of the city's rubble as a visual leitmotiv. As an attempt to explore Germany's immediate past, *In Those Days* represents a very cautious first step and, with the hindsight about Germany's post-war development we now enjoy, it is easy to be critical of its tentative approach.

Through the choice of a car as its principal character, the film goes a long way towards depersonalizing the whole Third Reich experience. The picaresque automobile is the only identification figure that links the various elements of the story. Although many of the characters in the film wonder about the nature of humanity in the face of their experiences, it is left to a mechanical object to provide any answers or guidance. Indeed, for a film attempting to deal with the period between 1933 and 1945, there are a number of notable absences. The word Nazi is entirely absent, as are swastikas and any portrayals of overtly brutal party members or officers. The few members of the state apparatus encountered are overly officious policemen. Physical violence is restricted to one scene in which a soldier is shot by unseen partisans while driving the car. Perpetrators are entirely absent and there is no mention of the concentration camps. Even the few German soldiers who appear are portrayed as frightened victims in a snow-covered nightmare landscape or as nostalgic car-lovers.

Questions of responsibility for the positions in which the car and its owners find themselves are left unasked, and the film's characters are depicted as victims of a superhuman evil akin to a natural disaster. The interweaving of subplots in the form of various love stories further weakens the film's attempts to deal with the past. Through these omissions the film takes on the quality of a fairy-tale with a mildly didactic tone that is accentuated by the use of a voice-over narrator. The final vignette even has clear Christian references as three characters – Marie (Bettina Moissi), Joseph (Carl Raddatz) and a baby – seek refuge in a barn before setting out on their long journey westward and what Joseph jokingly calls Egypt.

The film makes a clear appeal to humanity as the foundation of a new, post-war German society. These discourses were widespread at the time and, with its reluctance to deal with questions of responsibility and its hopeful end, *In Those Days* was typical of thinking in the Western zone in the first decade after the end of the war. The idea of 'drawing a line' under the past and moving on was to become paradigmatic in German public life during the 1950s.

Despite these criticisms, *In Those Days* does succeed in bringing disparate elements of the Third Reich into a single narrative, and its cautious and conciliatory approach certainly helped it maximize its popularity in post-war Germany: a society faced with the enormous task of trying to comprehend what had happened under the Nazi regime. In this sense, the film does make a pioneering, if cautious and tentative, contribution to the early cinematic attempts to come to terms with the past in post-war Germany.

Brian Long

...and the Sky Above Us

...und über uns der Himmel

Production Company:
Objektiv Film GmbH

Distributor:
Schorcht Filmverleih GmbH
(British and American zone)

Director:
Josef von Báky

Producer:
Richard König

Screenwriter:
Gerhard Grindel

Art Director:
Emil Hasler
Walter Kutz

Cinematographer:
Werner Krien

Composer:
Theo Mackeben

Editor:
Wolfgang Becker

Duration:
103 minutes

Genre:
Social Drama
Der Trümmerfilm

Cast:
Hans Albers
Paul Edwin Roth
Lotte Koch
Heidi Scharf

Year:
1947

Synopsis

When ex-crane operator Hans Richter (Albers) returns from World War II and a POW camp he finds his Berlin home in ruins. He soon learns that his son Werner (Roth) is also on his way home from the war. Meanwhile, a friend from the POW camp offers to employ Hans to haul some goods to the Haiti bar. When Hans realizes he has unwittingly trafficked in contraband, he demands more money, and is slowly pulled into a black market ring, as is his young, pretty neighbour, Mizzi (Scharf), another frequenter of the Haiti bar. His son Werner returns and witnesses in full horror the ruinous condition of his city and his family. He confronts his father about his black market work, and the rest of the film unfolds in the conflict between father and son, right and wrong, corruption and redemption, in post-war Germany. After this confrontation Hans retraces his steps around the ruined landscape and relearns the lesson of the rubble. He wanders around in a majestic overcoat and smart fedora, quietly taking in the rubble and those toiling away at it. It is his son's lessons of humility that teaches Hans that he has to be fully committed to the (legal) reconstruction of Germany.

Critique

Like many rubble films, ...and the Sky Above Us traces the post-war return and reintegration of a soldier returning home (Heimkehrer), but this time the Heimkehrer figure is played by a high-profile star, the much loved Hans Albers. Hans Albers counts as probably the greatest male star of the Third Reich, and the decision to cast him in the first US-licensed film drew harsh criticism: the criticism, however, was motivated not so much by Albers' work during the Nazi period, but by the casting of a star in a rubble film. In casting a star as its Heimkehrer, ...and the Sky Above Us took the rubble film in an altogether different direction because Hans stands in stark contrast to the recurrent and usually fatigued Heimkehrer-type familiar from the early eastern German rubble films. A big part of the earlier rubble films' coming to terms with the past seemed to be a cinema directed against the star-driven forms of both Hollywood and Nazi cinema – in deliberate contrast, the early rubble films cast relatively unknown actors to highlight the general, and therefore generalizable, plight and trauma of post-war Germans.

Due to these differences in the type of protagonist, Hans Albers as Hans Richter in ...and the Sky Above Us requires not the psychological and ideological jumpstart of the standard Heimkehrer sketched in the early DEFA films, but rather a severe downgrading of his exceptional ambition and activity. Albers, like many high-profile stars then and now, was famous for his performance of himself, rather than the scripted character of any given film. Many criticized his inability to subordinate his extra-filmic personality to the specific film role. While his role in ...and the Sky Above Us certainly played on his well-known charms, it also moved his career in an altogether different, although revealing direction: by Albers's own account, this was only the second time in his long and diverse film career he had played a father. In his celebrated outsider status, Albers was usually cast as single man and often maintained an uneasy relationship to the humbling social integration of family life. The film's casting of Albers as a father demonstrates the changed cinematic and social environment in which stars were then operating: from the very first sequence, conventional star status has been refigured by Hans' relationship to paternity and young people, which became central to his recommitment to the legal rebuilding of Germany.

How Hans learns from his son Werner is pretty clear, but, as critics at the time noted, the young neighbour Mizzi functions as the most dynamic and interesting character in the film. In her flight from the ruined private sphere to youthful indulgence she counteracts the flat and obviously normative depictions of female characters in other rubble films, including Susanne in *The Murderers Are Among Us* (1946), Grete Iller in *Somewhere in Berlin* (1946), and Lotte Behnke in *Rotation* (Staudte, 1949). She much more resembles Edmund's sister Eva in Roberto Rossellini's unflinching *Germany Year Zero* (1948), a strong female who demonstrates and acts upon both sexual desire and economic ambition.

The film allows for the complexity of Mizzi's reaction to the post-war context, but ultimately favours Werner's reaction. As Werner walks through the rubble, the film cuts from him looking to documentary shots of ruins, wounded and maimed bodies, and *Trümmerfrauen* ('rubble women') labouring atop mountains of rubble. The moment echoes those in numerous other rubble films, in which the male learns to assimilate the lessons of the rubble by looking in an altogether different way at the context. But in this very different film the star Albers, as Hans Richter, learns from his son. It is a rags-to-riches back to rags story for the protagonist Hans that refigures the usual graced ascent of the star by way of a deliberately modest post-war reconstruction.

Jaimey Fisher

Rotation

Production Company:
Deutsche Film (DEFA)

Distributors:
Deutsche Film (DEFA)
Sovexport-Film GmbH
Westfalen-Film

Director:
Wolfgang Staudte

Synopsis

The film opens with the 1945 battle of Berlin. Prisoner Hans Behnke (Esser) stares blankly at some graffiti in his cell, from which a dissolve begins an hour-long flashback. This flashback to the Weimar and Nazi periods begins by recounting Hans's marriage to Lotte (Korb) and introduces Lotte's communist brother Kurt (Bernt), as well as a social circle that turns increasingly Nazi. After they have a son, Hellmuth (Deickert), Hans seeks work in the degenerating economic situation. While communist Kurt actively resists the Nazis, Hans rejects any political involvement. Shots of a newspaper press announce the changing times – 'Hitler comes to power' – and economic matters have improved substantially for the Behnkes. Although not a convinced Nazi, Hans cooperates with them, including turning his back on Jewish neighbours as they are deported. When Kurt asks Hans to help print anti-war leaflets, the Behnke's

Screenwriters:
Wolfgang Staudte
Erwin Klein
Fritz Staudte

Cinematographer:
Bruno Mondi

Composer:
H. W. Wiemann

Editor:
Lilian Seng

Duration:
80 minutes

Genre:
Social Drama
Der Trümmerfilm

Cast:
Paul Esser
Irene Korb
Karl-Heinz Deickert
Reinhold Bernt
Reinhard Kolldehoff
Brigitte Krause

Year:
1949

son Hellmuth reports his parents, and Hans is forced to turn in his brother-in-law. When Hellmuth denounces his father again, Hans is confronted with his own son in front of a Security Service (SD or *Sicherheitsdienst*) official, which ends the flashback.

Back in 1945, Lotte is killed amid the Berlin chaos, while Hans is liberated by Soviet soldiers. After his post-war release, young Hellmuth finds Hans, who is not sure how to react to the son who turned him over to the Nazis. But then, after a few moments of hesitation, he embraces him. The film closes with Hellmuth and girlfriend Inge (Krause) in the countryside, recalling Hans and Lotte's first date, though Hellmuth promises not to repeat the mistakes of history.

Critique

At the time if its release, *Rotation* was the most expensive film DEFA had made, and it counted as probably the most popular of its anti-fascist films in the 1945–49 period. The film's goal, as described by Staudte, was certainly one shared by many anti-fascist films: to galvanize historical consciousness and activate political resistance in the average German. In much of the contemporary and later reception of the film *Rotation* is praised for shifting the post-war films' political emphasis out of the private house into a more public forum, particularly for thematizing the public sphere and the various media constituting it. In fact, the title refers to the rotation of the newspaper printing presses of the Nazi daily, *Völkischer Beobachter*, where Hans eventually takes a job; a clear and stark admonishment against political compromises made for economic stability.

In terms of film style and genre the first two post-war films, *The Murderers Are Among Us* (1946) and *Somewhere in Berlin* (1946), both deliberately tried to circumvent the compromised years of 1933–45 by returning to the Weimar era. *Rotation* similarly returns to a genre from the late-1920s/early-1930s, but instead engages the Weimar worker film, which foregrounds the economic struggles of the working-class between 1919 and 1933. Indeed, among *Rotation*'s most memorable montages are poignant depictions of the material and psychological struggles of the unemployed. For example, one particularly celebrated sequence offers scenes of Hans literally being locked out (by a recurring visual motif of bars) from work and economic plenitude. The film, however, later matches such memorable sequences with scenes that highlight the political compromises Hans makes to overcome economic challenges. For example, after Hans is forced to renounce his communist brother Kurt, another arresting sequence pans over Kurt's death certificate to the shocked and then despairing Lotte, to Hans staring at the *Führerbild* (required picture of Hitler) in the dinning room. A tea kettle screams, Hellmuth, outfitted in Hitler Youth regalia, comes in to turn it off and to witness Hans throw an ashtray at the picture of Hitler, which leads to the child's final denunciation of his own father.

In its depiction of National Socialism and its aftermath, then, *Rotation* approaches coming to terms with the past through the relationship between a politically passive man and a threatening youth who provides a conduit for Nazi propaganda and ideology to infiltrate the family home. In this respect, the film also takes up a fairly direct dialogue with the 1933 Nazi propaganda film *Hitlerjunge Quex* (dir. Hans Steinhoff), which also depicted the crises of late Weimar and the rise of National Socialism as a largely youth affair, with a similar son's flight from the family's private sphere into a youth-dominated, Nazi public sphere.

Rotation, however, also bears the marks of its particular late 1940s historical moment, one still dominated by the Allies but now in an increasingly politicized, proto-Cold War moment: the film's original ending had Hans burning his son's uniform after giving him his old suit and saying, 'That was the last uniform you'll ever wear.' The Soviet authorities resisted this declaration and, apparently with their own plans for German soldiers and uniforms, insisted that Staudte remove the burning of the uniform and Hans' declaration about it. By 1949, *Rotation*'s coming to terms with the past was already imbricated in a political planning for the Cold War future.

Jaimey Fisher

The Last Illusion
Der Ruf

Production Company:
Objectiv Film

Distributors:
Schorcht Filmverleih GmbH (Germany)
Films International (USA)

Director:
Josef von Báky

Producer:
Richard König

Screenwriter:
Fritz Kortner

Art Director:
Fritz Lück
Fritz Maurischat
Hans Sohlne

Cinematographer:
Werner Krien

Composer:
Georg Haentzschel

Synopsis

An exiled Jewish professor, Mauthner (Kortner), receives a call back to his former German university after World War II. In Berlin, Mauthner seeks his estranged wife, Lina (Hofer), and viewers learn only then that they have a son who remained in Germany with his mother: Lina remarried and raised him as an Aryan without revealing who his real father was. Back at his university, a resentful faculty member is apparently planning some kind of action against Mauthner with the students, one of whom, Walter (Schröder), is also Mauthner's son, although neither knows it. Mauthner gives his (re-)inaugural lecture on a topic about which he last spoke at the university: Plato and the teachability of virtue. At the end of the lecture the vast majority of the German students deliberately refuse to applaud.

At a post-lecture reception a brawl breaks out between German and American students, with the Americans defending Mauthner and the Germans attacking him. Walter confronts Mauthner and causes him to have a heart attack. Now bedridden, Mauthner asks Lina to stay with him. Walter visits Mauthner to apologize and sees his mother there. When Walter addresses her as 'mother,' Mauthner recognizes his son, but dies at this realization. The film closes with his funeral procession, which formerly anti-Semitic students now join.

Critique

Josef von Baky's *The Last Illusion* was the first post-war film released in both German and English versions, and celebrated the triumphant homecoming of the famous theatre and film actor, Fritz Kortner. After von Báky's somewhat controversial *...and the Sky Above Us*, *The Last Illusion* reflects how other rubble films from the Western

Editor:
Wolfgang Becker

Duration:
100 minutes

Genre:
Social Drama
Der Trümmerfilm

Cast:
Fritz Kortner
Rosemary Murphy
Johanna Hofer
Ernst Schröder

Year:
1949

sectors began to cast stars as their male leads. For instance, one critic observed that with *Illusion* von Báky was continuing the trend started with *Sky Above*: a 'Starfilm' of international calibre.

Kortner was one of the biggest stars of the Weimar stage and screen, having been a favourite of famed theatre director Max Reinhardt, and a regular player in films, including important pictures like Wiene's *The Hands of Orlac* (1924) and Pabst's *Pandora's Box* (1929). Vilified by the Nazis for being Jewish, as well as for his theatrical and film work, Kortner left Germany in the early 1930s for England and then the United States, where he worked from 1933 to 1949 with relative success. *The Last Illusion* was closely identified with the real-life exile of Kortner: its focus on the experience and homecoming of an exile also resonated with a number of prominent figures including Thomas Mann, Bertolt Brecht and Alfred Döblin.

Kortner's own exile biography seemed to inform the representational approach of the film. In most German rubble films of the late 1940s the opening sequences offer images of the ruins of Germany as a succinct symbol for the post-war social and cultural crisis. *The Last Illusion*, however, begins with an image that, for that historical moment, proves far more startling: establishing shots of an efficiently operating modern Los Angeles and an intact, handsome bourgeois home surrounded by a white picket fence. This surprising opening invokes the stereotype that many Germans in Germany had about life in exile, which was, in reality, severely impoverished for the vast majority of exiles.

More than in *Sky Above* or a film like *Ways into Twilight* (1948) (which was directed by and starred matinee heartthrob Gustav Fröhlich), however, *The Last Illusion*'s star becomes a transfer point for (*Kultur-*)national identity – a face with which the nation could identify. In his classical training and his commitment to high German culture despite the Nazis, Kortner and his character could help the national community in Anderson's memorable phrase, 'imagine itself.' Perhaps because the star comes to play such a nationally central role, *The Last Illusion* radicalizes the humbling of the star actors manifest in *Sky* and *Ways*. It traces a trajectory of Mauthner from optimism about reconstruction to an utterly failed effort to return and contribute.

This failure is, tellingly, not so much Mauthner's, but rather the failure of German students to learn the lessons of the war. In this regard, the film reflects the widespread post-war belief that universities were hotbeds of persistent Nazi beliefs. In its memorable lecture sequence, *The Last Illusion* seems to refer explicitly to the famous case of Pastor Martin Niemöller. In 1946 Niemöller lectured to students in Erlangen and advocated acknowledging German guilt for the war. The address, however, became infamous not so much for Niemöller's controversial calls for acknowledging the guilt of all Germans, but rather for the reaction of the students, whose dismissive booing and stomping allegedly drowned out Niemöller entirely. In the wake of such controversies the 'German youth' became an essential means for Germany to stage and narrate its problems with persisting Nazi beliefs, and therefore a central forum, as in *The Last Illusion*, for early post-war coming to terms with the past.

Jaimey Fisher

WAR FILM
DER KRIEGSFILM

Left: *Europa Europa*, Central Cinema Company Film (CCC)/Les Films du Losange.

The Bridge

Die Brücke

Production Company:
Fono Film

Distributors:
Deutsche Film Hansa (Germany)
Allied Artist Pictures (USA)

Director:
Bernhard Wicki

Producer:
Hermann Schwerin

Screenwriters:
Michael Mansfeld
Karl-Wilhelm Vivier
Bernhard Wicki (uncredited),
based on the novel by Manfred Gregor

Cinematographer:
Gerd von Bonin

Composer:
Hans-Martin Majewski

Editor:
Carl Otto Bartning

Duration:
103 minutes

Genre:
War
Social Drama

Cast:
Folker Bohnet
Fritz Wepper
Michael Hinz
Frank Glaubrecht
Karl Michael Balzer
Volker Lechtenbrink
Günther Hoffmann
Wolfgang Stumpf

Year:
1959

Synopsis

Set in a small Bavarian town in April 1945, *The Bridge* recounts the desperate moment when the home front became the actual front in Germany's wartime collapse. Despite the inevitable defeat, seven teenage boys are, with differing levels of enthusiasm, drafted into the Germany army. With their fathers largely absent due to the war, their mothers manifest assorted reactions, ranging from dogged commitment to resignation and despair. The boys are given a mere day of training before being shipped off to the front, but a former teacher, now captain, gives a corporal the verbal order to take the boys to defend their own hometown bridge, primarily to keep them away from the front and likely death. This apparently merciful plan falls apart, however, when the corporal is shot by the town's military police, who are convinced, given that he is hanging around a small town of little strategic importance, that he is a deserter. His death leaves the boy without an actual commander who could call off their senseless defence of a bridge that is, in any case, slated for demolition. When US tanks roll into the town, the boys fight heroically but senselessly until only one of the seven survives, underscoring the squandered idealism and senseless loss of their generation.

Critique

One of the best-known and most celebrated films of West Germany, the popular *The Bridge* was Germany's Oscar nominee in 1959, and established Bernhard Wicki as one of German cinema's best known and most beloved figures. In many ways, given its profile and approach, *The Bridge* serves as a key transitional film between the (relatively) affirmative and non-critical films of the 1950s and the more self-consciously politicized and engaged films of the 1960s and 1970s; something confirmed in Wenders' and Fassbinder's casting of Wicki in some of their work from the 1970s.

The film was praised around the world for its crisp, unflinching realism as well as the small-scale location shooting befitting its serious subject. The film pivots on the absurd futility of the boys' mission, one that subverts their romantic longing for the front. While many of them dream of being shipped off to the distant front, they are ultimately dispatched to their hometown bridge – the added irony being that this familiar landmark is, in fact, now part of the collapsing front. The overarching absurdity is exacerbated by the fact that the captain and corporal who conceive and lead their mission, respectively, know that the bridge will be demolished anyway to prevent the Allied advance, but they never inform the boys, so that the boys do not realize what everyone around them recognizes, namely, that they would never have had to defend the bridge if their commander had not been murdered by other Germans.

The generational thematic depicting young people as firm believers until the end is familiar from the 'rubble films' of the late 1940s, but this film depicts the indoctrinated fanaticism of the

The Bridge, Fono Film.

youth with a lighter touch that exonerates them even more than those earlier films – here it is largely fate, along with the cynicism of a couple of older Nazis, that dooms them. But, as in the rubble films, concentrating on (relatively innocent) young people allows the film to evade tougher political questions. Even if the film is relatively light politically, however, particularly poignant is the film's portrait of small-town life in 1945, including key aspects of the war years that must have been fading in the rear view mirror of the 1950s 'economic miracle': the experience of the bombing, food rationing, and, interestingly, 'foreign workers' (actually slave labour that kept Germany's economy going in the years when many of its able-bodied men were serving in the military). Although it does not go into detail about these slave labourers, it makes clear how important and visible they were, right up until the last moments of the war, when many of them used the chaos of the collapse to escape and join one of the largest displacements of refugees in history (estimated at c.15 million at the end and shortly after the war).

The popularity of the film, combined with its Oscar nomination, brought Wicki considerable international renown, something in fairly short supply for German film culture in the 1950s. Wicki had studied art at the Bauhaus in Dessau and then acting under Gustaf Gründgens, the former of which led to his internment in a concentration camp, Sachsenhausen, outside Berlin in 1938/39. After *The Bridge* he worked on international productions, but eventually returned to work primarily in Germany. Today, the legacy of Wicki and the stature of the film is confirmed by the 'Bernhard Wicki Prize – The Bridge – Peace Prize for German Film,' given annually for the promotion of 'humanity, tolerance, and education' at Germany's second most important film festival, the Munich Film Festival. It was remade for German television in 2008 and viewed by over 3.5 million viewers.

Jaimey Fisher

The Tin Drum
Die Blechtrommel

Production Companies:
Argos Films
Artémis Productions
Bioskop Film
Film Polski Film Agency
Franz Seitz Filmproduktion
GGB-14
Hallelujah Films
Jadran Film

Distributors:
United Artists

Director:
Volker Schlöndorff

Producers:
Franz Seitz
Anatole Dauman
Volker Schlöndorff

Screenwriters:
Jean-Claude Carrière
Volker Schlöndorff
Franz Seitz, based on the novel by Günter Grass

Art Director:
Nicos Perakis

Synopsis

The precocious Oskar (Bennent) stunts his own growth at age 3 by hurling himself down the cellar steps. This rejection of the adult world of 1930s Germany, fast being caught up by the approach of World War II, is also his drastic form of inner emigration. The twin channels of protest are his glass-shattering voice, and the cacophony of his tin drum; most notably when his off-centre rhythms rout a Nazi rally in the satirical high point of the film. A child of various literary traditions in Günter Grass' novel, on which the film is based, Oskar is also of contested biological ancestry, and is indirectly responsible for the death of both his possible fathers (one German, one Polish). The confused lineages continue when his cousin, Maria (Thalbach), falls pregnant, either to Oskar or to his father, Matzerath (Adorf), meaning that her son Kurt is either Oskar's son or his brother. Emerging from the chaos of such family life as microcosm of society; Oskar's amoral, anarchic stance threads a dubious line of survival through the catastrophes of the war, as enacted in the city of Danzig.

Critique

This is the most successful in a series of literary adaptations by director Schlöndorff. It is unusual among adaptations inasmuch as the author Grass was heavily involved some two decades after first publication of his novel. The film gained West Germany's first award for Best Foreign Language Film at the 1980 Oscars. It wisely omits the last third of an already sprawling novel, thereby confining itself to Danzig, a longstanding crucible for Polish-German tensions, and hence a problem in Hitler's new order. As the site of Oskar's unnaturally protracted childhood, Danzig becomes outright mythological by the end, tinged with nostalgia. Screen images of the city challenged contemporary western audiences, above all in the concrete setting – the poignancy of the real Danzig's remoteness – on the other side of the Iron Curtain.

Cinematographer:
Igor Luther

Composer:
Maurice Jarre

Editor:
Suzanne Baron

Duration:
142 minutes

Genre:
History
Melodrama
War
Comedy

Cast:
David Bennent
Mario Adorf
Angela Winkler
Daniel Obrychski
Katharine Thalbach

Year:
1979

Within a strong cast, the performance of David Bennent as Oskar steals the show and lends this gothic Peter Pan the quality of a gargoyle prophet. He alone disqualifies any documentary aspect of the narrative, which keeps alluding to horrors beneath the surface of the adult world. The death of Sigismund Markus (Charles Aznavour), for Oskar the proprietor of a magic toyshop, indelibly marks the turning point of the Kristallnacht ('Crystal Night') in the outer world. The gallows humour of the Polish post office sequence underscores the futile courage of resistance, as an infernal card game prevails. Matching Grass' Rabelaisian momentum and indulgence in a reinvigorated German language, the film chooses some of the most extreme incidents and images (e.g. the eels scene) for grotesquely realistic depiction. The resulting tone is best conveyed by the sheer confusion of genre categorization above – the film spans these genres (often in tension with one another) and more. That in turn reflects the profusion of humanity in this film: the tapestry of bit parts, the montage of episodes, which combine to create a sense of an underplayed epic, of history as a motley cabaret revue. One linking device is Oskar's voice-overs. Characteristically he is not seen in dialogue with others, but heard via a disembodied commentary that styles him as a patently unreliable narrator. The cinematography lends itself to Oskar's view from below, progressing naturally to a picaresque view of history. The camera lingers on sexual advances made beneath the card table, in the line of vision of a crouching Oskar; an arresting POV shot takes us with Oskar through the final stage of the birth canal, headed inexorably towards the soon-to-be-shattered light bulb above; Oskar's peephole view of the rostrum at the Nazi rally is an iris-shot of history, focusing but also strongly filtering.

The layer of society dissected is closest to Christa Wolf's novel *Pattern of Childhood*, but without her moral earnestness. The film took the often introverted agonizing over Germany's past, as evidenced in much of the New German Cinema, into more carnivalistic territory. A narrative refrain intones that Poland will never be lost, a claim belied both by the narrative events and world history. And yet a European audience was acutely aware that beyond the narrative time frame, Danzig had indeed reverted to Polish hands. In pre-war Germany, according to this narrative, most citizens were remarkably ordinary in their foibles, and interchangeable in their national and political blind spots, rather than their fanaticism.

Roger Hillman

The Boat

Das Boot

Production Companies:
Bavaria Film
Radiant Film GmbH

Synopsis

After a raucous celebration in the French port city of La Rochelle, the crew of the German U-boat *U-96* set out to sea in search of the British enemy. Lieutenant Werner (Grönemeyer), a naval war correspondent who is there to 'watch respectable German heroes', joins the crew, which consists of a few seasoned sailors, among them

Süddeutscher Rundfunk (SDR)
Twin Bros. Productions
(Director's Cut)
Westdeutscher Rundfunk (WDR)

Distributors:
Neue Constantin Film (West Germany), Triumph Releasing Corporation (USA)

Director:
Wolfgang Petersen

Producers:
Günter Rohrbach
Ortwin Freyermuth (Director's Cut)

Screenwriters:
Wolfgang Petersen
Dean Riesner (uncredited), based on the novel by Lothar-Günther Buchheim

Art Director:
Götz Weidner

Cinematographer:
Jost Vacano

Composer:
Klaus Doldinger

Editor:
Hannes Nikel

Duration:
149 minutes (original release), 209 minutes (director's cut), 293 minutes (original uncut version)

Genre:
Anti-war Drama

Cast:
Jürgen Prochnow
Herbert Grönemeyer
Klaus Wennemann
Hubertus Bengsch
Martin Semmelrogge
Erwin Leder
Bernd Tauber
Martin May

Year:
1981

Captain Lehmann-Willenbrock (Prochnow) and Chief Engineer Grade (Wennemann), and many inexperienced submariners. Initially, the sub does not encounter enemy ships and the crew suffers from boredom and claustrophobia. After a drill, which tests the seaworthiness of the sub as well as the hardiness of the crew, they encounter a British convoy and are engaged by an enemy destroyer. After a lengthy storm, the sub comes across a British convoy and, having sunk two ships, is attacked and damaged by a destroyer. U-96 has to dive to such dangerous depths that the crew's endurance is severely tested. When the Chief Mechanic, Johann (Leder), suffers a panic attack, the Captain is on the verge of shooting him before the sub is finally able to surface safely. The crew's original order to spend Christmas in La Rochelle is rescinded and instead they are sent to La Spezia, Italy. While trying to pass through the dangerous Strait of Gibraltar, the sub is attacked by a British fighter plane and has to dive to such a depth that it is severely damaged. Knowing that it is running out of time and oxygen, the crew works feverishly to repair the sub. After sixteen hours they manage to raise the sub from the ocean floor and to surface. When U-96 arrives at the port in La Rochelle, an air raid by British planes destroys the sub and kills most of its crew.

Critique

Das Boot is not only a most exciting and convincing anti-war film, it is also an indictment of Nazi war strategy. The opening credits, which state that '40,000 German sailors served on U-boats during World War II. 30,000 never returned,' leave no doubt as to what the outcome of the story is going to be. While the viewers cannot help but admire the crew's valour and loyalty, they are always aware of the historic context. The scene in which the sailors get drunk in a French nightclub suggests that only a few of them believe in Nazi ideology. Captain Thomsen (Otto Sander), who has just been honoured for his bravery with a Ritterkreuz medal, mocks Adolf Hitler in a drunken speech and calls him sarcastically 'the world's greatest battle strategist and great naval expert.' There is only one ardent Nazi among the crew of U-96, the First Watch Officer (Bengsch). He is treated as an outsider by the other submariners, and his outsider status is underlined by the fact that he proudly wears an immaculate Nazi uniform even under the most trying circumstances, while the other members of the crew wear clothing appropriate for their surroundings. While the young sailors are mostly apolitical and primarily intent on surviving the war, the Captain and the Lieutenant are openly critical of the Nazi leadership and its war strategy. The most telling scene depicting the disconnect between the decision makers, who are far removed from any danger, and the sailors, who have to risk their lives on a daily basis, occurs on the *SS Weser*, a German merchant ship anchored in Vigo, Spain. The officers of the sub, who had to make do with mouldy bread and canned food are shocked when they are offered a cornucopia of hard-to-come-by delicacies such as fresh figs, sausages, herring salad and Christmas cake. Having experienced extreme hardship, deprivation and

The Boat, Bavaria Film/Radiant Film GmbH/Süddeutscher Rundfunk (SDR)/Twin Bros. Productions (Director's Cut)/Westdeutscher Rundfunk (WDR).

mortal danger they are told by the Nazi representative, 'It's not an easy life here, appearances to the contrary.' Having witnessed the luxuries and comforts their superiors enjoy, the officers of the sub are extremely disappointed when they are informed of the new order by headquarters: their Christmas vacation in France has been cancelled and they are sent on an extremely dangerous mission instead. It is telling that the submarine crew does not sing a patriotic German song on their way back to La Rochelle after their near-death experience on the bottom of the ocean, but rather 'It's a Long Way to Tipperary,' a song made popular by the British Army during World War I. The fact that most sailors die during a British air raid just after they have arrived safely in La Rochelle is a poignant reminder of the futility of war.

The ending is also necessitated by the film's narrative perspective. Since the viewers have come to empathize with the crew of *U-96*, they need to be reminded that the sailors ultimately were a part of the German war effort. In the final scene the disillusioned war correspondent, Werner, through whose eyes the viewer has watched the events unfold, witnesses the Captain's death as the submarine sinks in the harbour. In order to get his message across, Wolfgang Petersen had to diverge from historical fact: the real Captain of *U-96* survived the airplane attack.

Karl L. Stenger

Europa Europa

Hitlerjunge Salomon

Production Companies:
Central Cinema Company Film (CCC)
Les Films du Losange

Distributor:
Les Films du Losange

Director:
Agnieszka Holland

Producers:
Artur Brauner
Margaret Ménégoz

Screenwriters:
Agnieszka Holland, based on the autobiography by Salomon Perel

Cinematographer:
Jacek Petrycki

Composer:
Zbigniew Preisner

Editor:
Ewa Smal
Isabelle Lorente

Duration:
112 minutes

Genre:
Drama
History

Cast:
Marco Hofschneider
René Hofschneider
Julie Delpy
André Wilms
Ashley Wanninger
Klaus Abramowsky
Michele Gleizer

Year:
1990

Synopsis

Salomon Perel (Marco Hofschneider) – also called 'Solek' and 'Solly' – is born 20 April 1925, in Peine, Germany, the fourth child of devout Jewish parents. When his family is attacked during *Kristallnacht*, the infamous pogrom against Jewish people, on 9 November 1938, and his sister Bertha (Marta Sandrowicz) is killed, the family moves to Lodz, Poland. When the Germans invade Poland, Solly and his brother Isaak (René Hofschneider) are sent to the eastern part of the state, which is occupied by the Russians. While crossing a river, the brothers are separated and a Russian soldier rescues Solly. He is sent to an orphanage in Grodno and indoctrinated with communist propaganda. He is turned into an avowed communist and accepted into the Komsomol, the youth wing of the Communist Party. When the Soviet Union is attacked by German troops in 1941, Solly is separated from the fleeing orphans and captured by the Germans. He convinces them that he is a *Volksdeutscher*, an ethnic German living outside the Reich, named Josef Peters. Being able to speak Russian fluently, he identifies one of the captured prisoners as Stalin's son. The German soldiers consider him their 'good luck charm' and use him as an interpreter. Solly/Jupp is eventually sent to a Hitler Youth school in Berlin, where he is indoctrinated with Nazi propaganda. When he is forced to take up arms against the Russians during the last months of the war, he refuses to fight and deserts his unit. He surrenders to Red Army soldiers who want to execute him, believing that he is a Nazi. As he is about to die, Solly is recognized and saved by Isaak, who has just been freed from a concentration camp. The brothers make their way to the American troops and Solly eventually emigrates to Palestine with the goal of being true to his Jewish faith.

Critique

The film, whose German title *Hitlerjunge Salomon* ('Hitler Youth Salomon') encapsulates the protagonist's dilemma of pretending to be a Nazi while Jewish in order to survive, is based on the autobiography of Salomon Perel, published in 1989. To stress the authenticity of the unbelievable story the director has the protagonist narrate the events. Solly's gift of recall almost strains credulity when he states: 'You won't believe it but I remember my circumcision.' The appearance of an aged Salomon Perel in the last scene of the film, singing a Jewish song, leaves no doubt that the film portrays real events.

Holland signals the various transformations of the film's protagonist in scenes that depict his birth/rebirth. The film opens with a dream sequence, which shows Solly swimming under water, dressed in a Nazi uniform, struggling with a male figure and eventually surfacing. Since this sequence is immediately followed by Solly's circumcision, it can be read as an allusion to his birth. It simultaneously foreshadows two subsequent scenes of rebirth and transformation. In the first scene Solly, while taking a bath before his bar mitzvah, the Jewish rite of passage, has to flee the house naked during an attack by the Nazis and to don a Nazi uniform before he can return home. In the second scene Solly almost drowns in a river while fleeing the Nazis and is saved by a Russian soldier. Two additional scenes of birth/rebirth show Solly covered by motor oil resembling amniotic fluid before he is picked up by German soldiers, as well as swimming in a pool at the elite Nazi Youth school. Another leitmotiv is Solly's need to hide the fact that he is circumcised because it signals his Jewish background. When a group of German soldiers relieve themselves in the open, Solly must hide behind a tree. While taking a bath he is revealed as a Jew to Robert (Wilms), a German soldier, but because Robert has a secret of his own – he is gay – he does not expose Solly. At the Nazi Youth school, Solly avoids a physical by pretending that he has a toothache, only to have a healthy tooth pulled. He is unable to be intimate with Leni (Delpy), a girl he fancies, and he ties skin over his penis in an attempt to be like everyone else. However, his penis becomes infected and Solly has to acknowledge, 'I couldn't escape my own body. I still had to hide.' In a dream sequence Solly finds Hitler hiding in a closet with his hands covering his genitalia, a reference to the Führer's rumoured Jewish background. It is not until he is in the Russian prisoner of war camp that Solly can be open about his Jewish identity when he and his brother relieve themselves joyously out in the open. The film was awarded the Golden Globe Award for Best Foreign Language Film in 1992, but was not nominated for an Academy Award by the German jury, which caused a considerable controversy in Germany.

Karl L. Stenger

Rosenstrasse

Production Companies:
Studio Hamburg Letterbox Filmproduktion
Tele München Fernseh Produktionsgesellschaft (TMG)

Distributor:
Studio Canal (Worldwide),
Concorde Filmverleih (Germany)

Director:
Margarethe von Trotta

Producers:
Richard Schöps
Henrik Meyer
Marcus Zimmer

Screenwriter:
Margarethe von Trotta
Pamela Katz

Cinematographer:
Franz Rath

Synopsis

After the death of her husband, Robert, Ruth Weinstein (Lampe) insists on performing the Jewish mourning ritual of Shiva for seven days, which includes covering mirrors, sitting on the floor and keeping a candle burning. The sudden discovery of her Jewishness comes as a complete surprise to her children, Hannah (Schrader) and Ben (Conen), as does Ruth's rejection of Hannah's fiancé, Luis (van Huêt), because he is a Gentile. When Hannah tries to uncover the reasons for her mother's unusual behaviour, she learns from Rachel (Regnier), Ruth's cousin, that Ruth had been taken in by a German woman called Lena Fischer (Riemann) when her mother was deported to the Auschwitz concentration camp in 1943. Hannah travels to Berlin and meets with 90-year-old Lena Fischer (Schade), pretending to conduct historical research but in reality researching her mother's fate. She discovers that both Miriam Suessmann (Stolze), Ruth's mother, and Fabian Israel Fischer (Feifel), Lena's husband, were arrested and taken to a collection centre at Rosenstrasse during the 'Final Roundup of Jews.' In an unprecedented act of resistance a large number of Aryan wives stood watch in front of the building, demanding that their Jewish husbands be returned to them. After a seven-day standoff between the courageous women and German soldiers, and the intervention by propaganda minister Joseph Goebbels, whom Lena and her brother Arthur von Eschenbach (Vogel), a highly decorated officer, asked for help, the prisoners are released. Ruth, however, waits in vain for her mother and is accepted into the Fischer family. When Ruth's relatives in the United States send for her after the war, the girl feels that she has lost her mother for the second

Composer:
Loek Dikker

Editor:
Corina Dietz

Duration:
136 minutes

Genre:
Drama
War

Cast:
Katja Riemann
Maria Schrader
Doris Schade
Jutta Lampe
Jürgen Vogel
Martin Feifel
Lena Stolze
Romijn Conen
Fedja van Huêt
Carole Regnier

Year:
2003

time. After Hannah's return to New York her discoveries enable her mother to make peace with the past and the film ends with the joyous Jewish wedding of Hannah and Luis.

Critique

Like many of Margarethe von Trotta's films, *Rosenstrasse* features strong women whose personal stories are intricately intertwined with historical events. Even though the script is based on interviews with participants in the Rosenstrasse protest, von Trotta uses fictional characters to broaden the scope of the film's theme. It not only depicts two examples of courageous resistance against the Nazi regime – one public, when the women stage a protest against the rounding-up of their Jewish husbands; one private, when Lena Fischer takes in the motherless Jewish girl – it also explores the theme of personal coming to terms with the past. The use of the framing device set in present-day New York signals that the film is not merely a reconstruction of a historic event, but also an investigation of how the past affects the present. Since Ruth initially refuses to confront the past, even though memory flashes indicate that she is not entirely able to suppress it, it falls to her daughter Hannah to unearth the truth. She proceeds like a detective, unravelling a mystery and takes the viewer along on her journey of discovery. To guide the viewer through the challenging, non-linear structure of the film von Trotta and her cameraman, Franz Rath, employ a 'bleach-out procedure', which gives those scenes set during the 1940s a bleached-out, bluish tint, differentiating them from the scenes set in pre-Nazi Berlin, which depict Lena and Fabian Fischer's successes as classical musicians and their courtship, as well as those set in present-day New York and Berlin. It is telling that most scenes in which ninety-year-old Lena Fischer recounts the events surrounding the Rosenstrasse protest are set in her dark apartment, an indication that the old woman is still haunted by the ghosts of the past. Through Lena's narration Hannah comes to understand her mother's suffering, which she has never revealed to her children. Because Ruth's father divorced his Jewish wife, caving under the pressure exerted by the Nazis on those living in mixed marriages, the protection afforded to wife and daughter no longer applies. They are forced to wear the yellow star and Miriam is taken to the collection centre in Rosenstrasse, where Ruth is able to visit her one last time before she is deported to Auschwitz facing certain death. In contrast to Ruth's father, Lena refuses to divorce her Jewish husband even though she has to endure rejection by her father, a staunch Nazi officer, the loss of her career as a classical pianist and the confiscation of her belongings. She shows great courage when she takes in the motherless Jewish girl and when she attempts to join her husband in the collection centre, wearing the yellow star. Being able to appreciate both her mother's childhood trauma and Lena's courage and selflessness, Hannah can bridge the past and present when she returns to New York. Not only does she enable her mother to make peace with the past but she also accepts and appreciates her racial background when she gets married in a Jewish wedding ceremony.

Karl L. Stenger

Downfall

Der Untergang

Production Company:
Constantin Film Produktion

Distributors:
Constantin Film (Germany), Momentum Pictures (UK)

Director:
Oliver Hirschbiegel

Producer:
Bernd Eichinger

Screenwriters:
Bernd Eichinger, based on the book by Joachim Fest, and the book by Traudl Junge and Melissa Müller

Cinematographer:
Rainer Klausmann

Composer:
Stephan Zacharias

Editor:
Hans Funck

Duration:
156 minutes, 178 minutes (extended version)

Genre:
Drama
War

Cast:
Bruno Ganz
Alexandra Maria Lara
Ulrich Matthes
Corinna Harfouch
Juliane Köhler
Heino Ferch
Christian Berkel
Matthias Habich
Ulrich Noethen
André Hennicke

Year:
2004

Synopsis

Set in April 1945 as the Red Army enters Berlin, the film narrates the fall of the Nazi regime on two different spatial levels: underground in a secret bunker, it depicts the Führer's (Ganz) final days and the rampant hysteria among his closest collaborators; above ground on Berlin's streets, it follows three parallel stories. The first deals with a group of child soldiers from the Hitler Youth, who struggle in their attempt to resist the advancing enemy. The second story concerns a doctor, Professor Ernst-Günter Schenck (Berkel), who witnesses the cruelty of some SS guards toward civilians while trying to retrieve medical provision for his hospital. The third story centres on the clash between SS officer Wilhelm Mohnke (Hennicke) and propaganda minister Joseph Goebbels (Matthes), concerning the use of volunteers, the *Volkssturm*, in the final battle to defend the Reich Chancellery. Adopting a circular narrative structure, *Downfall*'s narrator and main character is Traudl Junge (Lara), Hitler's personal secretary, while scenes from a documentary interview with the real Junge frame the fictional reconstructions. After the suicides of Hitler, his wife Eva Braun (Köhler) and the Goebbels family, the film concludes with Junge fleeing the Soviet infantrymen along with Peter (Donevan Gunia), the only survivor of the Hitler Youth group.

Critique

Downfall is one of the most successful German films of the last decade in terms of festival presentations, awards and international audience figures. Since its initial theatrical release, it has continued its prominence as a result of various DVD editions and television re-runs. At the same time, Hirschbiegel's film has been controversial. Fiercely attacked by some critics for humanizing a Parkinson-debilitated Führer, who in his last days appreciated a popular song sung by children or a slice of cake for his birthday, *Downfall* also depicts a cruel dictator who despises the German people for failing to live up to his exaggerated expectations. As a result, the final image of Hitler is of a simple person who managed to understand the mood of the people and lead the Germans into a self-destructive war sustained by military strategists and propaganda experts.

In its attempt to create the most authentic reconstruction of the last days of the Third Reich, the film reinforces the duality between good and evil. The representation of space in *Downfall* reflects this black and white division: the German people versus the Nazi elites, victims versus perpetrators, which, according to Paul Cooke, alludes to the earlier representations of the regime in the immediate aftermath of the Second World War (2007: 247–61). The binary opposition between good and bad Germans is made explicit through the parallelism of the narrative strands above and below the ground level. While in the bunker the evil manifests itself through senseless military plans as well as in Magda Goebbels's (Harfouch) chilling decision to kill her children and commit suicide in order to avoid a life without National Socialism, on the surface various sequences show the suffering of ordinary Germans.

Specifically, *Downfall* constructs a clear vision of the population as defenceless victims of Hitler's and Goebbels's insanity by showing the massacre of child soldiers on Berlin streets, and the senseless use of volunteer civilians in the firing line between the Red Army and the remnants of the German military forces. Nevertheless, the film does not cover the trauma of millions of German women raped by Soviet soldiers, even though it is mentioned by some women present in the bunker, and alludes very vaguely in the last sequence to the atrocities committed by the Red Army.

Traudl Junge constitutes the connection between the two worlds the film depicts: the suffocating and sinister bunker and the bloody rubble-covered streets of Berlin. The film culminates in her acknowledgment of her naïve belief in National Socialism, and of her thoughtless involvement with Hitler's activities. As she ponders the consequences of her actions and the question of her personal responsibility, her character becomes a symbol for larger issues of national guilt and the banality of evil.

Elena Caoduro

The Ninth Day

Der neunte Tag

Production Companies:
Provobis Film
Videopress S.A.
Bayerrischer Rundfunk (BR)
BeltFilm
ARTE

Distributors:
Progress Film-Verleih (Germany)
Kino International (USA)

Director:
Volker Schlöndorff

Producer:
Jürgen Haase
Jakob Hausmann

Screenwriters:
Eberhard Görner
Andreas Pflüger, based on the memoir by Jean Bernard

Cinematographer:
Tomas Erhart

Synopsis

Henri Kremer (Matthes) is a Catholic priest from Luxembourg who has been sent to the Dachau concentration camp along with other clerics from the German occupied areas of Europe. In February 1942 he is allowed to return home for nine days, ostensibly to attend his mother's funeral. But Kremer's 'leave' comes with conditions. His fellow inmates and his family will be executed if he flees. But he and his fellow internees will be allowed to go free if he can convince the Bishop of Luxembourg (Thate) to drop his resistance to the Nazi occupation of their country and publicly support Nazi policy. Nine days are all he has.

Kremer's counterpart is the head of the Gestapo in Luxembourg, SS *Untersturmführer* Gebhardt (Diehl). He, too, is a man of faith, having been ordained as a deacon before joining the followers of his new saviour, Adolf Hitler. Kremer and Gebhardt meet regularly during the nine days and a wide-ranging philosophical duel develops between them. Kremer eventually meets Bishop Philippe, who refuses to drop his resistance. Left to deal with his own conscience, and after much agonising, Kremer decides against collaborating with the Nazis and on the ninth day returns to Dachau.

Critique

The Ninth Day tackles a difficult and still controversial area of Third Reich history: the relationship between National Socialism and the Christian churches, in this case the Catholics in Luxembourg. The film is based on the memoirs of Jean Bernard, a priest who was interned at Dachau between May 1941 and August 1942.

Schlöndorff's camera takes us inside the concentration camp,

Composer:
Alfred Schnitke

Editor:
Peter R. Adam

Duration:
98 minutes

Genre:
Historical Drama
Thriller, War

Cast:
Ulrich Matthes
August Diehl
Bibiana Beglau
Hilmar Thate
Germain Wagner
Jean-Paul Raths
Michael König

Year:
2004

but the portrayal of the Holocaust is much more concentrated and focussed than a film such as *Schindler's List* (Spielberg, 1993). With the exception of a gruelling eleven-minute opening sequence as Kremer is delivered to the camp and a fellow priest is brutally crucified, the violence in *The Ninth Day* is almost entirely psychological, and the film comes close to being a thriller. The two main characters – Kremer and Gebhardt – are complex human beings, and the film is more successful in its portrayal of moral dilemmas than many films dealing with the Holocaust and the Third Reich. There are no black and white divisions here. Kremer is tormented by his decision to deny potentially life-saving water to a fellow internee, and Gebhardt comes across as a genuine man of faith who follows his convictions, even when they lead him to support a genocidal regime.

All too often film directors are over-enthusiastic in their depiction of the Nazis as irredeemably evil and uncultured brutes. The figure of Amon Goeth (Ralph Fiennes) in *Schindler's List* is a good example. In reality, many of them – including figures such as Gebhardt – enjoyed an enlightened education in the western tradition, and appear to have had little problem assimilating their participation in genocide with an appreciation of western culture and Christianity. A pillar of the post-war settlement has been the idea that exposure to the cultural traditions of Western Europe would protect the world from the re-emergence of fascism. Schlöndorff questions this belief through his humanisation of Gebhardt, a man who moved seamlessly from seminarist to SS officer and sees the Nazis as crusaders against godless Bolshevism. It is this questioning of simple explanations of National Socialism that represents *The Ninth Day's* greatest contribution to the cinema's attempts to come to terms with Germany's past.

The film is visually restrained, particularly in the use of colour and its portrayal of Luxembourg in winter. Ulrich Matthes, with his penetrating eyes and drawn face, is ideal for the role of Henri Kremer, although in a strange twist of fate he also appeared as the leading Nazi Joseph Goebbels in *Downfall*, Oliver Hirschbiegel's film that appeared in German cinemas just two months before *The Ninth Day*. The use of the music of Alfred Schnitke in the opening camp sequence – and subsequent flashbacks – is particularly telling and powerful.

Attempts to come to terms with the past are not helped by over-simplification and generalisation. In *The Ninth Day* Volker Schlöndorff consciously focuses on a single and relatively minor event in the history of the Third Reich. He resists the temptation to try and capture the enormity of the Holocaust and the complex relationship between the Christian churches and Hitler's regime. In doing so he gives us a taut and compelling insight into the psychological torment suffered by many who fell victim to the terrors of National Socialism.

Brian Long

References

Cooke, Paul (2007), '*Der Untergang* (2004): Victims, Perpetrators and the Continuing Fascination of Fascism', *German Monitors*, 67, pp. 247–61.

HISTORICAL DRAMA

Left: *The Marriage of Maria Braun*, Albatross Filmproduktion, Fengler Films/Filmverlag der Autoren/Tango Film/Trio Film/Westdeutscher Rundfunk (WDR).

Zero Hour

Stunde Null

Production Companies:
Edgar Reitz Film (ERF)
Solaris Film
Westdeutscher Rundfunk (WDR)

Distributors:
Atlas Film Verleih (West Germany)
Prokino Filmverleih (West Germany)

Director:
Edgar Reitz

Producer:
Bernd Eichinger

Screenwriters:
Karsten Witte
Petra Kiener
Edgar Reitz

Art Director:
Winfried Hennig

Cinematographer:
Gernot Roll

Composer:
Nikos Mamangakis

Editor:
Ingrid Broszat

Duration:
108 minutes

Genre:
Historical Drama
post-WWII

Cast:
Kai Taschner
Herbert Weissbach
Günter Schiemann
Anette Jünger

Year:
1977

Synopsis

It is September 1945, the end of World War II. In a small village near Leipzig the inhabitants experience a brief moment of calm after American troops have withdrawn and before Soviet forces arrive to occupy the area. Many have abandoned their village for fear of 'Stalin's red cohorts' whose reputation precedes them. The few remaining villagers slowly begin to enjoy the fact that the war is over and that they are still alive. They find food and enjoy simple pleasures. Joschi (Taschner), an ex-Hitler Youth, is looking for buried Nazi treasure and seeks to join his new-found heroes, the Americans, without success.

Critique

Edgar Reitz' 'filmic novel' *Heimat* (1984) was so successful that it has always overshadowed the earlier and much smaller *Zero Hour*, although they are related in many ways. Where the sprawling epic *Heimat* chronicles the history of a German village and its inhabitants over the course of 30 years, *Zero Hour* is more of a short story covering a few days in the life of a handful of villagers. Like *Heimat*, but as a *Momentaufnahme* ('snapshot') of an important historical moment, *Zero Hour* focuses on ordinary people who are not aware of the magnitude of events unfolding around them; they concentrate on surviving. What is so compelling about Reitz's *Alltagsgeschichte* ('history of the everyday') is that his history lessons are quite different from the top-down approach to which we are normally exposed. The fact that Reitz likes to use non-professional actors adds another layer of realism.

The microcosm of *Zero Hour* is strictly confined geographically to a small village, within which pivotal scenes are set at the disused railway station. The precise location is matched by the precise moment in history. Here, at this clearly defined intersection of time and space, the station and the railway track lie dead in the landscape – a remnant of what was once a timetabled certainty of departures and arrivals, of objectives now defunct, deserted without purpose. It could stand for the whole country: lacking clear direction after the collapse of the National Socialist regime. The time for ideology and heroism is over. The people who were left behind are left with many unanswered questions, but also with thoughts of what might have been and fear of what lies ahead.

The focal point of the railway crossing is used to great effect in several scenes. It is the transitional point through which everyone has to pass: mostly refugees and their handcarts, Joschi on his motorbike, a small boy on his bicycle, other inhabitants. Later, the Russians use it to play pranks under the fearful eyes of the villagers. Sometimes it seems to open and close for no reason at all – the old stationmaster is fulfilling his duty, even though not a single train passes, a clear sign of his redundant role. He has taken to mending bicycles, a much more useful mode of transport given the post-war situation.

Actions that might signal a new start are counteracted with powerful symbols of stagnation. An example of this is the merry-go-round. It provides much-needed relief: people socialise around its lights at night, it symbolises stirrings of both life in general and new business opportunities more generally. At the same time, though, its circular movement, which is underlined when the small boy cycles repeatedly around and around, symbolises stagnation. This is a time of confusion, contradiction, lack of orientation, not an unequivocal 'zero hour'.

On the narrative level continuation of the past in the form of an unearthed Nazi treasure, which should provide the basis of Joschi's future, is shown to be misguided: the Americans confiscate the treasure and abandon the young man. His world collapses. The irony of his thwarted euphoria is painful to watch, but stands for the disillusionment of many of that generation. Without being moralistic Reitz represents human nature and the necessity of 'coming to terms with the past,' but he does not profess to know how to do it. However, neither euphoria nor amnesia offers solutions.

All the characters in the film are quite understandably disorientated by this 'chance' event of a zero hour. In order to achieve closure and seize the opportunities inherent in a new beginning we need time for reflection. Reitz (among other German film-makers of his generation) is critical of the fact that in post-war Germany one system (the Nazis) was replaced by another (the occupying forces) without achieving proper closure. When the identification of a whole nation with a system is as strong as it was in the case of the Nazis, many simply transfer their loyalty from one system to the next (in Joschi's case the occupying Americans), without first attempting to come to terms with the loss. That, to Reitz, is not a fresh start.

Maggie Hoffgen

Death Is My Trade

Aus einem deutschen Leben

Production Companies:
Iduna Film Produktiongesellschaft
Westdeutscher Rundfunk (WDR)

Distributors:
Filmverlag der Autoren (West Germany)
Arthaus Filmverleih (Germany)

Synopsis

Death Is My Trade is a semi-fictionalized account of the life of Auschwitz commandant Rudolf Höss from age 16 until shortly before his execution in Poland in 1947. Based on Kotulla's script, which he based on Höss' memoirs and the French novel *La mort est mon metier* by Robert Merle, the film tells the story of Franz Lang (George) (a false name Höss assumed when he went into hiding in 1945) and picks up in 1916, with the teenager Lang working in a field hospital during World War I. The film then moves through fifteen episodes in Lang's life spanning 30 years. Each episode is introduced by a title announcing the respective year and what will happen next. The first and the last titles read: '1916 Franz Lang wants to go to war,' '1946 The Americans have handed Franz Lang over to the Poles, on whose territory Auschwitz is located. In Cracow, he is being tried (after the trial's conclusion, he will be

Director:
Theodor Kotulla

Producers:
Volker Canaris
Nils Nilson

Screenwriters:
Theodor Kotulla, based on the novel by Robert Merle

Cinematographer:
Dieter Naujeck

Composer:
Eberhard Weber

Editor:
Wolfgang Richter

Duration:
145 minutes

Genre:
Historical Drama, Biography

Cast:
Götz George
Elisabeth Schwarz
Hans Korte
Kurt Hübner
Matthias Fuchs

Year:
1977

executed in 1947.) In his prison cell, he wrote autobiographical notes.'

The thirteen titles in between broadly tell Lang's/Höss' life story, making chronological leaps between less than one and more than seven years from World War I, to his rise and ultimate fall with the Third Reich.

Critique

Death Is My Trade was one of the first West German feature films aimed at a broad public audience to focus on the Holocaust and the Germany that brought about its existence. Formally and aesthetically the film is largely a study in realist cinema: it is restrained, unadorned and fact-oriented, with no musical soundtrack and a colour palette so drained it almost seems black-and-white. However, the film is also infused with traces of Brechtian theatre: it illuminates and comments on the factual linear narrative by way of selective fictionalization and alienation techniques, such as the episodic narrative structure and the use of intertitles, thus straddling the precarious line between a biography and its artistic interpretation in an imaginative and elucidating manner.

The plot oscillates between portraying the ordinary, the banal and mundane of Lang's daily existence, and the extraordinary, momentous and crucial inhumanness that manifests itself leading up to and during his pivotal part in the murderous Nazi regime. There are scenes of him sowing a button back onto his uniform shirt after joining the SS in 1922; of him having lunch with his family or dinner with a fellow concentration camp commandant in his house in Auschwitz, talking about French cognac; or of him exhausted and late in the evening poring over papers and files in his office, rubbing his eyes and gratefully thanking his adjutant for bringing in a cup of coffee while going over numbers of people to be killed. These scenes are juxtaposed with episodes in which Lang murders a helpless man in cold blood, meets with Himmler and Eichmann to discuss the 'Final Solution,' and conducts his first test of the use of Zyklon B with a group of prisoners. Some episodes appear to be vitally important to Lang's development, the portrayal of his character, or his role in the history of the Holocaust. Other scenes seem insignificant, narrative asides, quotidian experiences of an Everyman. By thus interweaving the everyday and private life of Lang/Höss with his administrative and public life as a Nazi official, the film accomplishes a rare and difficult feat: it effectively combines the representation of the Third Reich with the representation of the Holocaust, and *Alltagsgeschichte* ('history of the everyday') with a form of 'left-wing historicization' (Elsaesser 1996: 142) of fascism that is one not designed to normalise and relativise, but to contextualize in regard to German history. *Death Is My Trade*, cognizant of the impossibility of such a project, does not attempt to be an 'authentic' representation of Nazi Germany and the Holocaust. It does, however, successfully attempt to problematise and articulate crucial issues involved not only in the genesis of Nazism and the Shoah, but also in their representation. The film's sophistication and insightfulness are even more remarkable in light of the fact that it was made over 30 years ago, at a time when public discourse on the Third Reich and the Holocaust in Germany, especially in regard to the then limited number of mass cultural products dealing with these issues, was still largely non-existent.

Christine Haase

The Marriage of Maria Braun

Die Ehe der Maria Braun

Production Companies:
Albatross Filmproduktion
Fengler Films
Filmverlag der Autoren
Tango Film
Trio Film
Westdeutscher Rundfunk (WDR)

Distributor:
United Artists

Director:
Rainer Werner Fassbinder

Producers:
Michael Fengler
Wolf-Dietrich Brücker
Michael Fengler

Screenwriters:
Rainer Werner Fassbinder
Pea Fröhlich
Peter Märthesheimer
Kurt Raab

Cinematographer:
Michael Ballhaus

Composer:
Peer Raben

Editor:
Rainer Werner Fassbinder
Juliane Lorenz

Duration:
120 minutes

Synopsis

This marriage lasts from 1945 until 1954, though husband and wife are together little more than a few hours during that time. As Allied bombs destroy the building around them, Maria (Schygulla) and Corporal Hermann Braun (Löwitsch) are married. He is immediately redeployed to Russia and lost in battle. When Maria's brother-in-law, Willi (John), returns from the front he says Hermann is dead. But Maria continues to search for him as she works to support her family by pawning things or renting herself as a dancer in an Allied club. At the club she meets Sergeant Bill (Eagles), an American GI who is part of the occupation forces, and they begin an affair. Bill provides material security for the family and love and friendship for Maria. However, when Hermann suddenly returns, Maria strikes Bill dead. Hermann takes the blame for the murder and is imprisoned. Afterwards, Maria meets businessman Karl Oswald (Desny). They agree to a business/sexual relationship, but Maria cautions him that she remains married to Hermann. Meanwhile, Hermann is released from jail and leaves for Canada to make a success of himself. In the end, Oswald dies and leaves half his fortune to Maria. Hermann returns and reveals that Oswald has left the other half to him as part of the men's arrangements. As Hermann and Maria prepare for bed, the radio announces Germany's victory in the World Cup, and Maria lights a cigarette that blows up the house that had been filling with gas from the kitchen stove.

Critique

The Marriage of Maria Braun is the first instalment in Fassbinder's BRD trilogy. Along with *Lola* (1981) and *Veronika Voss* (1982), it critiques the years of the German economic, social and political recovery after World War II through the lives of three eponymous women. *Maria Braun* was Fassbinder's most appreciated and most profitable production and remains his most widely known film, for its portrayal of the German 'economic miracle' and its concern, for the struggles of German women during the period, and especially for its complex depiction of one of Fassbinder's most engaging characters.

At the centre of this film lies Maria's dedication to her marriage: not to her husband, her family, the state, capitalism, another person, nor another institution. She views everyone and everything through the lens of her marriage. However, it is not because Maria

Genre:
Historical Drama
Melodrama

Cast:
Hanna Schygulla
Ivan Desny
Klaus Löwitsch
Gisela Uhlen
Elisabeth Trissenaar
Gottfried John
Hark Bohm
George Eagles

Year:
1979

views marriage through a romantic or idealistic prism that she sees the world this way, but because her marriage grounds her against the unstable present and uncertain future that is Germany after World War II. Maria's marriage stands against the stream of costume changes and ruined architecture littering the *mise-en-scène*, and provides her with a centre around which to reconstruct herself. In this way Maria's outlook reflects the outlook of a nation attempting to reform itself against its recent history and seeking an institution by which to re-establish its place in the world. Additionally, it provides us with a lens through which to view the (claustrophobic) space and hear the (restricting) music and radio and public address system announcements.

Although Maria's marriage and Germany's history reflect one another throughout the film, they intersect with disastrous results in the final scene. As Germany regains its place on the world stage of football and Chancellor Adenauer announces that Germany will rearm itself, Maria's marriage literally explodes. What had served as an alternative foundation or centrepiece is incompatible with these other institutions. As Maria races through the house and from costume to costume, trying to match her attire to her new position as wife, she learns the secret of the men's contract, and the Chancellor's decision that have undone her own arrangements. Despite her best efforts, she cannot match the situation. Germany cannot resist rearming itself. In the final moments the whole house explodes, and the film repeats its opening gesture of the exploding building as Germany returns to a past it had tried to escape. In the end, the opening portrait of Hitler returns through the portraits (in negative) of the post-war Chancellors, illustrating Fassbinder's contention that the BRD remained a thin veneer covering ingrained Nazi sentiments. Even if they do not repeat the war years, the post-war regimes do not completely break with them either.

As with Fox, in *Fox and His Friends* (1975), Maria Braun is undone by a contract. The marriage contract she signed with Hermann was undone by the one between Hermann and Oswald. In the end, the German people are also undone by a contract. The one between themselves and their state is torn apart by the state's turn to NATO and the rise of Cold War antagonism.

Brian K. Bergen-Aurand

Hunger Years in a Land of Plenty

Hungerjahre – in einem reichen Land

Synopsis

13-year-old Ursula (Ulrich) struggles with puberty in the Germany of the early 1950s. With her first menstrual cycle, Ursula becomes more aware of her own sexuality and has many unanswered questions. But her mother (Pohland), who struggles with her own sexuality, silences her every time a question about the changing female body comes up. The silence leads Ursula to a peculiar relationship with a North African man (Ismail Mahdu), with whom

Production Companies:
Jutte Brückner Filmproduktion
Zweites Deutsches Fernsehen (ZDF)

Distributor:
Basis-Film-Verleih GmbH

Director:
Jutta Brückner

Producer:
Jutta Brückner

Screenwriter:
Jutta Brückner

Cinematographer:
Jörg Jeshel
Rainer März

Composer:
Johannes Schmölling

Editor:
Anneliese Krigar

Duration:
113 minutes

Genre:
Drama
Feminist

Cast:
Britta Pohland
Sylvia Ulrich
Helga Lehner
Claus Jurichs

Year:
1980

she tries to explore her newly gained sexuality. Her physical transformation is overshadowed by the political and economic changes of Chancellor Adenauer's post-World War II Germany that become cause for familial tensions. On one hand these tensions are caused by her mother, who attempts to restrain any signs of Ursula's sexual development, instead focusing on consumption and capitalist gain. On the other hand, the tensions develop with her father's (Jurich) lies about his political past and the turmoil brought about by a romantic affair he has with another woman, both of which distance him from Ursula and her mother. Domestic and political realities make it hard for Ursula to find a place as a woman in the fast changing world around her.

Critique

Brückner's ironic title for the film poses an important question fundamental for understanding the film: how can a there be hunger in a land of plenty? As Ursula's story develops, the spectator realizes that the answer to this question is complex. Germany's economic boom in the 1950s is, from the start of the film, closely connected to Ursula's life. Germany's economic miracle of the 1950s is highly problematic in the context of World War II. Efforts to rebuild the country after the war were successful and the economy recovered swiftly; however, coming to terms with what had happened during the war was not sufficiently addressed in the public sphere. It became very easy to forget about the past during a time of fast economic and political change, especially if this change helped distance Germany from its Nazi past. From outside, Germany seemed changed and prospering, while inside it was still struggling with and haunted by its past.

Ursula's story assists us to look at this period of German history critically and, in particular, attempts to illuminate uniquely female struggles during this time. As a result, questions of female emancipation become a central theme in the film and are intricately tied to its economic themes. Ursula's mother is central for the analysis of emancipation in the context of the economic boom. She is the first one to realize that the family should take advantage of the good economy with excess purchase and consumption. Convincing her husband that getting a job for herself is the only way to keep up financially with the spending programme she has created, Ursula's mother takes the first step away from the stove and hence the first step toward emancipation.

No longer just a housewife, Ursula's mother now earns money just like her husband, yet still feels and is inferior to him. The mother's unsuccessful 'emancipation' is in fact revealed to be nothing more than modified oppression. The spectator becomes aware of this while she is intimate with her husband. It becomes obvious that sex for her is an obligation and not pleasure, which clarifies her motives for trying to prevent Ursula of ever having to deal with it. The mother's negative regard to sex is stifling when the time comes to help her daughter deal with it. She tries everything to repress Ursula's sexual development, advocating instead that Ursula should focus on school. For her mother it is clear that Ursula will have everything once she has a means to earn money. But for Brückner this poses a problem, because the economic principles that the mother thinks will help Ursula find a better place in the world than she has do not necessarily foster emancipation. Brückner exposes the faults in the mother's worldview but without demonizing her as a person. The film carefully depicts the complex mother-daughter relationship by portraying the mother as victim of a system unsympathetic and oppressive toward women.

As Ursula learns more about her own sexuality and about Germany's political past and present, her questions become more intense and reveal many of the underlying problems in her parents' lives. The political and the private narratives collapse into one and are negotiated on and through Ursula's body: Ursula becomes the metaphor for Germany's struggle during a time of plenty, especially at the end of the film when she develops bulimia. Obsessive and excessive consumption that is followed by violent purging engender a sharp social critique and foreshadow a bleak future for both Ursula and Germany.

Ervin Malakaj

Jadup and Boel

Jadup und Boel

Production Company:
Deutsche Film (DEFA)

Director:
Rainer Simon

Screenwriters:
Rainer Simon
Paul Kanut Schäfer

Cinematographer:
Roland Dressel

Composer:
Reiner Bredemeyer

Editor:
Helga Gentz

Duration:
103 minutes

Genre:
Gegenwartsfilm
Drama

Synopsis

Jadup and Boel is set in a small East German town in the late 1970s, depicted as corrupt and decaying. The middle-aged mayor (Kurt Böwe) is reminded by chance of a young girl (Knappe) he had known in the time immediately after Germany's surrender in 1945, who was raped in circumstances that had never been clarified. He feels guilty for not having helped her and tries to investigate, but meets only with frustration. Through his remembrances, he sees that he has become too set in his ways, acquiring a new perspective on life and a better relationship with his own son (Jakob). The film is structured via a series of subjective flashbacks from the present to 1945.

Critique

Jadup and Boel is perhaps Rainer Simon's most important film and, notably, the last film to be banned in East Germany. Simon had intended it as an intervention into public political debates, yet its delayed release prevented this effect. It is adapted from the novel *Jadup* (1975) that paints a devastating picture of life in the GDR provinces, far from the positive image desired by the authorities. Although Simon repeatedly made the cuts requested by the censors, the film was finally shelved for nearly eight years.

The flashback structure of the film is not in the novel, and was added to the script. Flashback scenes are marked by the use of added colour (yellow and blue) at the edge of the lens. The image of the past that emerges is cryptic and fragmentary, largely due to the sheer brevity of the flashbacks. Two different actors play Jadup:

Cast:
Kurt Böwe
Gudrun Ritter
Katrin Knappe
Timo Jakob
Käthe Reichel
Franciszek Pieczka
Heide Kipp
Michael Gwisdek

Year:
1980

Kurt Böwe for the middle-aged man in the present, and his son Christian Böwe for the younger man in 1945. Simon also added a mythological dimension to the film by having it begin in the basement of Mayor Jadup's house and end in a church tower, thus implying a literal journey from darkness into light; he also inserted scenes with Jadup's son Max on a river ferry suggesting the river Styx. Along with the story of the main character, his wife and son, and the girl Boel and her mother, there are also subplots about a local historian (Willi Unger) and a visiting antiques collector (Herr Gwissen) who pursues an 'investigation' of the town parallel to Jadup's.

Simon began his career in the late 1960s making documentary fiction films, a genre also practiced by DEFA director Lothar Warneke and Polish director Krzysztof Zanussi. This genre – influenced by neorealism and *cinéma vérité* – sought to remain close to the surface of everyday life, using non-professional actors, episodic narratives and documentary inserts. Although *Jadup and Boel* is more poetically stylized than such films, its aesthetic is still one of understated realism. This is particularly evident in the performances of the main actors, especially Kurt Böwe, whose gruff but likeable persona earned him the nickname 'Columbo of the East.' *Jadup* was also influenced by the Polish 'cinema of moral concern,' which included directors Andrzej Wajda as well as Zanussi. (The presence of Polish actor Franciszek Pieczka in *Jadup* also points to this influence). Like them, Simon saw himself as an ethical investigator of the everyday life of his country, of the moral decisions made by individuals in socialist society. It was precisely this 'reduction of the revolution to morals' instead of Marxist historical processes to which the GDR's last Film Minister, Horst Pehnert, objected. This moral interest gives the film's narrative a parabolic quality often found in the best DEFA films. The parabolic aspect is heightened by the allegorical name of the antiques collector Mr. Gwissen, whose name in German resembles the word for 'conscience.' The hero Jadup is, like the heroes of many other Simon films, a rebellious outsider figure who refuses to fit in or toe the line. Simon called his film a work of 'honest self-questioning,' which shows its moral engagement with the society around it. Rather than being a dissident film, this is a film that seeks to reform everyday socialism through moral reflection.

Larson Powell

Peppermint Peace

Peppermint-Frieden

Director:
Marianne Rosenbaum

Screenplay:
Marianne Rosenbaum

Cinematographer:
Alfred Tichawsky

Composer:
Konstantin Wecker

Editor:
Gerard Samaan

Duration:
112 minutes

Genre:
Historical Drama

Cast:
Saskia Tyroller
Peter Fonda
Gesine Strempel
Hans-Peter Korff
Cleo Kretschmer
Konstantin Wecker

Year:
1983

Synopsis

The story takes place between 1943 and 1950. Little Marianne's (Tyroller) father (Korff) goes to war, a fact that causes her great anxiety. At the end of the war mother (Strempel) and daughter are reunited with her father, who has become the teacher in a village in Bavaria. Here the girl meets a friendly GI called Mr. Frieden (Mr. Peace) (Fonda) by the children, who has an affair with Nilla (Kretschmer), a young village woman. Marianne's process of growing up involves exploring and questioning social conventions, in particular the rules of the Catholic Church, and the way the adults handle the legacy of the past. Her fears of war are kept alive with the onset of the Cold War and the Korean War.

Critique

Peppermint Peace can be seen as part of a wider trend in West German cinema from the mid-1970s to the early 1980s, when several film-makers of the New German Cinema began to explore German history, namely National Socialism. Before this time only very few attempts had been made to confront this difficult subject in film culture, and not just there – in the main, the whole of West Germany seemed to be in the grip of an amnesia which was, in the Sixties, described as 'the inability to mourn' and related to Freud's theory of repression. A younger generation insisted that 'memory work' had to be done.

Some women film-makers were among those who tackled the issues, most notably Helma Sanders-Brahms with *Germany, Pale Mother* (1980). Feminists were seeking alternatives to dominant (male) modes of representation. Their different approaches were particularly suited to the radical exploration of themes that (most of) their male counterparts had not been able (or willing) to 'crack.' Women film-makers uncovered not just male dominance, but also took a critical look at the collusion of women in their own subjugation.

Rosenbaum tackles a complex array of issues by fusing the process of growing up in rural post-war Catholic Bavaria with the historical dimension of the memory of Nazi times and the effects of war. In doing so, she uses the device of showing it all through the eyes of a girl. The consistent privileging of the child's perspective results in a radical departure from classical narrative conventions and visual style. We are only privy to scenes that are significant for Marianne. The film, therefore, exhibits little continuity of storytelling; rather, the approach is non-linear, montage-style. Some scenes are only later revealed to be the little girl's dreams or visions. The visual style complements this radical approach: a hand-held camera, often wide-angled to accommodate Marianne's somewhat distorted view, is always lowered to a child's height; correspondingly, dialogue scenes in shot/reverse shot are filmed in low/high angle. Often the child looks straight at the camera (and thus at us) and asks uncomfortable questions.

Very early on it becomes apparent that Marianne has clear memories of Dr Klug's (Gérard Seamaan) fate, even though the adults 'protect' her (and themselves) from this knowledge – as a Jew, he has been deported to a concentration camp. Marianne knows that he has not 'gone travelling' and in nightmares she is plagued by her memories to the point of personally feeling guilty for his deportation. This is a very interesting example of 'the return of the repressed,' which, ironically, she experiences but the adults do not. This is possible because she has not yet been 'stitched' into the dominant discourse.

The women's collusion with the regime and, at the same time, their failure to limit their offspring's knowledge is shown in a poignant scene in which Marianne's mother pushes her against a shop window in order to keep her from seeing concentration camp prisoners being marched by. Again, Marianne realises what is happening, this time as a reflection in the window. This provides a beautiful commentary on the way the child experiences and interprets the world: filtered through conventions and interventions and yet shrewdly gaining an understanding that her as yet 'unfixed' place in society/history allows her to gain. Here, as in other scenes, her perspective is at once reduced and strangely widened, with subversive results.

The subversive potential of a child's view is also revealed in the children's discussions of adult terminology. Stock phrases are interpreted to humorous effect. For instance 'freedom' is translated as '*Frieden*' ('peace') – part of the film's title – because the English term cannot be assimilated. Religious and political concepts are applied by declaring 'fraternisation' to be a 'deadly sin'. Here, the children definitely have the last laugh.

The Church looms large in the children's lives. As a potent social institution it seeks to indoctrinate them, and is able to instil fear in the recipients. However, in partly comical, partly nightmarish actions, visions and dreams, Marianne questions the unconditional and conventionalised power of the Church: 'Where was God in the war?' she asks.

Maggie Hoffgen

The Harmonists

Comedian Harmonists

Production Companies:
Bavaria Film
Beta Film

Distributors:
Senator Film (Germany)
Miramax Films (USA)

Synopsis

The Comedian Harmonists were one of the most accomplished and popular male singing groups of the 1930s. They modelled themselves after the American group The Revellers, recorded countless popular songs in their inimitable four-part harmonies, toured Europe and the United States, and appeared in twenty-one films. Vilsmaier's film traces the story of the sextet from its first clumsy try-outs in the economically ravaged Berlin of the Weimar Republic to its sold-out performances in pre-Nazi Germany, and its eventual demise when the group's three Jewish members are banned from performing. The film's central character is Harry Frommermann

Director:
Joseph Vilsmaier

Producers:
Hanno Huth, Reinhard Klooss
Danny Krausz

Screenwriters:
Klaus Richter
Jürgen Egger, based on the story by Jürgen Büscher

Art Director:
Cornelia Ott

Cinematographer:
Joseph Vilsmaier

Composer:
Harold Kloser

Editor:
Peter R. Adam

Duration:
126 minutes

Genre:
Historical Drama

Cast:
Ulrich Noethen
Ben Becker
Heinrich Schafmeister
Kai Wiesinger
Heino Ferch
Max Tidof
Meret Becker
Katja Riemann
Otto Sander

Year:
1997

(Noethen), an unemployed Jewish actor who places an ad in a local Berlin paper in search for talented singers. He is joined by Robert Biberti (Ben Becker), a bass of Aryan descent, who introduces Frommermann to three of his friends (Schafmeister, Ferch and Tidof). When the pianist Erwin Bootz (Wiesinger) joins them, the group gradually develops its signature sound. The forceful Biberti not only quickly takes control from Frommermann by declaring himself the business manager and arranging concerts, recordings and salaries, he also disrupts Frommermann's courtship with Erna Eggstein (Meret Becker), a student who works in a music shop run by an elderly Jewish couple. Erna is flattered by Biberti's attentions and moves in with him. Only when Frommermann, along with the two other Jewish members of the group, is no longer allowed to perform after the Nazis' rise to power and is forced to leave Germany does Erna realize that she loves him and joins him on his journey to the United States of America.

Critique

The film represents an, at times, uneasy mixture of Hollywood-style entertainment and the exploration of Germany's Nazi past. Vilsmaier stated in an interview that his film depicts German history situated between comedy and tragedy. Even though he considers the historical background an essential element of the film, he expects a certain amount of background knowledge from the viewers. Instead of preaching or teaching he wants to entertain. Nevertheless, the director takes great pains to lend an air of authenticity to the production. The viewers are informed at the outset that the film is based on a true story and the film concludes with original photos of the Comedian Harmonists, along with captions which describe the eventual fates of the men, albeit in a simplified and not entirely accurate fashion. Vilsmaier also employs the broadcast of a Hitler speech, in which the dictator boasts of his party's intolerance towards those who do not subscribe to the Nazi agenda, along with the appearance of the infamous *Gauleiter* Julius Streicher (Rolf Hoppe), founder of the rabidly anti-Semitic newspaper *Der Stürmer*, to lend the film verisimilitude. The use of original, digitally enhanced recordings by the Comedian Harmonists during the concert sequences gives viewers the illusion that they are witnessing the actual event. While the group is touring New York City the 1934 skyline of the city is conjured up by means of digital effects. On occasion, however, Vilsmaier manipulates the facts. He transposes, for example, the artistic rivalry between the instinctively gifted Frommermann and the well-trained pianist Erwin Bootz, which is documented in Eberhard Fechner's 1975 made-for-television documentary, by focusing on the rivalry between Frommermann and the blonde, blue-eyed Robert Biberti instead. Erna's temporary turning away from the sensitive and reserved Jew Frommermann and moving in with the take-charge Aryan Biberti takes on a symbolic meaning when considered in its historical context. Vilsmaier uses the opposing world view of the two men to great effect when he contrasts a sequence during in

The Harmonists, Bavaria Film/Beta Film.

which Biberti takes Erna out on a date to a brutal boxing match with a joyous Jewish wedding celebration. Frommermann's and Biberti's conflict reaches a climax during their stay in New York: whereas the other members of the group consider remaining in the United States, Biberti insists on returning to Germany. When Frommermann expresses his fear of being sent to a labour camp, Biberti accuses him of suffering from a persecution complex. Unlike Biberti, Frommermann subordinated his own needs to the group's credo that 'the group is more important than the individual' (which throughout the film is symbolized by the men joining hands). Whereas Vilsmaier's intention to present his audience with an entertaining film rather than a history lesson caused some critics to accuse him of trivialization, the general audience embraced the story of the Comedian Harmonists. The film, along with Eberhard Fechner's documentary, revived interest in the singing group: young audiences started listening to their recordings and imitators like the Berlin Comedian Harmonists and the Italian Harmonists kept their memory alive.

Karl L. Stenger

Nowhere in Africa

Nirgendwo in Afrika

Production Companies:
Bavaria Film
MTM Cineteve

Distributors:
Constantin Film (Germany)
Optimum Releasing (UK)

Director:
Caroline Link

Producer:
Peter Herrmann

Screenwriters:
Caroline Link, based on the autobiographical novel by Stefanie Zweig

Cinematographer:
Gernot Roll

Composer:
Niki Reiser

Editor:
Patricia Rommel

Duration:
141 minutes

Genre:
Historical Drama

Cast:
Juliane Köhler
Merab Ninidze
Lea Kurka
Karoline Eckertz
Matthias Habich
Sidede Onyulo

Year:
2001

Synopsis

In 1937 Walter Redlich (Ninidze), a Jewish lawyer who is no longer allowed to practice, leaves Breslau for Kenya in order to escape persecution by the Nazis. He finds work as manager of Rongai, a farm owned by the British. Six months later his wife, Jettel (Köhler), and daughter, Regina (Kurka and Eckertz), are able to join him under the sponsorship of the Jewish community in Nairobi. Whereas Regina immediately takes to her new surroundings, spoiled Jettel refuses to adjust, expecting their stay to be a temporary one. When war breaks out in Europe, the family is interned along with other German refugees in Nairobi. Walter is fired from his job, but Jettel is able to secure a position for him on another farm with the help of a British officer in exchange for sexual favours. When Walter enlists in the British Army and participates in Operation J, Jettel takes charge of the farm. Her transformation from a spoiled and selfish socialite to an independent and empowered woman able to appreciate cultural difference is complete. When the war is over and Walter decides to return to Germany, where he plans to participate in the rebuilding of his homeland as a judge, Jettel at first refuses to join him, having lost her entire family to the Nazis. However, when she realizes that she is pregnant, she reluctantly agrees to return to a country that no longer feels like home. On 6 June 1947 a son is born and named Max in honour of his grandfather.

Critique

The film is based on Stefanie Zweig's memoir, which recounts her family's nine-year long exile in Kenya from a child's perspective. Caroline Link follows the book's narrative strategy by having the film narrated by Regina, who is introduced in the opening sequences in Germany as a shy and anxious girl. Regina has only dim memories of her homeland, which she describes as 'a dark place, not as bright and hot as Kenya, a place with large buildings and dismal rooms.' Her narration alerts the viewer that the girl's focus is going to be Africa, which she considers her true home. Here she is no longer shy and anxious: she quickly makes friends with Owuor (Onyulo), the family's Masai cook, and with the local children. Whereas she was afraid of a little dachshund in Breslau, she now adopts a young gazelle and a wild dog. Link shows the girl's immediate acceptance of her new surroundings visually by recurring close-ups of her feet touching the ground, first clad in shoes, then naked, and eventually exploring warm cow dung. Regina quickly learns to speak Swahili, observes local rites like the slaughtering of a sheep, and starts thinking like the natives. Süßkind (Habich), another German Jew who emigrated to Kenya and who, unlike Walter Redlich, considers Africa his home, predicts a great future for the girl because she is 'already talking like a Negro.' Even though Regina is the narrator of the film Charlotte Link makes Jettel, the mother, its focal point. The director has

Nowhere in Africa, Bavaria Film/MTM Cineteve.

stated that one of the reasons for the shift in perspective was the fact that her previous two films featured girls at the centre of the story and that she did not want to repeat herself. More importantly, Jettel is a more interesting character than either her daughter or her husband because she undergoes the most radical transformation. At the beginning she refuses to adjust to her new, stark surroundings because she naïvely believes that Hitler and the Nazis will not last long. She wears inappropriate clothes, refuses to speak Swahili, and treats proud Owuor like a servant. She is rebuked by her husband who accuses her of treating the locals with the arrogance of 'some people in Germany you wouldn't like to be compared to.' Only when bad news reaches the family in the form of letters and radio broadcasts does Jettel begin to realize that Africa represents her family's salvation. She gradually opens herself to the local customs and language and befriends Owuor. She also takes an active role in running the farm and is instrumental in saving the harvest from a swarm of invading locusts.

Two pivotal scenes show her newfound appreciation of her surroundings. When she finds an abandoned dying woman, she understands and accepts the local custom. Participating in a big local feast, Jettel wears an expensive evening gown, which she frivolously brought to Africa instead of a much-needed refrigerator, as a way of honouring the celebration. She has learned 'how valuable differences are.' As she begins her train journey back to an uncertain future in Germany, she tells a local woman who sells bananas that she cannot afford one because she is 'as poor as a monkey,' indicating that she has become one with the country that she rejected at the beginning but ultimately embraced. The film received an Academy Award in 2002 for Best Foreign Language Film.

Karl L. Stenger

And Along Come Tourists

Am Ende kommen Touristen

Production Companies:
23/5 Filmproduktion GmbH
Das Kleinfernsehspiel

Distributors:
Bavaria Film International (Worldwide)
X Verleih AG (Germany)

Director:
Robert Thalheim

Producers:
Britta Knöller
Hans-Christian Schmid

Screenwriters:
Robert Thalheim
Bernd Lange
Hans-Christian Schmid

Art Director:
Christian Cloos

Cinematographer:
Yoliswa Gärtig

Composer:
Uwe Bossenz

Editor:
Stefan Kobe

Duration:
85 minutes

Synopsis

Sven (Fehling), a young German, arrives in the Polish town of Oswiecim to begin civil service at the former concentration camp Auschwitz. As part of his duties he looks after a former inmate, Stanisław Krzemiński (Ronczewski), who is in his eighties and lives close to the camp grounds, repairing exhibition objects for the Auschwitz museum. In spending time with the initially brusque and taciturn Krzemiński, Sven begins to understand that the old man's work has become his reason for living, and notices a lack of respect and interest for him and his suffering. Sven falls in love with Ania (Wysocka), a young Polish woman who works as a tour guide in Auschwitz. Exploring the countryside around Oswiecim with her, Sven learns how the Auschwitz legacy still affects the lives of the local Polish population. Ania announces that she is leaving for a job in Brussels and ends her relationship with Sven. Meanwhile, his efforts at keeping Krzemiński's memories alive end in failure. Frustrated, Sven intends to leave but waiting for his train at the local station, he opts to return.

Critique

And Along Come Tourists examines the ongoing social and cultural conflicts between Poland and Germany on the grounds of their historical relationship as victim and perpetrator during World War II. The film depicts how the atrocities of the past loom over contemporary Polish-German relations. Thalheim's first feature film, *Netto* (2005) focused on the German East-West divide and reunification, and indicated his interest in the ubiquitous presence and impact of history on the lives of ordinary people. Locating this film in Auschwitz, Thalheim approaches the most traumatic event in modern European history in its most symbolic location. Many issues the film addresses are anchored in the relationship between Sven and Stanisław. The young German is seen walking aimlessly around the concentration camp, unsure what to do with his life. Krzemiński, on the other hand, is determined to preserve and communicate history, speaking at commemorative events and mending victims' suitcases with feverish zeal.

The film posits language as a key for cultural understanding and respect. Krzemiński, his sister Zofia (Kwiatkowska) and Sven's friend Ania speak fluent German. In Krzemiński's passion for Franz

Genre:
Melodrama
memory
post-war
holocaust

Cast:
Alexander Fehling
Ryszard Ronczewski
Barbara Wysocka
Piotr Rogucki
Rainer Sellien
Lena Stolze
Halina Kwiatkowska

Year:
2007

Schubert's *Liederzyklus* ('*Ich hört ein Bächlein rauschen*') one can detect an appreciation of the 'enemy's' language and culture. In contrast, Sven's deficient command of Polish keeps the town and most of its inhabitants at a distance. But language, as the film suggests, can also be used to avoid actual engagement. The film ironically comments on official discourses of reconciliation and commemoration, which in their meaningless invocation cover up a refusal to face up to the past. A prime example for this strategy is the director of the German company that runs a chemical plant in town. Superficially subscribing to a politically correct discourse of guilt and atonement, during the inauguration of a memorial stone in the grounds of a former forced labour camp she sidelines Krzemiński as his presence shows up her rhetoric as insincere and empty. Thalheim's film suggests that young Germans have difficulties in understanding history as lived experience. In seminars that accompany visits of youth groups to the concentration camp, students replicate the factory director's empty phrases. Throughout the film, Krzemiński's attempts to convey his experiences as a concentration camp prisoner fail to truly affect his listeners.

Exposing the inadequacies of language to articulate the Holocaust as human experience, *And Along Come Tourists* revisits a long-standing philosophical discourse. A quiet film that does not lecture its audience, its visual journey through idyllic summer landscapes takes on an unsettling note as these landscapes include the remnants of barbed wire and observation towers. Thalheim's film can be contrasted with other recent film engagements with World War II as predominantly entertainment, both in German cinema and in Hollywood – *Downfall* (2004), *Mein Führer* (2007), *Inglourious Basterds* (2009), *Valkyrie* (2008) – in that it approaches the presence of the past as a timely and urgent issue.

Claudia Sandberg

References

Elsaesser, Thomas (1996), *Fassbinder's Germany: History, Identity, Subject*, Amsterdam: Amsterdam University Press.

POLITICAL DRAMA

Left: *The Baader Meinhof Complex*, Constantin Film Produktion/Dune Films.

The Lost Honour of Katharina Blum

Die verlorene Ehre der Katharina Blum

Production Companies:
Bioskop Film
Paramount-Orion Filmproduktion
Westdeutscher Rundfunk (WDR)

Distributor:
CIC

Directors:
Volker Schlöndorff
Margarethe von Trotta

Producers:
Willi Benninger
Eberhard Junkersdorf

Screenwriters:
Volker Schlöndorff
Margarethe von Trotta, based on the novella by Heinrich Böll

Cinematographer:
Jost Vacano

Composer:
Hans Werner Henze

Editor:
Peter Przygodda

Duration:
100 minutes

Genre:
Political Drama

Cast:
Angela Winkler
Jürgen Prochnow
Mario Adorf
Heinz Bennent
Hannelore Hoger
Dieter Laser
Rolf Becker

Year:
1975

Synopsis

During a carnival party in Cologne, shy and reserved Katharina Blum (Winkler), whom friends call 'the nun,' meets Ludwig Götten (Prochnow), a young man under police surveillance. Forming an immediate attraction, they spend the night together at her apartment. The next morning heavily armed policemen break into the apartment in search of suspected bank robber and anarchist Götten, but he is nowhere to be found. Katharina is taken in for questioning and treated as a terrorist sympathizer and eventually an accomplice. Katharina is not only demeaned and victimized by the police but also by the press, who work in collusion with the police and the District Attorney. Werner Tötges (Laser), reporter for the right-wing tabloid *Die Zeitung*, interviews Katharina's friends, employers, ex-husband and critically ill mother and twists their words, turning Katharina into a whore, atheist and terrorist sympathizer. Katharina receives threats and obscene messages and is no longer able to show her face in public. She has lost her honour. When Götten is discovered by the police in a country house owned by Alois Sträubleder (Karl Heinz Vosgerau), an influential industrialist and former admirer of Katharina, it is revealed that he is not an anarchist but rather a deserter from the army. Katharina, whose life has been destroyed by the press, invites Tötges to her apartment under the pretence of giving him an exclusive interview, and shoots him repeatedly when he boasts of making her famous and suggests a quickie in order 'to get to know each other better.' Katharina is arrested and the film ends with Tötges' funeral, during which Dr. Lüding (Achim Strietzel), the owner of *Die Zeitung*, rails against 'the violence which is undermining the foundations of our liberal-democratic order,' and cynically asserts that 'the shots that killed Werner Tötges didn't hit him alone, they were aimed at the Freedom of the Press, one of the most precious values of our young Democracy.'

Critique

The film, along with the Heinrich Böll novella on which it is based, grew out of the author's painful experience with the right-wing press; above all, the widely read tabloid *BILD-Zeitung*. Nobel Prize recipient Böll was savagely attacked by the right-wing press when he published an article titled 'Does Ulrike Want Mercy or Safe Conduct?' in the left-leaning magazine *Der Spiegel*. There he attacked right-wing publications for demonizing the Baader-Meinhof group and creating mass hysteria. His aim was to urge a more measured response by the authorities. *The Lost Honour of Katharina Blum* (published in 1974) is both Böll's artistic treatment of his own experiences, as well as his renewed warning of a repressive and intrusive government and an irresponsible and out-of-control right-wing media. Since Ludwig Götten is not a terrorist his treatment by the police is completely disproportional to the crime he has committed; namely, stealing money while deserting from the army. When the police arrive at the country house to arrest the

The Lost Honour of Katharina Blum, Bioskop Film/Paramount-Orion Filmproduktion/Westdeutscher Rundfunk (WDR).

unarmed Götten, the viewer is shown hundreds of policemen, a helicopter and dozens of police vehicles, among them armoured trucks. Katharina's treatment by the police is even more egregious and brutal, especially since she has no connection with terrorists. Her only 'crime' is falling in love with Götten and helping him evade the police. The film thus suggests that the government's indiscriminate repression threatens the democratic foundations of the state, and leads to a radicalization of those groups that are merely critical of the social order.

The film also links the repressive government with the country's Nazi past: when the boyfriend of Katharina's aunt offers her the key to his place because she can no longer tolerate living in her violated apartment, he states: 'They only spared me, perhaps just because I'm an old Nazi.' Several scenes show members of the press working hand in glove with the police and brutalizing and defaming Katharina. Werner Tötges has no qualms manipulating the words of Katharina's friends and employers to suit his purpose, and he does not hesitate disturbing her critically ill mother disguised as a doctor, hastening her death. Even though the woman was only able to utter an ambiguous 'Why?' the newspaper informs its readers that the sick mother collapsed in tears, complaining that her daughter had not visited her for a long time and sighing: 'It had to come to this.' Katharina gives voice to the film's central message when she states after her mother's unexpected death: 'These people are murderers. All of them. It's their very business to rob innocent people of their honour, often to take their lives. Otherwise nobody would buy their papers.' Having witnessed the destruction of a human being and the manipulation of the public in the name of profit, the viewer can only marvel at the hypocrisy of *Die Zeitung*'s owner when he stresses in the final scene, which does not appear in Böll's novella, that freedom of the press is 'the core of everything: prosperity, social progress, democracy, pluralism, diversity of opinions.'

Karl L. Stenger

Germany in Autumn

Deutschland im Herbst

Production Company:
Filmverlag der Autoren

Distributor:
Concorde Film (Netherlands)

Directors:
Alexander Kluge
Volker Schlöndorff
Rainer Werner Fassbinder
Alf Brustellin
Bernhard Sinkel
Katja Rupé
Hans Peter Cloos
Edgar Reitz
Maximiliane Mainka
Peter Schubert
Beate Mainka-Jellinghaus

Producers:
Theo Hinz
Eberhard Junkersdorf

Screenwriters:
Alexander Kluge
Volker Schlöndorff

Critique

Germany in Autumn is one in a series of three collaborative films (including *The Candidate* [Aust, Kluge, Schlöndorff and von Eschwege, 1980] and *War and Peace* [Aust, Engstfeld, Kluge and Schlöndorff, 1982]) that were produced by collectives of directors and writers in an attempt to establish, what Alexander Kluge describes as, 'counter public-spheres'; that is to say, spaces independent of the mainstream media that encourage the audience to actively participate in the meaning-making process surrounding issues, policies, events and ideas that impact on the world in which they live. While *The Candidate* and *War and Peace* focus on the 1980 federal German election campaign and the American installation of nuclear weapons on West German soil, *Germany in Autumn* was produced in response to a series of terrorist related events that took place in the German Autumn of 1977, including: the kidnapping and subsequent murder of Hanns Martin Schleyer by members of the Red Army Faction (RAF); the hijacking of a Lufthansa plane en route to Frankfurt and the subsequent liberation of the passengers in Mogadishu; and the alleged suicides of key RAF members Andreas Baader, Gudrun Ensslin, and Jan-Karl Raspe in Stammheim prison.

As the directors point out in their analysis of the project, in making the film it was not their intention to provide the audience with a definitive analysis of the period in question: '[I]t is not our concern to provide another statement about terror here and abroad' nor 'to add to the hundred thousand theories the first correct one' (Brustellin et. al. 1988: 132). Rather, what motivated the production of the film was the degree to which the activities of both the RAF and the state had, by the end of 1977, rapidly dissipated in public consciousness (ibid.). The aim of the film is thus to

Rainer Werner Fassbinder
Alf Brustellin
Bernhard Sinkel
Katja Rupé
Hans Peter Cloos
Edgar Reitz
Heinrich Böll
Peter Steinbach
Maximiliane Mainka
Beate Mainka-Jellinghaus
Peter Schubert

Cinematographers:

Jörg Schmidt-Reitwein
Michael Ballhaus
Jürgen Jürges
Bodo Kessler
Dietrich Lohmann
Colin Mounier
Werner Lüring
Gunter Hoermann

Editors:

Beata Mainka-Jellinghaus
Heidi Genée
Mulle Goetz-Dickopp
Tanja Schmidbauer
Christina Warnck
Juliane Lorenz

Duration:

123 minutes

Genre:

Experimental Documentary
Political Drama

Cast:

Hannelore Hoger
Helmut Griem
Katja Rupé
Vadim Glowna
Angela Winkler
Heinz Bennent
Mario Adorf
Manfred Zapatka
Enno Patalas

Year:

1978

mobilise public debate by posing a series of questions about the period (and, in particular, its relationship to Germany's Nazi past) without providing the audience with any clear-cut answers or firm conclusions. The directors argue, 'Autumn 1977 is the history of confusion,' and if the film is to do justice to the complexities of the situation, then it is '[e]xactly this [confusion which] must be held on to' (ibid.: 133).

The film itself is very experimental in its form and is constructed out of an eclectic collection of fictional and documentary footage, as well as photographs, drawings, paintings and interviews with figures as diverse as Horst Mahler (the co-founder of the RAF) and the mother of Rainer Werner Fassbinder, the latter of whom compares the atmosphere of fear, repression and self-censorship characteristic of the German autumn to her experience of life during the Nazi period. Along with material shot at a Social Democrat Party convention and footage of the Bundeswehr in action, we also view workers at a Daimler-Benz assembly plant observing three minutes of silence in honour of former company executive Hanns Martin Schleyer, and we hear Kluge's voice reading out a letter from Schleyer to his son over footage of Schleyer's state funeral. Among other documentary material included in the film is footage of the burial of Baader, Ensslin and Raspe in Dornhalden cemetery, which is preceded by a fictional segment about a television production of Sophocle's *Antigone* that is shelved by management out of a concern that 'the youth will misinterpret it as a call to subversion.' The television executives' anxiety about Antigone's attempt to defy the state by burying her brother is followed by photographs of Baader and Ensslin, and another of Ensslin after her death, as we learn via voice-over of the difficulties experienced by her father in finding a burial site for his daughter and her friends.

As these brief examples demonstrate, it is through the juxtaposition of fictional and documentary material, and through the layering of the image with voice-over text that seeks to complicate and/or open up (rather than explain or reinforce) the image on-screen that the viewer is encouraged to become an active participant in the meaning-making process: to question the motives and activities of the terrorists; to reflect on the security measures put in place by the state; to query the atmosphere of fear and self-censorship generated, in part, by the media; and to consider the relationship between the German autumn of 1977 and Germany's then, still very recent, fascist past.

Tara Forrest

The Third Generation

Die dritte Generation

Production Companies:
Filmverlag der Autoren
Pro-ject Filmproduktion
Tango Film

Distributor:
New Yorker Films (USA)

Director:
Rainer Werner Fassbinder

Producer:
Rainer Werner Fassbinder

Screenwriter:
Rainer Werner Fassbinder

Art Director:
Volker Spengler

Cinematographer:
Rainer Werner Fassbinder

Composer:
Peer Raben

Editor:
Juliane Lorenz

Duration:
105 minutes

Genre:
Political Drama
Satire
Crime
Thriller
Terrorism

Cast:
Harry Baer
Hark Bohm
Margit Carstensen
Eddie Constantine
Jürgen Draeger
Raúl Gimenez
Claus Holm
Günther Kaufmann
Udo Kiel

Synopsis

Set in Berlin in the mid 1970s, *The Third Generation* deals with the criminal activities of a middle-class group of young political activists and drug addicts. When the radicals suspect there is a traitor in their midst the gang strikes by kidnapping the CEO of an American computer company. They do not realize, however, that they are being manipulated by the industrialist himself, who lured them into a trap to generate terror among the political leadership and increase his company's revenue by selling surveillance equipment to the government. The outcome of the terrorists' plan is tragic: during the joyful celebrations of the carnival the last members of the group are assassinated.

Critique

The Third Generation constitutes an additional fragment to the mapping of German history from the Wilhelmine era to the present undertaken by Rainer Werner Fassbinder throughout his career. In his attempts to describe the West German situation at the end of the 1970s and the experience of urban terrorism, the *enfant terrible* of the New German Cinema used the contemporary political circumstances to investigate the legacy of the Nazi past in the new democratic state and the origins of the social troubles beginning in 1967 with the student movements. After his contribution to the collective film *Germany in Autumn* (1978) – where the director showed some sympathy towards the first wave of terrorists – Fassbinder returns to the theme of political violence, producing a satirical critique of the revolutionary group, focusing in particular on the last generation, which follows the escalation into armed fight by the Baader-Meinhof gang and the idealist radicals of 1968.

The ferocious portrait of bourgeois youngsters turned into urban terrorists echoes the parody of Maoist revolutionaries of *La Chinoise* (1967) by Jean Luc Godard. Both films centre on the representation of unresolved tensions and political contradictions within the groups, and focus on the slogans and empty words uttered by the characters. Like Godard's film, where the red walls and the propaganda posters become protagonists alongside the human figures, the *mise-en-scène* of *The Third Generation* is instrumental in stylistically mirroring the conflicts. The rich and saturated colours employed in the depiction of the apartment's environment intensify the carnivalesque and puzzling atmosphere. Moreover, the abrupt cuts that characterize the film's montage and the rather odd camera angles contribute further to the loss of coherence and the sense of estrangement.

However, it is through the 'sound montage', one of the most recurrent stylistic resources in Fassbinder's oeuvre, that the most uncanny elements emerge. Besides the weird *mise-en-scène* of the interiors, dialogues are overlapped by noises and sounds coming from radio and television sets, rendering the elliptical plot even more incomprehensible. The film-maker combines three levels of

Bulle Ogier
Lilo Pempeit
Hanna Schygulla

Year:
1979

sound mixing – mood music, audio registrations and TV broadcastings – in order to reveal the mediated world the protagonists are living in. In its use of electronic music and the continuous presence of technologies, such as computers and television screens, *The Third Generation* pays homage to a tradition of science fiction thrillers and conspiracy films. Evoking the atmosphere of films set in an imaginary future, Fassbinder reflects on the emergence of a surveillance society.

The conspiracy genre may be considered the favourite form to deal with the Cold War and the representation of state violence and international intrigues. In light of the events of the German Autumn, the conspiracy theories that developed in the immediate aftermath seem to be a reaction to human impotency and a fantastic projection to orientate people in a socially complex system. In this sense, the character of P.J. Lurz (Eddie Constantine) embodies the impermeability of the historical facts through the figure of an obscure puppeteer, who manipulates the organized crime and the secret services for personal advantage. As a result, *The Third Generation* reflects the anxieties of a society controlled by electronic systems that still need to solve some of the mysteries from its recent past.

Elena Caoduro

The German Sisters

Die bleierne Zeit

Production Companies:
Bioskop Film
Sender Freies Berlin (SFB)

Distributor:
Filmverlag der Autoren

Director:
Margarethe von Trotta

Producer:
Eberhard Junkersdorf

Screenwriter:
Margarethe von Trotta

Cinematographer:
Franz Rath

Composer:
Nicolas Economou

Synopsis

West Germany 1970s: Marrianne (Sukowa) and Juliane (Lampe) are two politically engaged sisters who choose different means of protest. The former, married and with a child (Vogler), decides to embrace the armed struggle by becoming a terrorist member of the Red Army Faction (RAF); the latter is a reporter dealing with women's issues. After the arrest of Marianne, Juliane visits her sister in jail and they discuss their strict education, their choices and their beliefs. However, when Juliane is informed that Marianne and other terrorists have committed suicide, she does not believe the official cause of death and starts investigating the events on her own. Finding no support from the press, she dedicates herself to taking care of her nephew, victim of arson for being son of a terrorist, who finally wants to know the truth about his mother.

Critique

Based on the true lives of sisters Christiane and Gudrun Ensslin, *The German Sisters* portrays the fictional account of Gudrun's experience as daughter of an Evangelical pastor and founding member of the RAF. The film makes explicit reference to her adolescence, political activism and the mysterious deaths of German terrorists that took place in Stammheim high-security prison in 1977. The obsessive research of the truth and motives behind the suicide in the film reflects the widespread conspiracy theories

Editor:
Dagmar Hitz

Duration:
106 minutes

Genre:
Political Drama
Terrorism

Cast:
Barbara Sukowa
Jutta Lampe
Rüdiger Vogler
Doris Schade
Franz Rudnick
Vérénice Rudolph
Luc Bondy

Year:
1981

developed by sympathizers of the Baader-Meinhof gang and intellectuals not aligned with conservative media in the aftermath of Stammheim's 'Death Night'.

The German title of the film originates from the poem 'Der Gang aufs Lang' by Friederich Hölderlin,[1] but Margarethe von Trotta adopted it to refer to the metaphorical weight of the past, suggesting the atmosphere of the 1950s; the period when the Ensslin sisters and herself grew up with a deep sense of guilt and shame about the Nazi regime. The various translations of the title are interesting in shedding light on different marketing strategies of the film and how the expression '*bleierne Zeit*' became a formulaic temporal label and *lieu de memoire*. When presented at the International Venice Film Festival in 1981, the Italian translation, '*anni di piombo*,' altered the original meaning alluding to the 'years of the lead bullets' as the phase of domestic political violence perpetrated by the Red Brigades in the 1970s. While, for the German audience, the leaden years correspond to the post-war historical situation where amnesia about Germany's fascist past developed and where little fundamental change took place in public life, the Italian press adopted the expression to describe the most turbulent decade in Italian and West German history: the 1970s. The two English titles misled the British and American audience, suggesting that the film was more about the sisterly relationship; in fact, the marketing of *The German Sisters* and *Marianne and Juliane* (the

The German Sisters, Bioskop Film, Sender Freies Berlin (SFB).

US title) stressed the dramatization of their childhood, the feminist nature of the film and the women's issues addressed, rather than emphasising the role of the film as a sociological analysis of terrorism in West Germany.

The victory of the Golden Lion at the festival consecrated von Trotta as female director and a key critical figure of the New German Cinema, since then overshadowed by her male colleagues. Although the film was well received, she was not immune to criticism, especially for avoiding direct references to specific historical facts and for privileging the personalization of conflicts. Nevertheless, *The German Sisters* offers a powerful commentary on the origins of left-wing terrorism, linking it to the immense guilt felt by those who grew up toward the end of the 1950s and early 1960s. Since the end of the war the Allied propaganda officers forced the German population to view concentration camp films, especially to 're-educate' the new generations. Moreover, the obligation in the following years to screen these overwhelming and revolting images in schools and parish halls is illustrative of the educational strategy of the young German republic and the trauma that it caused. In *The German Sisters*, the viewing of *Night and Fog* (Resnais, 1956) and some shocking news footage of massacres in Vietnam constitutes the turning point in Marianne's life who starts in that moment her process of radicalization, which transforms her from daddy's girl to a less tender-hearted young woman.

In addition, the excerpt from Resnais' documentary aims to show the inner contradictions within the Ensslin family, and the permeating 'leaden silence' in school classes and homes. Marianne and Juliane's father, protestant pastor Klein (Rudnick), is not able to discuss the tragic scenes shown by the projector and neither to talk about the Nazi past with his daughters, but he reproduces instead dictatorial behaviours toward his wife and children.

Nevertheless, the final sequence of *The German Sisters* overrules the burden of incommunicability within the family as Juliane explains to her nephew Jan the reasons for Marianne's violent actions and recounts his mother's life. The dialogue between generations, which was denied to the two sisters and their father represents the moral command left by the director.

Elena Caoduro

Note

1. 'It is dim today, the roads and alleys slumber, and it almost seems to me as if I am in a leaden time' [my translation].

Legend of Rita

Die Stille nach dem Schuß

Production Companies:
ARTE, Babelsberg Film
Mitteldeutscher Rundfunk (MDR)
Mitteldeutsches Filmkontor (MDF)

Distributors:
Arthaus Filmverleih (Germany)
Kino International (USA)

Director:
Volker Schlöndorff

Producers:
Arthur Hofer, Emmo Lempert
Friedrich-Carl Wachs

Screenwriters:
Wolfgang Kohlhaase
Volker Schlöndorff

Cinematographer:
Andreas Höfer

Editor:
Peter Przygodda

Duration:
103 minutes

Genre:
Political Drama
Thriller
Romance

Cast:
Bibiana Beglau
Martin Wuttke
Nadja Uhl
Harald Schrott
Alexander Beyer
Jenny Schily
Franca Kastein
Mario Irrek

Year:
2000

Synopsis

West Germany in the early 1980s: following a number of terrorist acts with fatal consequences, members of the left-wing Movement 2 June (a terrorist group allied with the RAF) seek refuge in East Germany. The East German secret police, the Stasi, help them by offering new identities in the Middle East or in the GDR. One of the radicals, Rita Vogt (Beglau), takes up a job as a factory worker with a clothing manufacturer in East Germany, where she experiences the privations of the communist regime but begins to sympathize with its cause. Unpopular for her naïve political beliefs, she befriends another young girl, Tatjana (Uhl), who struggles with alcohol addiction. The two outsiders develop a sexual relationship, which ends when Tatjana learns of Rita's true identity and terrorist past. Again with the help of the Stasi, Rita is transferred to a children's day care centre. During a summer camp, Rita falls in love with a student, Jochen (Beyer), and makes plans for the future. But her true identity once again scuttles her opportunities. After the fall of the Berlin Wall and the capture of other former terrorists, Rita flees again but is fatally shot when she tries to escape during a hold-up at a border police checkpoint.

Critique

A key figure of the 1970s and 1980s, director Volker Schlöndorff returned to the issue of political violence after *The Lost Honour of Katharina Blum* (1975), made with Margarethe von Trotta, and his participation in the portmanteau film *Germany in Autumn* (1978) in 2000 with *Legend of Rita*, which inaugurated a new wave of films about terrorism and the German past that flourished in the subsequent decade. Following the fall of the Berlin Wall and with new documents from East German archives becoming available, new evidence emerged that shed light on a hidden history. Schlöndorff's film deals with the historical turning point of the end of the Cold War, and Rita's death at the end of the film can be read in terms of a sense of grief for the loss of reference points and the victory of capitalism over communist utopias.

Although criticized for its nostalgia – particularly in the opening sequence where, accompanied by the Rolling Stone's music, Rita and the other terrorists rob a bank Bonny-and-Clyde style – *Legend of Rita* represents a passionate expression of sorrow for the loss of ideals, and the absence of a strong counter-cultural movement in contemporary Germany at the precipice of a new millennium. The romanticisation of the young rebels does not appear apologetic for the terrorists' actions, but functions as a cry against the victory of lowbrow culture in making the terrorists commodities and pop icons during the 1990s, as the 'Prada-Meinhof' phenomenon testifies.

Adopting conventions of the road movie genre in depicting Rita's nomadic life and her continuous search for a new identity, Schlöndorff explores spatial boundaries, specifically the relationship between East and West Germany. The audience is shown the daily routine of GDR workers from a western perspective, through the naïve gaze of Rita; but one gets a detailed portrait of domestic and social life, especially in the sequences of Tatjana's family reunion and in the summer camp by the Baltic Sea, calling to mind the *mise-en-scène* of East German melodramas. Wolfgang Kohlhaase, veteran DEFA screenwriter of films such as *A Berlin Romance* (Klein, 1956) and *Berlin around the Corner* (Klein, 1965), collaborated with Schlöndorff, assisting to improve the authenticity of the script, in particular the portrait of everyday life in the GDR. At the beginning of the new millennium, not only does Schlöndorff reconcile with issues from the past, he also engages with a forgotten East German cinema heritage. The cooperation with Kohlhaase in *Legend of Rita* seals a new harmonious phase of post-unification cinema, where finally the DEFA tradition can occupy an honourable position.

Elena Caoduro

The State I Am In

Die innere Sicherheit

Production Companies:
Schramm Film
Hessischer Rundfunk (HR)
Arte

Distributor:
Pegasos Film

Director:
Christian Petzold

Producers:
Florian Koerner von Gustorf
Michael Weber
Liane Jessen
Andreas Schreitmüller

Screenwriters:
Christian Petzold
Harun Farocki

Cinematographer:
Hans Fromm

Composer:
Stefan Will

Synopsis

Somewhere in Portugal a German family, father Hans (Müller), mother Clara (Auer) and their teenage daughter Jeanne (Hummer) are staying in a holiday flat, but they are not on holiday. It becomes clear gradually that they are on the run from the law. Although never stated explicitly, a series of hints reveals that they are terrorists wanted by the German state. Jeanne wants to break out of the confinements of living underground. This includes a relationship with a young man, Heinrich (Bingül). Because of Jeanne's indiscretions, the family's relative security is jeopardised, and they are forced to flee to Germany to secure money for their emigration to Brazil. After a failed bank robbery, a car accident likely kills the parents; Jeanne survives.

Critique

If a home is the mark of a fully integrated human being, Petzold's protagonists are only half-human. These zombie-like beings live in holiday apartments, deserted houses and cars, and are thus removed from everyday reality and from interaction with other people. Living underground means danger and necessitates perfect understanding between them. Petzold's pared down style captures their situation perfectly: the parents communicate through furtive glances, oblique dialogue and well-synchronised body language. The audience needs to fill in unspoken or vague details. Within the narrative cause and effect are often presented in reverse or are only hinted at.

The most striking example of ghostliness and minimalism is a scene during the family's car journey through Germany. At a crossroads the traffic lights are on red and the car stops. Nobody

Editor:
Bettina Böhler

Duration:
106 minutes

Genre:
Political Drama
Terrorism

Cast:
Julia Hummer
Barbara Auer
Richie Müller
Bilge Bingül

Year:
2000

talks; the only sound is the running engine. What ensues is a peculiar incident: the traffic lights stay on red, obviously broken, but the parents, as if in a trance, step out of their car with both hands raised in the air, as if to turn themselves in. But to whom? The driver of the car behind them ignores their bizarre behaviour; he simply moves out and drives through the red light, almost as if their car did not exist. This is filmed as one single take in a long static shot; head-on, unremitting.

Hans and Clara's back-story is part of the history of West Germany. During the 1970s and 1980s the country was plagued by successive generations of urban terrorists whose main aim was to destroy the manifestations of capitalism, and to end the continued occupation of West Germany by the French, British and US Allied forces who provided the dominant representatives of capitalism and militarism. The terrorists kidnapped and murdered several heads of industry and banking, and blew up military targets. The West German state reacted to these violent outgrowths of the student movement of the 1960s with extreme measures in the name of 'Innere Sicherheit' ('Inner/State Security'), which is also the German title of the film. The civil liberties of moderate citizens were eroded in order to catch a handful of extremists, in many people's eyes a hysterical over-reaction, which according to some observers led to even more radicalisation. Judging by their age, the adults of *The State I Am In* must have been members of the third generation of terrorists.

Apart from their terrorist actions, the parents have committed another crime: they were selfish enough to raise a child in such circumstances. This child is now at an age when she wants to live her own life. Things that a young girl takes for granted, like clothes, friends, the beginnings of a romance perhaps, are all but inaccessible to Jeanne. Her loneliness is apparent in the very first scene of the film. It is off-season in a Portuguese resort; against the background of the sea Jeanne sits alone in a windy beach café with her drink and her cigarettes, listening to Tim Hardin's 'How Can We Hang On To a Dream' from the jukebox. This song immediately conjures up the period of political unrest of the 1960s, out of which the West German terrorist scene grew at the beginning of the 1970s. Thus, in simple film language, Jeanne's situation and the political background are introduced.

Trouble begins when Jeanne breaks out of the strict code imposed on her by her parents' predicament. She begins to interact with the outside world and threatens the 'Inner Security' of the family unit. Her relationship with a boy finally leads to his betrayal of them. The film ends with a car accident after a police chase. Slowly Jeanne emerges from the car wreck, injured and confused, and looks straight at the camera, as if to ask: 'What now?' – reminiscent of Truffaut's young protagonist (Jeanne-Pierre Léaud) in *Les quatre cents coups/The 400 Blows* (1959). He, like Jeanne, has escaped but is utterly alone.

Just as Truffaut's first feature marked the beginning of the French nouvelle vague, *The State I Am In* is generally regarded as the founding film of the so-called Berlin School, a loose group of film-makers who focus on low-key representations of human relationships, where social and political critique is rendered implicitly rather than overtly, as it was during the 1960s to 1980s.

Maggie Hoffgen

The Edukators

Die fetten Jahre sind vorbei

Production Company:
Y3 Film

Distributors:
Celluloid Dreams (Worldwide)
Delphi Filmverleih Produktion (Germany)

Director:
Hans Weingartner

Producers:
Hans Weingartner
Antonin Svoboda

Screenwriters:
Katharina Held
Hans Weingartner

Cinematographers:
Matthias Schellenberg
Daniela Knapp

Composer:
Andreas Wodraschke

Editors:
Dirk Oetelshoven
Andreas Wodraschke

Duration:
126 minutes

Genre:
Social Satire

Cast:
Daniel Brühl
Julia Jentsch
Stipe Erceg
Burghart Klaußner

Year:
2004

Synopsis

Jan and Peter (Brühl and Erceg), two young activists who live in a commune in Berlin, use non-violent means to oppose social injustice. They break into villas of affluent Berliners, disable the alarms, and rearrange the furniture, leaving notes stating, 'Your days of plenty are over' or 'You have too much money.' The friends' aim is to frighten the owners so they 'feel less safe in their high security neighbourhoods' when they find their stereos in their refrigerators and their Meissen porcelain figurines in their toilet bowls. Their motto is: 'Reach 1, educate 100.' Jule Lindner (Jentsch), Peter's girlfriend, is evicted from her apartment because she is late with her rent. Moreover, she has been fired from her waitressing job in a swanky restaurant and she owes 94,500 to Justus Hardenberg (Klaußner), a rich businessman whose S-Class Mercedes-Benz she totalled. Jule moves into the commune and, when Peter is away scouting their next project, she and Jan discover a mutual attraction. Jan reveals his and Peter's nocturnal activities to Jule and she talks him into entering Hardenberg's villa. They redecorate the mansion and throw a sofa in the indoor swimming pool. The next day Jule realizes that she left her cell phone behind and, during the attempt to retrieve it, she and Jan are surprised by Hardenberg, who recognizes Jule. In a panic, they knock him unconscious. On Peter's suggestion they take the businessman hostage and move him to a remote cabin in the Austrian Alps. During their stay in the cabin Hardenberg reveals that he was one of the leaders of the Socialist German Student Union and that he had similar views as the three activists. However, he insists that everyone changes and becomes more conservative over time. The friends realize that the kidnapping was not done 'to save the world but rather our own asses' and return to Berlin, where they release Hardenberg. The manager gives Jule a waiver of debt and promises not to contact the police. However, he breaks his promise and a group of heavily-armed policemen storms the activists' apartment, only to find it abandoned. They find only a note that reads: 'Some people never change.' It is revealed to the viewer that the three friends have made their way to Spain where they plan to destroy a control centre for Europe's main satellites.

Critique

The most striking element of the film is its ambiguity. Hans Weingartner does not supply the viewers with easy answers and pat solutions, but his goal is rather to elicit critical discussions. The idea for the film grew out of the real-life story of a French physician who broke into Parisian villas over a two-decade-long period and stored stolen items in his cellar without turning them into cash. In addition, Weingartner wanted to deal with his personal experience of trying to be politically active but not knowing how to go about it. The central theme of the film is stated in the activists' note, which is quite ambiguous. First of all, it can be read as a comment on Hardenberg's deceptive behaviour: he pretends to empathize with the activists while he is at the same time plotting their arrest. Twice he assures the friends that he will not contact the police and twice he breaks his promise.

'Some people never change' can also be applied to Jan's and Peter's political involvement. Despite Jan's temporary urge to abandon their cause, he ultimately decides to keep pursuing it because 'the best ideas survive.' While the two men raise their subversive activities to a new level at the end of the film, they remain committed to non-violent protest. Jule is the only character in the film who undergoes a profound transformation. While her protest against Asian sweatshops seems perfunctory at the beginning of the film, she gradually radicalizes when she feels she has become a victim of an unjust society. The fact that payment for Weingartner's damaged Mercedes-Benz will ruin her prospects for the next eight years while the car is petty cash for the manager, it is seen as a profound injustice by Jule's friends. While at first Jule rejects Jan's assertion that she is 'paying for some jerk's lifestyle' by stating that 'I screwed up, now I pay the price,' she eventually agrees with him when he says, 'You are still some rich bastard's slave.' She convinces a reluctant Jan to break into Weingartner's villa where she smashes several bottles of wine. The political discussions between her and the businessman in the Alpine chalet show that her view of society has changed. The fact that she is in the van's driver seat when the group returns to Berlin is an indication that she is now in charge of her life. The director leaves it open whether the activists are going to change as they age. Will they become more radical or will they become more conservative over time? It is up to the viewer to ponder these possibilities.

Karl L. Stenger

Sophie Scholl: The Final Days

Sophie Scholl – Die letzten Tage

Production Companies:
Broth Film
Goldkind Filmproduktion

Synopsis:

Set in 1943 Munich, the film recounts the final days of Sophia Magdalena Scholl (Jentsch), a 21-year-old university student and member of the secret organization the White Rose, an anti-Nazi non-violent resistance group. Accompanied by her brother Hans (Hinrichs), Sophie plans to distribute some leaflets in the main building of Munich University while classes are in session, but they are caught by a janitor as they leave the hall mingling with other students. Sophie is arrested by the police. Accused of high treason and interrogated by the Gestapo, Sophie demonstrates

Distributor:
X Verleih AG (Germany)
Zeitgeist Films (USA)

Director:
Marc Rothemund

Producers:
Fred Breinersdorfer
Sven Burgemeister
Christoph Müller
Marc Rothemund.

Screenwriter:
Fred Breinersdorfer

Cinematographer:
Martin Langer

Composers:
Reinhold Heil
Johnny Klimek

Editor:
Hans Funck

Duration:
120 minutes

Genre:
Political Drama
Biopic
History

Cast:
Julia Jentsch
Gerald Alexander Held
Fabian Hinrichs
Johanna Gastdorf
André Hennicke
Anne Clausen
Florian Stetter
Maximilian Brückner
Johannes Suhm
Lili Jung

Year:
2005

great strength of spirit, moral integrity and courage. Trapped in a nightmare, she finds empathy from other inmates, guards and even the Gestapo investigator who offers her a last chance to be saved. After a show trial, Sophie, her brother and an Austrian friend involved in the resistance movement are found guilty and sentenced to death penalty by guillotine.

Critique

In the documentary *Blind Spot: Hitler's Secretary* (Helle and Schmiderer, 2002) that frames the fictionalization of *Downfall* (2004), Junge Traudl claims that she was unaware of the Nazi atrocities while she was employed as Hitler's personal secretary. She also acknowledges how young and politically naïve she was when she came to work for Hitler. However, she recounts an epiphanic moment of her life: the visit to the memorial for Sophie Scholl in Munich. In that moment Junge realized the member of the White Rose movement died the same year the Chancellery employed her and that they were born only one year apart. Being young was not an excuse and Junge admitted her individual responsibility, but also the guilt of an entire generation that did not follow the message of the Scholl siblings.

Sophie Scholl constitutes a veritable hagiography of the German student, a celebration of her fight for freedom and her courage, as the film emphasizes the psychological profile of the female protagonist. Moreover, the film underlines the beneficial role of the White Rose sacrifice for the anti-Nazi resistance when, in the last scene, we see an Allied plane flying over a German town disseminating propaganda such as the manifesto of the Munich students. Following the last six days from the preparation of the leaflets to Sophie's capture, interrogation, trial and execution the film portrays a vivacious young woman who leads a relatively normal life in 1943 Munich. Sustained by deep religious faith and a strong belief in morality, Sophie is presented as a contemporary Joan of Arc, who fights for her ideas with great civic courage and approaches her execution with serenity, having a natural sense of right and wrong.

Like *Last Five Days* (Adlon, 1982) *Sophie Scholl – The Last Days* devotes itself to the final days of Sophie Scholl; but while Adlon's film frames the events from the perspective of Else Gebel, the political prisoner who shared a cell with Sophie, Rothemund's work gives a more rounded overview of the case, focusing in particular on the interrogations by the Gestapo officer Robert Mohr (Held) and the subsequent trial. In a certain sense it continues *Last Five Days*, which terminates when Scholl is conducted to the courthouse, adding also the depiction of her stay in Stadelheim prison: her last meal, the farewell to her parents, the visit of the prison's pastor and the last cigarette with her brother and their Austrian friend, Christoph Probst (Stetter). The story of the Scholl siblings and the Munich resistance movement in 1942–43 was the basis of another 1980s film, *The White Rose* (1982), which describes the formation of the anti-Nazi group, its organisation, its ideals and its end.

Screenwriter Fred Breinersdorfer, who practiced law for many years, was able to consult the original minutes of the Gestapo interrogation and the legal proceedings of the trial hidden away in

East German archives until 1990, in order to compose an authentic and moving script. Thanks to these recent sources, *Sophie* adds new dimensions to Sophie's personal tragedy rather than focusing on the history and activities of the resistance group, White Rose. In addition, the filmed interviews used for research purposes with Sophie's sister, Elisabeth, and the son of Gestapo interrogator, Willy Mohr, who opened their private archives and revealed personal anecdotes of their relatives, gave further insight into the main characters of the film, resulting in rounded and psychologically developed portraits.

Elena Caoduro

The Baader Meinhof Complex

Der Baader Meinhof Komplex

Production Companies:
Constantin Film Produktion
Dune Films

Distributors:
Constantin Film Verleih (Germany)
Momentum Pictures (UK)

Director:
Uli Edel

Producer:
Bernd Eichinger

Screenwriters:
Uli Edel
Bernd Eichinger, based on the book by Stefan Aust

Art Director:
Hucky Hornberger

Cinematographer:
Rainer Klausmann

Composers:
Peter Hinderthür
Florian Tessloff

Synopsis

The film covers ten years of German history from the student revolts in 1967/68 and the visit of the Shah of Iran to Berlin until the tragic epilogue of the German Autumn in 1977, culminating in the assassination of kidnapped Hans-Martin Schleyer (Bernd Stegemann), president of the Confederation of German Employers' Association, and the liberation of a hijacked Lufthansa aircraft in Mogadishu. Charting the descent into violence of Gudrun Ensslin (Wokalek), Andreas Baader (Bleibtreu) and Ulrike Meinhof (Gedeck), the film retells in numerous dramatic sequences the attacks by the urban guerrilla group that challenged the young West German democracy. Depicting the incarceration of the first wave of radicals, the film also addresses the issue of the treatment of political prisoners in German high-security jails, the degeneration of the second generation of terrorists and the political legacy of the 1970s in the Bonn Republic.

Critique

Referring to Hegel's theory of repeating history, Karl Marx said that history repeats itself the first time as tragedy, the second as farce. Soon after its release in European cinemas the official website[1] of *The Baader Meinhof Complex* welcomed visitors with a reworked version of this famous quote: 'History repeats itself first as tragedy and then as fashion.' The film tackles a difficult and still unresolved topic – the political violence of the 1970s – through generic conventions, mixing gangster and action movies in order to please popular tastes and to attract a young audience. The film works as a site of distraction and relies primarily on archival material and reproductions of iconographies generated by other media. While some critics labelled the film as an example of 'terrorist chic' (or 'Prada-Meinhof') – emphasising the aestheticization of violence and the glamorisation of its protagonists over a serious reflection on the Red Army Faction – others defended the film on account that it offered a new take on the subject: the fascination the Baader-Meinhof group exerted as counter-cultural icons in the 1970s, and their legacy in pop culture today.[2]

Editor:
Alexander Berner

Duration:
150 minutes

Genre:
Political Drama
Action
Biopic
Terrorism

Cast:
Martina Gedeck
Moritz Bleibtreu
Johanna Wokalek
Niels-Bruno Schmidt
Stipe Erceg
Nadja Uhl
Vinzenz Kiefer
Simon Licht
Sebastian Blomberg
Alexandra Maria Lara
Bruno Ganz

Year:
2008

The Baader Meinhof Complex is a film about clothes and masquerade; the objects of fetishism and nostalgic adoration are neither the charismatic characters, nor the illusion of a political revolution, or even the idea of a lost youth, but the various types of sunglasses and leather jackets worn in opposition to the ordinary and bourgeois uniform of suit, tie and shirt. Any empathy created towards the main characters of the film is channelled through the concept of vintage in its connotation with fashion. Ulrike, Andreas and Gudrun (and other secondary characters) are shown in synchronicity with their times: they are 'cool' in interpreting their zeitgeist through clothes. In this context the film conforms to Stella Bruzzi's observations with regard to the differences between French and American gangster films: 'Costumes do not support but rather substitute characterisation' (1997: 76). Similarly, in Edel's film we might say that the terrorists' clothes, often associated with status, revolutionary philosophy and style are part of the process of constructing an identity.

Previously depicted in the fictionalised biopic *Baader* (2002), Baader's iconography in Edel's film is constructed through the continuous use of props, such as fast models of Porsche and BMW and, particularly, clothes such as tight trousers and leather jackets. Vintage clothing is adopted as a cinematic trope, like flashbacks, to achieve the desired style of an era. But fashions do not work merely as temporal anchorage; they are important signifiers in the whole narrative structure. Baader's leading role within the gang is signalled by the abundance of fashion signifiers of his status, such as the cigar smoked during the first trial for arson. In addition, his leather jackets have several functions. Firstly, they attest to his status. The eagle on the back of one of his jackets serves as a metaphor for his role as principal male protagonist of the film and leader of the terrorist gang. Secondly, and contradicting its function as symbol of opposition to bourgeois tradition, the leather jacket becomes a narcissistic object of attraction for Baader who is more worried about some scratches on a sleeve than the fact that he was almost hit by a bullet.

The obsession with objects associated with the 1970s might be interpreted as a way to control time: a nostalgic reconstruction of the past allows us to experience a sanitised and regulated version of the past. *The Baader Meinhof Complex* is therefore symptomatic of the present collage culture of archive photographs and video clips, since much of its *mise-en-scène* is inspired by other mediated images. Vintage associated with mass nostalgia evoked by media is in reality an effective surrogate; a denial or an exorcism for not facing the images of the past and the tragedies of history.

Elena Caoduro

Notes

1. http://www.bmcmovie.com/#preloader
2. See for instance Andrea Dittgen, (2008), 'Radical chic', in *Sight and Sound*, 18, 12, pp. 24-26.

The Wave

Die Welle

Production Company:
Rat Pack Filmproduktion GmbH

Distributor:
Constantin Film (Germany)
Momentum Film (UK)

Director:
Dennis Gansel

Producer:
Christian Becker

Screenwriters:
Dennis Gansel
Peter Thorwarth
Todd Strasser

Art Director:
Petra Ringleb

Cinematographer:
Torsten Breuer

Composer:
Heiko Maile

Editor:
Ueli Christen

Duration:
107 minutes

Genre:
Political Drama
Thriller

Cast:
Jürgen Vogel
Frederick Lau
Max Riemelt
Jennifer Ulrich
Amelie Kiefer
Christiane Paul
Jacob Matschenz
Cristina do Rogo

Synopsis

Rainer Wengler (Vogel) is a beloved high school teacher and coach of the local water polo team. During project week, he decides to treat the topic of autocracy differently from the usually boring classes about National Socialism. His students, who do not believe a dictatorship could emerge again in Germany, reluctantly and then eagerly take part in an experiment that will ultimately prove them wrong. First, strict discipline and more formal manners are introduced. Then the students decide a name for the group, 'Die Welle' ('The Wave') and adopt a uniform – white shirts and blue jeans – along with a salute and a logo. The participants of the project start vandalizing the town, spraying their logo everywhere and bullying whoever is not part of the group. While Karo (Ulrich) and Mona (Kiefer), two students who initially abandoned Die Welle, try to reveal how they are instead falling victim to fascism, another student, Tim (Lau), becomes obsessed with the social group, burning all his other clothes and proposing to become Wengler's bodyguard. When the situation starts to degenerate, Wengler calls all the Wave members into the auditorium to demonstrate how their predictions were wrong and to call an end to the movement. However, Tim cannot accept the end of Die Welle and shoots a fellow student before committing suicide. At the end, Wengler realizes how destructive his experiment has been and is escorted to a car by the police.

Critique

The Wave is a remake of a teleplay by Johnny Dawkins based on the book *The Wave* by Todd Strasser (1981), a fictional account of a teaching experiment in a California high school. The sociological procedure undertaken by an American history teacher during the first week of April 1967 proved the appeal of fascism to the masses to the participating students, who could not understand why the German population endorsed for so long a dictatorship and ignored the genocide of the Jewish people and other minorities. Moving the setting to modern day Germany in a quiet suburban high school surrounded by lush nature, the film deals more directly with the German past, addressing a delicate issue in an apparently quiet bourgeois environment, and showing how a country, which identifies itself as guilty, cannot avoid the possibility that a similar event could occur again.

While in the teleplay a portrait of Hitler is shown at the last Wave meeting to reveal the fascist evolution of the group, *The Wave* concludes with the teacher giving a vigorous speech, which only echoes the fervent voice of the Führer on the radio. In addition, the tragic finale of the film with the suicide of Tim substantially differs from the end of the book, where the student most affected by the dissolution of the movement reconciles instead with the teacher. *The Wave* builds up the tension in a subtler way, engaging the audience with a climax of terror episodes, such as the dangerous

Joseph M'Barek
Maximilian Vollmar
Max Mauff

Year:
2008

expedition on the construction scaffold and the night-time incursion of Karo into the school building. In particular, this scene recalls the teen-thriller sub-genre in the creation of suspense through the music, low lighting and the creepy setting.

Die Welle confirms the interests of director Dennis Gansel in exploring group dynamics and psychologies. After *Before the Fall* (2004), which recounts the experience of two gifted boys from an exclusive school who become the future Nazi elites in the 1930s and 1940s, Gansel goes back to the issue of group power and its influence on individuals and offers an intense portrait of the present generation. The film excels for its socio-anthropological picture of the high school class, which represents a microcosm of contemporary Germany with all its contradictions. Solid performances from the young cast produce a powerful survey of various youngsters, including the representation of 'outsiders' such as the son of Turkish immigrants and an *Ossi* boy originally from East Germany. In this sense, *The Wave* addresses several public issues, which go beyond the problem of the rebirth of fascism in Germany, and engages with contemporary topics like bullying, social integration and dysfunctional families.

Elena Caoduro

References

Brustellin, Alf, Fassbinder, Rainer Werner, Kluge, Alexander, Schlöndorff, Volker and Sinkel, Bernhard (1988), '*Germany in Autumn:* What is the Film's Boast? (1978)', in Eric Rentschler (ed.), *West German Filmmakers on Film: Visions and Voices*, New York and London: Holmes & Meier, pp. 132–33.

Bruzzi, Stella (1997), *Undressing Cinema: Clothing and Identity in the Movies*, London and New York: Routledge.

Dittgen, Andrea (2008), 'Radical chic', *Sight and Sound*, 18: 12, pp. 24–26.

THE BERLIN WALL
DIE BERLINER MAUER

How interesting can a wall be? How many images can be made of it? If it's the Berlin Wall, the number must reach the millions: encoded on video, flickering through a projector, set into a still image, sketched on paper. A *very* important wall. A wall that was both grand and quotidian – said to have divided Europe and families. Political and personal, it was a miserable and paranoid construction, but a great setting for cinema.

Twenty years after its fall, relations between Germans are still riven by this East-West axis. This is apparent in one striking phenomena: the persistence of what Peter Schneider prophetically called 'the Wall in the mind' (1982). This, clearly, is about more than the Wall. It predates its construction for one. The fundamental and banal differences of the two sides of post-war Germany were notable even before the Wall went up, as we see in Helmut Käutner's *Sky Without Stars* (1955). This early entry into a long history of Wall films tells the story of a family split across two borderline villages, divided by the carve-up of Germany into Soviet and Allied sectors.

Sky Without Stars explores with prescience a thematic that recurs for at least another 55 years: the East-West division's intrusion into the lives of families and lovers. The Wall film is often about the traffic between East and West, generally its blockages and interruptions. *Beloved Berlin Wall* (dir. Peter Timm), a tepid romantic comedy from 2009 is only the most recent, obvious example of a story that German film-makers have returned to repeatedly. We find it also in Margarethe von Trotta's *The Promise* (1995). This is a typically thoughtful, if melodramatic and schematic, telling of an East-West division of lovers. Respected GDR film-maker Heiner Carow directed *Missing* (1992), a story of a middle-aged, pre-unification love affair between an East German woman and a West German dockworker. Other works used the device of twins or siblings – one in the East, one in the West – to play out how Germany developed over the period after World War II. Reunification was commonly depicted as a marriage of (female) East and (masculine) West – or at least a flirtation, a courtship, a jilted affair.

But just as common in the first ten years after the Wall's fall were films that saw no interaction at all between East Germans and West Germans – a kind of 'cultural apartheid,' in Leonie Naughton's words (2002: 112). It wasn't quite as if the Wall had not fallen – 'Ossis' ('easterners') could travel to Italy and New York, as in the *Trabi* films (*Go, Trabi Go* [Timm, 1991], *Go Trabi Go 2* [Büld and Klooss, 1992]) – but intra-German dialogue was minimal. *Adamski* (Becker, 1993), for example, tells the story of a love triangle composed solely of East Berliners. The German family also broke down regularly in the plots of films made during unification, as in Carow's *Missing*, but also *Lost Landscape* (Kleinert, 1992), *Apple Trees* (Sanders-Brahms, 1992), *Little Angel* (Misselwitz, 1996), *Herzsprung* (Misselwitz, 1992), *Ostkreuz* (Klier, 1991) and *Jana and Jan* (Dziuba, 1992).

While it's not always helpful to reduce cinema to socio-political determinants, it is worth noticing the industrial arrangements of film in post-unification Germany. Leonie Naughton's book *That Was the Wild East* (published 2002) details the sale of the GDR production studios (DEFA). The films produced there during the GDR era were

Left: *The Promise*, Bioskop Film, Canal+/Centre National de la Cinématographie (CNC)/Les Productions JMH/Odessa Films/Studio Babelsberg/Westdeutscher Rundfunk (WDR).

long denigrated as mere propaganda, either co-opted by the state or deformed by censorship – just as the country's people were said to be. That attitude toward GDR cinema seems to be changing and East Germany's own Wall films may yet make it into volumes like this. Nevertheless, in the moment of reunification, DEFA was discredited and its directors faced baptism-by-market. Brought up on the generous state patronage of the studio, GDR directors struggled to articulate their ideas and visions in the terms favoured by the capitalist culture industry i.e. dominated by the big commercial film houses of Munich. Equally difficult to convince were the capitalist state bureaucracies which subsidise so much German film production. Consequently, only a minority of films were helmed by 'Ossis' after the Wall fell. In the initial years of unification, as GDR cinemas closed or re-oriented their programmes to western fare, many of these failed to even find an audience in the former GDR. This collapse is allegorised on-screen in *Apple Trees* (1992) – a sympathetic West German production.

It is this history that makes *Sonnenallee* (Hau mann, 1999) all the more remarkable: a huge domestic box office success about East Germany directed and written by East Germans. East Germans tended to make sombre, alienated films about the unification process. *Sonnenallee*, by contrast, superficially fit with the many western comedies made about the trials of reunification, many of which were fish out of water stories dedicated to folk heroes or flights of fancy. Indeed, these unification comedies traded on clichés of westernness and easternness. The most generous thing that can be said of them is that they perhaps helped to 'normalise' German-German relations after unification: many of the western unification comedies asserted a certain moral superiority of the '*Ossis*,' even as they depicted them as naïve, backward and simplistic: a nation of idiot children and rigid bureaucracy. These films emerged while popular, contemporary German comedies flattered the ascendant, yuppie lifestyles: the period was later to be dubbed the 'cinema of consensus.'

There is no one, definitive film that has managed to encapsulate the experiences of reunification and the 'new Germany.' As Katharina Gerstenberger (2008) has argued about the failure of the great, post-Wall 'Berlin novel' to appear, these experiences were too diffuse, diverse and imbricated in global developments to be captured in one text. The many documentaries about the 'New Berlin' suggest an attempt to find the truth of the city and the lives of its inhabitants. In feature films of the same period we find the failed romances of '*Ossis*' and '*Wessis*', the steady trade in historical dramas of both Nazism and the Stasi (*The Lives of Others* [von Donnersmark, 2006], *Sophie Scholl – The Final Days* [2005]) and the cosmopolitan and immigrant stories of Germany today. Germany's double dictatorship, Berlin's vacant metropolis and the Turkish proletariat all vie for attention.

The diffusion is understandable. The loss of the Wall was a traumatic moment in recent German history; one that rent German identity, which was predicated in both Germanys on another, *more* German Germany on the other side of the Wall. Havoc ensues when this literal and metaphorical border breaks down. Such a loss of stable identity plays across many post-Wall films. In *Goodbye Lenin!* (2003), a loving family attempts to maintain the mother's attachment to the no longer existing socialism of the GDR. The elaborate ruse attempts to cover over the literal and metaphorical hole in German identity: the rupture in the Wall. Other comic films tell the story from the West German side, as in *Berlin Blues*, (2003), one of a growing number of films where we find a West German equivalent ('*Westalgie*') of a nostalgia for the East ('*Ostalgie*'). In *Berlin Blues*, as in many other films and novels where we find this narrative, this takes the form of nostalgia for the Berlin district of Kreuzberg. This district, encircled by the wall on three sides, is here a kind of Wild West; a dead end populated by artists, draft dodgers and ex-pats, before the return of capital and the onrush of gentrification after 1989. There is an inevitability to the failure of these earnest attempts to find the *real* Germany. No language – in the cinema or novels or whatever – could adequately capture the overwhelming quality of this transition from a divided to reunified (not reunited) Germany.

This failure, then, was as much aesthetic as it was thematic. Perhaps a more fruitful engagement with post-Wall Germany will develop in the corpus of works associated with the Berlin School. This school is a loose grouping of film-makers who began orbiting around the city's film schools in the years after reunification, or drifted to the city around the same time (Christian Petzold, Angela Schanelec, Thomas Arslan, Christoph Hochhäusler, Maren Ade, Valeska Grisebach and editor, Bettina Böhler). Marco Abel has argued persuasively that the films of this school possess a 'cartographic' quality (2008); not the representation of Germany seen in tourist shots, but a network of images that emerge from a subjective experience of reunified Germany and Europe.

After the tame offerings of German cinema in the 1990s – that cinema of consensus – the new school of film-makers displayed an aesthetic of reduction, a language beyond the TV-flavoured offerings of German cinema in the 1990s. The story of the School's emergence echoes that of the New German Cinema revolt against 'Papa Kino' in the 1970s. The Berlin School favours observation over assertion, alert to the dialectic of form and content. They move away from a literal, thematic (sociological) concern with 'Germany today.' In contrast to dominant modes, the films of the new School are oblique and elusive, but all the more intriguing for that. Mastery over meaning or 'reality' is always an illusion of wholeness – the directors of these films are willing to acknowledge that. But they still index a Germany that is absolutely *after* the Wall (*This Very Moment* [Hochhäusler, 2003], *Yella* [Petzold, 2007]). Not historical dramas, but life today. The country's internal border may no longer be visible, but the blocked traffic between East and West is still present in German cinema.

Ben Gook

Sky Without Stars

Himmel ohne Sterne

Production Company:
Neue Deutsche Filmgesellschaft (NDF)

Distributor:
Europa-Filmverleih AG

Director:
Helmut Käutner

Producer:
Harald Braun

Screenwriter:
Helmut Käutner (based on his play)

Cinematographer:
Kurt Hasse

Composer:
Bernhard Eichhorn

Editor:
Anneliese Schönnenbeck

Duration:
108 minutes

Genre:
Wall Film

Cast:
Eva Kotthaus, Erik Schumann, Horst Buchholz

Year:
1955

Synopsis

It is the year 1952. Anna Kaminski (Kotthaus) lives in East Germany, Karl Altmann (Schumann) is a border policeman on the West German side. They meet when she crosses the border illegally in order to see her young son, who currently lives with his grandparents in the West. Mother and son were separated when Germany was divided into East and West. The border is becoming more and more fortified because of countless attempts of East Germans to flee the communist East to the capitalist West. Anna resolves to take her son back to the East where her grandparents live and where she feels needed. Anna and Karl fall in love. He assists and protects her and loses his job as a result. In order to be with him, Anna decides to take her grandparents and her son to the West. Tragically, they don't make it.

Critique

Originally working in the theatre, Käutner began directing films in 1939 with the aim of maintaining control of his own screenplays. His early career may stand as an example of a film-maker who worked during the period of National Socialism and yet was not a Nazi. He was a relatively apolitical artist and, unlike many of his colleagues, he did not emigrate. However, he had constant problems with the censors. Some of his films were never finished or were taken out of distribution very quickly. Generally speaking, though, it was possible for him (and others) to steer a neutral course within the Nazi film industry. This fact, that not every film-maker working in Germany at that time was an active Nazi or indeed collaborated with the Nazis, is now acknowledged in scholarly circles, after a long period of equating all cultural production of the years between 1933 and 1945 with fascism. After the war, when the Allies imposed strict controls, Käutner was able to continue working in West Germany because of his neutral stance and the quality of his films.

Sky Without Stars is significant as the first film to deal with the impact on both East and West Germans of a border dividing two contrasting political systems. The film covers the years of 1952–53, when the Wall had not yet been built but the border was being increasingly guarded. Apart from being a gripping drama in itself, it is also an important historical document of political developments rarely seen on film. The German-German border was hardly represented on-screen during its lifetime, mirroring the way in which it was treated by the general population: it was all but ignored. One of the aims of the film would have been to educate West Germans about the extraordinary events leading to a nation's division, and make them aware of the human cost of this. Unfortunately, West German audiences did not seem ready to deal with such issues and Käutner gained a reputation for being 'box office poison' with films that ask questions about Germany's recent past, most notably in the aptly titled *In Those Days* (1947), *The Last Bridge* (1954) and *The Devil's General* (1955).

In his depiction of East and West Käutner is surprisingly even-handed, painting subtle portraits of people on both sides. He shows the negative accompaniments of West Germany's 'economic miracle,' namely selfishness and materialism, but also the great humanity of individuals. On the East German side, a Russian soldier tries to help Anna escape, but earlier horrific deeds of the occupying Russians are also referred to. All in all, the film, though made during the Cold War, eschews expedient ideology. Käutner's sensitive portrayal of the two sides is to a large extent achieved by his nuanced screenplay, based on his own play, in which one word or small gesture can suggest a person's political or historical standing. The love story itself is convincing through very fine acting and never becomes a tearjerker. It is rather a dark story of impossible happiness.

The film is grounded in realism through its *mise-en-scène*, filmed on location near the German-German border in Bavaria. An abandoned train station with its overgrown tracks becomes one of the focal points. It is one of the places where crossing the border is still possible and where Anna and Karl meet regularly. Dilapidated buildings, foggy rivers and dark woods characterise the no man's land between the two German states. Käutner's voice-over accompanies the opening images and recurs later in the film. He laments how the once-fertile land stretching between Bavaria and Thuringia now lies fallow, disused and divided by this monstrous border. With astonishing insight the voice declares that this geographical division was beginning to affect the minds of the people that not long ago had been one nation. Käutner must have been one of the first to realise this.

Maggie Hoffgen

Wings of Desire

Der Himmel über Berlin

Production Companies:
Road Movies Filmproduktion
Argos Films
Westdeutscher Rundfunk (WDR)

Distributors:
Basis-Film-Verleih GmbH (West Germany)
Image Entertainment (USA)

Director:
Wim Wenders

Producers:
Wim Wenders, Anatole Dauman

Synopsis

The film is set in West Berlin in the late 1980s, towards the end of the Cold War. We follow two angels, Damiel (Ganz) and Cassiel (Sander) as they roam the war-scarred city, unseen and unheard by the people, observing and listening to the diverse thoughts of Berliners and trying to comfort them. Although Damiel and Cassiel are purely observers, invisible to all but children, and incapable of any physical interaction with the human world, Damiel begins to fall in love with a circus trapeze artist named Marion (Dommartin), who is talented and lovely but profoundly lonely. A significant subplot of the film follows Peter Falk, cast as himself, who has arrived in Berlin to make a film about Berlin's Nazi past.

Eventually, Damiel too longs for physicality, and to experience humanity he breaks through into the mortal world to pursue a life with Marion. In addressing the story of two angels, the film delves deeply into a contemplation of humanist concerns, and also acts as a meditation on Berlin's past, present and future.

Wings of Desire, Road Movies Filmproduktion/Argos Films/Westdeutscher Rundfunk (WDR).

Screenwriters:
Wim Wenders
Richard Reitinger
Peter Handke

Cinematographer:
Henri Alekan

Composer:
Jürgen Knieper

Editor:
Peter Przygodda

Duration:
128 minutes

Genre:
Fantasy
Romance
Drama

Critique

Many film history surveys describe the 1980s as a period of decline in German cinema, with the death of Rainer Werner Fassbinder in 1982 unofficially bringing an end to the New German Cinema and marking the end of German cinema of the period as a formally innovative and politically provocative force. The election in 1982 of the CDU-dominated government under Chancellor Helmut Kohl had coincided with a conservative turn in social and economic policies as well as cultural tastes. The film industry endured a steady erosion of support with the further reduction of public subsidies, along with an intensified competition for audiences after the introduction of home video and, later, cable television. The pursuit of commercial success and the appeal of big budgets were also contributing to the exodus of yet another generation of German film-makers to Hollywood.

Nevertheless, Wim Wenders rode the international success of the New German Cinema into the 1980s, with his *Paris, Texas* (1984) dominating the Cannes awards in the year of its release. As one of the three key figures in New German Cinema (along with Fassbinder and Herzog), Wenders has developed a filmic style that combines generic conventions, literary influences, avant-garde traditions and counter-cultural sensibilities in highly innovative ways.

In *Wings of Desire*, we can discern many of Wenders' characteristic themes, motifs and stylistic signatures. The film explores the

Cast:
Bruno Ganz
Solveig Dommartin
Otto Sander
Curt Bois
Peter Falk

Year:
1987

tension between alienation from contemporary society and the quest for authenticity, immediacy and belonging, coupled with the desire for freedom and movement. We also find an open-ended narrative typical of his films, structured here around a search for authentic life, existence and reality.

With *Wings of Desire*, the imagery and sound moves deftly between subjective and objective realities, predominantly in black-and-white to show the angels' sepia-tinged monochromatic point-of-view, switching to colour only with the turn to mortal perspectives. Wenders' long-term collaborator, Dutch cinematographer Robby Müller, is absent; the film is instead exquisitely shot by veteran cinematographer Henri Alekan, who had famously worked on Jean Cocteau's visually stunning *Beauty and the Beast* (1946). It retains the distinctive cinematography of Wenders' movies, distinguished by contemplative long takes, elaborate camera movements and composed still images. Jurgen Knieper's score builds a wall of sound composed of harps, cellos and a chorus that buttresses the other-worldly feel.

The film's German title, *Der Himmel über Berlin*, can be literally translated as *The Sky over Berlin* or *Heaven over Berlin*. It is a film about a Berlin that is not simply haunted by angels, but a Berlin as a site of history, haunted by a troubled past, difficult present and insubstantial future. The beginning of the film provides us with slow, sweeping airborne camera shots, as we look down upon Berlin in autumn. Berlin, divided into East and West, is a city wasteland caught up in the long struggle of the Cold War, still marked by conflict and in the throes of a historicised physical and political schizophrenia symbolised by the Wall itself. The Berlin Wall – snaking through the urban spaces, covered with graffiti, which would fall two years after the film was released – has isolated the city and blurred its history. The notion of yesterday and beyond appears untouchable or sealed off despite Berlin's abundantly visible scars, and its future seems always deferred.

Wings of Desire became one of the most iconic art house films of the 1980s. Critically acclaimed and garnering multiple awards (including Best Director for Wenders at Cannes 1987), it was given a Hollywood remake in 1998 (*City of Angels* [dir. Brad Silberling] starring Nicolas Cage and Meg Ryan). Its well-received sequel, *Faraway, So Close!*, set in a unified Berlin, was released in 1993.

Collin Chua

The Architects

Die Architekten

Production Company:
Deutsche Film (DEFA)

Synopsis

In Peter Kahane's 1990 film *The Architects*, the 39-year-old East Berlin architect Daniel Brenner (Naumann) has won awards for designing buildings, but none of his buildings have actually been built. That's until he receives funding from the state to build a youth and cultural centre, consisting of a menagerie of buildings to accompany a new housing block. He rounds up a posse of friends from his

Director:
Peter Kahane

Producer:
Herbert Ehler

Screenwriters:
Peter Kahane
Thomas Knauf

Cinematographers:
Andreas Köfer
Christoph Prochnow

Composer:
Tomas Kahane

Editor:
Ilse Peters

Duration:
102 minutes

Genre:
Drama

Cast:
Kurt Naumann
Rita Feldmeier
Uta Eisold
Ute Lubosch

Year:
1990

days in architecture school, friends who have all since left the profession, and he aims to construct buildings that are environmentally friendly and aesthetically different from the *Plattenbau* so common in the German Democratic Republic. In the process of designing the centre Brenner's wife, Wanda (Feldmeier), has an affair with a Swiss man, divorces Brenner and leaves with their daughter to Switzerland. He must make painful compromises regarding his building project, constantly being insulted by older *apparatchiks* (Communist Party bureaucrats). Members of his young team of architects leave the project. He receives a call from his daughter who is on a school trip in West Berlin, telling him she will be at the Berlin Wall in an hour and that he should look for her. He rushes to the Wall and, of course, can see nothing because of the distance, the guards and the tourists. The final scene shows Brenner with a bottle of liquor, walking through the proposed – and still barren – building site at night. Finally, he vomits and passes out.

Critique

'Bauen ist Politik, Machtdarstellung' ('Building is politics, a representation of power'), says Brenner's mentor. And this comparison gets to the heart of *The Architects*. Architecture and city planning in the film are metaphors for several things. On a basic level constructing a building is like constructing a socialist state. The *Plattenbau* buildings – big, rectangular and monotonous, designed for housing many people – provide a more concrete image of this metaphor at work. The planning that accompanies building, however, gets deeper into the notion of building as politics, as the German Democratic Republic had a planned economy. Furthermore, there was a teleological, utopian push in the GDR regarding economics and technology, including engineering and architecture –the New Economic System – that began in 1963 and lasted until Honecker took over in 1971. There was a backlash against the NES in much of GDR literature and culture in the 1970s and 1980s, and *The Architects*, with its pessimistic view of architecture and politics in the GDR is part of that backlash. The scenes with older *apparatchik* architects telling Brenner what he must change in his designs – with an older Party member even being assigned to watch over Brenner's group to make sure they follow the Party line – reveals much of the paradox of any notion that the Party in the late 1980s represents progress regarding technology. Furthermore, the film points towards the self-destructive nature of the GDR project. Not only do the older architects forbid Brenner from building a statue representing the difficulties of family life, they even forbid him from constructing buildings that are more energy-efficient and would save the state money. They also forbid him from including a Vietnamese restaurant. Far from being a politics of idealism, the politics of building in the GDR, as Brenner's mentor goes on to tell him, is the politics of compromise. And Brenner compromises to the point of self-destruction.

Peter Kahane began work on the film while Erich Honecker was still in power, but the film was not finished until after the fall of the

Berlin Wall. This shift in power meant that the film was not subjected to censorship in the ways that earlier DEFA films had been. The shift in power also meant, however, that the film was largely overlooked, as it appeared in cinemas as Germany was rapidly reunifying. The film includes chilling footage of the Wall and the way that people interacted with it late in its history. The film also includes footage of other parts of East Berlin including Karl-Marx-Allee, and the dreary background of East Berlin, combined with the impossibly staid demands made by older *apparatchiks* in the film, makes watching the movie a rather claustrophobic experience. This is another reason why the film was overlooked at the time. Although the film is critical of the GDR, it resembles, in sight, cinematography and narrative, so many other DEFA films.

Robert Blankenship

Latest from the DaDaeR

Letztes aus der DaDaeR

Production Company:
Deutsche Film (DEFA)

Distributor:
Filmverlag der Autoren

Director:
Jörg Foth

Producer:
Manfred Renger

Screenwriters:
Steffen Mensching
Hans-Eckardt Wenzel

Cinematographer:
Thomas Plenert

Editor:
Renate Schäfer

Duration:
86 minutes

Genre:
Wall Film
Musical
Comedy

Synopsis

Letztes aus der DaDaeR presents the surreal odyssey of the clowns Meh and Weh (Mensching and Wenzel) through the final year of the GDR, mixing comedy sketches and musical revue with biting satire, its two protagonists at times being filmed participating in real events that would, in retrospect, be defined as the *Wende*, or the moment when German history 'turned' from Cold War division towards unification. Each day the two clowns are released from their prison cell to travel the country and entertain the population as it rebels against its aged leaders. In the process the film gives a snapshot of everyday life for the whole of society: from its geriatric ruling elite who begin the year attempting to cling on to authority, continuing to believe in the power of the moribund bureaucracy they have built around themselves; to those who maintain the state's rubbish heaps, a far better reflection of society's real values to be found, we learn, in what it discards than in its corridors of power. On the way Meh and Weh reflect the population's joy as it celebrates its growing freedoms, as well as the clowns' anxieties about what they see as the uncertainties that lie ahead.

Critique

This film is based on Steffen Mensching and Hans-Eckardt Wenzel's highly acclaimed cabaret act that had been satirising life in the GDR since the early 1980s. The popularity of these artists, along with their fundamental belief in the value of the state's socialist project, protected them from imprisonment or exile, the fate meted out to many of their cultural colleagues before them. Their act was, however, transformed by the film's director Jörg Foth into a piece of cinematic performance art, engaging with the events of the time as they were happening. In reviews, *Letztes aus der DaDaeR* was taken as a sign of the exciting artistic experimentation to come from the likes of Mensching, Wenzel and Foth in an East

Cast:
Steffen Mensching
Hans-Eckardt Wenzel
Irm Hermann
Christoph Hein
André Hennicke
Täve Schur
Peter Dommisch
Gerd Wolf

Year:
1990

German system freed from the yoke of the censor. In the event, however, much of this potential was not realised, as the GDR state film industry (DEFA) was wound up, leaving a generation of DEFA-trained artists floundering in the western-dominated mediascape of the unified Federal Republic.

Meh and Weh resonate with the power of Samuel Beckett's clowns as they wait for the GDR's own version of Godot to appear from the detritus that surrounds them. Filmed between March and May 1990, when it was only just becoming clear that the country was heading towards unification, the clowns offer a point of critical reflection on the events they witness, counselling a re-evaluation of socialist principles rather than their complete rejection in favour of western capitalism. They pass the time quoting texts from the German literary canon that, to the broader population, seem entirely out of step with the times, but, to the cinema audience, foreground the seismic significance of the events we are witnessing. We see, for example, the first mass celebration of the German festival of Walpurgis Night on the Brocken Mountain. The mountain, made famous to the world by Goethe's *Faust*, had always been the traditional location for the festival but had been closed off to revellers during the rule of the East German Communist Party, situated as it was in the 'no man's land' between the East and West German border. The critical potential of the clowns' presence, however, disturbs the revellers who clearly have no wish to reflect upon the process of unification that they hope is now under way. Nevertheless, even by the time of the film's release on 7 October 1990 – only 4 days after unification – many of those living in what had now become the 'new Federal regions' of the unified country would already be beginning to demand just such a process of reflection, as they found it harder to adjust to life in this new capitalist system than they had expected.

Paul Cooke

Faraway, So Close!

In weiter Ferne, So Nah!

Production Company:
Bioskop Film
Road Movies Filmproduktion

Distributor:
Sony Pictures Classics (USA)

Director:
Wim Wenders

Synopsis

Angels watch over a reunited Berlin, among them Cassiel and Raphaela (Sander and Kinski). They are able to hear the thoughts of humans but are not allowed to intervene in their lives. Witnessing the happiness of his friend and former angel, Damiel (Ganz), who is married to Marion (Dommartin), a trapeze artist who owns a pizza restaurant called Casa dell' Angelo ('House of the Angel'), Cassiel yearns 'to be one of them' and to experience the joys of human existence. When he saves Raissa Becker (Aline Krajewski), a girl whom he has been watching, from plunging to her death from a high-rise building, he becomes human, losing his armour and ponytail. While attending a Lou Reed concert, Cassiel decides that he 'wants to be good, to act like a man.' At first he succeeds, but soon he succumbs to human desires and follies led on by the mysterious Emit Flesti (Dafoe), who later reveals himself as 'time itself.' Cassiel takes a handgun away from a teenager, who

Producers:
Ulrich Felsberg
Wim Wenders

Screenplay:
Wim Wenders
Ulrich Zieger
Richard Reitinger

Art Director:
Martin Schreiber

Cinematographer:
Jürgen Jürges

Composer:
David Darling
Laurent Petitgand
Graeme Revell

Editor:
Peter Przygodda

Duration:
144 minutes

Genre:
Drama

Cast:
Otto Sander
Bruno Ganz
Solveig Dommartin
Horst Buchholz
Nastassja Kinski
Willem Dafoe
Peter Falk
Heinz Rühmann

Year:
1993

wants to shoot his father, but when he is unable to obtain alcohol from a corner store because he has no money, he uses the gun to threaten the store-owner. Cassiel eventually becomes entangled with Anton Baker (Ingo Schmitz), an American gangster who was born in Germany but who left the country at the end of World War II with his father, a Nazi. When Cassiel realizes that Baker trades in weapons and pornography, he decides 'to be good' and destroys Baker's business by stealing the arms with the help of Damiel and his circus friends, and by blowing up the underground facility which houses the pornography. When Raissa Becker, who turns out to be Anton Baker's niece, is kidnapped, Cassiel sacrifices his life in order to save the girl a second time. He is reunited with Raphaela.

Critique

Faraway, So Close! is the continuation of Wim Wenders' 1987 film *Wings of Desire*. As in the previous film, Wenders presents the realm of angels in black-and-white and that of humans in colour. The director indicated in an interview that seeing in colour is, in his opinion, a superficial way of seeing things, while the use of black-and-white shows that angels see the essence of things. Whereas *Wings of Desire* focuses above all on the search for personal happiness and love (the angel Damiel falls in love with the aerialist Marion and renounces immortality in order to be with her), *Faraway, So Close!* has a decidedly political slant by exploring Germany's Nazi past, and the continued (negative) influence of the past on the present: a re-unified Berlin. Unlike Damiel, Cassiel does not become human in order to find happiness with a woman but rather to be a force of good in the world, taking his cue from a song by Lou Reed whose concert he attends. This turns out to be much more difficult than Cassiel originally expected because the country is ruled by such negative forces as Time and criminal organizations. What makes matters worse is the fact that the film's central gangster, Anton Baker/Becker, has a direct connection with Nazi Germany: at the end of the war he and his father, a prominent Nazi, escaped to the United States, while his mother and sister Hanna stayed behind. A flashback in which Cassiel witnesses the escape makes the connection between past and present clear, as does the scene in which Cassiel follows Baker into a museum and, looking at a Max Beckmann painting of fallen angels, is transported back to the infamous Nazi exhibition of 'degenerate art' which was mounted in Munich in 1937. Baker's return to Germany and his unsavoury business practices are signs that Germany has not learned from the mistakes of the past and has squandered the opportunity of a new, positive beginning. The fact that Baker's business is destroyed at the end of the film and that he and his sister and niece renounce the past and become a family again is an indication that a positive future is possible: 'the cycle is broken.'

The film, however, does not provide the viewer with concrete ideas as to how a better post-unification Germany can be achieved. While the angels stress that 'the message is love' and while their presence points to the importance of faith and religion, Mikhail Gorbachev, the last General Secretary of the Communist Party of the Soviet Union, states, 'I'm certain that a secure world can't be built on blood, only on harmony.' It is the viewers' task to ponder how this harmony can be achieved and how society can be bettered. The film was awarded the Grand Jury Prize of the Cannes Film Festival in 1993.

Karl L. Stenger

The Promise

Das Versprechen

Production Companies:
Bioskop Film
Canal+
Centre National de la Cinématographie (CNC)
Les Productions JMH
Odessa Films
Studio Babelsberg
Westdeutscher Rundfunk (WDR)

Distributors:
Concorde-Castle Rock/Turner (Germany)
Fine Line Features (USA)

Director:
Margarethe von Trotta

Producer:
Eberhard Junkersdorf

Screenwriters:
Peter Schneider
Felice Laudadio
Margarethe von Trotta

Art Director:
Martin Dostal

Cinematographer:
Franz Rath

Composer:
Jürgen Knieper

Editor:
Suzanne Baron

Duration:
115 minutes

Synopsis

Autumn, 1961: in the aftermath of the newly-built Berlin Wall, some young people plan their escape from East to West Berlin, among them two lovers, Sophie and Konrad (Becker and Zollner). Of the two only Sophie manages to flee, Konrad is too late to reach the manhole cover of the sewage system. This is the first in a series of his failed attempts to join Sophie in the West. In the following 29 years they only meet four times altogether. One of these meetings, in Prague in 1968, results in Sophie becoming pregnant. She continues to live in West Berlin with her son Alexander and her partner. Meanwhile, Konrad is married with a daughter and follows a successful career as a physicist, living a very different life in East Berlin. Alexander sees his father only twice, most significantly towards the end of the film, where he finds him amongst the crowd on the night of 9 November 1989, when the Wall opens and Konrad and Sophie meet again.

Critique

As the first German post-Wall film *The Promise* is an important contribution to the discussion about the Wall. The film brings into focus the separation of Germany into two very different political systems, and the consequences of a divided country on its people(s). During its lifetime the Wall hardly figured in feature films, either East or West German. Indeed, for more than a decade after German unification *The Promise* was exceptional in its serious treatment of the divided Germany. The so-called '*Ostalgie*' (nostalgia for the East) comedies predominated.

The title's 'promise' works on two levels: it concerns the pledge the two protagonists give to each other, but also the undertaking of successive West German governments to unite Germany once again, physically and spiritually. On both levels, von Trotta and screenwriter Peter Schneider are sceptical as to the fulfilment of these promises. This scepticism is written on the faces of the lovers as they meet again on the night of 9 November 1989 in the melee of Berliners as they stream to the Oberbaumbrücke, whose border control was the first to open. The uncertainty is also expressed in the final words by an East German woman: 'When the cage has been opened after such a long time you cannot fly any more.' Will the younger people be able to fly? The film does not tell us.

The lovers are caught up in the maelstrom of political events. Their story is consistently embedded in these events by the *mise-*

Genre:
Wall Film
Drama
Romance

Cast:
Meret Becker
Corinna Harfouch
Anian Zollner
August Zirner

Year:
1995

en-scène and cinematography, which contrasts the intimacy of their rare meetings with their separate lives, all set against larger historical events. This duality is mirrored by the reasons for their continued separation: a combination of individual decisions and circumstances beyond their control. Further narrative strands focus on other characters such as Konrad's sister (a pastor) and her husband Harald (Pierre Besson). They stand for resistance against the repressive East German state and are contrasted with a Stasi agent's vile behaviour. In fact, key historical events and their individual manifestations are portrayed so prominently that the characters could be seen as functions of history rather than complex individuals.

It is an ambitious project to trace, in two hours, key events of the history of both Germanys as experienced by two characters. Despite the meticulous research and attempts towards a balanced representation of East and West Germany by, for example, casting actors from both East and West, the critical response to the film was mixed. As West Germans, von Trotta and Schneider were criticised for representing the East too schematically and negatively. However, the same could be said for the way the film treats the West: material wealth, libertarianism and its negative consequences are contrasted with signs of repression in the East. One such instance is Harald's deportation to the West. Konrad has been blackmailed by a Stasi agent into putting pressure on his sister and her husband to leave the East because they are troublemakers. They refuse and Harald is deported. At West Berlin's Zoo train station he emerges, somewhat dazed, among the homeless, drug addicts, alcoholics and beggars who used to populate this final stop and outpost of the Federal Republic of Germany during the life of the Wall; a shocking representation of the fallout of capitalism and a sight Harald has never encountered before. A 'wanted' poster of terrorists of the 'Red Army Faction' graces the wall. Every West German citizen would have been familiar with such posters in the 1970s and 1980s. Outside the station the Memorial Church looms. The film-makers sought to capture what they perceived as essential differences between the two German states and in such formulaic representations might have gone too far at times. With the benefit of hindsight it could be argued that such an approach was unavoidable, so soon after unification, when normalisation had hardly begun.

Maggie Hoffgen

Heroes Like Us

Helden wie wir

Production Company:
Senator Film Produktion

Synopsis

The story begins with an outrageous assertion. The first person narrator with the unpronounceable name, Klaus Uhltzscht (Heidenreich and Borgwardt), claims that he alone had brought about the fall of the Berlin Wall on 9 November 1989 and, moreover, that he did it with his oversized penis. How he managed to do this is only revealed to his fictive listener, a journalist for the *New York Times*, at the end of seven spoken audiotapes. Klaus Uhltzscht

Distributor:
Senator Film

Director:
Sebastian Peterson

Producers:
Hanno Huth
Alfred Holighaus
Gerhard von Halem

Screenwriters:
Christian Eisele
Markus Dittrich, based on the novel by Thomas Brussig

Cinematographer:
Peter Przybylski

Composer:
Niki Reiser

Editor:
Peter Jurowski

Duration:
93 minutes

Genre:
Comedy
Satire

Cast:
Daniel Borgwardt
Xenia Snagowski
Adrian Heidenreich

Year:
1999

was symbolically born on 20 August 1968, just before the Warsaw Pact countries invaded Czechoslovakia to halt the Prague Spring reforms. He grows up as an introverted child in the GDR with his mother Lucie (Kirsten Block) – a hygiene inspector in Berlin-Lichtenberg – and his father Eberhard (Udo Kroschwald), a member of the Stasi, the secret state police. Living across the street from the Ministry of State Security, he dreams of becoming a heroic spy and playing his socialist part in winning the Cold War. After joining the Stasi himself his hopes of becoming an East German James Bond are rapidly dashed. Yet, his megalomaniac desires are ultimately realized by his gigantic penis, which grew to enormous proportion due to surgical error. In the turmoil of the *Wende*, Uhltzscht believes it was by showing his genitals to the dumbfounded border guards that the Berlin Wall was finally opened.

Critique

East German author Thomas Brussig's satire *Heroes Like Us* (1995) quickly became a bestseller, heralded by prominent German reviewers such as Wolf Biermann as the eagerly awaited reunification novel. Brussig himself wrote the screenplay for the film adaptation. The film premiered on 9 November 1999, the tenth anniversary of the fall of the Berlin Wall. Both novel and film reflect '*Ostalgie*' in contemporary German popular culture. The term refers to a specific feeling of nostalgia for certain aspects of everyday life and culture in the German Democratic Republic, and is a direct consequence of the rapid disposal of reminders of the communist regime. Leander Haußmann's film adaptation of another Brussig novel *Sonnenallee* (1999), or most prominently Wolfgang Becker's internationally successful film *Goodbye Lenin!* (2003) are filmic representations of the GDR that can equally be regarded as transporting audiences to a nostalgic and humorous view of the communist experience in former East Germany. The humour in the film is based on the coupling of the protagonist's awkward sexual preoccupations with the political context of totalitarianism and the *Wende* era. Performing useless espionage assignments on fellow citizens are sharply contrasted by Uhltzscht's dream of being a genuine state hero in the service of socialism. This dream ultimately, yet ironically, comes true in the anti-hero's conviction that the Berlin Wall was torn down thanks to his oversized penis. In the film version of *Heroes Like Us* there is little trace, however, of the irony inherent to the novel or this rage over fellow travellers or the objectionable character of the novel's hero. Uhltzscht is presented in such a way that the viewer can still identify with him.

The protagonist Klaus Uhltzscht is a grossly exaggerated, larger than life embodiment of a fellow traveller who unites the fates of all the normal fellow travellers in the former GDR in his person. The clueless character hovers unsteadily between nullity and megalomania, between insecurity and arrogance. In tracing the protagonist's hilarious evolution from childhood to young adulthood, *Heroes Like Us* can be regarded as a parodic *Bildungsroman*, but also stands in the tradition of the picaresque novel. It is a mild parody of military and bureaucratic hierarchy in the communist regime. The actors – Adrian Heidenreich as the boy and Daniel Borgwardt as the neurotic teenager and young man Klaus Uhltzscht – appear more good-natured, more human even than the zombie-like original. Unlike the book, the central theme of the film is provided by an adolescent love story, which is gradually replaced by the plot of a conventional thriller complete with a wild car chase in a Trabant and a conspiracy among white-coated, faithful followers of the Stasi. Brussig's successful reunification novel is a burlesque comedy replete with malicious allusions to prominent turncoats. It drastically depicts the programmatic stultification of its protagonist and is full of quirky anecdotes from everyday life under the Stasi. The many scurrilous details are pieced together and presented like stage props from an East German theatre. The director, Sebastian Peterson, is extremely inventive in the use of various film techniques and materials. He links live-action film and animated cartoons, documentary and fictional materials, his own shootings, newsreels and old television images from the 1970s and 1980s, maintaining the forms and the colours of the times when the pictures were produced. Time-lapse techniques condense the images into ironic mosaics. Peterson thus creates a very personal view of the late GDR, which is an amusing and instructive alternative to the official historiography.

Arvi Sepp

Sun Alley

Sonnenallee

Production Company:
Boje Buck Produktion

Distributors:
Beta Film (Worldwide),
Delphi Filmverleih Produktion (Germany)

Director:
Leander Haußmann

Producers:
Claus Boje, Detlev Buck

Screenwriters:
Detlev Buck, Leander Haußmann, based on the novel by Thomas Brussig

Cinematographer:
Peter Krause

Synopsis

Michael ('Micha') (Scheer) is a 17-year-old living an ordinary teenage life in 1970s East Berlin. He dreams of a girl, he fawns over banned rock LPs and he schemes with friends. Micha lives life pressed up against the Berlin Wall, a border crossing just outside his window, on the street of the film's title. Corruption, bureaucracy, suspicion and the Party – all the stereotypes of East German life – swirl around him, but his one goal is to woo Miriam Sommer (Weißbach), the dreamiest, blondest, least attainable girl at school. As Micha and his friends go about fulfilling their teenage wishes, the film is littered with absurd scenarios, slapstick, musical numbers and political irreverence. A sombre, discreet undertaker is mistaken for a Stasi man; zealous party members stay up all night, dosed on the narcotic of Western television. Micha, meanwhile, gets the girl.

Critique

Sonnenallee is a popular post-unification film about East Germany written by, directed by and starring East Germans. It is remarkable for this alone. The marketing of the East German film industry during reunification marginalised most GDR film workers. This meant a paucity of Eastern voices addressing topics of unification and life in the GDR. Both writer Thomas Brussig and director Leander Haußmann have engaged in filling-out the record of

Composers:
Stephen Keusch
Paul Lemp

Editor:
Sandy Saffeels

Duration:
101 minutes

Genre:
Wall Film
Comedy
Teen Film

Cast:
Alexander Scheer
Alexander Beyer
Katharina Thalbach
Teresa Weißbach
Henry Hübchen

Year:
1999

GDR experience. Brussig has been a forthright critic of reducing the GDR to simplistic portraits of despair, Stasi surveillance and boredom. Another two of his novels – *Heroes Like Us* (1999) and *NVA* (Haußmann, 2005) – have been turned into screen comedies about the GDR. Brussig has said of *Sonnenallee*, 'it was supposed to be a film which would make westerners jealous that they weren't allowed to live in the East' (in Cooke 2005: 111).

Sonnenallee was a successful film by market measures: it sold over 1.8 million tickets in Germany in the year of release. This put it in third place for gross sales in its first year, behind two Hollywood blockbusters. Part of the reason for this success was its superficial fit within the foremost domestic genre of the era: the New German Comedy. It also boasts a lineage reaching back to 1950s' Hollywood teen films (e.g. *Rebel Without a Cause* [Ray, 1955]) and earlier GDR productions (*Berlin Schönhauser Corner*, [Klein, 1957] and *The Legend of Paul and Paula*, [Carow, 1973]).

Domestically, *Sonnenallee* was caught up in a debate about *Ostalgie* Alongside *Goodbye Lenin!* (2003) and *The Lives of Others* (2006), it is one of the best-known post-unification films about the GDR. Yet, despite its goofball stylistics, the film is in some ways more incisive than either *Lenin!* or *The Lives of Others*. This is because *Sonnenallee* is a reclamation of life in the GDR. It carries cutting moments of commentary critiquing both the naïve reappropriation at the heart of some *Ostalgie*, and the set of capitalist norms presumed to trump those of the East.

Sonnenallee thus occupies an ambiguous position within the field of *Ostalgie*, It can be seen as a 'reactionary' film; its existence is predicated on injecting humour into a grim image of the East. It very much comes out of an *Ostalgie* industry: it is a part of this field of commercialised, aestheticized renderings of an East German past. Yet *Sonnenallee* is also a celebration of East German quotidian culture. It judiciously weaves an anti-*Wessi*, and thus anti-unification, critique into an ambiguous text. Stylistically, the film deploys this subversive critique of post-unification triumphalism by echoing the form and appeal of New German Comedy in an Eastern setting. The film seems to be affirming that 'we had fun over there too, you know.'

Indeed, *Sonnenallee* speaks back to its context of production, to the mainstream representations of *Ossis* in film and the media. *Sonnenallee* is a corrective to the fundamental misunderstandings of the GDR in the first stage of unification. During this time, as Dominic Boyer has argued, one saw 'the wholesale public discrediting of the social, cultural and political legacies of state socialism as criminal, totalitarian and destructive of human integrity' (2006: 377). Over the past two decades, 'West Germans [have] often [been] unable to imagine the GDR as normal life in any respect, and their imagery for the GDR tends to revolve around enclosure, privation, and bareness' (ibid.). *Sonnenallee* may carry its share of quaint '*ostalgic*' moments, but it ultimately seeks to redress this crude picture of penury and denial of life to paint in some colour where a bleak grey had come to dominate. In light of the lost and rapidly de-legitimated GDR public realm, film becomes a place to reinstate lost symbols and material existence; a place for lost community and wistful teenage love affairs.

Ben Gook

No Place to Go

Die Unberührbare

Production companies:
Distant Dreams Filmproduktion
Zweites Deutsches Fernsehen (ZDF)

Distributor:
Advanced

Director:
Oskar Roehler

Producers:
Kaete Casper
Ulrich Casper

Screenwriter:
Oskar Roehler

Art Director:
Birgit Kniep

Cinematographer:
Hagen Bogdanski

Composer:
Martin Todsharow

Editor:
Isabel Meier

Duration:
110 minutes

Genre:
Drama

Cast:
Hannelore Elsner
Vadim Glowna
Jasmin Tabatabai
Lars Rudolph

Year:
2000

Synopsis

Hanna Flanders (Elsner) is a communist-sympathizing novelist living in Munich when the Berlin Wall is torn down. She clings onto her naïve Leninist beliefs and becomes depressed because of the disintegration of the East German state. She complains about East Germans rummaging through bins of western goods and does not understand why the East Germans are happy about their newly granted access to the West. All of this is ironic, because she herself lives in the West and compulsively spends money on luxury items. She also compulsively gives up her apartment in Munich and spends all of her money moving her things to Berlin to observe the political upheaval there more closely, having decided to move in with an old friend without asking him. She arrives in Berlin and is told that she cannot move in with him, is temporarily offered a brief stay in a writers' residence, and is later taken in by a hospitable East German family who eagerly celebrate German unification. She returns to Bavaria and asks her wealthy parents for money, then moves in, for one night, with another old friend who drinks too much even for Hanna. A chain-smoker, who also has problems with alcohol and pills, Hanna collapses in public because she underestimates how long it will take for a sleeping pill to take effect and wakes up in a hospital – where she is examined while unconscious – and is told that she has extreme hardening of the arteries in one leg due to smoking too much. She is forced to quit smoking and is told that her leg might have to be amputated. She is moved to a sanatorium, where she experiences intense nicotine withdrawals, and she eventually kills herself by purposefully falling out of a window, but not without first smoking her final cigarette. The film is based around the events leading up to the death of the director's mother, the writer Gisela Elsner.

Critique

The plot of this character-study is already dark enough, but cinematographic means are used to amplify the film's darkness. The film is black-and-white. There is a close-up of Hanna's face near the end of the film, where the viewer can see Hanna's deep wrinkles. In the final scene, in which Hanna falls out of the top-floor window at the sanatorium, she simply falls seemingly without emotion into light. The film's minimal soundtrack also contributes to its impressively cold feeling and allows other sounds to come to the fore and assume relevance, such as a clock in the sanatorium that, according to Hanna, is ticking too loudly. Music is played when a character plays a record, for example, but is otherwise mostly absent, which is especially notable in the final scene. The combination of the black-and-white film, close-up shots and the sparse soundtrack lends the film an intensely gloomy atmosphere.

The film was well received in Germany and abroad, having won thirteen awards including awards for directing, cinematography, and Hannalore Elsner's (no relation to Gisela Elsner) convincing performance. It has been compared to films by legendary New German Cinema film-maker Rainer Werner Fassbinder, both because of its concern with dark, social and psychological issues, and because of its thoughtfully composed, slowly moving, black-and-white pictures, as well as to the neo-noir films of the 1990s. The film, however, eschews categorization. The film is also unlike any other cinematic response to German unification in that it avoids comedy and *Ostalgie* and in that it addresses the issue of leftist melancholy. The film also represents a sharp break with German films of the 1990s that portray youth and popular culture with humour. From start to finish, the film achieves an earnest, gloomy portrayal of leftist melancholy in the wake of the fall of the Berlin Wall.

Robert Blankenship

The Tunnel

Der Tunnel

Production Companies:
Sat. 1, teamWorx Produktion für Kino und Fernsehen GmbH

Distributor:
K Films

Director:
Roland Suso Richter

Producers:
Nico Hofmann
Ariane Krampe

Screenwriter:
Johannes W. Betz

Cinematographer:
Martin Langer

Composers:
Harold Kloser
Thomas Wanker

Editor:
Peter R. Adam

Synopsis

Harry Melchior (Ferch), a decorated GDR swimmer who spent four years in prison for his participation in the June 1953 uprising, crosses over to West Berlin on 26 August 1961 with a forged Swiss passport. He has to leave his sister, Lotte (Lara), behind because her husband, Theo (Schmieder), is not willing to leave East Germany, and the couple considers it too dangerous for their young daughter, Ina. Harry vows to get her family out once Ina is older. Harry's closest friend, Matthis Hiller (Koch), an engineer, and his pregnant girlfriend, Carola Langensiep (Michelsen), try to escape through the underground sewer system, but they are separated and Carola is arrested. Once settled in West Berlin the two friends hatch a plan to dig a 145-metres-long tunnel underneath the Wall to facilitate the escape of their loved ones. They are joined by Vittorio 'Vic' Constanza (Kurtulus), an American soldier who lost his right leg to a landmine and who plans to sell his story to Hollywood; Fred van Klausnitz (Eitner) who wants to get his mother out of East Berlin; and Fritzi Scholz (Krebitz), whose fiancé Heiner (Panzner) is drafted to help build the Wall. Despite careful planning by Matthis, the engineer, the group has to face unexpected setbacks such as a concrete wall and a burst pipe. In addition, their mission is endangered by several informers who are drafted by Colonel Krüger (Kokisch) to uncover the plot. First, Carola agrees to be an informant when she is offered a release from prison. When Carola is no longer useful to the secret police, Lotte's husband, Theo, is drafted to spy on his wife. The growing attraction between Harry and Fritzi also creates a distraction. When Fritzi's fiancé, Heiner, hears about their relationship, he tries to escape to West Berlin and dies at the foot of the

Duration:
150 minutes

Genre:
Drama
Escape Film

Cast:
Felix Eitner
Heino Ferch
Sebastian Koch
Uwe Kokisch
Nicolette Krebitz
Mehmet Kurtulus
Alexandra Maria Lara
Claudia Michelsen
Heinrich Schmieder
Florian Panzner

Year:
2001

Wall after he is shot by guards. After a failed attempt to take her own life Fritzi dedicates herself to the group's mission. In an act of extreme courage she and Harry, disguised as an East German guard, help 29 people escape to West Berlin through the tunnel, among them Lotte and her family as well as Carola's and Matthis' newborn son. Carola has made the ultimate sacrifice by staying behind and leading the secret police to a remote location, thus buying time for the escapees.

Critique

While the events depicted in *The Tunnel* are based on historical fact, some of the details and characters have been changed. For example, the character Harry Melchior's real-life equivalent was Hasso Herschel. The storyline of the film combines the construction of 'Tunnel 57', which was dug in 1964, and that of an earlier tunnel, which was documented by an NBC film crew. The documentary, entitled *The Tunnel*, was presented on American television in 1963 as part of the 'White Paper' series. In order to anchor the film's fictional elements in reality, the director uses newsreel excerpts as well as newspaper headlines. He also recreates scenes from the documentary in grainy black-and-white. The scene in which an East German soldier jumps across a barbed wire barrier to freedom replicates one of the best-known images of the time, and Heiner's shocking death at the foot of the Wall alludes to the foiled escape attempt of Peter Fechter. He was an 18-year-old bricklayer shot by border guards on 17 August 1962 while scaling the Wall, and who bled to death after an hour (the border guards were convicted of manslaughter in 1997). End titles, which inform the viewer of the fate of the principle characters, also serve to lend the film an air of verisimilitude.

The director's primary goal, however, is not to replicate in detail a specific historical event, but rather he uses the escape story as the basis for a study of human courage, faith and loyalty in the face of oppression and injustice. Even though the scenes depicting the digging of the tunnel are riveting and realistic, the director's primary interest is the exploration of the multifaceted and courageous personalities. The director states in the 'Making of *Der Tunnel*' documentary that 'action movies are not for me' and the scenes in which various characters slip in and out of East Berlin while risking their lives are more riveting than the excavation of the tunnel itself. Those characters that develop in the course of the film and that, despite occasional stumbles and falls, ultimately exhibit astounding courage are more interesting than those whose determination does not waver. While Fritzi's initial motivation to join the conspirators is self-serving – she wants to help her fiancé escape – she puts her life on the line without ulterior motives after her boyfriend is killed. Carola Langensiep eventually becomes the film's heroine when she sacrifices her own future in order to give the gift of freedom not only to her newborn baby but also to 28 strangers.

Karl L. Stenger

Goodbye Lenin!

Production Company:
X-Filme Creative Pool

Distributors:
X Verleih AG (Germany), UGC Films (UK)

Director:
Wolfgang Becker

Producers:
Andreas Schreitmüller
Stefan Arndt
Katja De Bock

Screenwriters:
Bernd Lichtenberg
Wolfgang Becker

Art Director:
Matthias Klemme

Cinematographer:
Martin Kukula

Composer:
Yann Tiersen

Editors:
Peter R. Adam
Antje Zynga

Duration:
121 minutes

Genre:
Comedy
Drama

Cast:
Daniel Brühl
Katrin Saß
Stefan Walz
Chulpan Khamatova

Year:
2003

Synopsis

Goodbye Lenin! is a light-hearted and, at times, poignant film that reflects upon the changes forced upon a fictional family living in the former East Berlin. The film employs a discourse of the family and of the home to discuss the tumultuous events leading up to the fall of the Berlin Wall, and the subsequent unification of Germany. After witnessing her son, Alex (Brühl), being arrested by the Stasi during an anti-government demonstration on the eve of the GDR's 40th anniversary celebrations, Christiane Kerner (Saß), a seemingly committed party member, suffers a heart attack and falls into a coma for eight months. When she awakes, the Berlin Wall has fallen and the GDR is no more. Alex, fearing the shock of these events might cause his mother to have another heart attack, decides to keep the realities of German unification from his mother, creating the illusion that nothing has changed. To maintain this illusion, Alex enlists family and friends, along with the defunct products and facsimiles of life under the former regime, as well as an alternative narrative, to keep his mother cocooned from the monumental changes. His machinations highlight, in a tragi-comic style, the complexities of personal, social and cultural change, and address the problematic of 'official' histories and 'official' information.

Critique

Goodbye Lenin! portrays the scenario of a heterogeneous reaction to global hegemonic forces; primarily, one person's perpetuation of a now-defunct culture through processes that refer to the recent German phenomenon of *Ostalgie*. The film offers a humorous alternative history and interpretation of the events surrounding the fall of the Berlin Wall and, in doing so, ruminates on a changing nation and its culture. The film tacitly acknowledges the nature of utopian ideals in a post-industrial/post-traditional world, and questions perceptions of historical processes, as well as perceived wisdoms regarding ideal societies.

Despite being a box office success, some critics have taken issue with the film's playful subversion of historical events, footage and historical narratives, leading to accusations that the film glosses over the veracities of life in the former GDR and encourages nostalgia for, what was to some, a totalitarian regime. However, the film may be read not so much as a problematic expression of loss, but rather as a commentary on popular contemporary thought and practice. In particular the film shows how, through the increasing use of various media and new technology, the past is repeatedly made to live again both off- and on-screen and in a variety of contexts; something that is alluded to in the German subtitle to the film 'The GDR lives again – in 79 square metres. Honestly!' As Jozwiak and Mermann state, *Goodbye Lenin!* 'engages viewers in how and why we retrospectively and uncritically recreate the past' (2006: 780–95), rather than in the idealisation of certain moments in the past itself.

Similarly, the popularity of *Goodbye Lenin!*, both in and beyond the borders of Germany, further serves to show how the film

Goodbye Lenin!, X-Filme Creative Pool.

manages to broach more universal issues. Of interest is how the film plays with traditional ideas and constructs of utopia. In fact, the phenomenon of *Ostalgie*, as alluded to in the film, has been described as less a symptom of East German nostalgia, than of western utopia (Boyer 2006: 361–81). It is, therefore, through themes of utopia that *Goodbye Lenin!* provides a more insightful perspective on social, cultural and individual change. The film not only portrays the disillusionment with one experimental utopian society and the embracing of another seemingly more successful one, but it also portrays utopian desire and change on a more personal and individual level.

Throughout the film, references to former modes of living and technology show how traditional concepts of utopia gradually change from political/state-sponsored exercises into more individual (heterogeneous) and personal projects. Further, the imaginative use of archival footage and, more importantly, its subversion draws attention to how both film and television are unreliable narrators – especially where history is involved. *Goodbye Lenin!* illustrates how film-makers willingly recycle past images, icons and emblems for use as new icons for new historical narratives (Ebbrecht 2007: 221–34). The 'doctored' television programmes that Alex feeds to his mother provide a reassuring sense of continuity, as well as offering an alternative and more palatable version of events. Ironically, therefore, Alex's attempts to shield his mother from the veracities of the outside world mirror the same processes employed by the former communist regime to do the same, and the audience is left to infer that such practices are not just the preserve of defunct ideologies or states. *Goodbye Lenin!* therefore refers to wider meaning-making processes, both on- and off-screen, but it does so to illustrate how contemporary life is experienced through a heavily mediated landscape.

Kenneth A. Longden

The Lives of Others

Das Leben der Anderen

Production Companies:
Arte
Bayerischer Rundfunk (BR)
Creado Film
Wiedemann & Berg Filmproduktion

Distributors:
Buena Vista International (Germany)
Sony Pictures Classics (USA)

Director:
Florian Henckel von Donnersmarck

Producers:
Quirin Berg
Max Wiedemann

Screenwriter:
Florian Henckel von Donnersmarck

Art Director:
Christiane Rothe

Cinematographer:
Hagen Bogdanski

Composers:
Stéphane Moucha
Gabriel Yared

Editor:
Patricia Rommel

Duration:
137 minutes

Synopsis

Set in 1984, the film offers the spectator a suitably Orwellian image of the former East German State, in which the writer Georg Dreyman (Koch) is placed under surveillance by the state's infamous security service, the Stasi, on the advice of a corrupt party official Minister Hempf (Thieme). Hempf claims to suspect the man of dissidence – an accusation that at the start of the narrative is entirely false. However, Hempf's real motivation is his attraction to Dreyman's lover, the actress Christa-Maria Sieland (Gedeck). During the surveillance operation, the controlling Stasi officer, Captain Gerd Wiesler (Mühe), initially a devout believer in the GDR's status as the better of the two post-war German states begins to lose faith in the GDR's draconian understanding of its 'socialist' project. He is drawn, instead, to the humanist artistic worldview to which he is introduced by spying on the writer and his partner. As a result, rather than relaying to his superiors Dreymann's gradual turn to dissidence, Wiesler protects him, writing innocuous reports. He can, however, not protect Christa-Maria, whose is destroyed by her relationship with Hempf, the full truth of which Dreyman does not realise until after unification, when he gains access to his Stasi file and learns of the officer who was his guardian angel.

Critique

The film was a surprise recipient of the 2006 Oscar for Best Foreign Language Film, not least because it was not set during the Nazi period – the common denominator in both Germany's previous winners. That said, it did deal with Germany's other problematic past, while also conforming to the international genre conventions of melodrama and the 'heritage' film, thus following the 'rules' of winning in this category which decree, as Georg Seeßlen puts it, that a 'film has to be "foreign enough," but must also not flout the aesthetic codes of the dream factory too flagrantly.' Thus, in line with the trend of 'heritage' cinema to fetishize 'authenticity' in its quest to turn the past into a straightforwardly consumable form, the film constructs a hyper-authentic *mise-en-scène* in which the GDR of the 1980s is carefully recreated in every detail. This authenticity was further enhanced by Bogdanski's use of a colour palette of grey and brown tones, which helps to transport the spectator back to the GDR of the 1980s, replicating the hue of images we see today in old television footage. The film's attention to detail with regard to *mise-en-scène* was, however, considered problematic for some since it was not supported by a similarly accurate narrative. While

Genre:
Wall Film
Melodrama, Heritage Film

Cast:
Sebastian Koch
Martina Gedeck
Ulrich Mühe
Ulrich Tukur
Thomas Thieme

Year:
2006

internationally the film was widely praised, in Germany its reception was more mixed, with Rüdiger Suchsland, for example, dismissing it as 'Disney's GDR-Melo [drama]' – a reference to the film's distribution in Germany by Buena Vista – which turned Wiesler, in Günter Jenschonnek's words, into 'a State Security Schindler.' The key problem with presenting Wiesler in this light was that, unlike Spielberg's hero, Wiesler is a fictional character. Indeed, there is no substantial evidence of any such conversions by members of the Stasi. Consequently for its critics, the film was seen as a worrying form of revisionism that sought to trivialise the devastating effect the Stasi had on its real victims. For others, however, it was praised for its ability to communicate the oppressive mood of the time to a generation of Germans brought up on *Ostalgie* comedies such as Wolfgang Becker's *Goodbye, Lenin!* (2003), who connect the GDR with quirky consumer goods and funny-looking traffic lights in the eastern part of Berlin, rather than with the authoritarian oppression of the GDR authorities. In this regard the use of melodrama could be defended, it was argued, as it allowed the film to speak effectively to mainstream cinema audiences. In the process, the film moreover became embroiled in debates around the very status of German national cinema, with Günter Rohrbach, President of the German Film Academy, decrying the likes of Suchsland and Jenschonnek as 'autistic' and out of touch with a cinema-going public that is increasingly attracted to such films; an attraction that is helping to put German cinema back onto the international map.

Paul Cooke

References

Abel, Marco (2008), 'Intensifying Life: The Cinema of the "Berlin School"', *Cineaste*, 33: 4.
Boyer, Dominic (2006), 'Ostalgie and the Politics of the Future in Eastern Germany', *Public Culture*, 18: 2.
Cooke, Paul (2005), *Representing East Germany since Unification: From Colonization to Nostalgia*, Oxford and New York: Berg.
Ebbrecht, Tobias (2007), 'History, Public Memory and Media Event: Codes and Conventions of Historical Event-Television in Germany', *Media History*, 13: 2/3, pp. 221–234.
Gerstenberger, Katharina (2008), *Writing the New Berlin: The German Capital in Post-Wall Literature*, Rochester, NY: Camden House.
Jozwiak, Joseph F. and Mermann, Elisabeth (2006), 'The Wall in Our Minds? Colonization, integration, and nostalgia', *Journal of Popular Culture*, 39: 5, pp. 780–95.
Naughton, Leonie (2002), *That Was the Wild East: Film Culture, Unification, and The 'New' Germany*, Ann Arbor, MI: University of Michigan Press.
Schneider, Peter (1982) *Der Mauerspringer: Erzählung*, in Peter Schneider and Leigh Hafrey (1998), *The Wall Jumper: A Berlin Story*, Chicago: University of Chicago Press.

RECOMMENDED READING

Baer, Hester (2009), *Dismantling the Dream Factory: Gender, German Cinema and the Postwar Quest for a New Film Language*, New York and Oxford: Berghahn Books.
Barlow, John D. (1982), *German Expressionist Film*, Boston: Twayne.
Bergfelder, Tim, Carter, Erica and Göktürk, Deniz (eds.) (2002), *The German Cinema Book*, London: BFI.
Bergfelder, Tim, (2005), *International Adventures: German Popular Cinema and European co-productions in the 1960s*, New York: Berghahn Books.
Berghahn, Daniela (2005), *Hollywood Behind the Wall: The Cinema of East Germany,* Manchester and New York: Manchester University Press.
Boa, Elizabeth (2000), *Heimat – A German Dream: Regional Loyalties and National Identity in German Culture, 1890–1990*, Oxford and New York: Oxford University Press.
Bock, Hans-Michael and Bergfelder, Tim (2009), *The Concise Cinegraph: Encyclopaedia of German Cinema*, New York: Berghahn Books.
Brockmann, Stephen (2010), *A Critical History of German Film*, Rochester, NY: Camden House.
Byg, Barton (1995), *Landscapes of Resistance: The German Films of Daniele Huillet and Jean-Marie Straub*, Berkeley: University of California Press.
Clarke, David (2006), *German Cinema: Since Unification*, London and New York: Continuum.
Coates, Paul (1991), *The Gorgon's Gaze: German Cinema, Expressionism and the Image of Horror*, Cambridge, UK and New York: Cambridge University Press.
Cooke, Paul (2005), *Representing East Germany since Unification: From Colonization to Nostalgia*, Oxford and New York: Berg.
Corrigan, Timothy (1994), *New German Film: The Displaced Image*, Second Edition, Indianapolis: Indiana University Press.
Corrigan, Timothy (1986), *The Films of Werner Herzog: Between Mirage and History*, New York: Methuen.
Davidson, John E. (1999), *Deterritorializing the New German Cinema*, Minneapolis: University of Minnesota Press.
Eisner, Lotte H. (1969), *The Haunted Screen: Expressionism in the German Cinema and the Influence of Max Reinhardt*, Berkeley: University of California Press.
Elsaesser, Thomas (1989), *New German Cinema: A History*, New Brunswick, NJ: Rutgers University Press.
Elsaesser, Thomas (1996), *Fassbinder's Germany: History, Identity, Subject*, Amsterdam: Amsterdam University Press.

Elsaesser, Thomas and Wedel, Michael (1996), *A Second Life: German Cinema's First Decades*, Amsterdam: Amsterdam University Press.

Elsaesser, Thomas, (2000), *Weimar Cinema and After: Germany's Historical Imaginary*, London and New York: Routledge.

Fassbinder, Rainer Werner, Töteberg, Michael and Lensin, Leo A. (eds.) (1992), *The Anarchy of the Imagination: Interviews, Essays, Notes*, Baltimore: Johns Hopkins University Press.

Fehrenbach, Heide (1995), *Cinema in Democratizing Germany: Reconstructing National Identity After Hitler*, Chapel Hill: University of North Carolina Press.

Feinstein, Joshua (2002), *The Triumph of the Ordinary: Depictions of Daily Life in the East German Cinema, 1949–1989*, Chapel Hill: University of North Carolina Press.

Fisher, Jaimey and Prager, Brad (eds.) (2010), *The Collapse of the Conventional: German Film and its Politics at the Turn of the Twenty-first Century*, Detroit: Wayne State University Press.

Flinn, Caryl (2003), *The New German Cinema: Music, History and the Matter of Style*, Berkeley: University of California Press.

Frieden, Sandra, McCormick, Richard W. and Petersen, Vibeke R. (eds.) (1993), *Gender and German Cinema (Volume II): Feminist Interventions*, Providence, RI: Berg.

Fuchs, Anne (2007), *Phantoms of War in Contemporary German Literature, Films and Discourse: The Politics of Memory*, Basingstoke: Palgrave Macmillan.

Ginsberg, Terri and Thompson, Kirsten Moana (eds.) (1996), *Perspectives on German Cinema*, New York: G.K. Hall; London: Prentice Hall International.

Guerin, Frances (2005), *A Culture of Light: Cinema and Technology in 1920s Germany*, Minneapolis: University of Minnesota Press.

Hake, Sabine (2002), *German National Cinema*, Second Edition, London and New York: Routledge.

Halle, Randall (2008), *German Film After Germany: Toward a Transnational Aesthetic*, Urbana: University of Illinois Press.

Halle, Randall and McCarthy, Margaret (eds.) (2003), *Light Motives: German Popular Film in Perspective*, Detroit: Wayne State University Press.

Hantke, Steffen (ed.) (2007), *Caligari's Heirs: The German Cinema of Fear After 1945*, Lanham, MD: Scarecrow Press.

Hardt, Ursula (1996), *From Caligari to California: Erich Pommer's Life in the International Film Wars*, Providence, RI: Berghahn Books.

Hillman, Roger (2005), *Unsettling Scores: German Film, Music and Ideology*, Indianapolis: Indiana University Press.

Hoffgen, Maggie (2009), *Studying German Cinema*, Leighton Buzzard, UK: Auteur Publishing.

Isenberg, Noah William (ed.) (2009), *Weimar Cinema: An Essential Guide to Classic Films of the Era*, New York: Columbia University Press.

Kaes, Anton (1989), *From Hitler to Heimat: The Return of History as Film*, Cambridge, MA and London: Harvard University Press.

Kaes, Anton (2009), *Shell Shock Cinema: Weimar Culture and the Wounds of War*, Princeton, NJ: Princeton University Press.

Knight, Julia (1992), *Women and the New German Cinema*, London and New York: Verso.

Kracauer, Siegfried (1947 [2004]), *From Caligari to Hitler: A Psychological History of the German Film*, Princeton, NJ: Princeton University Press.

Kuzniar, Alice A. (2000), *The Queer German Cinema*, Stanford, CA: Stanford University Press.

Langford, Michelle (2006), *Allegorical Images: Tableau, Time and Gesture in the Cinema of Werner Schroeter*, Bristol: Intellect.

Majer-O'Sickey, Ingeborg and von Zadow, Ingeborg (eds.) (1998), *Triangulated Visions: Women in Recent German Cinema*, Albany, NY: State University of New York Press.

McCormick, Richard W. (2001), *Gender and Sexuality in Weimar Modernity: Film, Literature and 'New Objectivity'*, New York: Palgrave.

McCormick, Richard W. and Guenther-Pal, Alison (eds.) (2004), *German Essays on Film*, New York: Continuum.

von Moltke, Johannes (2005), *No Place Like Home: Locations of Heimat in German Cinema*, Berkeley, CA: University of California Press.

Petro, Patrice (1989), *Joyless Streets: Women and Melodramatic Representation in Weimar Germany*, Princeton, NJ: Princeton University Press.

Pflaum, Hans Günther (1990), *Germany on Film: Theme and Content in the Cinema of the Federal Republic of Germany*, Detroit: Wayne State University Press.

Phillips, Klaus (1984), *New German Filmmakers: From Oberhausen through the 1970s*, New York: Ungar.

Pinkert, Anke (2008), *Film and Memory in East Germany*, Bloomington: Indiana University Press.

Rentschler, Eric, (1984), *West German Film in the Course of Time: Reflections on the Twenty Years Since Oberhausen*, Bedford Hills, NY: Redgrave.

Rentschler, Eric (ed.) (1986), *German Film & Literature: Adaptations and Transformations*, New York: Methuen.

Rentschler, Eric (ed.) (1988), *West German Filmmakers on Film: Visions and Voices*, New York and London: Holmes & Meier.

Rinke, Andrea (2006), *Images of Women in East German Cinema, 1972–1982: Socialist Models, Private Dreamers and Rebels*, Lewiston, NY and Lampeter, UK: Edwin Mellen Press.

Sandford, John and Allan, Seán (eds.) (1999), *DEFA: East German Cinema, 1946–1992*, New York and London: Berghahn Books.

Santner, Eric L. (1990), *Stranded Objects: Mourning, Memory and Film in Postwar Germany*, Ithaca, NY: Cornell University Press.

Scharf, Inga (2008), *Nation and Identity in the New German Cinema: Homeless at Home*, New York: Routledge.

Schindler, Stephan K. and Koepnick, Lutz (eds.) (2007), *The Cosmopolitan Screen: German Cinema and the Global Imaginary, 1945 to the Present*, Ann Arbor, MI: University of Michigan Press.

Shandley, Robert R. (2001), *Rubble Films: German Cinema in the Shadow of the Third Reich*, Philadelphia: Temple University Press.

GERMAN CINEMA ONLINE

Berlinale – Internationale Filmfestpiele Berlin/Berlin International Film Festival
http://www.berlinale.de
The official site of the Berlinale – the Berlin International Film Festival – the largest film festival in Germany and also one the largest film festivals in the world.

Bright Lights Film Journal
http://www.brightlightsfilm.com/
Bright Lights Film Journal is a popular-academic online hybrid of movie analysis, history, and commentary, looking at classic and commercial, independent, exploitation, and international film from a wide range of vantage points from the aesthetic to the political.

Bundesarchiv
http://www.bundesarchiv.de
The official website of the Bundesarchiv (Federal Archives) including The Department of Film Archives.

CineFest
www.cinefest.de/
The official website CineFest – International Festival of German Film Heritage. In close collaboration with international scholars and archives, CineGraph and Bundesarchiv-Filmarchiv expanded their conference to incorporate a film festival.

CineGraph
http://www.cinegraph.de/
CineGraph is an encyclopaedia of German cinema. The website has news and an extensive list of useful links to resources

DEFA Film Library at the University of Massachusetts Amherst
http://www.umass.edu/defa/
The DEFA Film Library at the University of Massachusetts Amherst is the only archive and study centre outside Europe devoted to the study of a broad

spectrum of film-making by East German film-makers and films related to East Germany from 1946 to the present.

DEFA Foundation
http://www.defa-stiftung.de/
The mission of the DEFA Foundation is to preserve the films of DEFA, the former East German film studios, and oversee their use for the public good as part of Germany's national cultural heritage. The website includes a database (German only), which includes all films for which the DEFA Foundation holds copyright or part copyright.

Deutsche Kinemathek and Museum für Film und Fernsehen (Berlin)
http://www.filmmuseum-berlin.de/
Official website of the Berlin Film Museum and German Cinematheque in English and German. The site features information on current and past exhibitions. While there is no searchable database of the film archive there is a chronological and alphabetical list of the films contained within the collection. There is also information on publications by the museum. Part of the holdings in the museum's library are also searchable through this site.

Directory of World Cinema
www.worldcinemadirectory.org/
The website for the *Directory of World Cinema* series, featuring reviews and biographies of directors. An ideal starting point for students of world cinema.

Edition Filmmuseum
http://www.edition-filmmuseum.com/
This is a joint project of film archives and cultural institutions in the German-speaking part of Europe. Its ambition is to publish film works of artistic, cultural and historical value in DVD editions that both utilise the possibilities of digital media and meet the quality demands of the archival profession.

Goethe-Institut
http://www.goethe.de
The Goethe-Institut is the Federal Republic of Germany's cultural institution operating worldwide. It promotes the study of German abroad and encourages international cultural exchange. It also fosters knowledge about Germany by providing information on its culture, society and politics. The Goethe-Institut is involved in the organization of several festivals of German cinema worldwide.

Filmarchives Online
http://www.filmarchives-online.eu/
Filmarchives Online provides easy and free access to catalogue information of film archives from all over Europe. Via the multilingual web portal film works can be searched for by content, filmographic data and physical characteristics. Search results provide information about existence and location of the materials, as well as contact details to facilitate access. The focus of the database is on non-fiction material; i.e. documentary and educational films, newsreels, travelogue, advertising, scientific, industrial, experimental, sports films, as well as animation films.

Filmmuseum München (Munich)
http://www.stadtmuseum-online.de/filmmu.htm
The Munich Film Museum is part of the Munich City Museum. On the German-only website are links to the ongoing film programme and also a link to 'Edition Filmmuseum' where many hard to get DVD titles can be purchased with English subtitles.

German Films
http://www.german-films.de/
An English language site by German Films Service + Marketing (GmbH). A national information and advisory centre for the promotion of German film worldwide. The site offers information about new German films, a film archive, as well as information and links to German and international film festivals and institutions, international market analyses and special festival brochures.

German/Austrian Cinema: A Selected Bibliography of Materials in the UC Berkeley Library
http://www.lib.berkeley.edu/MRC/Germanfilmbib.html
A list of resources contained within the UC Berkeley Library.

German Film Institute (DIF)
www.deutsches-filminstitut.de/
Founded in 1949, the Deutsches Filminstitut (DIF) is the oldest cinematic institution in Germany and also one of the country's largest. One of the main purposes of the DIF is to collect, process and analyse information on film. A second purpose is the collection of films, their preservation and, if necessary, restoration in order to bring them back to the screen.

Internationale Kurzfilmtage Oberhausen/International Short Film Festival Oberhausen
http://www.kurzfilmtage.de/
Over the course of more than five decades, the International Short Film Festival in Oberhausen has become one of the world's most respected film events. The festival is a catalyst and a showcase for contemporary developments, a forum for what are often heated discussions, a discoverer of new trends and talent, and, not least, one of the most important short film institutions anywhere in the world.

International Film Festival Mannheim-Heidelberg
http://www.mannheim-filmfestival.com
The official site of the International Film Festival Mannheim-Heidelberg. The festival was founded in 1952 and is one of the oldest film festivals in Germany

Senses of Cinema
www.sensesofcinema.com/
Senses of Cinema is an online journal devoted to the serious and eclectic discussion of cinema. *Senses of Cinema* is primarily concerned with ideas about particular films or bodies of work, but also with the regimes (ideological, economic and so forth) under which films are produced and viewed, and with the more abstract theoretical and philosophical issues raised by film study.

Screening the Past
http://www.latrobe.edu.au/screeningthepast/
Published online by La Trobe University, Australia, *Screening the Past* is a leading, fully refereed international film studies journal dedicated to publishing outstanding scholarship on screen history.

TEST YOUR KNOWLEDGE

Questions

1. Who directed Germany's international post-war hit *The Cabinet of Dr. Caligari* (1920)?
2. Which film genre is considered 'uniquely German', and best associated with films such as Hans Deppe's *Black Forest Girl* (1950), *The Heath is Green* (1951) and *When the White Lilacs Bloom Again* (1953)?
3. Which brothers were responsible for the first projection event of celluloid films for a public, paying audience, in November 1895?
4. Which director has a self-professed 'innate sense of picture composition'?
5. Which 1927 Walter Ruttmann documentary was remade by Thomas Schadt 75 years after its original release?
6. Which February film festival is famed for its historic controversies and the Golden Bear awards?
7. Which two directors are famous for their contribution to music-based film, such as *Die Chronik der Anna Magdalena Bach/The Chronicle of Anna Magdalena Bach* (1968)?
8. Which television programme's title sequence features a metamorphic animation by Heinz Edelmann?
9. Which example of the German *phantastische film* features a man driven mad by his autonomous reflection?
10. Which Fritz Lang film was originally subtitled 'A German folksong in six verses'?
11. How many stories are contained within Paul Leni's *Waxworks*?
12. Depicting a fight between an archangel and the Devil, which German film was F. W. Murnau's last before leaving for Hollywood?
13. What traditional children's story was Konrad Petzold's *The Dress* adapted from?
14. After Patrick Süskind's initial refusal to sell the rights to his novel 'Perfume: The Story of a Murderer' to directors Kubrick and Scorsese, who finally directed the film adaptation?
15. Which film genre does Brian Taves divide into the following: swashbuckler, pirate, sea, empire, and fortune hunter?
16. Under which adventure sub-genre is Arnold Fanck's *Storm Over Mont Blanc* commonly classified?
17. Which two-part Indian epic was shot in Berlin?
18. *Aguirre: The Wrath of God* tells the story of the Conquistador Lope de Aguirre searching for which mythical land?
19. The popular *Indianerfilme* all starred which Serbian actor and stuntman?
20. What is the literal translation of 'Heimat'?

21. Which film, set in Bavaria and telling the story of a love affair between a mayor's son and a gypsy, has been hailed as the perfect example of a *Heimatfilm*?
22. Which unconventional 1953 film explores themes such as divorce and female independence?
23. What controversial technique did Werner Herzog claim to have used on his actors prior to filming *Heart of Glass*?
24. The comedy genre is responsible for how many out of Germany's top twenty grossing films?
25. Peter F. Bringmann's *Invitation to Dance* and *Theo Against the Rest of the World* both star which German rock icon?
26. Who wrote, directed and acted in the 1938 film *Napoleon Is to Blame for Everything*?
27. What is the German term given to the post-war trips made into the countryside to barter for food (illustrated in Frank Beyer's *Carbide and Sorrel*)?
28. Who plays the lead role in the 1999 remake of Frank Beyer's *Jacob the Liar*?
29. Which 1979 film features a soldier's knee as its narrator?
30. What is the name of the alien in Michael Herbig's film *Dreamship Surprise – Period 1*?
31. Which comedy features Hitler wearing a yellow tracksuit and crouching on all fours, barking like a dog?
32. *Short Cut to Hollywood* was made famous by which ill-judged publicity stunt on 10 September 2009?
33. The term 'Gastarbeiter' refers to whom?
34. Which R. W. Fassbinder film begins with the assertion that happiness is not always fun?
35. Berlinale-winning *Head On* was the creation of which Turkish-German director?
36. Richard Oswald's *Different from the Others* is hailed as the beginning of what cinematic movement?
37. 'Each man kills the thing he loves' is an Oscar Wilde quotation echoed throughout the narrative of which film?
38. *A Virus Has No Morals* deals with which recurrent theme?
39. What colour scheme features heavily in Angelina Maccarone's *Unveiled*, hinting towards the central character's Iranian background?
40. During what decade were *Trümmerfilme* (rubble films) released?
41. At which 1962 event did a group of 26 German film-makers, writers, artists and intellectuals publicly state "The old film is dead. We believe in the new one"?
42. In which post-war ruined city was 1947 film *In Those Days* shot?
43. Which war film by Bernhard Wicki was Germany's Oscar nomination in 1959?
44. *Jadup and Boel* features Kurt Böwe as the present day Jadup. Who plays the Jadup seen in flashbacks of the character's past?
45. *Nowhere in Africa* is narrated by Regina, daughter of a family fleeing Nazi Germany. But which character did director Caroline Link choose as the film's focal point?
46. Which Nobel Prize-winning author wrote the novella on which *The Lost Honour of Katharina Blum* was based?
47. The German title of which film originates from Friederich Hölderlin's poem 'Der Gang aufs Lang'?
48. Dennis Gansel's *The Wave* takes place in Germany. Where was the 1981 book of the same name set?
49. Departing from his frequent collaboration with Robby Müller, Wim Wenders' *Wings of Desire* was shot instead by which veteran cinematographer?
50. In which category did *The Lives of Others* win an Oscar in 2006?

Answers
1. Robert Wiene.
2. *Der Heimatfilm.*
3. Max and Emil Skladanowsky.
4. Arnold Fanck.
5. *Berlin, Symphony of a Great City.*
6. The Berlinale.
7. Straub and Huillet.
8. *Der Phantastische Film.*
9. *The Student of Prague.*
10. *Destiny.*
11. Three: the Oriental, Russian, and Jack the Ripper episodes.
12. *Faust.*
13. 'The Emperor's New Clothes'.
14. Tom Tykwer.
15. *Abenteuerfilm* (adventure film).
16. *Bergfilm* (mountain film).
17. *The Tiger of Eschnapur/ The Indian Tomb.*
18. El Dorado.
19. Gojko Mitic.
20. Homeland.
21. *When the Evening Bells Ring.*
22. *When the White Lilacs Bloom again.*
23. Hypnosis.
24. Fifteen.
25. Marius Müller-Westernhagen.
26. Curt Goetz.
27. *Hamsterfahrt* ("hamster trip").
28. Robin Williams.
29. *The Female Patriot.*
30. Spucky.
31. *Mein Führer – The Truly Truest Truth About Adolf Hitler.*
32. The 'Bluewater Attack'.
33. Guest-workers.
34. *Ali: Fear Eats the Soul.*
35. Faith Akin.
36. Queer cinema.
37. *Querelle.*
38. HIV/AIDS.
39. Green and red.
40. 1940s.
41. Oberhausen short film festival.
42. Hamburg.
43. *The Bridge.*
44. Kurt's son, Christian Böwe.
45. Jettel, the mother.
46. Heinrich Böll.
47. *Die bleierne Zeit* (The German Sisters).
48. California.
49. Henri Alekan.
50. Best Foreign Language Film.

NOTES ON CONTRIBUTORS

The Editor
Michelle Langford lectures in film studies at the University of New South Wales in Sydney, Australia. She has published widely on Iranian and German cinema and is the author of *Allegorical Images: Tableau, Time and Gesture in the Cinema of Werner Schroeter* (2006) also published by Intellect.

Contributors
Nicholas Baer is a Ph.D. student in Film and Media at UC Berkeley with a Designated Emphasis in Critical Theory.

Stephen Barber is a Professor in the Visual and Material Culture Research Centre at Kingston University in London. His recent books include *Abandoned Images* (Reaktion, 2010). His research in Berlin was supported by the DAAD.

Rebecca Beirne teaches Film, Television, Gender and Cultural Studies at the University of Newcastle, Australia. She is author of *Lesbians in Television and Text After the Millennium* (Palgrave Macmillan, 2008).

Brian Bergen-Aurand teaches film, ethics and embodiment at Nanyang Technological University, Singapore. In 2004, he earned his Ph.D. in Comparative Literature from the University of Maryland. His current projects include *Cinematic Provocations: Ethics, Justice, and the Body*, *The Encyclopedia of Queer Cinema*, and a volume on film-maker Jay Rosenblatt.

Robert Blankenship is a Ph.D. candidate in the Department of Germanic Languages and Literatures at the University of North Carolina at Chapel Hill. His research interests include East German literature, film and culture.

Elena Caoduro holds a BA in Communication studies from the University of Padua, Italy and a Research MA in Media Studies from the University of Amsterdam, The Netherlands. She is currently a Ph.D. candidate in Film Studies at the University of Southampton. Her dissertation is entitled 'Do you Remember Terrorism? Memory and Representation of left-wing political violence in recent Italian and German Cinema.'

Colin Chua teaches film and media at the University of New South Wales, in Sydney. His research focus is currently on the art, politics and commerce of Mainland Chinese and Hong Kong cinema.

Paul Cooke is Professor of German Cultural Studies at the University of Leeds. He is the author of *Speaking the Taboo: A Study of the Work of Wolfgang Hilbig* (Rodopi, 2000), *The Pocket Essential to German Expressionist Film* (Pocket Essential Press, 2002), *Representing East Germany: From Colonization to Nostalgia* (Berg, 2005) and *Contemporary German Cinema* (MUP, 2012).

Klemens Czyzydlo is a Ph.D. candidate at the University of Leeds, Department of German and the Centre for World Cinemas. As a visiting lecturer he taught film at the University of Leeds, Royal Holloway University of London, Northern Film School in Leeds, and the University of Southampton.

Jaimey Fisher is Associate Professor of German and Director of Film Studies at the University of California, Davis. He is the author of *Disciplining German: Youth, Reeducation and Reconstruction after the Second World War* and co-editor of *Critical Theory: Current State and Future Prospects*, *Collapse of the Conventional: German Film and its Politics at the Turn of the Twenty-first Century* and *Spatial Turns: Space, Place, and Mobility in German Literary and Visual Culture*.

Tara Forrest is Senior Lecturer in Cultural Studies at the University of Technology, Sydney. She is the author of *The Politics of Imagination: Benjamin, Kracauer, Kluge* (2007), co-editor of *Christoph Schlingensief: Art Without Borders* (Intellect, 2010), and editor of *Alexander Kluge: Raw Materials for the Imagination* (forthcoming 2012).

Kyle Frackman is a Lecturer in German and Scandinavian Studies at the University of Massachusetts, Amherst. His teaching and research focus on eighteenth to early twentieth century German literature, German and Nordic film, and German and Swedish language.

Adrian Gerber is a Ph.D. candidate in Film Studies at the University of Zurich. He is currently working on his dissertation, which explores film reception in Switzerland during World War I.

Ben Gook is a Ph.D. candidate in Social Theory and Cultural Studies at the University of Melbourne. He is currently writing his thesis about remembrance of the GDR in reunified Germany.

Alison Guenther-Pal is an Assistant Professor of German and Film Studies at Lawrence University in Appleton, Wisconsin. She has published on 1950s film, queer German cinema, and feminist detective fiction; she also co-edited a sourcebook on German film with Richard W. McCormick.

Christine Haase is an Associate Professor of German Studies at the University of Georgia in Athens, USA. Her teaching and research focus on twentieth and twenty-first century German literature and culture and German national cinema, in particular cinematic representations of the Holocaust and the Third Reich, German-American film relations, and German film comedy.

Habiba Hadziavdic is an Adjunct Faculty in German Studies in the Department of Modern and Classical Languages at the University of St. Thomas, St. Paul, Minnesota. Her research interests include Sinti and Roma Studies and German Cinema.

Brían Hanrahan works in the Department of Theatre and Film at Cornell University, where he teaches media history and film studies. His research interests include German cinema and the early history of radio and sound.

Roger Hillman is a reader in the German Studies Program in the School of Language Studies and in the Film Studies Program in the School of Cultural Inquiry at the Australian National University. He is author of *Unsettling Scores: German Film, Music, and Ideology* (Indiana UP, 2005).

Maggie Hoffgen has until recently taught German language and culture for the Goethe-Institut and the University of Manchester, where she also completed her MA in film/cultural studies. She now works as a freelance film lecturer and author. Her areas of expertise are German and European cinema.

Alina Hoyne's research interests include re-enactment and repetition in performance, film and art. In 2009 she was awarded a Ph.D. from Melbourne University with a dissertation on re-enactment in contemporary British art. She lives and works in Berlin.

Darlene A. Inkster was awarded a Ph.D. in Art History, Curatorship and Film Studies by the Australian National University in 2009. She currently resides in Los Angeles and is preparing a book on early cinema for publication

Maria Irchenhauser received her Ph.D. in German language and Literature from Queen's University, Canada. Her dissertation explored recent German *Heimat* film and *Heimat* texts in the context of globalization. Maria currently holds a position as a Visiting Fellow at the Bader International Study Centre (Queen's University) in Hailsham, East Sussex.

Ilinca Iurascu holds a doctoral degree in Comparative Literature from the University of Pennsylvania. She is currently researching postal networks in German cinema at the Bauhaus-Universität in Weimar.

Alice Kuzniar is author of *The Queer German Cinema* (2000) and *Melancholia's Dog: Reflections on our Animal Kinship* (2006). She has taught at the University of North Carolina at Chapel Hill and the University of Waterloo in Canada, with guest professorships at Princeton, Rutgers and the University of Minnesota.

Katharina Loew is an Assistant Professor in Germanic Studies and Cinema Studies at the University of Oregon. Her teaching and research focuses on German silent film theory and practice in a transnational and interdisciplinary context as well as film technology and special effects.

Brian Long teaches in the arts management program at the University of Melbourne. His research interests focus on cultural diplomacy in post-war Germany.

Kenneth Longden has taught in media, critical and creative arts for ten years and is currently researching for a Ph.D. in contemporary popular narratives and transnational identities at the University of Winchester, Hampshire. His research has looked at popular genre narratives, utopian narratives and German film.

Martina Lüke is an Assistant Professor-in-Residence for German and Comparative Literature and Cultural Studies at the University of Connecticut. Her research and publications include the use of Prussian history for propaganda purposes in the Weimar Republic and in National Socialism, the romantic adaptation of *Nosferatu* by Werner Herzog, as well as representations of warfare in German literature.

Ervin Malakaj is a Ph.D. student in the Department of Germanic Languages and Literatures at Washington University in St. Louis, where he is also completing a certificate in Film and Media Studies. His primary research interests include literature of the nineteenth century, film and film history.

Louise Malcolm is a Ph.D. candidate at the University of New South Wales. Her Ph.D. thesis centres on in the films of Wong Kar-wai, specifically looking at the ways in which spectators engage affectively with film performance in his films.

Isolde Mueller is a Professor of German at St. Cloud State University. Her teaching and research focus on eighteenth-century women writers, contemporary Austrian literature, and community-based learning forms such as service learning and education abroad.

Ruediger Mueller is an Associate Professor of German Studies and the Associate Director of the School of Languages and Literatures, University of Guelph, Canada. His research and publications focus on German and Austrian literature of the fin de siècle as well as the eighteenth and twentieth centuries.

Tyson Namow is a Tutor, Research Assistant and Ph.D. candidate in the Department of Cinema and Media Studies at La Trobe University, Melbourne. His research focus is on the work of German film-maker Werner Herzog, nature and landscape in cinema, and classic film theory.

Larson Powell is Assistant Professor of German, University of Missouri, Kansas City. His first book was on modern German poetry; a second on post-1945 electronic media art is nearing completion. He has published and lectured on German film and literature as well as on musicology and philosophical aesthetics.

Samantha Michele Riley is a Ph.D. candidate in Comparative Literature at the University of North Carolina, Chapel Hill. She is currently working on her dissertation on a 'Global AIDS Cinema.'

Claudia Sandberg teaches German language and German film at the University of Southampton. She is currently completing her Ph.D. dissertation about German-Jewish film-maker Peter Lilienthal, and has presented several papers on this subject at conferences in Europe and the United States. Her further research concerns cinemas in and of exile.

Arvi Sepp is Assistant Professor in German Literature and Culture at the University of Antwerp and the Erasmus University College of Brussels (Belgium). His teaching and research centre on comparative literature, literature and politics, twentieth-century German (Jewish) literature, autobiography, and popular (German and American) culture.

Qinna Shen received her Ph.D. in German from Yale University in 2008, and is Visiting Assistant Professor at Miami University. She is currently working on a book entitled *The Politics of Magic: East German Fairy-Tale Films*. Her articles are published in peer-reviewed journals including *German Studies Review*, *Brecht Yearbook 2010* and *Marvels and Tales*.

Sunka Simon is Associate Professor of German, Film and Media Studies at Swarthmore College. She is the author of *Mail-Orders: The Fiction of Letters in Postmodern Culture* (2003) and articles on German film and popular culture. She is currently working on a book on regionalism and globalization in German TV formats.

Karl L. Stenger is Associate Professor of German at the University of South Carolina Aiken. He has published a book on Friedrich Theodor Vischer and articles on African American literature, mystery and detective novels and gay literature.

Evan Torner is a Ph.D. candidate in German and Scandinavian Studies and Film Studies at the University of Massachusetts, Amherst. He is currently finishing his dissertation entitled 'The Race-Time Continuum: Race Projection in DEFA Genre Cinema.'

Chantal Wright is Assistant Professor of German and Translation at the University of Wisconsin, Milwaukee. Her research centres on migrant and exophonic texts in the German-speaking world.

FILMOGRAPHY

4 Minutes/Vier Minuten (2006)	201
Aguirre: The Wrath of God/Aguirre, Der Zorn Gottes (1972)	84
Ali: Fear Eats the Soul/Angst essen Seele auf (1974)	151
And Along Come Tourists/Am Ende kommen Touristen (2007)	258
...and the Sky Above Us/...und über uns der Himmel (1947)	223
A Virus Has No Morals/Ein Virus kennt keine Moral (1986)	187
Berlin – Buenos Aires/Die Tränen meiner Mutter (2008)	166
Beste Gegend (2008)	120
Brothers and Sisters/Geschwister – Kardesler (1997)	159
Carbide and Sorrel/Karbid und Sauerampfer (1963)	130
Cerro Torre: Scream of Stone/Cerro Torre: Schrei aus Stein (1991)	90
City of Lost Souls/Die Stadt der verlorenen Seelen (1983)	185
Death Is My Trade/Aus einem deutschen Leben (1977)	245
Destiny/Der müde Tod (1921)	48
Die Mädels vom Immenhof (1955)	107
Different from the Others/Anders als die Andern (1919)	172
Downfall/Der Untergang (2004)	239
Dreamship Surprise – Period 1/(T)raumschiff Surprise – Periode 1 (2004)	140
Europa Europa/Hitlerjunge Salomon (1990)	236
Faraway, So Close!/In weiter Ferne, So Nah! (1993)	290
Faust/Faust – Eine Deutsche Volkssage (1926)	54
Fitzcarraldo (1982)	88
Friends/Freunde (2000)	161
Fox and His Friends/Faustrecht der Freiheit (1975)	180
Germany in Autumn/Deutschland im Herbst (1978)	264
Girls in Uniform/Mädchen in Uniform (1931)	173
Goodbye Lenin! (2003)	200
Good Times/Beste Zeit (2007)	119
Grave Decisions/Wer früher stirbt, ist länger tot (2006)	142
Happy Birthday, Türke! (1992)	158
Heart of Glass/Herz aus Glas (1976)	111
Head On/Gegen die Wand (2004)	162
Heimat (1938)	100
Heroes Like Us/Helden wie wir (1999)	293
Hunger Years in a Land of Plenty/Hungerjahre – in einem reichen Land (1980)	248

Hunting Scenes from Bavaria/Jagdszenen aus Niederbayern (1969)	109
In Those Days (or Seven Journeys)/In jenen Tagen (1947)	221
It Is Not the Homosexual Who Is Perverse, But the Society in Which He Lives/Nicht der Homosexuelle ist pervers, sondern die Situation, in der er lebt (1971)	176
Jacob the Liar/Jakob, der Lügner (1975)	132
Jadup and Boel/Jadup und Boel (1980)	250
Krabat (2008)	64
Latest from the DaDaeR/Letztes aus der DaDaeR (1990)	289
Legend of Rita/Die Stille nach dem Schuß (2000)	270
Lola and Billy the Kid/Lola und Bilidikid (1999)	192
Madame X: An Absolute Ruler/Madame X – Eine absolute Herrscherin (1978)	182
Mailman Müller/Briefträger Müller (1953)	104
Mein Führer – The Truly Truest Truth About Adolf Hitler/Mein Führer – Die wirklich wahrste Wahrheit über Adolf Hitler (2007)	143
My Father is Coming/Ein Bayer in New York (1991)	190
Napoleon Is to Blame for Everything/Napoleon Ist an Allem Schuld (1938)	127
No Place to Go/Die Unberührbare (2000)	297
Nosferatu the Vampyre/Nosferatu: Phantom Der Nacht (1979)	59
Nowhere in Africa/Nirgendwo in Afrika (2001)	256
Palermo or Wolfsburg/Palermo oder Wolfsburg (1980)	155
People on Sunday: a film without actors/Menschen am Sonntag: Ein Film ohne Schauspieler (1930)	98
Peppermint Peace/Peppermint-Frieden (1983)	252
Perfume: The Story of a Murderer/Das Parfum – Die Geschichte eines Mörders (2006)	63
Querelle (1982)	184
Return to Go/Zurück auf los! (2000)	196
Rosenstrasse (2003)	237
Rotation (1949)	224
Schultze Gets the Blues (2003)	117
Shirin's Wedding/Shirins Hochzeit (1976)	153
Short Cut to Hollywood (2009)	146
Sky Without Stars/Himmel ohne Sterne (1955)	284
Somewhere in Berlin/Irgendwo in Berlin (1946)	220
Sophie Scholl: The Final Days/Sophie Scholl – Die letzten Tage (2005)	274
S.O.S. Iceberg/S.O.S. Eisberg (1933)	79
Storm Over Mont Blanc (or Avalanche)/Stürme über dem Mont Blanc (1930)	74
Sun Alley/Sonnenallee (1999)	295
Tecumseh (1972)	86
The Adventures of Prince Achmed/Die Abenteuer des Prinzen Achmed (1926)	52
The Architects/Die Architekten (1990)	287
The Baader Meinhof Complex/Der Baader Meinhof Komplex (2008)	276
The Bitter Tears of Petra von Kant/Die Bitteren Tränen der Petra von Kant (1972)	177
The Blue Light/Das blaue Licht (1932)	77
The Boat/Das Boot (1981)	233
The Bridge/Die Brücke (1959)	230
The Cabinet of Dr. Caligari/Das Cabinet des Dr. Caligari (1920)	46
The Dress/Das Kleid (1961/1991)	57
The Edge of Heaven/Auf der anderen Seite (2007)	164

The Edukators/Die fetten Jahre sind vorbei (2004)	273
The Einstein of Sex: Life and Work of Dr. M. Hirschfeld/Der Einstein des Sex: Leben und Werk des Dr. Hirschfeld (1999)	193
The Female Patriot/Die Patriotin (1979)	134
The German Sisters/Die bleierne Zeit (1981)	267
The Golem: How He Came into the World/Der Golem, wie er in die Welt kam (1920)	44
The Harmonists/Comedian Harmonists (1997)	253
The Heath is Green/Grün ist die Heide (1951)	103
The House in Montevideo/Das Haus in Montevideo (1951)	129
The Hypocrites/Die Scheinheiligen (2001)	115
The Last Illusion/Der Ruf (1949)	226
The Lives of Others/Das Leben der Anderen (2006)	302
The Lost Honour of Katharina Blum/Die verlorene Ehre der Katharina Blum (1975)	262
The Murderers Are Among Us/Die Mörder sind unter uns (1946)	218
The Nasty Girl/Das Schreckliche Mädchen (1990)	135
The NeverEnding Story/Die unendliche Geschichte (1984)	61
The Ninth Day/Der neunte Tag (2004)	240
The Promise/Das Versprechen (1995)	292
The Raspberry Reich/The Revolution is My Boyfriend (hardcore version)/ The Raspberry Reich (2004)	197
The State I Am In/Die innere Sicherheit (2000)	271
The Story of Little Mook/Die Geschichte vom kleinen Muck (1953)	56
The Student of Prague/Der Student von Prag (1913)	40
The Third Generation/Die dritte Generation (1979)	266
The Tiger of Eschnapur/The Indian Tomb/Der Tiger von Eschnapur/ Das indische Grabmal (1959)	82
The Tin Drum/Die Blechtrommel (1979)	232
The Tunnel/Der Tunnel (2001)	298
The Wave/Die Welle (2008)	278
The White Ecstasy – New Ski Miracles/Der weisse Rausch – neue Wunder des Schneeschuhs (1931)	76
To New Shores/Zu neuen Ufern (1937)	81
Virgin Machine/Die Jungfrauenmaschine (1988)	189
Waxworks/Das Wachsfigurenkabinett (1924)	50
Weird Tales/Unheimliche Geschichten (1919)	42
What to do in case of fire?/Was tun, wenn's brennt? (2001)	138
When the Evening Bells Ring/Wenn die Abendglocken läuten (1930)	97
When the White Lilacs Bloom Again/Wenn der weiße Flieder wieder blüht (1953)	105
White Hell of Pitz Palü/Die weiße Hölle vom Piz Palü (1929)	72
Wings of Desire/Der Himmel über Berlin (1987)	285
Winter Sleepers/Winterschläfer (1997)	112
Zero Hour/Stunde Null (1977)	244